The Making of a Permabear

The Making of a Permabear

THE PERILS OF LONG-TERM INVESTING IN A SHORT-TERM WORLD

Jeremy Grantham

with

Edward Chancellor

Grove Press UK

First published in the United States of America in 2026 by
Atlantic Monthly Press, an imprint of Grove Atlantic

First published in the United Kingdom in 2026 by
Grove Press UK, an imprint of Grove Atlantic

Copyright © Jeremy Grantham, 2026

The moral right of Jeremy Grantham to be identified as the author of this work has been asserted by him in accordance with the Copyright, Designs and Patents Act of 1988.

All rights reserved. No part of this publication may be reproduced, stored in a retrieval system, or transmitted in any form or by any means, electronic, mechanical, photocopying, recording, or otherwise, without the prior permission of both the copyright owner and the above publisher of the book.

No part of this book may be used in any manner in the learning, training or development of generative artificial intelligence technologies (including but not limited to machine learning models and large language models (LLMs)), whether by data scraping, data mining or use in any way to create or form a part of data sets or in any other way.

1 3 5 7 9 8 6 4 2

A CIP record for this book is available from the British Library.

Hardback ISBN 978 1 80471 119 4
E-book ISBN 978 1 80471 120 0

Printed and bound by CPI Group (UK) Ltd, Croydon CR0 4YY

Grove Press UK
Ormond House
26–27 Boswell Street
London WC1N 3JZ

www.atlantic-books.co.uk

Product safety EU representative: Authorised Rep Compliance Ltd., Ground Floor, 71 Lower Baggot Street, Dublin, D02 P593, Ireland. www.arccompliance.com

*To the memory of my grandfather
Joseph Cook, who instilled in me
some of his Quaker values*

and

*To Hanne, who has nurtured me for the
past 60 years and counting*

The author circa 2000

Contents

Prologue	9
1 Gasbag	11
2 The Zero-Sum Game	50
3 Grantham, Mayo, Van Otterloo	94
4 The Sausage Factory	128
5 Markets Can Remain Irrational Longer than You Can Remain Solvent	166
6 Vindication	213
7 The Greatest Sucker Rally in History	239
8 Lessons Not Learned	272
9 Spaceship Earth	282
10 The Race of Our Lives	319
11 Waiting for the Last Dance	353
Epilogue: And You Thought the Stock Market Was Important!	384
ACKNOWLEDGEMENTS	397
INDEX	399

Prologue

The low point came in late 1974 when Dean and I traveled to New York to visit our most prestigious client, the Rockefeller Family Fund. They had a few million dollars with Batterymarch, perhaps $4 million of our $48 million. They were our only well-known name, so it was critical for us to retain them. Anyway, we went into their offices in Rockefeller Center to justify our terrible performance, which was no more terrible than anyone else's. For the first time ever Laurance Rockefeller attended the meeting. He was a grandson of the Standard Oil titan and brother to the politician Nelson and the banker David. Their wealth was held in the Rockefeller Brothers Fund, which was much larger. The Family Fund was for their children's generation. Laurance Rockefeller was the honorary chairman or something and was keeping an eye on his children's affairs.

They had a committee of about nine very smart, agreeable people, including my good friend Bevis Longstreth and Jon Hagler (who later became a GMO colleague) and a very smart and agreeable hired gun with Mr. Rockefeller, making sure they all stayed on the straight and narrow. I made a fairly impassioned pitch for why small cap value would come back. The actual case for small cap stocks was that to go back to trend, they would have to rise 100 percentage points against the market. Right. One hundred percentage points of outperformance. I couldn't bring myself to say it because it felt inherently unbelievable. So I presented the data that to the eye suggested this but said out loud we were counting on 50 percentage points of outperformance. I showed the data of the ebb and flow and how cheap small caps were. They were at an absolutely all-time low. Why would you want to quit now? I mean, this was one of those rare opportunities that comes once or twice in a lifetime. And it was, by the way.

At the end of my harangue, Mr. Rockefeller said, in a stage whisper, "Well, it's a lot of words, but what does it mean?" I was looking down at this piece of paper. I remember that moment, absolutely, vividly. My eyes watered, I was so mad. I was really pissed off. I flushed and couldn't hear what was being said, but I was vaguely aware that Dean had started to talk. I interrupted Dean. And I heard someone talking, then a little part of my brain said, that's me. What's he going to say? I've gone on automatic pilot only a couple of times in my life, when I've had this out-of-body experience in which I'm talking and I'm thinking, oh my God, at the same time.

I looked up at the crowd, stared down the table so I wouldn't be looking straight at Mr. Rockefeller (who was sitting next to me), and said, "Well, I have the impression that I have completely missed my target. I think this is probably the most important thing that we've ever had to say about the stock market, and I'd really like to have another go." So I recapped the argument, boiled it down, spat out the points, and behind Mr. Rockefeller were these nine people all nodding sympathetically at me, which was pretty cool of them. He couldn't see them, because they were sitting behind him, but they were very supportive. With them still nodding encouragement, I went through my pitch and finished. We left. As Dean and I walked down Fifth Avenue after the meeting, silently contemplating the high probability of losing our most prestigious account, he said, "Well, if you've got to go, you might as well go with style." A pretty generous comment under pressure. Dean always had a soft spot for style.

CHAPTER 1

Gasbag

By background I'm both a Quaker and a Yorkshireman, which I like to call double jeopardy. People from Yorkshire are known for their bloody-mindedness and independence of mind – they call a spade a spade. Quakers consider thrift a virtue. So maybe I was destined by birth to become a value investor.

I was born on October 6, 1938 in Great Amwell, a little village outside Ware in the southern county of Hertfordshire, and christened Robert Jeremy Goltho Grantham. My father's family came from Lincolnshire. Goltho is a town in Lincolnshire established in 850 AD, only 25 miles from Grantham, where Margaret Thatcher was born and raised. Goltho's main claim to fame is that it was one of the few villages in the country not included in the Domesday Book, which took a record of every person, every sheep, every cow so the conquering Normans could tax them. Presumably in the case of Goltho an effective bribe was received. (As an addendum to my arrival on this earth, *The Times* of London on October 6 carried the story of "the Cassandra-like" Mr. Churchill complaining that Herr Hitler appeared to want to devour Europe piece by piece, having just moved into Czechoslovakia the day before.)

My father was a civil engineer and, at a very young age, was appointed town surveyor for Thurnscoe in Yorkshire. It was said that he was the youngest surveyor in the country. Later, in 1931, he became the town surveyor for Ware in Hertfordshire. And, I think reading between the lines, he was extremely ambitious. He pioneered the use of concrete, helping to build some of the first concrete roads in England while also trying to build cheap council housing that would be good value for the money. He came from the junior branch of an upper-class family, but he was the youngest son of the youngest son. His father had a country inn and his uncle was a kind of country squire. When he was working up in Yorkshire, he met my mother, she became pregnant and they married, not necessarily to the great satisfaction of his family.

After the war started, my father joined the Royal Engineers and was posted to Egypt, based in Cairo, where there were plenty of bridge-building possibilities. He died there in 1942, having caught a disease that wouldn't kill you if you had decent medicine. But in wartime conditions it did. He'd been away for two years so I must have last seen him when I was one and a half. We were living at the time in a rather fancy house in Ware, Hertfordshire. Very shortly after my father died, my mother, three sisters and I piled into a substantial truck with bits of furniture and off we went to live with her parents in Doncaster, a mining town in Yorkshire.

My mother's parents came from a resolutely working-class background. Both of them had left school at 12 or 13. Her mother was registered in the census as a houseworker. Her father had started working life as a wheelwright and had lost an eye in an industrial accident. He received a decent settlement and used it to buy a little corner bakery store. He took the first shilling from the first loaf of bread they sold and nailed it to the counter. (By a nice twist of fate, that first delivery of bread came by a pony and trap driven by my grandmother's brother Henry Douse, who was building a very successful regional bread company, "Douse's Bread." He later sold the business to J. Arthur Rank, the famous moviemaker and bread company, who even later sold on to Xerox, much to my great-uncle's financial benefit.) My grandfather had been brought up a Quaker. Although apostate, he led the life of a Quaker. Because Quakers don't approve of flashy spending and do approve of hard work (believing the devil finds work for idle hands), they got to be pretty well off.

After a few years – a typical story of thriftiness – they opened a second store but didn't stay in one specialty. To the little bakery they added a greengrocer and then a liquor store. They eventually ended up with 17 stores. A few decades later they traded them all to a chain for quite a lot of money and bought a big restaurant on the Great North Road that ran from London to Edinburgh, right through the middle of the town in the days before the bypass. As soon as they had done that, the war broke out. Restaurants had an extra ration of food, which meant that if you wanted to eat off your ration book, you had to go out and pay up. Being in the restaurant business was a license to steal.

But my grandfather refused to profiteer. As I like to say, capitalism being what it is, they cleared the market the hard way by having lines outside the restaurant every lunchtime that would stretch up the high street. And they had marvelously highly trained waitresses, all dressed in dark blue with little lacy things around their heads and aprons. They would scurry around, very impressively, with three big dishes of meat, potatoes and cabbage on one hand and three on the other. They responded to this crazy demand caused by the cheap price by being very, very quick and slick.

Wartime propaganda forced frugality on the nation. There was a government program to get people to stop wasting. We had big posters in the streets showing a Squander Bug, which was a big, ugly-looking spidery thing. It said to the general public, "Do not waste." In my view, this is how one should live. You didn't need to tell Yorkshire Quakers not to waste. Of course, you had to clear your dinner plate. You couldn't throw anything away. You darned socks over and over again. Till they were all darn and no sock. And why not? Waste not, want not.

Even if you'd wanted to waste money during the war, it was pretty hard. I didn't know at the time that the toy shops had once been full of toys. When I looked through their windows, they were always very sparse. I thought that was normal so I didn't suffer. My mother took me to buy a toy when I was four. But there were no toys. She wept but I didn't know why she was weeping. She only told me years later. All they had was a pathetic wooden sword and an army revolver holster. She wanted me to buy that nice leather

Me with my favorite stuffed toy in Doncaster, Yorkshire, in 1942

holster without a gun. I thought what on earth would I want with an empty holster? I went for the sword. And then, mysteriously, the sword disappeared about two days later. I looked everywhere for it but it had gone. Of course, I must have been racing around the house, waving that damn sword, threatening to knock over everything precious. They just mysteriously vanished it for me. Decades later I told that story to my nephew and his son, and the son, who was about six years old, was so moved that he and his father made me a wooden sword that we proudly display in our house in Westport, Massachusetts. It's an unlikely little codicil to that story.

Even after the war, everything was rationed – potatoes, bread, sugar. The only exotic things that were sometimes available were oranges, which we had at Christmas. But after I turned seven, life got better every year. The main aspect was food becoming more available: potatoes would come off the ration list, then bread would come off, and, finally, candy came off years later, when I was nine or ten. I remember the whole family driving around from shop to shop that first Saturday with freely available sweets and chocolate, trying mostly unsuccessfully to buy whatever scraps were left in the stampede. I remember my first banana, my first melon, my first grapes. Cars came back on the road and toy shops filled up. Everything zooming upwards at a rate they could never keep up, what the French call the *Trente Glorieuses*, the three decades of rising post-war prosperity. As Prime Minister Macmillan said, "You've never had it so good." Of course we'd never had it so good: the comparison period was pre-war depression, war and post-war austerity.

Looking back, the early experiences of childhood seem to me a kind of brainwashing that was impossible to shake off. Take my Yorkshire grandfather, who was brought up as a Quaker and later became a diehard apostate. But he retained near-perfect Quaker principles to the end of his life. He could reject the notion of the ever-lasting life, one of the key tenets of faith, but he couldn't shake off the rest of the cultural brainwashing. He treated everyone so well and he was so modest and unassuming, despite being a substantially self-made man. As my grandfather lay on his deathbed, his believing wife, my wonderfully warm and friendly grandmother, who really brought me up on her apron strings, said to him, "Joe, Joe, you'll soon be with the angels." To which he replied, "Florie, I'll be happy enough just pushing up daisies." They say there are no atheists in foxholes, yet even though a deathbed is the foxiest of holes, he didn't flinch. That still seems to me pretty cool.

In Doncaster we lived in a terraced Victorian house, three floors with stained-glass windows at the front and an extended area at the back, big kitchen and scullery, an outhouse where the washing was done and a long, thin garden. My mother worked full-time in the restaurant, so I was mostly brought up by my grandmother, who took me to the movies almost every day. I saw more movies as a young boy than most people have seen in their entire lives. She used the cinema as a babysitting tool. After she was finished with the housework, she'd take me off to the movies and we'd see whatever was to be seen. I had to stand up most of the time, holding on to the seat in front, watching completely adult movies – gangster movies, Jimmy Cagney and all the classics, Humphrey Bogart as the bad guy – not really getting the point but being entertained. I wouldn't make a fuss, and my grandmother would sleep… soundly, every time. She never saw a single film. So, it worked out beautifully for both of us. Even now, watching old black and white movies on some cable channel, I'll think, "My God, this looks faintly familiar… I think I know what's going to happen next."

Having my grandfather as a father figure, I realize how much I was enveloped by his values. It's as if I had no choice. It's in my cortex. All my life I have been practicing a form of ancestor worship which, given the character of my grandparents, has not been such a bad thing. They, particularly my grandfather, brought me up with such a strong set of examples that I do things that I can't explain, as if I had no choice. I hate waste. I feel forced to be economical. To this day when visiting restaurants I still check the menu and order the thing that I think is a bargain. If I want a drink I have a glass of the cheapest wine. Years later, when I came to live in Boston I found that old-fashioned Yankee virtue was a very easy fit for a Yorkshireman. The fact that I later gave away most of my money is a further testament to my grandparents' powerful hold on me. My childhood experiences also influenced my approach to investment: as I like to say, every Yorkshireman worth his salt is born with the natural understanding that cheap is better than expensive.

SCHOOLING

My father had been a Freemason, which was a very fashionable thing back in the thirties. So, at the age of eight I was sent to the Royal Masonic Junior School for Boys in Bushey, near Watford. The school was run like a typical English prep school with one super-critical difference: everything from tuition to room and board to books to clothing to even rugby balls and cricket bats was paid for by the Freemasons. The unusual entry fee was that you had to have a dead Freemason father. At the end of the war, there were plenty of those. We were several hundred boys without a father between us.

I was one term behind the crowd because they wouldn't take you if you weren't eight, and because I'm an October birthday I didn't go until the Easter term. Just a handful of newbies arrived with me. What an alien, cold, cruel world we encountered. The food was barely edible – little pieces of meat with gristle, not fat, just gristle, with carrots and peas on the side. And gray bread – you still weren't allowed to make white bread because of rationing. During the war, bread was made with whole wheat and the wartime regulations continued for several years afterwards. When they finally brought out the unhealthy white bread, we all thought we'd died and gone to heaven.

I was raised at a time when the British still believed that a child should be seen and not heard. That didn't suit me at all. There are some of us who have a powerful urge to talk, and I was one of them. A trained psychologist given 20 hours of interviews might come up with a decent explanation, but I've come up with my own poor man's explanation. I grew up with three dominant sisters and a dominant mother, and no father. Put it this way: they ranged from normally strong characters to extremely strong. They had no mercy. If I couldn't get a word in, they didn't care. The topics over teatime, dinner and breakfast were overwhelmingly female topics. They were not going to spend that much time talking about football. The result was I hardly got a word in. For a while they gave me a bell to ring when I wanted attention. The bell was soon ignored.

When I got to boarding school, I couldn't wait to talk. Alas, that was forbidden. The school was like a Trappist monastery. We weren't allowed to talk anywhere – whether walking to and from meals, during prep or getting up from, or going to, bed. This was for the teachers' convenience. They didn't want to hear us kids yapping away. But because I couldn't talk at home, I made up for it at school and was duly punished. I became known as "Gasbag Grantham" and the teachers referred to me as "Gas." I was the only person in school whom the teachers uniformly referred to by a nickname.

Quite often I'd get stuck in the corner or take a beating for talking too much. The masters would hit us on the bottom and on the hand, any way they could. By general agreement, I was the most punished boy in the school. That went on for a couple of years until finally they grew tired of whacking me. I received something of a papal dispensation. A master would hear a voice and say, "Who's talking down there? Oh, Gas, shut up." If it had been anyone else, they'd have given him a whack on the hand. You could say that I enjoyed a mildly privileged position.

By 1947, when I arrived, almost all the boys' fathers had died in the war. After lights out we occasionally had the ritual "How did your father die?" My best buddy's father was shot down in the Bay of Biscay on a bombing mission. One boy had been on the beach with his family in Torquay in Devon when a German fighter, a Messerschmitt, came down the beach, machine-gunning the holidaymakers. They all ran for the breakwaters, which were huge. If you could get on the right side of one you'd be safe. This guy called Kestervan and his elder brother, father and mother were all running like mad. Then, little Kestervan fell and his father went back for him and put his body over him, which doesn't do any good against the kind of shells coming from a Messerschmitt. It killed his father and put a bullet through Kestervan's foot. At this stage of the story, he'd show us the scar on his foot and we boys were deadly impressed. Of course, he won the contest.

Not the best student, I finally got fed up with being a dunce. By the time I became a senior at the junior school, I began to make a determined effort. We had A, B and C streams. I worked my way up the class until in my last full year I made it to the top of the B stream. Unlike a boarding school of the normal kind, our school had to take everybody. Some of the boys were not very smart. Maybe I was a little dyslexic. Until multiple choice came along many years later, my results were never good. Multiple choice can make a poor student into a good student. I actually have a very substantial memory and remember much more than most people, but a retrieval system from hell. I simply cannot recall names at the spur of the moment. Exams were pure torture for me. I would hand in my papers with gaps. And I would write something like, "In 1704, the battle of blank took place." At the back of my mind, I knew it was the Battle of Blenheim, but I couldn't summon up the name. That's not how you do well at school. Later in life I'd find myself working with colleagues for many years and still not be able to recall their names. I remember my surprise and delight at meeting my first multiple choice quiz, which I took to get into Harvard Business School. I told my mother, "You won't believe it. They tell you the right answer!" Which, of course, they do.

VICTOR LUDORUM

I inherited my competitive side from my father. From what I gather, he was a real man's man, what we used to call a beer-drinking backslapper. He partied pretty well and played rugby for Eastern Counties and had a zero handicap at golf. His aristocratic great-uncle, Redding Grantham, didn't think it was gentlemanly to chase after little balls. Redding thought, damn it, the only dignified things were hunting, shooting and fishing.

Until about the age of 13, I was stocky with fair gingerish hair and sticking out ears. I could wrestle anyone who showed up. (Later, I shot up in height, grew skinny and stayed that way forever. There are people like me who fidget a lot, who are unable to sit still and burn off all their extra calories.) At boarding school I was the *victor ludorum* for overall sporting achievement. My sister Sally, at the Mason's girls' school, was awarded *victrix ludorum*. I won the 100 yards, equaling the school record. I established a new school record at 220 yards and I was slightly behind the record in the half- and quarter-mile. I won the hurdles. I came second in the high jump, the long jump and the mile. It was pretty hard to beat me.

My greatest competitive feat came in the half-mile. My best buddy, the Hertfordshire County champion over the distance, was in the same race. He ran a ridiculously fast first lap in well under a minute. A crazy thing to do, which seemed aimed at breaking my heart. I found myself at the back, so far away I could barely see him. But as he rounded a curve I noticed him slowing. I accelerated, overtaking a few runners and I thought, "Oh my God, this is going to kill me." I then jogged along in fourth or fifth place. On the next turn I saw that he had slowed even more. I made another dash and moved into third place, closing the gap. Into the final lap, he was so blasted that he practically started to walk. I took off in a sprint and by the time we reached the home straight, he was 10 yards ahead

The winners and runners-up of the 100-yard relay at the Royal Masonic Junior School for Boys in 1950. I'm in the middle of the top row.

with me closing in, eyes watering, chest burning, legs throbbing. Finally, he turned around and grimaced – the world's worst-looking grimace – and started to accelerate. Although totally exhausted, he had a little something left. The calculation was that he was moving more slowly, but accelerating; I was moving faster, but exhausted and decelerating. Could I catch him up before these two ratios shifted? As we crossed the tape, I was ahead by about a foot. Had it been another two yards or so, he would have won.

We lay on the middle of the grass track, the two most zapped, exhausted kids in England, with every part of our bodies aching. A little voice inside of me was saying, "Okay, big deal. You proved if you try much harder than anyone else and you nearly kill yourself, you can just beat them." If my buddy had put in as much as I had, he would have won. Maybe half the other runners could have beaten me. Yet I was the sucker who had put everything into it, every last drop of energy. I discovered that winning was not as big a deal as I had thought; not worth dying for, at least. This left me free to treat sport at college as casual and devote more energy to other things. At that moment, I vowed that I would never try that hard again – it just wasn't that important. And to the best of my knowledge, I never did. My nature didn't change, however. Decades later, my son Rupert told me that I was the most competitive person he'd ever met.

GAMING

Although I couldn't recall names and was a mediocre pupil, I always had a good head for figuring odds. At school on a Saturday evening, we played Monopoly, at which I was a complete whizz by the way. I won seven consecutive games of Monopoly with six people playing.

It was not an accident. We were fanatics and played whenever we could. I simply had a much better method playing the game given the rules that we had adopted. The end to each row had a higher rate of return than the beginning of the row. That alone was a helpful insight into winning the game. The end of each row from the Go had a higher return for the same price. The light blues had a much higher return than the browns, and the oranges had a much higher return than the pinks.

They were the value stocks, so to speak, and because they also were at the end of the first row and everyone was starting together, they were very likely to hit the light blue. If I could horse-trade for that set and get them developed before the game started, the poor suckers were paying me £550 on the first roll of the dice. If they survived that, I would quickly take my winnings and build hotels or houses on the oranges where, you know, my opponents are paying around £1,000. They are basically out of the game if they hit twice early in the match. Anyway, that battle plan was often sufficient.

Toward the end of junior school I added to my gaming repertoire and started a lottery. My fellow students were not sophisticated but they were very excited. It was just too much for the 10-, 11- and 12-year-olds to use their brains. The price of a ticket was a piece of candy or square of chocolate. The prize was a bar of chocolate. One guy, who later went to Cambridge, bought a whole bar of chocolate's worth of tickets to win a bar of chocolate. Some of the faculty were quite amused; others were horrified.

My buddies and I also played roulette. We used to go to cricket matches, pretending to watch the game but instead were hunkered around a roulette wheel, playing it, looking for a pattern. We tried to produce an infallible system, checking the numbers down in a little book. Needless to say, we didn't find an infallible system, but we did find out that the roulette wheel was skewed so that after playing for several weeks we found that certain numbers paid up. As I was to discover, the nice thing about the investment business is that it allows one to continue to hunt for infallible systems.

I also had a stamp-trading venture with my buddy, Norman Glass. We had a Stanley Gibbons catalog that was a great investment, though expensive. We knew what everything was theoretically worth and we would try and trade up with that information. We then became much more manipulative, returning from vacations with wonderful, pretty Central African Republic stamps, huge triangular colored things with camels and flowers. We would trade those wonderful, pretty stamps for nasty (but valuable) little penny blacks – fairly reprehensible, taking advantage of the callow nature of 10-year-olds. But they let us get away with it.

(Later, I became more and more serious as a stamp collector. At the age of 16 I was on the cusp of buying a whole collection from a dealer. When you buy a whole stamp collection you acquire many multiples of the theoretical Stanley Gibbons' value so that for me was an irresistible discount. I was palpitating at the thought, but the collection cost £4, which was quite a fortune. I had this money for my summer vacation. Did I want to have lots of money up my sleeve or this damn collection? I was in agony trying to make up my mind. And I decided that I would buy the collection but then I lost my wallet with the money in it. I was heartbroken. That was the end of my stamp-collecting days. I couldn't look at a stamp again without thinking of the loss.)

At that time, the school took the opportunity to suggest that I stay back a year. Their blatant reason was to get me out of the clutches of Norman Glass, who was obviously leading me into these terrible habits. The irony is that it was me, the crafty little Yorkshire boy, rather than Norman, who was responsible. He was blamed for my conniving character because he was Jewish. I discovered at a very visceral level the casual anti-Semitism and injustice that was typical of English schools in that period. There was a substantial degree of anti-Semitism back then, which I didn't share – two of my best friends at the junior school were Jewish, which took some doing as there was barely a handful at the school. I also felt the injustice of being forced to repeat a year unnecessarily, to separate me from this guy whom I had led astray, not the other way round. My education suffered. If I had gone up a year with the smarter boys, I would have been more engaged and focused.

UNIVERSITY

I failed my school leaving exams (known as A levels) and was sent to a crammer in London where I was finally able to take English. The Masonic School had no one available to teach English to the older boys. So my only academic talent was sidestepped; I was forced to take chemistry, which I failed gloriously. English literature was my favorite subject and the only one I was really good at. After my experience at the mediocre boarding school, I couldn't believe how exciting education could be. Our English teachers loved the language and loved literature. One even had a play on at the Royal Court Theatre. You could not help but pick up their enthusiasm. We would sit around during the coffee break, trading Chaucerian and Shakespearean quotes. It was dynamite. We did the two-year English course in one year. And the teaching was so brilliant that a motley crew of around 20 of us – housewives, refugees from Hungary, a Dutch Jesuit priest and three or four young girls who couldn't stand their convents any longer – all passed, every single one of us, even though half weren't even born English speakers. I got the top score in our class. I marched onward with confidence, at least in English.

My first three preferred choices for university turned me down. Sheffield was the only place prepared to take a risk on me. As it was the only offer, I didn't even need to visit their campus. I just replied, yes, thank you, packed up and arrived there for the first time as the semester started. I started out by reading English, but quickly saw the writing on the wall. Less than 10% of the entire year were women, and they were all concentrated in English. They were largely upper class, bright as whippets and from the top schools. I sensed the competition was going to be utterly deadly. We also had to do Anglo-Saxon, which is a complex language that declines like Latin, as well as Latin itself, to scholarship level. In a mad five-week course at the crammer I'd done enough Latin to meet the entrance qualifications for an English degree. But that combination was inconceivable to me, entailing lots of work and masses of competition.

To hell with that, I thought. Toward the end of my first semester, I switched to economics. One of my roommate buddies was taking economics and it looked like a piece of cake, which, as we all know, it is. I was lucky to get about the last minute of economics as a social science, just as the idea that you should actually use your brain was about to die on the vine in economics. We didn't do econometrics. There was one course in statistics, which was basic common sense and a few standard correlations. But the whole miserable business of pretending that humans are machines and can be treated by algorithms – I did none of it. What a relief. I did much more study in the history of economics – the general building blocks of the Pigou effect, Ricardo and the boys – which was much more interesting.

Although I read economics at university, I didn't find it of much help in my investment career. Economists today are always missing the point. They overexplain data without really understanding the quality of the data, or, I might add, the low quality of the data. They just will not use their common sense or perhaps they don't have any to use. Modern economics is like a brainwashing program: it teaches you to stop thinking and to accept the dominant theory that is being pushed by the teaching faculty. Nor is it useful training for investors. Back in the day, it used to take us two years to deprogram an economics PhD at GMO. They all arrived thinking the market was efficient. I mean, you can't get any more stupid than that.

Academically, I came alive in my second year at Sheffield, making a decent impression on the famous economist and future Nobel laureate, Sir John Hicks. Although he was an Oxford professor, for some reason he was given the job of marking our theory papers. He gave me a first on my theory papers. I did less well on some seriously boring papers. After graduating I was offered the opportunity to do a doctorate. My thesis proposal was on whether tax makes you work harder because some of your money has been taken away or whether it depresses you because the sweat of your brow is no longer rewarded. The study of taxation and incentives was right up my street and I should have done it. Instead, I went to work for my stepfather.

My mother had remarried just before my eighth birthday. She was a very likeable woman who must have appealed to almost every man. After my father died, she had three marriage proposals despite coming with four children in her train: one was from an air commodore; another from a captain, my favorite, who rode a motorbike and died in Burma behind enemy lines; and lastly from my stepfather, who was a captain in the Royal Army Service Corps. During the war he had led convoys of food and ammunition around Italy, including infamously taking a convoy of 18 heavy trucks up into a high mountain Italian village to a dead end. It was so tight all of them had to back down the mountain. It took hours and hours with people waving and shouting and screaming. It became a legend of military misfortune.

After the war, the family moved to South Croydon, on the outskirts of London. My stepfather ran a small supplier of catering and hospital equipment, A.W. Gregory. After my graduation he told me that if I didn't join the family business immediately, he would have to find someone to replace me in perpetuity. It seemed a mild form of blackmail but, being by nature conservative, I thought I had better comply. It just might be a great opportunity.

Instead, it turned out to be a succession of mishaps. One day I was sent to Harrods, the posh Knightsbridge store, to sell them a curious piece of equipment. It was a French commando's trenching tool, a little spade that went into your backpack and had all manner of instruments attached – wire cutters, bottle openers, snippers, you name it – a very impressive little gadget, lightweight, strong. When I tried to demonstrate it to the buyer at Harrods, I caught my tie in the snipper part and it was so tight that we could not get it open. The buyer had to borrow scissors from the kitchen department to cut my tie off. Anyway, he was so amused by the whole thing that he bought three of those damn tools and amazingly sold them eventually.

On another occasion we had this tea set – cups and saucers and mugs and plates for hospitals – made of polycarbonate. Polycarbonate was the up and coming super-strong plastic that could take all manner of colors. I wanted to demonstrate how absolutely indestructible polycarbonate was so I urged the guy at the hospital to jump on it. He jumped on it and the damn thing broke into a thousand pieces. But he bought some too. Apparently, the secret of my success was to make a complete ass of myself and then someone would buy something. These were the two most embarrassing episodes of my happily short career in the family business, which was complete misery.

There was a silver lining, though. After every appointment, I read a book for 15 minutes as a reward. I tried to learn languages from a primitive early tape recorder, which I would put on the driver's seat. I got recordings from foreign girlfriends who would record sections in their accent. If the girl was from Switzerland, I learned to recite lines from *All Quiet on the Western Front* in a Swiss-German accent. "*Mitten in der Nacht erwachen wir. Die Erde dröhnt.*" [We wake up in the middle of the night. The earth shakes.]

The worst part about working for my stepfather was, once in, how was I to get out? How do you tell your stepfather, who makes a point of saying that everything he's done has been to build up his business for you, treating you exactly like his real son, which, in a sense, he did, you want out? I knew that my leaving would hurt him and my mother too. Extricating myself was nerve-wracking beyond belief. In the end it happened by luck. After 18 months, I still hadn't summoned up the courage to tell him that I was planning to leave. But somehow he got wind of a job interview I had botched and threw such a hissy fit, assuming I'd made the decision to quit, that I had nothing to lose. It gave me the courage to take on the psychological family stress that I had so dreaded. Then I went out and hunted around for another job.

FROM SHELL TO HARVARD

One of the first things I did was visit a big consulting firm in the City of London. There I met a typical chinless twit – one forgets how much England has changed since then – but in the early sixties the City was full of upper-class types, who were so rude, so blatantly rude and demeaning and dismissive to everybody, it seemed. This one was typical; sneering at my résumé, he looked up and said, "Oh, Grantham, with this record you're no good to us. Come back when you've had 40 years of variegated business experience or been to the Harvard Business School." As I walked out of the office, I thought to myself, "Am I going to burn this building down and kill them all, or am I going to apply to the Harvard Business School?"

I chose the latter. I sent in an application to Harvard and then forgot about it. In the meantime, I had much better luck at a couple of enterprises. The first was at Hedley's, the makers of Fairy Soap, a company in Newcastle that had just been bought by Procter & Gamble. They offered me work as a researcher, digging through data and finding useful stuff about selling soap and other things. That would have been a serious job. Then Shell offered me a job. Shell was very upper class in those days – about three-quarters of its English management hires were from Oxbridge. The Honourable Hugh Arbuthnott (I'm not kidding) was my handler. He explained everything to me, took me here, there and everywhere. Tests included masses of English stuff, which I could ace and finish before other people were halfway through, particularly because many of them were Dutch, which didn't help them. I was then taken to the final selection meeting where the key personnel officer for the Royal Dutch group and eight other people sat along a table, like the Last Supper, and I sat on a little chair in front of them.

I'd recently had a miserable experience applying to the *Reader's Digest*, which was my first effort, where I disgraced myself by becoming so nervous that I became almost physically out of control and couldn't even find the chair to sit on. Very embarrassing. The rejection slip beat me home. This time, however, the Shell boss said, "Grantham, I see you went to Sheffield. Tell me, didn't you find that a cultural wilderness?" This is exactly what he said. A cultural wilderness. I'm happy to say I laughed. It was the only adequate response. I genuinely laughed and said, "Yes, you're right, I suppose it was." I went on to explain that Sheffield had more people who'd come from state secondary modern schools than from private schools. It was unique in that sense. To get to university from a secondary modern meant that in an obscure country village in Derbyshire some teacher had taken you under their wing and nursed you through A levels, as a kind of special gesture. You'd think such students were as rare as hen's teeth. But Sheffield had plenty. Some of my good friends were in that category. In that sense, it was almost a working-class university. After 11 years at boarding school, Sheffield was a chance to re-engage with, if not the real world, then at least a much less unreal one.

My laughter showed confidence and the answer hit them in a soft spot. So, they offered me a job and looked at my results and said this guy is clearly more analytical than executive, which, of course, is correct. They wanted to put me in the analytical category, which was the staff function, pointing out that I could aspire to become the boss of the economics department, that sort of thing. I said, nah, I want to be an executive. And they said, well, you know, everything suggests you're a staff guy. I replied to my friendly handler that I'd rather go and work for Procter & Gamble as a market researcher, my other job offer, up in Newcastle. Anyway, I went home and waited for the offer that I was going to reject. The letter arrived. "We're happy to offer you £1,200 a year as an executive stream trainee." This was £200 a year more than the staff job paid. Shell was about the highest paying big company in Britain, so that was all pretty good. Nine months later I left for Harvard Business School (HBS). At least I was decently paid for those nine months.

The only thing of note from my time at Shell was a paper I wrote on coal. I stumbled upon the fact that America had a monstrous amount of cheap coal. Even at the very substantial rate they were cranking it out, the U.S. had 800 years' supply of known reserves. By contrast, the rate at which they were pumping regular oil left them with only a few years' supply. I wrote this unexpected paper arguing that the United States should be a coal-based economy, dealing with the costs of delivering coal to ports and shipping it all over the world. There was a legal requirement that analysts could insist on sending research out to all the divisions – Deutsche Shell, French Shell, Italian Shell and so on. Over my boss's objections, I sent out this weird coal thing and it resonated like mad around the system because they all found it kind of strange and interesting. They checked the data and sent back responses, which never normally happened. It created a bit of a stir, and, in certain circles, must have marked me down as either a nitwit or a troublemaker.

Shortly afterwards, I received a message to go to London to take the Harvard entrance test. I traveled by train and arrived at the English Speaking Union where they were administering this entry test, a general knowledge multiple choice test. English people were terrified because we didn't do multiple choice in those days. But I had got a little book and had already practiced multiple choice, giving me an unfair advantage. Helpfully, one of the sections was about oil tankers. I knew the answers before I read the damn piece. Anyway, I sailed through that test. It turns out that they added 100 points to the score of the English people because they had no experience with multiple choice. So, 100 points added to my very decent score gave me a very high score indeed.

Next, I got a little note telling me to show up at the same place to be interviewed. I arrived with 18 or 20 people, two of whom were from universities established in industrial cities by the Victorians, such as Sheffield, known patronizingly as "red bricks," and the rest were from Oxbridge. We were to be interviewed by three HBS graduates, all of whom had been to Oxbridge, and then to business school where they had mutated, basically, into a different species. We were told to introduce ourselves. The first guy said, "I'm Roger Davenport.

I went to Balliol. My ambition in life is to sail up the Nile." Then the next guy said, you know, basically, "My name's also Roger Davenport. I also went to Balliol and my ambition is to sail up and down the Nile." I could not believe how ridiculous their ambitions were. Of course, they became more and more embroidered and competitive in their ambitions. Finally it was my turn. I said in my best Yorkshire accent, "Eeh by gum, the name's Grantham. I want to go to HBS to learn how to make money." I was being deliberately crass in order to play off these guys. The three adjudicators practically cheered because they had been pulling their hair out over how wonderfully off-topic these characters were. They must have been thinking why the hell are they applying to business school?

I hesitate to mention what happened next. It marks the extreme outer edge of my evil competitiveness. This was the only Brer Rabbit incident of my life. After the introductions, they asked us to take 10 minutes to pick a topic and then take half an hour to discuss it, after which we'd break for coffee. Then, we were to take another five or 10 minutes to pick another topic. I picked a reasonable first topic and threw myself into the argument pretty aggressively. Following the break the Oxbridgey types gathered around the coffee urn, giving me dirty looks. They'd marked me out as the uncouth Yorkshire git who had to be stomped on. They started to discuss what topic to choose next. One of them suggested transportation. I was working at Shell, for heaven's sake. I spent my whole day reading about transportation. Naturally, I tell them that transportation is the worst damn idea I had ever heard. Instead, I proposed South America as a general topic as a red herring. Of course, they gathered behind transportation and railroaded it in.

This is too much, I'm thinking. This kind of thing only happens in movies. Anyway, it gets worse. The leader of the bad guys is holding forth about the recent Crowther report on transportation, one of these giant government reports that makes its author a peer. This report had been written up everywhere, but I had read the damn thing cover to cover because that was my job. This is getting better and better, I think to myself. I say to this guy, "Have you read it?" He squirms around, saying he'd not really actually read it but had seen several reviews. Then, of course, I say, "Well, I've actually read it and this is what it says, bang, bang, bang." There were no survivors from this group when I got to Harvard. I never saw any of them again, but I've never managed to repress the guilty feelings I had about being so completely ruthless. It was a level of ruthlessness that I never reached again, which is a pity because perhaps I should have done. Since then I would say my career has suffered a little, but often, from being a patsy. Still, the incident changed my life by getting me accepted, with a mixed academic record, into HBS.

It was not, however, all work and no play. While I was working for my stepfather, on Friday evenings I would drop in at a bar in South Croydon, where foreign au pair girls would go after they'd had their English lessons. One night, having not been for a week or two, I dropped in and met a beautiful German girl, Hanne. We danced together. Her English was not good enough to talk much, but good enough for her to listen. And of course, talking was my specialty. I didn't stop talking and she got most of it; what she got was that I was having some family business trouble. Hanne came from a family business – her father ran a little printing enterprise attached to their big German house in Bremen. She was sympathetic and knew what it meant within the family for the son to say, "No, I'm not going to do this." I asked her out for a coffee, and we started seeing each other.

At the beginning of the summer before my start at Harvard, the time came for her to get on the train and make her way back to Germany. I went to London, put her on the train and said goodbye, as

I'd done a few times before, being something of an au pair specialist. It was good to have a relationship with such a nice clean end. They'd get on the boat train for France, known as the *Golden Arrow*, and disappear out of my life. In this case, it was the Harwich train and then a ship to Bremerhaven.

After Hanne had left, I felt a few pangs. I had felt pangs before, but they soon dissipated. These were different: they were relentless. Soon after, I called her up and proposed over the telephone. "Will you marry me?" I got to the point very quickly. And she replied, "I'm sorry. What was that?" I asked again, and she still couldn't hear. This time I practically shouted. Hanne was embarrassed because she took the call in the dining room, with the entire family sitting down for lunch. She knew the family would not be entirely happy at the prospect of their only daughter marrying an Englishman and that

Me with my mother (left) and Hanne (right) looking 1960s cool at the Shell Country Club in London in 1961

she would have to break the news gently. So she replied, "Oh, yes. How are you?" That's what she said, because I think she was trying to make our conversation sound commonplace.

She then came back to England and stayed with us for about a month, after which I got on a plane and flew off to Boston. At Christmas after my first semester, having written some pretty decent love letters, I got on an Icelandic Airways plane and flew to London. After a day or two to recover, I took the train and the ferry and the train to Bremen, where Hanne met me. Then I had a session with her father telling him that I wanted to marry his daughter. He got a little drunk and said there was no real lasting trouble between the Germans and the English. It was just their ridiculous leaders, Hitler and Churchill. Under the circumstances, I wasn't going to push him on this argument. The following summer, Hanne joined me in the States.

HARVARD BUSINESS SCHOOL

At Shell's headquarters in the spring of 1964, the elevator was a dangerous place to be at 5:01 as almost everyone in the executive block dashed to get home before dark, "to play with the kids." This was definitely not Goldman Sachs, and definitely pre-Thatcher, who in many ways Americanized Britain. After her, executives would, for better or worse, work a whole lot harder. But on this particular afternoon I was staying after 6 o'clock to eat dinner with a friend at our very good and heavily subsidized cafeteria, when the telephone rang and the secretary of my boss's boss's boss's boss said, to my amazement, that Mr. Bridges wanted to see me. It turned out that Mr. Bridges like me was a Yorkshireman and not educated at Oxford or Cambridge, unlike most Shell executives. Despite this disadvantage,

Mr. Bridges, then head of supply and planning at Royal Dutch, went on to become the boss of Shell Oil U.S. in 1971, an almost unique event for the completely autonomous U.S. division that presented itself as diehard Texan. We had an immediate friendly conversation, what a Yorkshireman calls a "thee and me," when we assume some tribal solidarity. He eventually asked me what my division was doing to help me go to HBS and I told him they had arranged for a tanker to take my trunk to Boston. "Well, Grantham," he says – this is how they talked in 1964, believe me – "how would it be if I kept you on the payroll?" Without taking any time, I said that I couldn't accept and explained to him, given he was clearly surprised, that two years was a long time and I had no idea whether I would want to return to Shell or to England. To this he said, "Grantham, when I place an order for a new tanker it takes five years to deliver and I have no idea what the tanker market will be like in five years," pause, "and, frankly Grantham, that's a much bigger decision."

I must say it was a very effective and memorable way to make the point. So immediately I replied that if he put it that way "I accept." And with that a third of my total business school costs were covered.

You need plenty of luck to get ahead in life. I had been lucky to get into Sheffield despite my poor school record and lucky to get into HBS and lucky that Shell offered to defray a fair bit of my costs. I also had the good fortune to avoid military service on two occasions due to some freak circumstances. Because I failed the school finishing exams, I spent an extra year at the crammer. During that time, Britain abolished National Service. So the rest of my school class had to do two years of military service and ended up a year behind me at university. Then, when I arrived in America, I was given a month to register for military service. Naturally, I waited until the last possible moment. I went along to register just after my 26th birthday, not knowing then that foreigners who were green card holders went to the top of the draft list. The rules stated that if you reached 26 without having received student deferment, which obviously I hadn't because I'd only just arrived in the country, you were deemed to be over age. I squeezed through this loophole very much to the disgust of the local officials. As a result, I was completely free of worrying about being sent to Vietnam, unlike almost all my other classmates.

I quickly realized that business school was not the intellectual challenge I had expected. It was more a spectacularly rigorous trade school. Our task was to race through cases of problems faced by individual companies, learning to view those cases through the eyes of individual executives while learning corporate jargon. It was a crash course in becoming familiar with every aspect of American business and not at all intellectual. There were hardly any questions about why something was going on, might it be different or even should it be different. We were certainly not there to question capitalism or suggest how it could be improved.

The school saw its job as getting the students up to speed as fast as possible so they could hold their own in business. It also gave us the very valuable opportunity to practice arguing cases against a relatively hostile, competitive crowd, leaving them with a sense of confidence, or rather overconfidence. Overconfidence is good for career development in regular business. But it's a pain in the butt for the people who have to deal with these overconfident people. They all reckon themselves more capable than they are. Me, too, no doubt. On the other hand, the last thing you want is someone lacking in confidence.

At business school I also got very valuable practice at public speaking. For six weeks, I didn't speak because I was too intimidated. Then one day, a perfect case arrived on ethics – the only one in the entire curriculum back then. I knew the regular guys would think that it was a waste of time. Happily, it was my kind of topic, a mixture of logic and philosophy. In any case, gamesmanship suggested that I had to do it. I studied every little nuance and worked hard to beat this soft topic into some sort of shape. When they asked for volunteers to present the case, which they always did, I put my hand up about four inches and there was only one other hand that went up. This guy had been waving his arms for six weeks. The professor looked down at the page because he didn't know who the hell I was and called on me. I made my presentation and then he did something very odd. He invited the rest of the class to ask me questions, to poke holes in my thesis. Seven or eight people asked me half-baked questions, which he allowed me to bury quickly. Then finally he threw it open and one of the highest status persons in the class said, "Well, one has to admit he nailed it." Thus he did no damage to my opening salvo. This was like walking on water. I floated back to my room with my roommate, gliding across the quadrangle when the visiting professor who had just taught the case, Mr. von Peterffy from Arthur D. Little, the consulting firm, saw us and changed direction slightly to intersect with us. He paused his walk briefly to say, "Good job today, Grantham."

It was worth waiting the six weeks of stomach-turning inability to make a point because you're intimidated – because you think you have no business being there. Apparently, this typically applies to about half the class. And, you know, you think you're an imposter, and by the end you think perhaps half the class are nitwits. It's an interesting process. It took me six weeks to catch up with the confident Princetonians and Harvardians who had already been indoctrinated to believe in their superiority. I actually recognized that a handful of the class were way over my pay grade. The Baker Scholars, recipients of the school's highest academic award, were drawn from the top 5% of the class. About half of them were so smart they didn't need to work hard to achieve that honor. The other half were particularly avoidable characters who focused everything on getting the scholarship; sucking up and working hard on even the most useless subjects and doing all those evil things.

The basic courses were not that interesting with one or two honorable exceptions. One was taught by a very famous guy, Theodore (Ted) Levitt, who wrote the state of the art marketing case study, *Marketing Myopia*. He was the guy who introduced the idea that you shouldn't define your job as buggy-whip manufacturer but as a transportation accessory manufacturer. That was the origin of the all-time cliché. Levitt also pointed out that oil companies were making a glorious mistake by not defining themselves as energy companies. And that was pretty cool for the mid-sixties. The oil companies still make that terrible error. If they'd defined themselves as energy companies and done it rigorously, forever, what different enterprises they would be today. Getting off your central skill proves to be very, very difficult. Anyway, that was a very important idea at the time.

The marketing class came with a really interesting and unique project that we performed at the end of the course. A small group was handed a consulting project: talking to outside people, asking questions and putting together a collective report and presentation to the company that posed the problem you were working on. Our problem was proposed by International Minerals and Chemicals (IMC) in Skokie, Illinois, which was a mass producer of farm fertilizer. They were interested in finding some tricks to get them to do better in the lawn and garden business, selling little bags of fertilizer to homeowners for their lawns. We had a brilliant taskmaster, Larry Selkovits, who would never take an easy answer. He would send you off to get a better one. We picked one guy because his typing skills were brilliant and someone else who was pretty good with numbers. I managed to get myself the plum job, which was to determine, if my colleagues decided there was not much juice to be had running on the current course, whether there was a deal to be had. Should they think in terms of buying into someone else's experience who was more focused on the lawn and garden market?

My colleagues soon realized that for 23 reasons there was little chance of IMC breaking into the business. There was only one player in the field, a specialist called O.M. Scott (Scott's), which had been around for a few decades, was doing perfectly well and had a very nice brand image, quality, dependability and all those good things. Scott's had an unassailable position. People only buy lawn and garden fertilizer once or twice a year – two weeks in the spring and maybe one week in the fall. Because that's the only time they use it. Scott's would do a wave of advertising at those times and otherwise remain out of view. IMC, Chevron and Shell all tried to break into the market and failed. It turns out that however much money you have, you can't make up for lost time. Scott's had a decades-long head start, which turned out to be the ultimate moat. It's still chugging along today.

I concluded, therefore, that the correct strategy for an industrial fertilizer company would be to buy the market leader. We presented this finding. Because the people from IMC who came to hear our presentation were all engaged in the lawn and garden effort, not surprisingly, they hated it. Afterwards, we had a hard time making polite chit-chat over drinks. But Ted Levitt much admired our balls, as well as our analysis. A few weeks later, the president and chairman of IMC arrived at HBS where he was on the visiting committee. We gave an impromptu pitch and completely convinced him. He flew all seven of us by corporate jet to Montreal and then by limo to a lodge by a lake. We had a weekend to present and discuss in infinite detail our findings to the boss and his personal consultant. Anyway, it was decided they should go ahead with this approach to

Scott's and we were vaguely promised a finder's fee that we calculated would amount to $100,000 for each of us. That was 50 times my salary when I left Shell. But before the deal could be completed, the IMC boss was ousted in a palace coup. We lost that huge fee, which would have changed our lives.

STATUS

The other course at HBS that stood out was destined to survive only a single year because it caused so much trouble. Our 90-member class was divided into small teams, which were then paired. One team was given the job of devising an experiment that would cast light on some social issue. The other team would observe how they did it, how leadership formed, how mistakes were made and so on. The school's secret plan was to see how leadership formed in an unstructured format with no designated leader. A noble experiment.

By then I understood that the business world comes in two flavors: a rather small group of people who are really invested in having a good idea, are into their own ideas for sure, but also into ideas in general; and a much bigger group who are into the implementation or management of ideas, regardless of where they originate. The second group is efficient, they write memos, they follow up on the telephone, they badger people, they move quickly, they hit deadlines. All the things that the great American executive does. As I like to say, they can't even spell the word patience: they must get everything done yesterday. At business school, there were mainly these impatient executive types, hard-driving and ambitious. The school had acquired, either deliberately or by accident, a small handful of ideas people, of which I was one. The ideas people in our section were pretty easily identified. They all sat on the back row and specialized in sniping at the stars, particularly the Baker Scholars. Most people were deferential to these scholars whenever they spoke, except, of course, the few of us at the back who would immediately start shooting arrows at them, rather effectively, I thought. Being a sniper was fun and exciting because the Baker Scholar types could really hit back and many had sharp claws.

Anyway, I found myself proposing that we should run an experiment based on our colleagues' perceived status. This notion came into my head as I started to talk, which is how I think ideas people often work. I started talking with a rough outline in my mind and the details fell into line of quite a complicated experiment: the same case would be presented by people of different status, allowing us to compare the scores given when persons of high and low status made identical points. I had a difficult time getting this experiment accepted by the executive types who always fought off the ideas guys. We got into a fight. I had one advantage, however. I was a vicious debater, partly from being English. (American debating style is more genteel, who knew?) After several meetings, knee-deep in blood, we took a break and when we reconvened the group agreed to implement my plan. I was given a pat on the head, and five minutes to explain the experiment at the beginning. I was happy as a clam. Of course, the executive types ran the show pretty damn efficiently.

Status was the big thing that year – one or two professors played a big role in deciding who were the big cheeses and who were ignored. There was this politically incorrect ranking. It must have been discouraging to be at the bottom of the list. So, we graded our 18 people by perceived status and found there was incredible unanimity in the ranking. The experiment proved a complete success. When a high-status person read a comment, they got a high score and when the same comment was read by a low-status person, they got a low score. It turned out that people were not listening to what was said, but responding to the standing of the person, no doubt influenced by body language, demeanor, reputation – all things relating to persuasiveness. We don't listen to what someone says. Instead, we listen to who the hell is saying it. My experiment proved this beyond a shadow of a doubt and put numbers on it. The class literally was not grading the comments. They were grading the speaker, over and over again.

The experience confirmed to me that I was an ideas guy and not an executive type, as Shell had realized when I applied to work there. The great American executive is always going to be good at dealing with crises like the great financial crash of 2008 after they've occurred. Always moving fast, focused, short-term-oriented, making quick decisions. Their weakness is that they never see outlier events coming. They're just not that kind of people. That's a more creative right-brained activity. Those whom I refer to as "the feet on the table with a coffee cup," bullshitting about the 1930s and 1970s – who take outliers seriously. I'm right-brained, incapable of managing my way out of a brown paper bag. The right brain is better suited for long-term investing than short-term management, or short-term investment for that matter.

WHAT'S GOING ON HERE?

Throughout my life I've always found myself asking the same question: What is going on here? You must be willing to ask embarrassingly simple questions, as well as more complicated ones. That comes easily to me. I also suffer from a kind of attention deficit disorder. After 20 minutes or half an hour max, I have to take a break or change the subject. But I always come back to the problem. And keep coming back, having allowed the brain time to mush it around in between. For me, it's important not to march forward with an idea till you've ground it to death.

My colleagues at the Grantham Foundation refer to this as my "butterfly effect." If you watch butterflies, which I do, you'll see them flitting around the garden as if they have no concentration. But they keep on their patch for a long time, certainly for hours, revisiting the same flowers. And that's what I do. I change the topic. Digress. Take a break. Tell stories, allow for digressions, allow for a change of subject, but always go back to the original topic. What I find is that each time I return to the subject, the digressions have freed up my brain cells. It's a much more profitable way to spend your time than focusing on a single topic. Because when you do that your brain runs dry, it becomes bored, however hard you try. Interspersing conversations with a kind of commercial break allows the brain to recycle, digest and have an insight.

If you're in an idea-generating business – which the investment business is – you need to generate ideas. Unless you deviate from the market in your opinion, and unless you deviate strongly and hold that opinion firmly, it's not worth the effort. And if you want to generate original ideas you need to set aside time for bullshitting or what the Brits more politely call brainstorming. The idea generation capability includes lots of half-baked ideas along with a few fully baked ideas. I'm very, very tolerant of half-baked ideas. I've never met anyone who only produces seriously good ideas. You must tolerate a lot of flaky ideas in order to get a few good ones.

Long bullshitting sessions often result eventually, at the end of a couple of hours, with some decent idea finally turning up. In my experience, one or two good ideas a year are more than enough. I also recognized early on that you need more than just having a few original ideas to succeed. You really need to defend them, to have the ability to dig in your heels and fight for your ideas, which is how I got the business school class to accept my status experiment. If you don't, you're screwed. If you think your ideas will speak for themselves in corporate America, you couldn't be more wrong. You may have a better chance of your ideas speaking for themselves in academic life. But even there, I think, you probably have to dig in your heels. By the time you enter the corporate world, the quality of the idea is of second order. The main issue is who has the idea and how well connected they are.

DOLPHIN

Three decades after leaving business school I attended a dinner held by one of our largest clients. At the same event were the investment heads of Morgan Stanley, J.P. Morgan and Goldman Sachs and some 50 other people. Before going into dinner everyone was invited to take a Myers-Briggs personality test. This test falls into this very interesting category that I really like, and that is that academics won't touch it with a 10-foot pole because the theory is lightweight. Yet it works. As the old joke goes, "Okay, so it works in practice. But tell me the theory."

My personality type turned out to be INFJ. I stands for introvert as opposed to extrovert. My nature is introverted, except when I'm on the soccer pitch where I can't help myself from shouting and ordering teammates around; N is intuitive as opposed to sensing; F is feeling as opposed to thinking. (I'm a feeler so I must worry about things like saving biodiversity.) Finally, J is judging as opposed to perceiving, which means you try to balance everything to make a judgment. These types are described as long-term strategists – and that's exactly what it says on my business card. But you could, if you wanted to be unfriendly, call them cold-blooded abstractionists.

At the dinner of this client's annual gathering, the guests were all sitting at tables with members of their own personality type. Except for the investment bosses who sat together at the high table. Each personality type was represented by an animal – among them foxes, lions, owls and dolphins. I was a dolphin. The only dolphin in the room apart from the woman organizing the event. At my table the investment bosses were all owls, the only owls in the room – which is a pretty amazing outcome for Myers-Briggs if you think about it. Owls are the natural leaders who want to crush your bones and tell everyone what to do. This told me what I already knew, which was that I was faking even those modest aspects of being an executive. I felt it in my stomach. I was the lone dolphin among the owls. I'm a delegator – an ardent delegator, who ruinously delegates on some occasions and brilliantly on others, somewhat randomly.

PAYING THE FREIGHT

I had a summer job after the first year at HBS for seven weeks at Arthur D. Little, working in their oil and gas group. Another oily Brit from business school worked with me. I remember when we got our first check and we sat back kind of glowing. Holding it in front of us, hardly able to believe how much it was. They had paid us at an absolutely splendid rate of $8,000 a year, about three times what we had earned in London just a year earlier.

In 1966, after my last year at HBS, I had a second summer job – the previously described position at IMC. It was even more lucrative than the first. Although we lost out on the dreams-of-avarice finder's fee, we were paid a then utterly unheard of $100 a day (probably about $1,200 a day in today's terms) plus a $15 a day living allowance along with a driving allowance. Hanne and I, who had been married at the registry office in Kingston, Jamaica, the previous Christmas, moved into a basement apartment in Wilmette, north of Chicago. By the end of the summer, I got a check for just over $6,000, almost exactly one year of school fees. Try doing that today! Unfortunately, as we shall see, I lost the money on foolish speculations.

After Harvard, I found a job at a consultancy, Cresap McCormick and Paget, which specialized in government work but had plenty of commercial work as well. At the time, they were quite close to the size of the big two consultancies, McKinsey and Booz Allen. Consultancy, as I soon learned, was, as then practiced, an inherently marginal activity in terms of usefulness. The work involved fairly superficial analysis. Consulting projects were designed to encourage another consulting contract. Profits were earned by doing repeat projects for the same client. The way you did that was by not upsetting the client. The great temptation was to tell them what they wanted to hear. If they wanted small changes, you gave them small changes and so on. What you didn't say is your whole premise is wrong, that you should adopt a completely different strategy – as we had done to IMC.

My first project was Old Spice, the aftershave brand. In those days everyone's father apparently wore Old Spice. It was a fine old brand, but mismanaged. The company was going downmarket with special deals and so on. They were looking for help. When we buzzed around, it soon became obvious that the big problem with Old Spice was incompetent top management, relatives of the founders. They had inadequate battle plans from top to toe. My project manager explained to me patiently that we couldn't say that. But in the end, he relented. I think he was old enough and senior enough in his career. Perhaps he wanted for once to do the right thing. We told them, "You had better sell out and become a decent brand in a long list of decent brands where they eat, sleep and breathe marketing and do everything right." Of course, they fired us.

By then my job with that dignified firm began to feel awfully tame. As I looked around for a better career, it quickly became obvious that my classmates who were having the most excitement were those in the investment business. Fortunately, I was quite efficient for one of the few times in my life and ran a comprehensive job-seeking program aimed at London, New York and Boston. There was a potential job offer in London and another from a hedge fund in New York but neither of them came through quickly enough. One was delayed waiting for S.E.C. approval for a new fund. But I couldn't wait. I headed for Boston, and after a refusal by Fidelity in an interview in which a then-famous fund manager could not stop looking at stock prices on his new Bunker-Ramo desktop device, I was offered a job at Keystone Funds.

High-paying industries, like the investment business, will casually pay you far more than you need. There is absolutely no relationship between the difficulty of your job, the social usefulness of your job and the relative rewards of your job. I realized in 1968 that I had jumped to the fortunate side of this equation. At my dopey consultancy job I had worked my way up to $12,000 a year, and these idiots at Keystone offered me the job at $18,000. I would have been thrilled to take it at $12,000. At the time, Fidelity and Keystone dominated the Boston mutual fund business, with the former managing $2 billion and Keystone nearly as large. Today, Fidelity has assets of around $5 trillion, while Keystone has disappeared. *Sic transit gloria…*

CHAPTER 2

The Zero-Sum Game

When I was a teenager, my parents had their friends over on most Sundays for a drink. (Actually, it was a 1950s version of "a few drinks.") During these sessions I was impressed by the confident expressions of current and future success laid out by my stepfather's closest buddy. His firm was a manufacturer of scaffolding, a patented, easily assembled variety, for which he was the main international salesman. After two or three years I could stand it no longer and at 16, because my parents did not invest in the market and for lack of a better idea, I arrived at a bank branch in a south London suburb with the bank book from my "home safe account," which was designed for children's savings and which I had had for as long as I could remember. Asking to see the branch manager, I surprised and amused him by asking for his help in investing everything in my account – £16. I remember the investment well: Acrow A shares. It was his first experience with investing for a home safe account but he could see no problem and without parental confirmation or any fuss at all did the trade. And so my first commission was paid out. And, by the way, £16 was a lot. I had been extremely frugal. (The exchange rate was 4:1 and $64 of buying power in 1954 translates to about $560 today.)

So far, so good. Years came and went as they do and presently I was 26 and unexpectedly heading to business school in America.

Equally unexpectedly and very generously I had been kept on the payroll of my employer, Royal Dutch Shell, but at £1,200 a year this was only going to cover one-third of my two-year expenses. As a result, everything I owned – as in every last thing – was cashed in. By this time my shares had blossomed to about £100 of value. Encouraged by the unabated enthusiasm from our scaffolding friend (who, after all, we had assumed must surely know the innermost secrets of his firm, particularly because we knew for a fact that he had most of his wealth, including his pension, tied up in the company's shares), and no doubt reinforced by past stock performance, my mother made me a proposition: to avoid paying the notorious commissions, I would transfer my shares to her account and she would pay me that day's closing price. So, off I went to the U.S. with enough to buy my ticket on a VC10, a faster crossing than you can get today by the way, but brutally expensive for a one-way trip. (My parents had bravely allowed me to take out a mortgage on their house to draw down as I needed.)

The following year, with little preamble, "our" company imploded to zero. My mother took a few hundred pounds' hit in her only (and last) stockholding, and our friend, right on the cusp of retirement, lost the great majority of his formerly comfortable nest egg. Almost until the last day he had known nothing about his impending doom, about big bets made and reckless debts assumed to make the corporate great leap forward. His own sales efforts in South America had continued promisingly into the last few months.

Later at business school, I had that well-paid summer job at Arthur D. Little with a fellow Englishman named Phillip. We were both living very cheaply, so what were we going to do with this sudden excess? We'd invest the money and turn it into the beginnings of a fortune. Phillip introduced me to the *Wall Street Digest*, which, amazingly to me, had all of this seemingly priceless information – the best research (presumably) that Wall Street had to offer. And it was all free in our business school library, along with a fair fraction of all the research out there. So we researched away, compared the most mouth-watering tips, shared a stockbroker and invested together.

Naturally, most of our stocks went up. Seduced by a bull market, we thought that either our advice from Wall Street was superior or we were, or, more likely, both. Time passed to the summer of graduation, when I had an even more ridiculously high-paying summer job, in this case for the large fertilizer company. The net effect was that at the end of summer, as I started my new job at the consulting firm in Manhattan, a check for $6,000 arrived, which was enough then to pay for a full year at business school and, interestingly, exactly what I owed on my parents' mortgage.

Paying off the mortgage seemed out of the question because by then I had convinced myself that I must have the touch for short-term investing. Hanne and I moved into an L-shaped, one-room apartment located almost in the Midtown Tunnel in Manhattan. My plan was to continue to save, spending nothing, and invest brilliantly in order to be able to return to Europe rich, or nearly so, and in a hurry. Because this plan could not be done with $6,000, it was necessary to borrow some more. Fortunately (or unfortunately, depending on the time horizon), there was a loan loophole that allowed you to pledge mutual fund certificates (the old type that you could actually touch as opposed to electronic impulses) and borrow 80% of their face value for "home improvements." Well, mine were for home improvements alright, but just not quite then. So, I borrowed and, after a little more good fortune, brought the new certificates to the bank and took another 80% against them too.

This period from late 1966 through to 1968 featured a normal bull market in large stocks, a more ebullient market in smaller stocks, and an epic silly season in tiny, under-the-counter pink sheet stocks. This was the age of the super-aggressive, go-go investors, known as the gunslingers. And I became a gunslinging nitwit in what was the last really crazy, silly stock market before the internet era. Most of the smaller stocks were newly minted and almost all ceased to exist in a few years. Many ventures had great names like "Palms of Pasadena." I joined a loose investing association of former classmates. With our buying and touting to all who would listen, our favorites tended to rise rapidly at first: rocket stocks that, like other rockets, would end up crashing back to earth quickly enough.

The defining event for me was in the summer of 1968, when my wife and I took a three-week holiday back in England and Germany, shortly after joining Keystone. Lunching with some of the hotshots – being a newbie I was by no means a fully-fledged member – I was fascinated, indeed, almost overwhelmed, by the story *du jour*: American Raceways. The company was going to introduce Formula 1 Grand Prix racing to the U.S. It had acquired one existing track and had one race that was hugely attended. With a few more tracks we could calculate how much money – a lot – the company could make. It seemed to me as a foreigner to have little chance of failure. With noise, speed, danger, and even the ultimate risk of death, it seemed, well, just so American. And every Brit's hero, Stirling Moss – one of the leading British drivers before his retirement in 1962 – was on the board. So I bought 300 shares at $7. (For defining events in your life you do remember the details. Sometimes even accurately.)

By the time we returned from our vacation, the stock was at $21. Here was my opportunity to show that I had internalized early lessons; to demonstrate my resolve. So I did what any aspiring value-oriented stock analyst would do: I sold everything else I owned and tripled up. Nine hundred shares at $21, mostly on borrowed money. In a Victorian novel aimed at improving morals, ethics and general behavior, this is where tragedy follows hubris. But real life is more confusing as to how it delivers lessons and it likes to tease, apparently. By Christmas, American Raceways hit $100 and we were rich by the standards of those days, and certainly compared to my expectations. Back then you could still buy a reasonable four-bedroom house in the London suburbs for £10,000 and in Boston for $40,000, and we had about $85,000 after margin borrowings and before taxes due.

In fact, in January 1970 came another nearly defining event: Hanne and I fell in love with a charming three-floor Victorian house in Newton, Massachusetts, on a very quiet street next to an apple orchard and backing on to some undeveloped hillside. Asking price: $40,000 (today's guess, perhaps $1 million or more). Our family capital account after its then recent decline would still have allowed us to: a) buy the house without a mortgage; b) buy a new BMW 2002 (small, fast, not too showy, and remarkably cheap); and c) have a few thousand left over. But our $37,000 offer was turned down and we backed off. And, even as we reconsidered, my stock began to crumble and I was lucky, with hindsight, to be able to scramble out of American Raceways in the low $60s. It turned out that Formula 1's original crowd was based almost completely on novelty and curiosity and had nearly no hard-core followers; Americans liked their motor racing to be in cars that looked not like real racing cars, but in vehicles that looked just like their own. Who knew?

Well, I was neither totally broke nor fully chastened and was eager to make back my losses. Naturally, I bumped immediately into a real winner. The new idea was called Market Monitor Data Systems and this really was a breakthrough technology, even with hindsight. It was going to put a "Monitor," an electronic screen, on every broker's desk, so that they could trade in options, making their own market. This brainchild of a mathematics professor had only one flaw: it was way ahead of its time. Fifteen years later the technology was completely accepted. Oh, well. After a good rise it became clear to stockholders that expenses rose rapidly with Monitors installed and no business followed. Almost none at all. And, following the developments far more hawk-like than was typical for me, I managed to leap out two weeks before bankruptcy with enough to pay down margin and bank loans, leaving me with about $5,000.

Hanne had not been amused by the frugality that characterized our 18 months in New York, a city then and now where some spending money makes a big difference in the quality of life. For her, to go back to Europe with a nest egg was maybe worth it. Maybe. Her biggest gripe was having to cook at home almost every day after work. No working wife today would stand for it, and rightly so. All I can say in my defense is that that was the style in the 1960s. Very weak, I know. But, when confronted with the near total loss of our savings and therefore our main plan – saving to go home well off – Hanne did not break into hysterics, rather she put herself to the task of keeping our financially leaky boat afloat. She, however, accrued an inexhaustible supply of IOUs. Well, inexhaustible so far.

Investing does seem to be an area where there are lessons that usually cannot be taught, only painfully learned on one's own. My motto in investing has always been cry over spilt milk, for analyzing errors is how you learn almost everything. My early investment disasters imparted some useful lessons:

From Acrow A:

1. Inside advice, legal in those days, from friends in the company is a particularly dangerous basis for decisions;

you don't know how limited their knowledge might be and you are overexposed to sustained enthusiasm.
2. Always diversify, particularly for your pension fund.
3. Fraud, near-fraud or colossal incompetence can always strike.
4. Don't buy stocks yourself if you're an amateur: invest with a relatively rare expert, if you can find one, or put your money in an index!
5. Investing when young will start your brain turning on things financial.
6. Painful errors teach you more than successful ones.
7. Luck helps, and finally…
8. Have a convenient mother to be the fall guy.

From American Raceways and other specs:

9. Local cultural differences can be very enduring even between Britain and the U.S. Formula 1 has tried repeatedly to break into the U.S. Soccer here has also been just around the corner for the past 50 years.
10. Sometimes even a great idea will fail, like Market Monitor, because the technology infrastructure is just not there; that it is simply ahead of its time. Much more importantly, investing is serious. It can and often is intellectually compelling. But it should not be driven by excitement, as it is for many individuals, and when treated that way will almost always end badly.

My experience with American Raceways and Market Monitor and, more importantly, my experience at painfully wiping out myself and my wife financially did far more than teach or re-teach some of the basic rules of investing. I got wiped out before anyone else knew the bear market started. After 1968, I became a great reader of history books. I was shocked and horrified to discover that I had just learned a lesson that was freely available all the way back to the South Sea Bubble. The experience turned me profoundly away from the speculative and gambling possibilities of investing and turned me permanently, and pretty much overnight, into a patient, long-term value investor. Luckily, the new style fitted nicely with my natural conservative and frugal upbringing. The value perspective is pretty much baked into the Yorkshire culture.

After my unsuccessful foray into GoGo stocks, it seemed obvious to me that buying cheap rather than expensive was a good idea. Ben Graham, the father of value investing, had noticed much earlier that for patient investors the important financial ratios (such as price-to-book and price-to-earnings) always went back to their old trends. He unsurprisingly preferred larger safety margins to smaller ones and, most importantly, more assets per dollar of stock price to fewer because he believed profit margins would tend to mean revert and make underperforming assets more valuable.

You do not have to be especially frugal to think, "What's not to like about that?" So in my training period I adopted the same biases. And they worked. It was not exactly shooting fish in a barrel, but close. For value managers the world was, for the most part, convenient, and even easy for decades. (Until around 2000 when things started to change.) I concentrated on knowing the long-term history of the stock market and tried to ignore short-term noise. I was constantly thinking: How does what I'm seeing now compare with earlier examples? What is the bedrock value underneath market price? What are the possible triggers for a crash?

KEYSTONE

After moving to Boston we took an apartment on Beacon Hill. It was a wonderful deal: $160 a month, two bedrooms. The apartment overlooked a little courtyard of a restaurant, which had a fountain. We would sit there in the summer with the window open and the fountain playing. From there it was a short walk to Keystone's offices in the downtown district.

The investment world in those days was terribly amateurish. There was very little talent. My fellow investment professionals were not the intellectual elite. They were people who, for one reason or another, had fumbled their way into the business. In the late 1960s, a career in investment was for the failed son of a rich family, who'd be packed off to Wall Street or London, where their job was to hold hands with rich clients. In short, investment management was a lowbrow enterprise and trading was even lower brow. That was the hierarchy.

The big institutional money in the U.S. in 1968, such as it was, was almost monopolized by the New York banks, particularly Morgan Guaranty Trust. Pension funds were just getting going. The New York banks appointed preppy younger sons to take clients out to dinner, buy them a fancy bottle of wine or two and then sell them some Exxon or Coca-Cola. That's how people invested money in those days. Several of my colleagues at Keystone at least were HBS grads, so by the standards of the investment business they were the elite. Smart enough, but not super smart. The super smart, it turned out, were mostly working for the government. In investing, if you just kept up a regular pace you could shine.

The business of investing was all new to me. You were given an industry or two to cover and introduced yourself to the famous analysts on Wall Street, who licked your boots because commissions in those days were fixed at a stunning 1% of the value of the trade. So, of course, they flattered us and treated us well. There was a mass of analyst dinners and lunches where Bear Stearns or Goldman Sachs would get an industry expert or a specialist professor to present. The one that I remember most was Franco Modigliani, the great economics professor – I say that thinking that most of them are complete turkeys – who got one of the few deserved Nobel Prizes and had a wonderful reputation for cooperating with everybody and being down to earth, practical and friendly. Almost too good to be true, you could argue.

Anyhow, Modigliani showed up to address this or that issue one lunchtime in the course of 1974, hired by some brokerage firm. I went to see him along with everybody else. He wandered into my territory while talking about small cap stocks and made a mistake. Shaking with excitement, I leapt up and pointed out his error. Well, you know what would normally happen when a cocky young kid does that to a prospective Nobel Prize winner or, indeed, any serious economist. But not this time. Instead of being slapped down and left to dislike him forever, he says, "Oh, that's interesting. So, if that's true then isn't the following also true…" "Yes, yes," I say and he goes on to dance with my data. He effortlessly proved in a few minutes that he could change his mind, incorporate new data at blinding speed and run with it all the while being unthreatened and abnormally generous and friendly. I'm left a fan for life.

From the start, it was very obvious to me that investors had no hard and fast rule as to what constituted value and what constituted the reason to buy a stock. The so-called professionals, the fund managers, themselves had no clue. Their standard was a whole series of rules of thumb. There was no options theory. Options prices were worked by gut feeling. The price-to-earnings (P/E) ratio was the standard valuation measure for stocks, but to me seemed quite arbitrary. So I immediately started asking what sense is there that everything is run by rules of thumb. How did investors decide that some industries deserve a higher P/E than others? What the hell is value and how should you measure it? What are the shortcomings of the existing measures? I tried to ask the right questions so as to better obsess about getting to the right answers.

Keystone was an interesting firm in that it had a great insight that could have made it a super fortune. Its funds were broken up into a series of in-house subdivisions. The market was divided into various groups. S1 were the super blue chips, S2 were medium blue chips, S3 were high yield stocks and S4 were the racy specs. The funds K1 and K2 were more diversified with K1 more of a value portfolio and K2 higher quality. This was a brilliant idea. They had exactly the same arrangement with their bond funds. Smart managers just managed against their benchmark, found a weak group to underweight, then would go out to lunch, have their three Martinis, come back and sleep at their desks. But they would still beat the benchmark. It was a good system and they never managed to make a fuss about it or promote it. They were selling purely on their record, which was not bad but they were missing this great opportunity to make a hullabaloo about a novel way in which the market could be segmented.

BRUNSWICK

I spent only nine months at Keystone, but that was long enough to nearly get me kicked out of the investment business. My first project came to my attention through a Brit friend whom we used to go skiing with. He was a stockbroker and had this nice idea about a company called Brunswick, which made equipment for bowling alleys. There had been a great bowling boom, a bubble, you might say, in the 1950s. In the early 1960s, the bubble blew up. Brunswick went from selling 100 alleys to selling none. Then, to make matters worse, the market shrank back to maybe half. There was chaos and confusion across the bowling world. Brunswick was on the hook because it had leased a lot of bowling lanes that were returned.

In its heyday, the company had been sensible enough to acquire the Mercury outboard motor business, which was then going very well and shared the market with Johnson. Even better, Brunswick had a medical instrument business, Sherwood Medical Instruments, which was growing rapidly. The company had gone public with Sherwood when the trouble started, but had only floated about 20% of the shares, using the cash proceeds to stay afloat and buy back the bowling lanes from failed operators. My broker friend pointed out that if you valued the remaining stake in Sherwood at the price its shares were trading for, it was worth more than Brunswick's entire market capitalization, giving you an outboard motor business and lots of bowling equipment for free.

The other interesting wrinkle was that the period for depreciating the bowling lanes was quite short and had just come to an end. Depreciation was a huge component of the accounting for bowling operations. Suddenly Brunswick had all these bowling lanes that were now fully depreciated so profits were set to pick up. It was not a particularly sexy business, but one with a positive and modestly growing cash flow. So, I plagiarized this idea, putting in quite a bit of extra thought and research that ultimately resulted in an eight-page note. It was a terrific, extremely underpriced opportunity, worth maybe three times what it was selling for. This attracted a lot of attention. Brunswick suddenly became a widely popular stock. Keystone bought the maximum amount of stock it could, which was 15%, and my friends at Fidelity, who enjoyed the story, also acquired a similarly sized stake.

I had plenty of acquaintances from business school who had gone into investment banking. A friend from my first year, Ed Gibbons, had started his own investment firm – Gibbons, Green, Van Amerongen – and it was doing deals and making good money. I called Ed and told him I had a good idea for a deal. I flew to New York to run through the rough outline for Brunswick. Ed saw it was a brilliant opportunity for a takeover and knew exactly the right people he was going to take it to. The potential buyer was a conglomerate named Bangor Punta, whose people were really interested. We stood to make a killing for shareholders and maybe I deserved to get a finder's fee (although given none had been discussed, this was just a teasing thought).

Unfortunately, Brunswick got a whiff of this. They thought they'd better do a counter deal. So they proposed to merge their business with Union Tank Car, which leased tank cars to carry oil and chemicals. It was a completely useless deal in every way except it would make an unattractive combined company, with the Brunswick people in charge, that no one would want to buy. In other words, management was screwing their stockholders but possibly helping themselves.

Fidelity and Keystone were actually not quite enough to block the deal ourselves, but with a few friends and acquaintances, Brunswick had no chance of getting it through without our agreement. So the telephone starts to ring. "What are you doing?" And I said, "Well, of course if it's a terrible deal, it's in our shareholders' best interests to have nothing to do with it." Fidelity, of course, said the same. The following day – this was moving very fast – the Brunswick CEO and his lawyers – a squad of five – arrived at Keystone to remonstrate. Eventually all the VIPs at Keystone joined the meeting and they called for this lowly, recently arrived analyst. I went in and they asked a lot of questions and I said it was a terrible deal and explained why the company was worth twice the price it was selling for. The next day Brunswick called off the merger with Union Tank Car.

Before our preferred deal could be tried, Saul Steinberg made an offer for Chemical Bank of New York, and overnight the mood on Wall Street changed. Who was this nasty nonentity attempting to buy one of the white shoe New York banks? The word went out to the Chase Manhattans and the Morgans to pull their damn commitments to all these upstart financial operators, like Steinberg. So Bangor Punta's funding for the Brunswick deal was also pulled.

Fast-forward 18 months, when I was no longer working at Keystone, I received a notice saying that the SEC was subpoenaing me. I flew down to Washington with a Keystone lawyer and walked into a smoke-filled room where happily, some really young fresh graduate types were beavering away. Our conversation was recorded on a little machine with a rubber tube that a woman talked quietly into so as not to upset the conversation. Every word that I said was recorded. They asked me whether I had been aware of a pending offer for Brunswick by Bangor Punta. And I replied, "Yeah, yeah, everyone was aware of the rumor." "When did you become aware of this? Did you immediately tell your superior that?" "No," I replied. They all sat forward in their seats. "Why didn't you tell them?" I replied to the effect that this was 1968. There was a deal being announced every few days. If I had rushed into my bosses and told them every market rumor, they would have fired me in a couple of weeks.

They all sat back in their chairs, satisfied with my answers. But they missed the key point. They did not ask, "Were you involved in any way?" They did not ask, "Did you mention this to your investment banking friends?" Because I had made up my mind that if they asked those questions, I would confess. The law of the land said mutual funds mustn't interfere in corporate affairs. The law also said that the behavior of mutual funds had to be in the best interests of their stockholders. In the Brunswick case, these two laws were completely contradictory. This was an opportunity to really make good money for our mutual fund investors. But I couldn't act in their best interests without interfering with corporate affairs. My defense was going to be that I had followed the latter rule, namely maximizing shareholders' returns. But my actions could have been construed as interfering with corporate affairs. It was still a little Wild West, shoot first and ask questions later. Things might not have worked out for me. The bullet whistled past my ear, which was exciting.

Although the Bangor Punta deal died, at least Keystone was able to sell its Brunswick stock for between two and three times what we had paid and I gained a reputation as the new hotshot who had written the Brunswick Report. The Keystone fund managers knew who I was. In the following months I was given the airlines to cover. I invited the leading bull and the leading bear on the industry to come to Boston and debate in front of all the fund managers. No one had ever done that before. It caused a minor sensation. The next thing I decided was that the entire airline industry was a buy. At the time, airline prices were fixed by the government. With fixed costs, a little bit of an increase in business would make the airlines a ton of money. This was not about nuances. This was about, "Dude, this is a big idea." So I wrote the first industry recommendation at Keystone and because of bureaucracy, I had to do one for every single airline. I wrote a pro forma one pager, duplicated for every airline, making the same case that this was a semi-government industry that had the opportunity to do very well if this and that happened. A couple of the Keystone fund managers, including Dean LeBaron, whom I eventually left with, seriously bought into this concept. Dean liked to make a striking statement so he took a large position in the airlines in the fund that he managed.

After seven or eight months, I was flying high. That fall there was a salary review. Normally new hires who had arrived in April were ignored. But Keystone gave me a jump to $20,000. This was a generous salary but I was restless. I had buddied up socially with a guy who was the son of the CEO of John Hancock, one of the most important commercial jobs in Boston, who worked for a competitor of Keystone. We would go skiing together with our wives and friends. We discussed starting our own fund. This was a very cocky thing, for sure. He'd had only a few years of investing experience and I'd had a princely nine months in the business. We hit on the idea of having Dean LeBaron as our chairman, while we'd run around and do the heavy lifting, picking stocks and making a fortune for our clients. I knew that Dean was at loggerheads with Keystone's chief investment officer. They didn't like each other at all. Dean didn't like being told what to do. The other guy didn't like someone who didn't like being told what to do. After some thought Dean agreed to join us. But then a few days later, he came back and said, "No, I won't do it. I'll start my own firm."

After Dean turned us down, I put our plans on hold. Dean then proposed that I join him. This put me in a dilemma. In the end I decided to go with Dean and offered my buddy a job but he wasn't interested. Ownership of the new firm, to be called Batterymarch Financial – named after the Batterymarch Building on Batterymarch Street in downtown Boston, where we rented an office – was split 60% to Dean and 40% to me, with the understanding that we would dilute our stakes as other people were hired. Dean had very grandiose ideas that the firm would manage a billion dollars by the end of the first year. To put that into perspective, Keystone only had a couple of billion after 40 years. So that was a ton of money. The reality was pretty sobering. We started out in June 1969 and a year later we had one account, $100,000 from Dean's friend, Charley Ellis, the investment consultant. Soon we were running through Dean's wife's money and I was working for nothing. By the end of 1974, over five years later, we were managing $48 million, still not enough to pay the freight.

Before leaving Keystone, I had this glorious investment portfolio worth $80,000, so I was in a good position to make a decision to go off on my own. But I hadn't really been counting on the fact that my $80,000 would become $5,000 after my gunslinging adventures, before six months had gone by. So really, before we put up our shingle and took our first account, I'd managed to wipe myself out, which made it fairly imperative that Hanne continued to earn an income. She worked, first at Berlitz teaching German where she did total immersion with the clients, spending every day for three or four days speaking nothing but German, which works, apparently. Hanne was an incredibly handsome woman and, of course, all her clients fell in love with her. One of her admirers was a former governor of Massachusetts, which was rather disconcerting. Then she got a job at MIT Press as assistant to the director working on their German translations.

This paid the rent and a bit else. I wasn't earning any material amount at Batterymarch for the next few years. I got paid what I'd call a half a salary when we had a research contract for a year. When that went away, I had no salary at all for two years, and then I got a half a salary again for a year. Those were frugal times. We didn't have enough money to go to the movies. I didn't buy a suit or a shirt or a tie for about three years. We were reduced to eating out once a week at the English Tearoom in Back Bay where they offered a kind of all you could eat at a fixed price. We would stoke up there for a day or two. I would only buy the *Boston Globe* when the Celtics had a game that I particularly wanted to read about. Otherwise I wouldn't buy the paper because it was too expensive. When I was moved to half a salary again, we noticed that the pay increase was like water and sponge. Our threadbare lifestyle would just soak up the money, so that every time we turned around we had nothing left. We didn't have any scrubbing brushes that weren't worn out. I would have to go and buy two or three suits to get a kind of passable wardrobe, and five shirts, and so on. Everything was worn out. The thing is, we didn't mind. We felt like students. I'd never had a lot of money and when I had more than needed never spent it. We were full of hope that eventually we would be just fine.

The year after Batterymarch started, we were joined by Dick Mayo who'd been with us at Keystone. Dick immediately made it clear that he would love to run the portfolio. He was a perfect portfolio manager. He had a great memory, was very hard-working, could understand valuation and all that stuff. Dick was perfectly sensible and could tell a cheap stock when he saw one. So he ran the portfolio – before we had any money, we were running a paper portfolio. Dick looked after 60% of the portfolio and I took charge of the rest. We didn't own a single stock unless we both agreed on it.

Dean was left to run the business. He had been a Baker Scholar at HBS, one of the top 5% in his year. Of these scholars, the super bright half were going to be stars whether they worked or not. (One of them who later worked in the government and taught at HBS was the only one who would play hooky with me to see the latest James Bond movie. Everyone else was too terrified not to be working.) The other half were typically very hard-working and focused, even for the least useful classes. They were also very good at examination technique and understood that who you know matters and, in general, were well suited to fight it out in corporate America. Dean was one of the latter group. He was given to ambitious ideas but hated to check the data consistently (although when moved to do it, did it well) and, as a result, was often wrong. In short, a bit flighty but an attractive, charismatic character whom most people were charmed by. Above all else, Dean understood that the investment business in those days was incredibly boring and that a little bit of flash would go a long way.

In the early days at Batterymarch, Dean was very good at spinning that we were more successful in terms of asset gathering than was the case. He taught me one very important lesson, which I wasn't able to capitalize on for quite a few years; and that was the importance of putting your best foot forward in terms of your public image. If you have a good idea don't hide it, don't be shy. If you have a good idea make it as clear as you can and polish it up. He was very good at propaganda, and I did learn that from him. Thank you, Dean.

It was an interesting experience to work with very little money. Hard times made us more cohesive. We managed to minimize our internal disagreements. Dean and I went for the big picture, and Dick went for detail and solidness. Initially Dean and I were on one side and Dick was on the other. But that shifted over time. My job description in those days was heaven. I didn't talk to anybody. I didn't have any responsibilities. I didn't manage the portfolio. Informally with Dick, I was expected to come up with a few decent ideas. Initially, I specialized in a few industries that fascinated me: little regional trucking companies, insurance companies, food retailers, and one or two other groups. I was free, though, for hours, days, sometimes weeks, just to burrow into any idea that seemed interesting. And they were all over the place. They all seemed interesting. I had no boring bureaucratic work to do. Pure heaven.

THE ZERO-SUM GAME

In my second year at Batterymarch, I stumbled across what turned out to be probably the most significant idea of my investment career.

One day we went off to HBS to hear a class taught by a guy called Lee Bodenhamer, from Little Rock, Arkansas, who was a friend of Dean's. Lee was leading a case discussion in an Easter break course for institutional managers, mainly small endowments, not Harvard and Yale, but the Swarthmores and Williamses. He'd written a case that compared Morgan Guaranty Trust (now J.P. Morgan) with T. Rowe Price, which in those days was a hotshot new company introducing growth stocks to a blue-chip-only culture, and added our flaky little Boston start-up (he didn't bother to mention Batterymarch's name) whose intention was to buy out-of-favor small companies.

The purpose of the presentation was to discuss the pros and cons of investing with these three different styles. At the end of the class, he said we've got these two guys from this flaky little firm; we should ask them what they think. So Dean said what he thought, whatever it was. Then it was my turn. I said the main thing that I had been thinking as I looked at the case was why no one in the class had suggested giving their money to the gentlemen from Standard and Poor's. Because if you lined up the three investment firms and then you threw in the data from the S&P benchmark index, all things considered, it looked like the bargain of them all, in terms of risk, potential returns and, above all, costs.

When we got back to the office we tossed around the idea of starting a fund that tracked the stock market index. Dean initially hated the idea. He told me he would kill me if I brought it up one more time. It was such a nice simple insight. But no one seemed to share it. All my friends thought it was loony; and the more they knew about finance the worse they thought it was and spent the time heaping abuse on the idea. One of my closest friends, Ezra Mager, who probably knew the most about investing, said it best: "Jeremy, Jeremy, you don't understand. Americans will never settle for mediocrity." He was a lot closer to being right than I realized at the time. For over 30 years later, the percentage of money in indexing was a rounding error.

Then one day a guy with no investing experience came into the office and told us that he was being sponsored to start a fund and was looking for ideas. Dean said to me, "I know what he should do. He should index because then people would trust that he couldn't screw it up." Batterymarch proposed a simplified fund. Although the client declined, at least we went on record as having been very early in offering such a product.* What we didn't know at the time was that a couple of other firms were also beavering away at indexing. Wells Fargo was clearly first in delivering an index fund but they did this in response to a direct request from the pension fund of Samsonite, the luggage company. In the "who was first" business, this was clearly cheating. There was also a little bank in Chicago, American National Bank. All three of us arrived at the idea of indexing independently. They didn't know much about us and we didn't know much about them. Besides, their underlying logic was utterly different. The underlying logic for the other two guys was that the market was efficient. The notion of market efficiency had started to be pushed a few years ago by finance academics, in particular by Eugene Fama in Chicago. Fama's efficient market hypothesis stipulated that securities fully reflect all known information, and the market cannot be beaten. Now, of course, if the market really were efficient, then of course you should buy the index, QED. But the market is still handsomely inefficient and back then in 1970 it was *gloriously* inefficient, as our performance for the next 15 years plus a hundred other things like the Japanese bubble of 1989 were later to prove.

---

* See Jeffrey Miller, *Program Trading: The New Age of Investing*, New York, J.K. Lasser Institute 1979, pp. 74–77.

My argument for indexing, in contrast, was not based on assumed efficiency. (Economists are at least very good at one thing: making assumptions. These are usually unrelated to real life and are almost always unproven by hard data. "Real life is merely an inconvenient special case," as the old joke goes.) Rather my argument was based on the undeniable reality that investing is a zero-sum game. It is like a game of poker. For every winner there is a loser. Obviously, the people who play the game will have friction – the costs of playing – and the people who don't play the game will not have friction. Because you can't collectively add value by money management, as you only shuffle the paper, it is clear that the group that has greater friction will sum to a lower number than the group sitting at the bar watching the poker players. As a group, money managers add nothing but costs. That's all the argument you need. If you buy the market you save extensive fees, which in those days were 1% management fee and 1% fixed commission on every transaction.

At Batterymarch, though, despite offering some of the first index accounts, we were also playing poker. We had to be reconciled that if our cost of doing business was 2% in order to win by 2% a year (which was our target, and we did much better than that), we had to get up every morning and ask, "Who is going to lose today?" We had to find someone to lose by 6% a year in order for us to win by 2%. The competition had to carry their 2% expenses, our 2% expenses and our 2% outperformance. In a game of poker, it feels a lot more intimidating to say every year, "Who's going to lose by six?" than it is to say, "Oh, I think I can win by two," but that's what it amounts to anyway. If the market is a zero-sum game and you have a lot of money, you should index, period. Yet the competition was practicing indexing because they said the market was efficient. We spat on the idea of market efficiency. Fama and other academics didn't emphasize the zero-sum case until very recently.

Fifteen years later in 1986 I put my thoughts down in a paper for *The Journal of Portfolio Management*: "The case for indexing is compelling," I wrote, "partly because large institutions, as a group, are a reasonable proxy for the market. If they are the market, they cannot beat themselves and therefore add no value for their efforts. Every dollar that money managers charge, that brokers charge, that specialists take and that goes to pay part of the salary of the pension officers, reduces the real wealth that would naturally accrue to the owners of equities if none of these services existed. Like a game of poker, it is a zero-sum game; the pie is fixed in size and the game consists of fighting over slices of the pie. My gain is your loss. Lucky players win on any particular evening, but slowly the wealth is transferred to the better players."*

We worried from day one what the end game for indexing would be like. Who do you think drops out of the poker game first, the best poker player or the worst? I've played poker with a group for 60 years. Now, over that 60 years, we lost a lot of really bad poker players. They would come, they would lose money, they would come again, they would lose money again and then one day they would not come. That's the nature of the beast. So the worst poker players drop out as indexing takes off, leaving you with the best poker players. The average quality of the players rises, until, as I like to say, only Buffett, Soros and you are left sitting around the poker table. Happy hunting! This is tough, but it's very efficient. They price stocks so damn well that you're going to have a hard time making money. Perhaps, when indexing reaches over 80% of investable assets, we will need to think about how to pay a few thousand analysts to keep stock prices reasonable, for it would do no one any good to have prices drift off

---

* Jeremy Grantham, "You Can't Fool All of the People All of the Time," *Journal of Portfolio Management*, Winter 1986.

randomly. Perhaps a few basis points tax on every transaction, or on asset value, to pay analysts in some reasonable way. Happily, this is someone else's problem.

At Batterymarch, in the early 1970s, I liked the novelty of the idea of indexing and Dean liked the potential for attracting attention, which was in short supply. For me, the great fascination was in the apparent inevitability of indexing. The idea seemed guaranteed to succeed based on what I naively perceived as its overpowering logic. Our new fund sat on the shelf for two years with no takers. The market was having nothing to do with inevitability. Batterymarch had no clout then, nor did the professors of finance touting market efficiency. The competition, in contrast, all picking stocks in the time-honored way, was openly derisory. The derision was justified probably, for there was little profit in indexing initially, and it did not take clairvoyance to see that potentially it was a commodity product that would end up as a cost-plus item.

The pull for indexing had to come, and finally came, from the clients. But even institutional clients had an axe to grind. Their hired guns had to justify their existence and fill up their day with honest toil. Indexing is very, very boring and takes no time at all. The officers of large pension funds exercise substantial power in the selection of managers, and that is a pleasant experience they would lose by indexing. To push for indexing also seemed an acknowledgment by these individuals that they could not do their job of picking good managers. The way to be noticed is to have your pack of managers deliver a good beating to the market. Senior management did not give enough weight to the job of pension fund performance. Back then they staffed the pension fund department with junior people, making it even easier to miss a good investment idea.

At the outset, indexing for the general public was a dead letter. Dean got the conversation into *The New York Times* Sunday magazine section. He got it everywhere. People were talking about indexing. They weren't doing it, but they were talking about it. They were thinking about it. *Pensions and Investments*, an industry magazine, in 1972 gave us a joke "Dubious Achievement Award" for having the most talked about product with no money. The next year, they gave us a second annual award for the most talked about product with no funds under management. It was only in 1973 that one of the local telephone companies signed up for what we called our "index-matching service." For a few years we split the business with Wells Fargo and American National Bank of Chicago. An article in *The New York Times* even referred to Batterymarch as one of the "Big Three" in indexing.

By February 1976, only $500 million was invested in index funds offered by BM, Wells Fargo and American National Bank. Six months later, Jack Bogle launched Vanguard's first index fund in August 1976. The First Index Investment Trust went live with a measly $11 million and was quickly dubbed "Bogle's Folly." "I can't believe that the great mass of investors are going to be satisfied with an ultimate goal of just achieving average returns on their funds," declared Ned Johnson, the chairman of Fidelity, which later became one of the largest managers of index funds. Some fund managers even dubbed it "un-American." Bogle's index proposition was emphatically based on the concept of a zero-sum game and the certainty that most active investors would underperform. I always respected Jack for being in favor of the common investor and trying to keep costs down and not taking no for an answer and being hated by the industry and driving forward with a singular intensity and focus. He drove Vanguard with a merciless will, and it was very slow to get going. Its index product was on the market for years with only a few million dollars under management. The joke was it had nothing but finance professors as clients for the first few years. But he kept going anyway. Today, Vanguard manages nearly $10 trillion, mostly in passive products.

In his booklet, *The First Index Mutual Fund* (1997), Bogle kindly credited Batterymarch, naming me and Dean, as a forerunner of Vanguard's index business. When he died in early 2019, I was interviewed by Bloomberg:

> What he [Bogle] meant to most people in the investment business was that he was a royal pain in the bottom. In a world where increasingly everyone is trying to maximize short-term profits, he was a complete outlier. He was more concerned about the long-term benefits for society. There were so few in that group. And he was the patron saint.
>
> His approach was, "How cheaply can we do this?" He made up his mind and pursued it with outrageously dogged, fixed focus. You didn't necessarily want to get in his way. I never got in his way. I watched his slow, painful start at Vanguard and then the steady success. I always thought it was inevitable that, if they steadily followed that path, they would win.

For me, indexing was a simple idea that came out of the woodwork. I realized that you can have an original idea in the investment business even if it is both obvious and simple. Like most decent, simple ideas, it's just there. It presents itself. Bang. Fully formed. Ready to go. By asking myself the simple question, "Where do investment returns come from?" the idea of indexing formed in my mind. Of course, nobody was interested, at first. But eventually the market discovers what works and what doesn't. The best ideas eventually come out on top, but sadly there's no guarantee you won't go out of business waiting.

Few money managers with a large pool of money, and possibly none with a very large pool, have beaten the broad market over a long period of time. For the average institution the costs (in terms of management fees and commissions) of trying to win are so large and the number of winners so small that one might even question the fiduciary prudence of not indexing. The cure is simple: repeat "We are the market" whenever you feel tempted to play the game, and act accordingly. For the record, indexing is what ordinary people should do. What's the downside to it? It's cheap. It's profitable in the long run, for the stock market has an almost mysteriously high return. Even before the last 20 odd years when the U.S. has freaked out and done particularly well.

BATTERYMARCH INVESTMENT STYLE

Indexing eventually grew to around half of our assets under management. But it soon became obvious to Dean and my other colleagues that the business was all bureaucracy and salesmanship. It was clear that to be successful you had to keep down custody charges and achieve scale. You had to be a trust bank or focus on individual investors, which is a very different world from the institutional one, and also be as single-minded as Bogle to succeed. I had no interest in doing that. Boring, boring, boring. My only involvement was coming up with the idea. Later, long after I had left Batterymarch, Dean realized there was no hope of competing with the big banks and got out of the index business.

Still, for Batterymarch being one of the original players brought our little firm notoriety during its precarious early years. Nevertheless, indexing was something of a distraction. We had established the firm as a value fund. Our aim was to construct portfolios with lower risk and higher returns. Our goal was to buy stocks that appeared cheap in relation to their fundamental value. This way, even if we were not always right, we hoped to minimize the risk of loss. Our approach was contrarian and conservative. Most people like to invest when prices are going up: it's like buying sweaters when they are on anti-sale. "Special offer: 30 percent more!" But we spent our time looking for the best bargains.

I tried reading Graham and Dodd's *Security Analysis* – the value investor's bible, first published in 1934 – but found it utterly boring. I tried quite hard because one year I was asked to give a talk at the famous Graham & Dodd annual breakfast at Columbia University. I opened my speech with the words: "Friends, Romans, countrymen, I come to tease Ben Graham not to praise him." I teased him for making such obvious comments: more value is better than less value and more yield is better than less yield and a margin of safety is better than no safety margin. It all seemed obvious and not very insightful, but sensible enough. Jesus Christ. Chapter after chapter telling you to be careful and get as much as you can per dollar. I mean, this is what I was brought up with. Anyone with a Yorkshire upbringing who thought anything else would be considered a crazy spendthrift and a lightweight.

In my talk, I compared Graham unfavorably to Keynes, who had a much better understanding of market psychology (see Chapter 5). Of course, I had to read quite a lot of Graham to cover my tail. Among other things, I found out that Graham never made the famous comment attributed to him that "in the short run the market is a voting machine, but in the long run a weighing machine." He said the first part, but the weighing machine was added later by wishful thinkers. Possibly Warren Buffett. Graham says quite clearly: in the short term, the market is a voting machine and therefore you have to act accordingly. The nice symmetry of the longer quote does not appear in the book.

The Batterymarch marketing material stated that "We agree that in the aggregate the market cannot be 'beaten' because all investment managers are the market, but we do believe that there are imperfections in the system that can be exploited." In our view, the structure of the investment industry was a source of market inefficiency. Institutional investment firms had come to own around 60% of the market and their focus was exclusively fixed on one-third of the stocks, which accounted for four-fifths of total market value. This was understandable: spending time on analyzing smaller companies was not profitable, nor was it efficient when administrative ease is considered. Brokerage research, in turn, was aimed at large investment companies because they generated more commissions. As a result, small- to medium-sized stocks were less closely followed.

At Batterymarch we moved away from the herd, specializing in neglected stocks, disliked stocks, unfashionable stocks, stocks that were not widely followed by others. That's how it was pitched, which was not unique but very rare at the time. We created the Batterymarch Universe of about 100 pretty good quality medium-to-small, but mainly small, companies. We'd go through the list and find the ones that were real bargains and buy them. We had the resources to get to know those hundred pretty well. The first thing we found was that no one was talking to most of them. We'd call up, and they'd spend an hour or so on the telephone with us. We often had a hard time getting off the telephone. So, we had an advantage – we really could know more about them than anybody else. We would call suppliers and cross-reference them and really get to understand them. These were durable, solid, almost micro-franchise companies that were small enough that we didn't have to compete to buy them, and where we had an information edge. Within two years of running mainly paper portfolios and a very modest amount of real money, the style had fallen into place.

SMALL CAP STOCKS

I delved into small cap stocks until I knew more about them than any living creature, I think. I would disappear for three or four months. Sometimes, I had a helper who would help me copy everything down longhand out of Value Line hard copy. We would take little samples of returns on equity (ROE) for 50 large companies and 50 small ones and calculate their ROE every five years for 30 years, because back then there was only 30 years of data. We would look at what happened to the profit margins of both large and small caps. The high and low margins on average regressed to average levels over time. I think we knew the average rates regression more accurately than anyone by 1973.

I owned a book by Fisher and Lorie called *Rates of Return on Investments in Common Stocks* that had historic stock market information. The Fisher-Lorie database provided the New York Stock Exchange data going back to 1926. The data was given on both a market-weighted and equal-weighted basis. Investment returns were provided from each starting year (1926, 1927, 1928, etc.) to 1965 when the book was published. By subtracting the difference in returns between one year and another, I was able to create an index of small cap stocks going back to 1926. As far as I know, this was the first small cap index ever created. This allowed me to compare the returns of small cap stocks with the market-weighted index (comparable to the S&P 500) over decades.

My calculations were put down on graph paper. This was quite a labor of love, as it all had to be done by hand. I stuck the chart on the wall of my office and obsessed about it for a month. What became obvious was the huge movement in this series over the decades. Small cap stocks delivered superior returns to the market over the whole period. But their relative performance moved in cycles, ebbing and flowing. I also saw that there were these fairly massive, odd events that caused small caps to do poorly for lengthy periods. In the Depression, for instance, small cap stocks were obliterated. They lost 93% of their value whereas the broad market declined by 84%. There may not seem to be much difference between losses of that magnitude. But, you have to ask, "What does it take when you have 7¢ left on the dollar to catch up with a guy who's got 16¢ left on the dollar?" You need to make 130% just to get back in the ball game. Put another way, if from the depths of the Depression small caps earned an extra two points a year it would take them 45 years to catch up. Because small caps were inherently riskier – flaky little companies more liable to go bust in hard times – it made sense that they should trade at a discount to the market and, in normal times, deliver superior returns.

SELLING WINNERS, BUYING LOSERS

My calculations also revealed that most of the extra returns from investing in small caps came entirely from reshuffling the pack. Every year, the small cap portfolio is rebalanced to make sure that its constituents remain small. Those companies that have done very well over the past 12 months are expelled because they've grown too large. Medium-sized companies that have done very badly are welcomed. Investors follow the aphorism, attributed to the classical economist David Ricardo, "cut your losses and let your profits run." We discovered this was the exact opposite of a winning strategy. With rebalancing, however, when cheap stocks get cheaper, you buy some more. When they get expensive, you sell.

Now, in a moderately mean-reverting world, any strategy of selling the winners and buying the losers should win. The fact that a company's depressed profitability reverts to its average level seemed to me just the fortunes of war. Say a firm is operating in an industry that turns down. Its managers scramble around looking for ways to stop the rot. They're working around the clock, they slash costs and eventually they get something right. They stem the damage and the firm's returns on equity go from, say, 4% to 4.5%. They're still making a miserable return, just enough to stay afloat. But it's 12% more profit margin than last year. And as profits recover, the stock price does too. Conversely, when a firm is super profitable its management become overconfident, it invests too much, costs rise faster than sales and margins decline.

We just didn't trust the theory. We asked how many of these failing companies survived. We studied companies that had nosedived as a separate group and found that very few of them actually dropped out of the small cap universe. When they did, it didn't really matter because they were so cheap you hardly noticed the difference. Most of them recovered. So we looked at our own portfolio and we said, let's say a quarter of the stocks go against you. How do they do? We found that a clear majority of them rallied handsomely and eventually made a higher return than the rest of the portfolio. Our initial purchases won by five points a year. That's just a number out of thin air, but approximately correct. The second lot, averaging down – buying the losers – won by 7% or 8% a year. We found that when you averaged down, about three-quarters of the stocks came out winners.

We looked at one more derivative: losers that crashed and burned a second time. We averaged down yet again and found that buying these serial losers produced even better returns. The odd one would go out of business from such a low level that it wasn't a catastrophe. So by averaging down, you made even more money than you did on your initial purchases, which was really cool. Rebalancing wasn't a topic in those days. We found that it was the best way to capture the mean reversion premium (more on this idea in the next chapter). Averaging down went against conventional wisdom, as per Ricardo, but back then it worked and probably had done since 1925 when decent data started.

SECTOR TILTING

Everyone knew that small cap stocks averaged cheaper than large caps over time. They were cheap for good reasons. On average, they have lower profit margins and are less seasoned. They don't have such brand strength. They are simply lower quality. My question was, "Are they sufficiently cheap to actually make good money?" And that was far from clear. My own work on the ebb and flow of small caps showed that after periods when small caps had badly lagged the market, they would eventually catch up. The pendulum swung back and forth. Bursts of superior performance weren't sustained indefinitely. But the small cap index on its own didn't have anything to say about valuation. We found that there was no "small cap effect." There was a reshuffling, mean reversion effect that had been very dependable. And there was a justified extra return to compensate for lower quality. Adjusting for these two facts, they probably underperformed. They were certainly no bargain in the long run. The reason to specialize in them in 1970 was also clear: there was no competition. No one followed them and you could get an easy edge. More importantly, in 1970 small caps were much cheaper than average.

We got through the first few years on a fairly old-fashioned value approach, using traditional ratios such as price-to-book (P/B). Then in 1975 we found a little operation called Ford Investor Services, run by a guy named David Morse. His firm was barely a year old.

Morse put out, at very modest expense, a weekly rating for every stock. He had a simple dividend discount model that assumed that a company's profits regressed steadily to the market's average over a 10-year period. Morse didn't have his own computer. He used to creep into one of the Silicon Valley companies at the weekend and finagle a way of using their hardware, either legitimately or not. We were never quite sure. He would then take the data on punch cards and turn it into print and send us a copy every two weeks. Every company would have its rating. No one was using a dividend discount model in those days. Bear in mind most investors didn't even understand any of this. It was all very avant-garde. As I've said, the competition was not sophisticated in any way. This gave us a huge advantage.

I would idly go through Morse's list, checking the 20 names that we owned against his valuations, and found that every single last one of them was spectacularly cheap in his model. I went to some trouble to understand the model, talking to Morse, and fell in love with it. It was clearly the way to go. So we ran it side by side. We started to look at the dividend discount score on anything we were interested in, and there was no disagreement. We never liked something that he didn't like and he never liked anything we didn't like. Pretty soon it became a screen, allowing us quickly and efficiently to know we were hunting in the right areas. Good research has always added value. We could take his quick screen and then check and fill out the data in a much more time-consuming way, simply getting to know the company, its leadership and its products as well as we could. In those glorious days from 1970 to 1990, 75% to 85% of our stocks beat the S&P 500 from purchase to sale.

One of the things Morse's service enabled me to do was to look at sectors (more commonly known today as factors), such as value, small and growth. We ranked the relative value of small caps by dividing them into 10 equal groups or deciles. When small was cheap, all 10 deciles by size would usually be ranked in perfect order of cheapness. And when there was a glitch in the data and, say, deciles 4 and 7 were out of sequence, they would almost invariably get back into sequence pretty quickly. An individual stock could be mispriced forever because the data was wonky but a whole decile was almost always reliable. This insight provided the basis for sector tilting, which involved tilting the portfolio toward sectors (factors) when they were cheap. Then we began to show how the pendulum swung back and forth in these sectors – size, quality and so on – between being cheap and expensive.

By 1972, small caps were very cheap by historical standards. We moved out of our fairly eclectic mix of cheap large and small cap stocks into a focused small cap portfolio. This had the added virtue of being incredibly contrarian because there were almost no other small cap managers around. (None, I think, in the institutional world.) Of course, we were young and foolish and we had 100% of our money in small stocks in the teeth of the Nifty Fifty era, history's greatest large cap boom. This is how I discovered footnote 23 of my view of the world: you find a good idea, for example, that small cap is very cheap, and then it gets a lot cheaper. It went from being nicely cheaper than normal to an all-time low in 1973. The valuation of large cap stocks, on the other hand, went to an all-time high.

THE NIFTY FIFTY

The Nifty Fifty was an informal grouping of 50 large cap, high-quality stocks. There was no definitive list; one broker would make a list but another list would have two or three different stocks. The key was their big, hefty size, which was unanimously agreed on.

Among them were some flashy tech firms: IBM, Polaroid, Eastman Kodak and Xerox; reputable drug makers: Eli Lilly, Schering-Plough, Merck and Johnson & Johnson; solid consumer goods companies: Coca-Cola, Procter & Gamble, Chesebrough-Ponds; and a handful of retailers, including a then little known chain store called Wal-Mart. These were the so-called "one decision stocks." After you'd made the decision to buy them, you didn't have to think again. Valuations didn't matter. They were such great companies you could own them forever.

The Nifty Fifty boom started to take shape in the early 1960s. By the middle of the decade, it was in full flower; these stocks withstood a bear market in 1967 and gathered speed during the conglomerate era. After the conglomerates waned toward the end of the decade, the true beauty of the Nifty Fifty was revealed: bigger was better. The stocks in the public eye that everyone talked about – IBM, Kodak, Polaroid, etc. – were going from strength to strength. They had a natural momentum. The American capitalist system was doing thrillingly well through all the 1960s, really. The economy didn't do anything dramatically uncomfortable. Other than some unpleasantness in Vietnam, everything was cool.

This group of stocks had also enjoyed an abnormally long run without notable corporate failures. A lucky streak, you might say. People started to tout the fact that they never failed. The whole idea of a one-decision stock involved taking the accidental good fortune that none had recently failed and extrapolating it forever. You couldn't be accused of being an idiot buying one of these companies. They not only had universal approval but they had impeccable histories and dividend records, and, by and large, very little debt. They were precisely the sort of quality stocks that a conservative institution would want to carry. The trust managers buying the fancy wine at dinner, all they had to do was make the occasional trade – sell a little Gillette, buy a little more Avon Products – and keep their noses clean.

How were you going to be disastrous with a strategy like that? Well, you weren't. No one was measuring performance in the way it was done later. As long as you weren't a complete outlier, you were fine.

By the early 1970s, the weight of speculation was in the Nifty Fifty. The stocks wouldn't shoot up like my American Raceways. They would grind slowly higher until they got to a valuation very much like that of 1929. We measured that beautifully. David Morse's dividend discount model showed they were at a 50% premium to fair value. The data was clear and accurate. The Nifty Fifty happens to be the only high-quality bubble in history. Quality stocks are so boring they don't typically participate in bubbles. By comparison, bubbles in sexy growth stocks are as common as dirt.

It needed everything to go right and for a while everything went right. There was nothing to get in the way. They were delivering a very satisfactory pattern of earnings growth and dividends and keeping everyone happy. Everyone, that is, except me, my Batterymarch colleagues and a handful of others. All good ideas in the investment business seem to have embedded career risk. The Nifty Fifty was all about career risk. As an investor, you kept your job if you bought expensive mega caps and you were in danger of losing your job if you bought cheap small caps. There's no free lunch for the value investor. You want to be careful, you want to avoid too much pain, you always take the risk of being too early.

Our portfolio of small, neglected stocks had a much better P/B ratio and much better yield. While everyone else was buying IBM and Eastman Kodak, we were buying the Hartford Steam Boiler Insurance and Inspection Company, the only company we ever found that had no footnotes to its annual report. The market's prejudice against small caps and favoritism toward large caps was highlighted by the valuation discrepancy in 1972 between Albertsons and Safeway. Here you had two almost identical companies doing identical things, namely, selling groceries. The one difference being that Safeway was much bigger. During the Nifty Fifty era you couldn't be respectable unless you were big. Safeway was respectable merely for being ten times bigger than Albertsons. Albertsons was more efficient, had a slightly higher return, lower debt and yet was half the price, measured by P/E ratio and twice the dividend yield. So if there'd ever been a headwind for value investors, this was it.

Batterymarch weathered the early Nifty Fifty storm because we had a huge alpha – outperformance relative to our index benchmark – in 1970 through to early 1972. Then in late 1972 we had sickening underperformance over a six-month period. But thankfully the two quarters fell in different years so clients didn't notice so much. In 1973 we lost by six points. That was the only year we lost. By then a fierce bear market had opened up. We had an oil crisis. A presidential crisis. A deep recession. We had high interest rates. We had dramatic inflation. One of the banks, Franklin National, was failing. What else do you want? The market hates high inflation and weak profit margins. When those two factors become extreme, the market should sell at seven or eight times earnings. And it did. At the trough, the S&P was down nearly 55%.

No one was interested in small caps, so they just lost touch with anything. We had companies at the bottom selling for four, three, two times earnings. I mean, they were giving them away. My favorite example is Security-Connecticut Life, a little specialty life insurance company in Hartford that was doing very, very well. I started to buy the stock myself in 1972. It was growing at 15% a year like clockwork. A life company could do that in those days because they fiddled assumptions, and it's easy to make money if you're selling a lot of product. So they had 15% managed earnings growth, year after year, and it was pretty cheap. I bought it at 7 and it went up to about 23. Naturally, I was very happy. Then the market came down and this thing just ticked down and down and down and down. I had sold 100 of my 300 shares in the 20s, so I'd made all my money back. On the other 200, I rode it down and it went down, 17, 12, 9, 7, 6, 5, to 2⅝. This was late 1974. Now, along the way, every quarter, its profits were gaining 15% from the year before. Every quarter on the way up, every quarter on the way down. The stock went from 23 to 2⅝, but the earnings did not ripple. Get your brain around that one. This, of course, was more spectacular than most. Most of the others only went down 60%, Security-Connecticut went down 90% on steadily rising, way above average, earnings. It was a growth stock, for God's sake. So when it got to 2⅝ I'm on the cusp of saying, "Well, it's going out of business. Its steady earnings must somehow be faked." But luckily I didn't bother to sell because it wasn't worth selling – even though it was clear to me that it must be going out of business because that was the only way I could explain its stock price.

Thank God, we outperformed the universe of small stocks quite handsomely with very little money, probably because our portfolio happened to have much higher quality than a typical basket of small caps. Still, we lost a third of our business. By the end of 1974, our performance was exactly breakeven with the S&P. The Nifty Fifty stocks were also crushed but they didn't fall by more than the market and because everyone who was anyone owned them, managers who owned them felt safe. In relative terms we were technically doing okay, but our first large account left us not because of the losses of 1973/4 but because "we lost the money so inelegantly." It was more acceptable to lose half of your dough in Coca-Cola or any other household name than in Great Lakes Dock and Dredge or Twin Disc Clutch. Our companies were pretty good businesses, but they were horribly off the radar screen, completely unknown companies.

Clients felt they were taking an unnecessary career risk with us. The only justification for them to be trying something new, even for just a year or so, would have been immediate and substantial outperformance. So, we lost quite a bit of business.

It was then, in late 1974, that we had our fateful meeting with Laurance Rockefeller. This was make or break for Batterymarch. They were our biggest and most reputable client. Despite what Dean and I had expected after our fraught meeting in Manhattan, we weren't fired. Rockefeller gave us a brief reprieve. We hung on. Then, the new year arrived, and on January 1, 1975, it was as if the man on Wall Street came out with a big bell and rang in a bull market, ding, ding, ding. Suddenly *everything* was going up, from the Nifty Fifty to the underpriced small stocks. The most painful, broad bear market since the Depression immediately ended and on cue everything went woosh. Small cap value leapt out of the starting block like a world champ. For January we were up 17% and off to the races. It was the broadest rally in history. We were 100% invested and no one else was. Everybody else had cash reserves. The blue chips came out, too, quite fast, but lagging a bit. Then the blue chips caught up and everyone had a thoroughly enjoyable year.

Security-Connecticut Life doubled and redoubled and by the summer it was at 10. This served to snap me out of my funk and I was saying to myself, "Oh my God, I was right after all and the market was stupid, not me. The earnings really are okay and even at 10 it's dirt cheap." So, coming out of my trance, I tripled up, feeling like a nitwit for having believed the market. After all, I had been the one checking up on the details regularly. Perhaps the only one. Within 18 months some large Hartford insurance company bought it for $35. What a lesson or two learned. Check the data and trust yourself. The market can be very, very inefficient, particularly on little companies not worth its trouble. This was an important experience for me. The realization that you can have an idea, a new idea, or a different idea, and you can be right, and the market, in general, can be wrong, is the single most powerful lesson, I think, that anyone can learn in this business.

Meanwhile, as to the broader market, the data on small cap seemed completely clear. The only cause for doubting the data was in myself. I just thought perhaps I don't know enough, perhaps I'm missing something. It's always the curse of a young person in the investment business. You can't believe the evidence of your own eyes. You assume the system is more efficient than it is. I had studied it enough, we had the data going back to 1925, showing the ebb and flow of small caps. We knew they ebbed and flowed, and we knew that they'd been ebbing like mad, and every measure of value showed that they were 30% cheap. But now, they had become 50% cheap, which nearly washed our firm away. But in comparison to my being bullied by the market into doubting Security-Connecticut, when it came to small caps in general, by the market low I was more confident about that bet than about anything else. This was yet another lesson: you can be much more confident about the data of a whole sector like small caps – and we had some quite proprietary data on small cap in the 1970s – than you should ever be with a single company, where there really could be important hidden factors. Of course, today you can say it's obvious – statistically guaranteed, even – but in the 1960s and early 1970s there was little intellectual discussion of principles and you discovered them on your own, often the hard way.

Later that year, Dean and I returned to New York to meet with the committee of the Rockefeller Family Fund. Laurance Rockefeller, for only the second time I ever saw him, showed up again. He started off the discussion by saying, "Well, I have to give you guys credit. You hung in and you got this right – the market's come back and

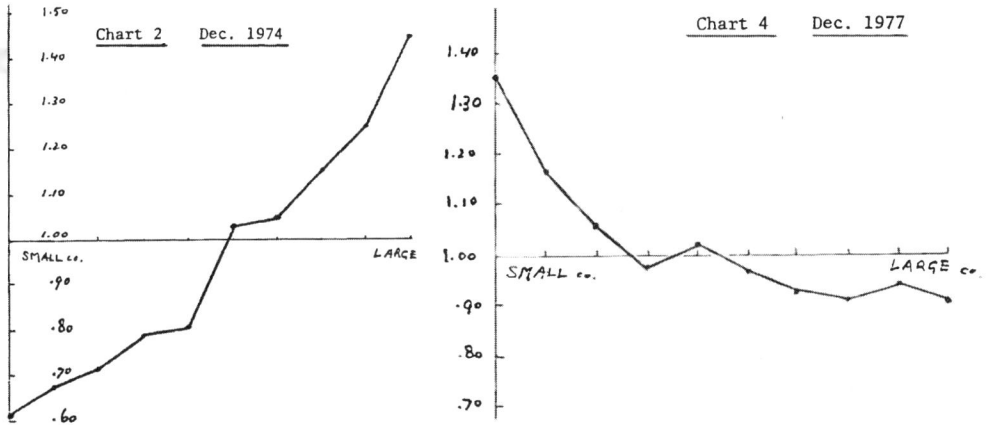

The ebb and flow of small caps. My contemporaneous hand-drawn decile run of small to large US stocks, showing the valuation discount or premium for each size decile of the US stock market compared to its historic average, at the end of 1974 (left panel) and the end of 1977 (right panel). In December 1974 the smallest stocks were trading at under 0.65x their historical average relative valuation, and the largest stocks trading at over 1.4x. In December 1977, after the bursting of the Nifty Fifty bubble and a great small cap rally, the smallest stocks were trading at over 1.3x their historical average relative valuation, and the largest stocks at less than 0.9x. Data from Batterymarch Financial Management, 1978

so have your stocks." At the end of the meeting, the hired gun put his arm around my shoulder as we walked out of the room and said, "You know, Jeremy, that is the closest I have ever heard Mr. Laurance come to making an apology in the investment business."

My bullish argument for small caps turned out to be understated. We were at the start of a historic rally in small stocks, which went on to outperform large stocks by 177% to the middle of 1983. For the year, the S&P 500 rose by 37% (including dividends) – and Batterymarch returned 41%, delivering four points of alpha. The next year the S&P's total return was 24% and we were up many points more. Then in 1977, the S&P declined by 11.5% but we continued to outperform, both in relative and absolute terms. This was the massacre of the innocents, with the innocents being the Nifty Fifty. They had bounced off the low together with us, and then we destroyed them at an accelerating rate.

We had survived by the narrowest of margins, helped by the fact that on the way down our stocks had higher quality than the average small cap. Our successful bet was rewarded by the most extraordinary success. Batterymarch went from doing pretty well in terms of performance to explosively well. Gradually times changed in our favor. In 1976, when we just continued to soar and the market slowed way down, people started to throw money at Batterymarch. We doubled our assets every six months for four consecutive six-month periods. Our $45 million went to $90 million, then from $90 million to $180 million. In a single year our assets quadrupled and continued rising to $720 million over the next couple of years. Batterymarch was on its way to becoming one of the most successful institutional fund managers in the business.

At last, I was paid a decent wage, a handsome wage you could say, by the standards of the time. I was getting $50,000, which in some ways seemed like a lot, but in some ways it seemed like a little. My income was now a whole lot more than the $28,000 Keystone offered me to not go to Batterymarch. But eight years had passed and I was now a fairly experienced money manager and we were doing very well. I knew that my senior partner was getting many multiples of what I was getting, even though I had a large stake in the firm. In a sense, as we prospered, Dean was underpaying Dick and me. More to the point really, he was under-crediting us. What an ideas person, like me, needs is a good pat on the head. If you do that we're pussycats. You don't even have to pay us that much. Just pat us on the head, publicly. Dean didn't get it. He wanted all the pats for himself. He wanted to take full credit for every Batterymarch idea – our innovative dividend discount model, sector selection (which was also quite novel), making very large bets – up to 100% – on small cap, quality, extreme value, etc. All standard issue for the last 20 years but not in the mid-1970s. Most significantly, he craved full credit for indexing, which, as I said, he thought was a terrible idea until it became useful.

Dick and I were also concerned that Batterymarch was growing too quickly, potentially hindering our ability to deliver decent returns in the capacity constrained world of small caps. So we decided to leave. Dean offered us an outrageously low price for our stakes. In the end, we took a deep breath and sold back our interest in Batterymarch at some three times earnings. For a company that was doubling every six months, it was not a very generous multiple. But we had to get on with our lives and stop haggling with Dean every day. Then at least we would get credit or discredit on our own.

CHAPTER 3

Grantham, Mayo, Van Otterloo

Dick Mayo and I teamed up with a close friend of mine, Eijk Van Otterloo, who'd worked with us at Keystone. Eijk was an aristocratic Dutchman who since leaving Keystone had served as director of common stock investment at a couple of Hartford insurance companies. The three of us had different investment styles and personalities. What we shared in common was a huge predisposition to be contrarian and to put value first, above everything else. At Batterymarch we had pre-committed to close our book of business. But when things started to fly, Dean changed his mind – that was one of our many disagreements. At GMO we decided to pick a limit of $250 million. Our initial goal was to raise at least $10 million by the end of the third year; if we didn't achieve that, whoever wanted to leave could do so.

Grantham, Mayo, Van Otterloo was incorporated on October 18, 1977. I joined officially at the end of that year. We brought with us several people from Batterymarch, all the early birds, including Dean's prep school buddy, Kingsley Durant. He'd been the treasurer at Batterymarch and became our treasurer. Kingsley was also the trustee of a family trust that owned the Batterymarch Building in

The founders of GMO in 1978 with (from left to right) me, Kingsley Durant (GMO's first CEO), Eijk Van Otterloo and Dick Mayo

downtown Boston and agreed, in exchange for a partnership stake, to pay the rent for three years for the little office we took in the building. We negotiated an agreement from our attorneys at Ropes & Gray to defer their start-up expenses until we got on our feet. Conning and Company, a Hartford-based brokerage, offered to cover three years of operating expenses, including a modest salary, in return for a 50.1% interest in the firm. But we didn't want to cede a majority share so this came to nothing. At the outset, no one was paid a salary apart from the administrator.

We started out with a single U.S. equity product, doing exactly as we had done back at Batterymarch. As I like to say, they kept the name, we kept the portfolio. I mean, literally, we started on day one with the same portfolio that we'd had on our last day there. They soon moved to an unrecognizable portfolio, but we had the same stocks slowly turning over in the old way. We picked the stocks by hand, using a filter system that over time was increasingly quantified and implemented systematically. I was in charge of building models and emphasizing what kind of stocks we should buy. Dick was in charge of picking the stocks, subcontracting 40% of the stock picking to me. For several years we coasted on the work we'd done at Batterymarch.

Although Batterymarch had lost its investment team lock, stock and barrel, the consultants didn't seem to notice. They continued to recommend Dean and didn't visit us or ask us a single question. Perhaps that was a testimonial to how well Dean had sweet-talked them. The dominant consulting firm never showed up until after we had closed the book of business for our first product, actively managed U.S. equities. When they eventually came to see us, I was quite rude and said, "You've been recommending Batterymarch to everybody even after half the engine room had left and you didn't come to see us once in five years. Now our book of business is closed. I mean, well, what the hell is your job description anyway?" This did not endear us to the consultant. They were our mortal enemies for quite a while after that because the boss didn't approve of being told off. Who does?

I had not realized until I went off on my own what a broadening experience starting a new business would be. It wasn't just that you had to write, but that you also had to deal with clients. Dean was the champion, a world-class client stroker, and had kept Dick and me like caged animals, where we did a handful of presentations to his hundreds. Now we were the suckers doing it. We had to learn how to run a little business in all its complexity in order to pay the running costs. There were a lot of interesting new things going on. Dick obsessed about running his paper portfolio. It soon became apparent we would have no prospectus or brochure unless I took on the job. I had a very hard time writing the prospectus. I put in a story about the ebb and flow of small cap and value. If anyone came to see us I'd show them that. A week later, I wrote something on the regression of profitability. I did another on the risk of stocks versus bonds over a 10-year holding period. Stocks had almost always won on the longer holding period. So if you had a 10-year horizon, how could you argue that stocks were much more dangerous than bonds? Which is an interesting thought. And, if stocks have a much higher return and don't have any bigger losses or probabilities of losses, why bother with bonds at all, other than as a modest portfolio diversifier? After a while I had about six or seven topics that I put in a brochure to show to anyone who was interested.

For the first few months we had little business, except a couple of wealthy individuals, a corporate client and an offer to run some money for a Canadian-based mutual fund company. We might have waited a terrible, long, miserable time to land some real assets. At Batterymarch, however, Dick and I had met with Cambridge Associates, the leading consultant to endowments and foundations. One day, one of their co-founders, Hunter Lewis, telephoned to say he was in the neighborhood and would like to drop in to see us. We went into a nervous frenzy at the thought. After all, we had no institutional business and the world was not beating a path to our door. The industry didn't really know Dick or me because we'd been hidden from the world at Batterymarch, and they didn't know Eijk, who'd been tucked away in his Hartford insurance companies.

Hunter Lewis, who's a very smooth guy, came in and we chatted him up. He stayed for about 20 minutes. We were very disappointed because we had expected a longer meeting. As he was going out the door, I handed him a scrappy copy of my working essays. Some of them were double-spaced and with drafting errors; others were fairly polished. I just kept updating them, one by one, as fast as I could. He took this strange-looking collection away and was perhaps the only person who ever read it seriously. Two or three weeks went by. Then one day Hunter called up. He has this rather British way about him and he said, "Sorry to call at such late notice. Really, I don't mean to disturb you, and if you don't want to play ball on this one, I'll completely understand. But we have this last-minute presentation at Swarthmore College in Philadelphia, and I would love to squeeze you into the finals. We're recommending you. I'm afraid it's tomorrow." We told him, yes, we thought we could find our way clear to attend.

Next day, all three of us went whizzing down to Swarthmore. Suddenly there I am, at the first big presentation for the new firm, looking at a table at which are seated a dozen or more committee members. I was completely unnerved by one woman at the table who stared straight at me, grinning, the entire time. I began to feel drops of sweat trickle down my sides. It was one of only two or three times in my entire career that I've sweated while making a presentation. I practically melted. Anyway, Dick and I staggered through the pitch. Dick told wonderful war stories and I got into the fancy sector-tilting, dividend discount stuff. It worked pretty nicely and we went home very, very excited.

Then, the very next day Hunter Lewis calls up and says, "Oh, I hate to do this to you again, but if you could get down here on Wednesday, I could just squeeze you in at the Corning Glass pension fund meeting in Manhattan. Oh, by the way, of course, you won the Swarthmore account. Yes, splendid job, splendid job." Two days later we're doing the same pitch to Corning Glass. No meltdown this time. I was very, very happy about landing our first institutional account, $5 million from Swarthmore when $5 million was $5 million. We presented to a very nice group, Jim Flynn and his people at Corning Glass. Then, the next day you would not believe it – Hunter calls up again. The same darn story! I've known him for 50 years and this was completely unique. He said, "I know that this is really quite bizarre. I keep calling up with these ridiculous requests for instant performance, but you've done so well and, of course, you've got the Corning Glass account. They're looking forward to having you work for them. I've been thinking about what a good match you might be for the World Bank. I know Hilda Ochoa, who runs it very well. She's been doing a three-month survey of redistributing all her business and I think she should talk to you – I think you guys are right up her street. But it's tomorrow." Down we went to Washington, D.C. and won the business. Hilda Ochoa became a good friend of the firm ever after.

We went from having essentially no business after 10 months to landing three accounts – all in one week. Not just any three but a major international institution, a pension fund, of the kind that everybody was fighting for in those days, and a nice prestigious college. It could not have been better. After that, it was all over, bar the shouting. We felt we had made it. We could pay the rent. All we had to do now was perform and the rest would take care of itself. If there's ever been a better week for an investment firm start-up, I've yet to hear of it.

During our first year in business, Dick and I believed that the extraordinary run-up in small cap value stocks was coming close to the end. We began to rotate the portfolio out of the stocks we had brought with us from Batterymarch. Over a 24-month period we moved almost completely out of small caps into large caps, which is what you'd expect if you were looking at our sector-tilting approach. During 1978 and 1979, the fund outperformed the S&P 500 by 10% and 17%, respectively. It was becoming clear to outsiders that we had played a key role in Batterymarch's success. After that week of landing three institutional accounts, it took us around two years before we closed the fund to new money. Then we had this wonderful period with consistently good performance.

We closed the fund when assets reached $250 million. Clients would beg us to take more money and we'd turn them down. Eventually over the following years we accepted a few special cases. But even without new inflows, the fund would still have grown to over $1 billion by 1988. Because over the following nine years the market doubled and our added value (alpha) of 8% per year doubled it again. With no down years for our first nine years this was certainly a very fortunate way to start a new enterprise. Over the following decades we were not always so lucky.

BUYING BONDS

There are only two stock market lows that count in my GMO career. The low in 1982 and the post-financial crisis low of 2009. Every market low in between is unimportant, in my view. There's no real bear market between those dates. In 1982, the U.S. stock market was selling at 7x earnings and bonds were getting crushed. The 30-year bond market peaked at 16%, and inflation peaked for a day at around 13%. The 30-year bond was saying that an inflation rate of 13%, which had been reached for one afternoon, would stay for the next 30 years.

I asked myself how the market could possibly think that inflation was going to stay so high, indefinitely. The bond market had extrapolated the historically high inflation rate years into the future, despite the fact that inflation had previously averaged around 1% to 2%. One might expect Treasury bills, which are short term, to yield 13%, but a rational investor would expect 30-Year Treasury bonds (which were supposed to be the most efficient forecast of inflation for the next 30 years) to reflect a more normal and, hence, lower interest rate. Even if long rates adjusted upwards for the possibility of much higher oil prices in the future, inflation would still likely only rise to 3% to 4% for a few years, nowhere near the 13% implied in the 16% yield on long bonds. I was certain about that. Everybody knew that the U.S. was not going to become Argentina. Fed chairman Paul Volcker was breathing fire. He was not just *threatening* to kill inflation but clearly doing his best to kill it. The Fed Funds rate was around 15%, having reached 19% the previous year. The economy was in recession. The consensus among economists was that long-term inflation would be 4.5% and the long bond was yielding 16%!

What had happened in this case is that, year after year, people had been willing to bet that interest rates would fall. They had taken out positions when the Fed Funds rate was 8%, which was heroically high, only to watch it climb to 9, 10, 11, 12, 13. Eventually, the Fed Funds rate reached 19%. By that time, most investors who had made those earlier painful bets were gone. It didn't matter how much Treasuries fell, the bond guys left standing had no fire left in their bellies. The only people who were prepared to go out and buy bonds with yields close to 16% were equity managers like us. Dick decided to build up a lot of fixed income in the fund, which I agreed with. We had some of our fixed income exposure in bonds denominated in the new European Currency Unit (ECU) that were also selling with huge double-digit yields. Our tiny institution became the largest single holder of those bonds. Dick also made the play of his life in his personal account when he bought 30-Year Treasuries on huge margins. He was paying 13% and receiving 16% and leveraging his position 10 to 1 or more. Had the bond yields gone to 18, he might have been wiped out. But they didn't. Interest rates peaked in the same week or two. Very quickly his margin costs went down. Dick made an outrageously brave bet and nailed it. It needed good luck, as well as bravery. I think he once said that after that bet he never really had to worry about money again.

Of course, we had no business playing the bond market in 1982. We were running a U.S. equities fund, for heaven's sake. It required nerves of steel because if we had lost, we'd have looked like idiots. But we won the bet and handsomely outperformed the S&P with our bonds all the while demonstrating a loss of investment discipline. But let's be fair, if you hit a home run, clients don't mind. If you lose the bet, then they're all concerned about discipline and benchmark deviation and all those things, as they should be. But in this case, because we won, they managed to swallow any earlier misgivings, and they probably always will.

The extraordinarily high bond yields and low earnings yields of 1982 left me with the lasting impression that markets are coincident indicators of comfort. The 30-year bond took the current inflation level and assumed it would last for 30 years. That's not a forecast, it's just a coincident indicator. That's how fixed income markets work; they do not make accurate predictions about the future. Anyway, it turns out the stock market is no different. The stock market, by and large, doesn't give a rat's tail about the future. What it cares about is the present. If there is very high inflation or profit margins are depressed, you find that earnings multiples are low, and vice versa. This is how the stock market works. But it isn't a prediction, because profit margins and stock valuations are demonstrably mean reverting. Things will get worse when they're perfect and get better when they're ugly.

So if you really want to make money in stocks, you buy when inflation is high and margins are low. That was the case in 1982. On June 28 of that year, a weekly investment newsletter, the "Portfolio Letter" (issued by *Institutional Investor* magazine), reported on its front page that the Goldman Sachs investment strategy team of Leon Cooperman was "telling clients that despite the technical rally last week, now is not the time to make any major commitments to stocks.

There appears to be no way interest rates can come down." I took a very different view. I thought we were looking at one of the biggest rallies in stocks and the bond market. On the side bar of the "Portfolio Letter" front page was a small notice that read "Grantham, Mayo Moves into Cyclicals." On page eight was my first ever interview with the press. The piece stated Dick and I were switching out of ultra-defensive stocks and buying cyclicals, selling Ralston Purina to buy Union Carbide. "Grantham added that he sees the stock market approaching a major rally, perhaps the biggest in a decade."

I was cited as saying that the real returns available from simply holding bonds were unsustainable, and that falling interest rates, combined with stocks selling at unprecedented lows, spelt a dramatic comeback from equities. "Right now, says Grantham, the firm's cash reserves in portfolios is nil. The portfolio is invested 80% in equities and 20% in long-term bonds." (Almost 40 years later I jokingly recalled this incident in one of my quarterly letters. Cooperman wrote me a testy note saying, in effect, "I haven't read your quarterly letter, but my friends tell me you're assassinating me and suggesting horrifically that I was bearish at the bottom." By way of reply, I sent him a copy of the original publication, which quoted him as saying it was too early to buy equities. I had thought 40 years on it would be seen as just a tease, but investing is a competitive business and the ultra-competitive can take it very seriously indeed. To be fair, I can be pretty thin-skinned on some issues, even though they took place long ago.)

As it turned out, the S&P did not beat the bond market; with U.S. governments at 16%, bonds were just about unbeatable. When interest rates fell, and they eventually fell like a stone, we had something close to a 100% gain on our ECU bonds. It was just amazing. Throw in a few ECU currency gains and it was a pretty high hurdle to surpass. Yet our equities fund jumped over it – our stocks outperformed bonds, the ECU notes and the S&P. Despite the incredible returns on fixed income, the 80% of the portfolio in equities actually beat the 20% in fixed income. It meant that one of our best and bravest ideas, at one of the rare times when we had almost perfect timing, actually cost the portfolio. Don't you love it?

Years later, my then colleague Forrest Berkley was doing an asset allocation pitch and engaged the prospective client in a discussion on the inefficiencies of the markets. Forrest made the point to their investment committee that the mispricing of bonds in 1982 was one of the greatest free lunches of all time. That investment committee included two prominent academics along with David Swensen and Dean Takahashi of Yale (the client was not Yale, however). Swensen revealed that in 1981 the former chairman of this very same committee had sold off *every* investment the institution owned and bought 30-Year Treasuries. That chairman turned out to be none other than Burton Malkiel, the author of the best-selling *A Random Walk Down Wall Street* (1973), which argues that market prices contain no information about prospective investment returns. Forrest said, "Wait a minute. How can someone who believes that markets are completely efficient engage in such speculative behavior?" One of the academics on the committee turned to him and said, "What academics say to sell books has nothing at all to do with the reality of what they do with their own money. And, Forrest, we're going to hire your firm because we hope you understand the difference."

AMATEUR'S ADVANTAGE

Forrest and I used to talk about what I call the amateur's advantage. If you're not a professional, you may easily miss something becoming very cheap, which allows you the luxury of having no position in it at all until it's extremely cheap and then finally it catches your attention. But if you're a professional, you will already own it when it's very cheap and you'll be hurting when it's very, very cheap. In 1982, Dick and I had that advantage buying bonds at extremely low prices. We were equity guys, of course. Not being fixed income professionals, we had not used up our ammunition. We enjoyed the amateur's advantage and benefited from getting into bonds very late, just as the market was about to turn.

Over the years I've also enjoyed the amateur's advantage to some extent in commodities, which I play in my own account from time to time and then forget about for a few years. My general principle is to wait for extraordinary outliers and then take a bet. For instance, one day in 1998, Dick came into my office and asked if I had seen the price of oil. Oil was just hitting $10 a barrel, down from over $40 in 1980; 17 years or so had gone by and it was hitting $10 a barrel. I had never bought an oil contract and he had never bought an oil contract, but looking at this price reaching $10, it seemed so impressive. Of course, I was prompted to say, "Yes, I have." Dick told me that when I called my broker, whom we shared, to buy one contract for him. I called the broker and bought several for myself and one for Dick. We turned out to be within 25 minutes of the low in oil.

Had we been value-oriented professionals, we would have gritted our teeth magnificently and we wouldn't have bought a barrel all the way down from $40 to, let's say, $20. But at $20, we would've been suitably conservative, accumulating slowly but surely. By $15, we would've been jumping in with both feet. By $12, clients would've been shooting us, and by $10, we would've been forced to cover, because we would've been sold out by our clients and life would've been miserable. This is what happens to professionals. When you hit the outlier, you are always going to bleed unless you are completely asleep at the switch. (It's even worse when you're selling short. In 2008, when oil was skyrocketing, our asset allocation team shorted oil at around $100 a barrel. A couple of months later, oil reached the pre-determined stop loss and we covered at $135. Six months later, after Lehman's failure, oil was touching $40.)

THE DEATH OF VALUE

Despite our fund's handsome performance, the move out of small caps proved premature. After beating the Nifty Fifty and the rest of the S&P in the market recovery, small caps and value stocks became highly fashionable. Clients had become more sophisticated: they knew about the small cap effect and the value effect (the outperformance of low P/E and low P/B stocks), and they knew that growth had underperformed. By the early 1980s, the value style was the investment flavor of choice. Yet value stocks, by their nature, are low quality. They go bust more often. They have lower returns on capital. Their earnings are more volatile. P/B is junk. P/E is semi-junk.

I had no confidence in P/B as a valuation measure even back then in 1980. A cheap book is the market's vote on the worst assets out there in the marketplace. These companies are failures, dogs, crap. Low P/B is capable of biting you on the leg in a 3-sigma event like the 1929 Crash and the Depression, where so many failed. The academics are right when they say that P/B is a risk factor. However you measure it, value stocks have lower profit margins, higher debt and less quality. They may not be higher beta (a measure of their volatility relative to the market as a whole) but beta is a complete mismeasurement of risk. For example, the high yields of marginal companies will tend to dampen their volatility. Another real weakness of simple P/B and P/E is that these measures are backward-looking; they are at the mercy of new information. Value stocks must be systematically very cheap indeed to win this struggle with their low quality. The "cheapest" value stocks can have another potential weakness. Sometimes they are not usefully cheap at all, but are so-called "value traps."

Buying wounded companies used to be considered imprudent. By 1983, however, it had become sanitized. In March of that year, I gave a talk in Boston called "The Death of Value" in which I argued that value was looking like a crowded trade. At the time, everybody wanted to be a value manager because it had done so dazzlingly well since 1974. Value had beaten the market by over 100 percentage points. The growth managers were hiding under the table. I suggested this was overdone. A new army of contrarian investors were overpaying for value. They threw their bodies in front of the value train as it traveled downhill and, as a result, by the sheer weight of their bodies the train stopped at a higher level. Because value investing had become so trendy, after 1983 you made no extra money from being in the cheapest value stocks, defined by P/B, for nearly two decades. Now that takes patience. You were paid absolutely nothing extra for carrying the poor fundamental quality that cheap P/B represents. I've always considered the death of value one of my best calls – 16 years later, value stocks were well behind their 1983 relative high.

The lesson from the long underperformance of value after 1982 is that there's no such thing as a small cap effect, or indeed a P/B effect; there is only a cheap effect. You don't get rewarded for taking risk or buying lousy companies; you get rewarded for buying cheap assets. And if the assets you bought got pushed up in price simply because they were in favor with investors, then you are not going to be rewarded for taking a risk; you are going to be punished for it. By the early 1980s, as value became very trendy as an investment style, this is exactly what happened. In the market investors can always overdo anything, and they usually do, with the same inevitable consequence of disappointing returns and, on extreme occasions, a market crash.

MY LIFE AS A QUANT

In 1978, my first year at GMO, I acquired a Hewlett-Packard programmable calculator with a little metal strip you slid in at the top. With this calculator, I managed to program a dividend discount model, which was very handy. This would allow us to put in the ROE of a firm, stock price and earnings and calculate its fair value. This was a pretty straightforward first-generation dividend discount model and the only programming I did in my life. The truth is that I have no math background. In fact, I have a more or less complete phobia of advanced mathematics. Completely blocked by a horrific math teacher at high school, I am anti-symbols. If there are more than a couple of symbols on the page, I don't even attempt to decode them. But I'm a good arithmetician. More importantly, I'm good at doing approximations in my head. When some quant comes up with an elaborate formula, I know when they've made a mistake. I was always comfortable with data, but I don't do equations or math in any traditional sense. I am, by no stretch of the imagination, a quant. Yet I ran a quant division for years. Fortunately, I had a brilliant mathematician, Chris Darnell, as my right hand.

When we started at GMO we were using David Morse's model. We offered him a job, but he turned us down. That's when Chris Darnell rode to the rescue. Chris isn't just smart. He is ridiculously smart. His father and brother are in the National Academy of Science.

There are only two father/son pairs in the National Academy and Chris was the smart one in the family – at least when I'm telling the story. He graduated number one at Yale by quite a bit and he did it in mathematics. Yale is not an easy place to be number one, certainly not in mathematics. Genius, I think is the technical description. At Yale, he wrote a graduate thesis in differential topology (which was accepted) but didn't stay to complete the PhD requirements. He then took an MBA at Harvard, where he was nearly bored to death. In fact, one of his professors called me and said he had an interesting candidate, who after acing it at Yale was doing his best to flunk out of HBS. Irresistible! He was the only hire I ever actively courted for GMO.

While looking around for an investment job, Chris met up with Hunter Lewis at Cambridge, who also pushed him in our direction. We met for the first time at a restaurant on Beacon Hill. Chris recalls that I was wearing a trench coat with the collar pulled up, looking tall, thin and intense. He thought I resembled a Cold War agent and wasn't sure whether he was going to be conscripted into the British Secret Service. Instead, I launched into my ideas about investing, some of which he found pretty outlandish. Within 30 minutes, however, he was hooked by the number of unusual, even weird, things we were trying. At least he didn't think he'd be bored.

Chris joined GMO in our second year, working out of our tiny space in the Batterymarch building. Dick was busy trading. Eijk and I were happy to have someone young and impressionable to share our ideas with. We tried to get across to him the idea of investment cycles – in particular, how value could vary cross-sectionally across the same parameter, like the size of companies. We talked to him about small and value. I showed him the valuation cycles made during my days at Batterymarch, where all my calculations were done laboriously by hand. Eijk and I would walk around the office bending our arms at various angles to show him where we were in the investment cycle.

One of the important things that Dick, Eijk and I agreed on – it was one of the rare times we agreed on anything – was to spend essentially all our firm's earnings on a computer. We bought a Prime computer with a five-megabyte hard drive. At the time this seemed like an enormous luxury. Our hard drive was about the same size as an industrial washing machine. I thought we could work our entire lifetimes and never fill it up. Today its capacity is less than that of the smallest thumb drive. That computer proved to be worth every penny. Because I had no mathematical training, I thought Chris could formalize things and test the rigor of my ideas utilizing the power of the computer.

By this date Wall Street was using computers for back office functions, like keeping clients' records, but wasn't using them for investment purposes. His first job was to build a database of U.S. stocks. We sent him off for months on end to the Boston Public Library to copy the key financial valuation metrics – profits, retained earnings, sales, stock prices, book value, etc. – by hand from old copies of Value Line going back to the early 1950s. Chris fed the data that he'd collected into what was perhaps the first mini-computer ever to be used for investment analysis. After he'd finished this project we got him to put Morse's data into the computer. So we ended up with a detailed computer database of company financial data; a database that showed when small caps collectively were expensive and when they were cheap; and when individual companies were cheap and when they were overpriced.

Chris and I used to ask ourselves, "What are we doing? What works? What doesn't work?" Everything was up for grabs. I fed Chris my hunches, things that might or might not work, and he'd apply the mathematical rigor. He was brilliant at shooting down my bad ideas. Most people can never persuade me that I am wrong. It's a hell of a skill to persuade people that they're wrong. If it can be done fast, brainstorming proceeds at a remarkable rate. The joke was that by the time I'd gotten up, taken a shower, walked across Boston Common – no cell phones in those days – and arrived at work, which took about 20 minutes, I almost always had a new set of ideas. I would take each idea to Chris, who in about 15 seconds would convince me that I had laid yet another egg. I'd kind of slap my face and forget about it. Then we'd go on to the next idea. Within an hour of arriving at the office, we had diagnosed all my new ideas as useless. The speed with which we could get through the five crazy ideas of a morning was just remarkable. Very occasionally something would go into the pot of things we were working on and genuinely didn't know the answer to. Chris and I felt we were moving faster than anybody else. It was paradise.

In return, I was sometimes able to keep Chris from making silly mistakes, which a lot of super quants are prone to do. After a while, as in several years, he knew that I could do one thing better than him. I could look at a page of numbers or a chart and sense that something was not quite right, that the model was not giving a plausible answer. I think there's something about being a serious mathematician which makes that quite hard to do. If you've gone through various processes, it's a bit of a jump to just say, "Is this approximately correct?" Sometimes he would show me a page and I'd say, "Well, I don't think this feels right to me." Chris would take a little convincing. Then he would go away and check his work and often discover a mistake, which made me happy.

It was important to both of us that our findings made sense in the real world. In other words, that we weren't building a black box. We both had business school degrees and were experienced at picking stocks the old-fashioned way. We knew what we were trying to do. Our first quant model in 1980 might be described as an expert system. We asked ourselves, "What are we trying to do?" Then we defined that for the computer. If the computer came up with a nonsense portfolio, we'd examine all the stocks that had been selected and change the model. This process continued until the portfolio only contained stocks that looked sensible to us. We were basically building a computer model to do what Dick, Chris and I were already doing by hand.

THE FIRST QUANT FUND

We closed our U.S. equity fund to new business in 1979. We were adamant about constraining the size of our assets under management, not only to prevent any impact on performance but also because we needed the freedom to do exotic things. One day, we were happily sitting around, not making any more presentations, when the telephone rang. It was the International Monetary Fund, whose pension managers had heard from Cambridge Associates that we were doing very well. They wanted to come and talk to us. No, no, absolutely closed, we told them, we didn't need any new business and we were not touting for it. Their guy, Charlie Schwartz, replied, "Oh, no, no, we understand that completely. It's just that your approach seems so interesting. We just wanted to come and chat with you." Of course, we invited them to visit us.

Charlie arrived with his assistant Paul Woolley, who later became a colleague and close friend. Paul recalls entering a small room in our office with a rickety table, a few bare chairs, piles of yellowing *Wall Street Journals* and a dead rubber plant. The table collapsed during the meeting. We had a corkboard on which a solitary exhibit was hung. The exhibit charted our performance relative to the market, updated quarter by quarter with different colored pencils or whatever happened to be at hand. The line went up very fast. I joked that if we continued to outperform by eight points a year, by my calculations our portfolio would exceed the S&P 500's total market cap by 2050, assuming the S&P grew at its normal long-term trend. This was my way of pointing out the complete improbability that such strong outperformance would continue.

We talked to Charlie and Paul for a couple of hours, spewing forth every little detail of our dividend discount model and sector-tilting, whipping out badly drawn tilts of small cap, growth and value as they ebbed and flowed over the years – and basically pointing out, bit by bit, all the nuances of our entire approach. At the end, we talked about the constraints of size and what we were trying to do. Later, Paul Woolley called up, saying they'd like to appoint GMO. "Didn't I tell you, we're closed," I replied. Paul said they understood the size constraints on what we were doing. He suggested instead that we take some of our macro ideas – the sector-tilting and the dividend discount model – and use our computer model to create a portfolio. "Would we just use our insights into which sectors were cheap and what was working?" he asked.

Naturally, I was drawn to the idea. Charlie and Paul were such a wonderful, well-informed pair. To be honest, I had been getting a little bored with the regular stock-picking business, which I'd been doing for over a dozen years. I was more interested in the top-down stuff and had always thought of myself as a strategist first and an assistant stock-picker second. I knew this change of direction would be a bit of a problem with Dick. Reasonably enough, he thought we should stick to our knitting. At the time, we were knitting rather well. Dick thought it was a distraction, which of course it was. He didn't fully approve of quant techniques because he lived for picking stocks by hand. I got that. But I thought it was an interesting concept and was intrigued to know whether it could be made to work. After I had caucused with Dick, and we had had our usual several rows on the topic, he reluctantly agreed that we would do this one account. He agreed to keep me happy. I had to push new ideas. That's how the IMF got us into the quant investment business, and 1979 was very, very early in the history of quantery.

The timing, though, was just superbly bad. As soon as the new quant product was launched we were hit right on the nose. Value suffered one of those occasional setbacks that come along every few years and always had done. The system we designed got off to a very bad start. After nine horrible months, we went to the IMF and told them it hadn't worked. We had some ideas that might work a lot better in future, but in the meantime, we offered to put them into our regular product that was otherwise tightly closed. We committed to not charging them any fees until we'd made up what we'd lost. This was fairly unusual treatment, but it seemed to us simple justice. After all, they'd been the guinea pig that had lost some fur.

Stung by our setback, Chris and I did a lot of thinking about how we could improve our model. We realized that the main culprit had been the turn-down in value that had impacted everybody. Dick hadn't done well either during this period. But our model felt amateurish anyway. So we did more work to get it right. Eighteen months later, we had polished up a relatively serious quant model with a few bells and whistles and the IMF's original money, now in our main, stock-picking-by-hand fund, had just made all its losses back. We went back to the IMF and said, "We know we messed up the first time, but if you're interested, we have a second-generation model." And Charlie, God bless him, said, "Sure, let's hear it." We described the second-generation model and they signed up, as did Corning Glass. The new fund, named U.S. Core, opened in late 1982. It has been described in a Harvard Business School study as "one of the pioneering computer-driven funds in the investment management industry."[*]

We pitched the fund as a low-cost alternative to indexing whose quantitative approach was designed to deliver modestly superior investment performance, with limited deviations from the S&P benchmark. Kingsley Durant, our treasurer, was dragooned into doing the trading. Because this stretched our limited resources, we decided to not trade that often. We developed a twice-a-year trading program, which actually had a lot going for it. It was seasonal – we traded in mid-November, early December. Then we traded again in mid-February, to get the year-end or January effect, which in those days was very strong but today, on average, is moderate. The second time around, the model worked. We started to grind out a fairly steady monthly performance, delivering around two points a year of alpha with modest volatility.

MEAN REVERSION

The model that Chris and I put together was built around mean reversion. The principle of mean reversion was first observed in biology by Sir Francis Galton, a cousin of Charles Darwin. In his book, *Hereditary Genius* (1869), Galton set out to prove that human ability passes through the generations. He found some confirmation that the descendants and relatives of distinguished people were likely to contain great achievers among them. The

---

[*] HBS GMO Case Study, 1994.

effect, however, diminished with time: only 36% of the sons of eminent men and only 9% of their grandsons were eminent. Galton also discovered that the same principle holds true of height. The children of abnormally tall people tend to be smaller than their parents, and vice versa. Without regression to the mean, the world would comprise geniuses and dolts, and giants and dwarves, with nothing in between.

Early in my career I came to the conclusion that everything important about markets is "mean reverting" or, if you prefer, wanders around a trend. Prices are pushed away from a fair price by a series of inefficiencies and eventually dragged back by the logic of value. In a free economy, the performance of companies reverts to the mean. In my very first investment job, when I pondered how P/B might work, I realized it was only because profitability, on average, reverts to the mean. I looked at the data in the Value Line hard copy and saw with my naked eye that in most cases when things get very, very profitable, they mean revert downwards. And after profits get wiped out, the reverse happens. The reason this happened was straightforward. Capital moves toward profits: excess returns attract competition and bad returns drive capital away. Pretty soon you have mean reversion. "Reversion is mean" was an idea always sticking in my head because it is a bit mean. It's a heartbreaking principle that good times always revert back to more boring, more ordinary times. On a more optimistic note, remarkably bad times don't last forever either.

The idea of mean reversion has dominated my entire career and back then I felt it was the main thing I really understood about investing. At Batterymarch I had discovered that the excess returns from small caps came from rebalancing the portfolio of stocks every year. Rebalancing picks up a lot of short-term mean reversion. A company has a great year, its market cap grows, we sell you. You have a terrible year, we buy you back.* Rebalancing only works because we live in a mean-reverting world. Later, when I entered the asset allocation business, we were able to identify bubbles in real time by showing that when an asset class moves rapidly away from its long-term trend, it sooner or later reverts to the mean. In layman's terms, the bubble bursts.

The investment world did not really get mean reversion when I entered the business. It got that you should buy solid companies and tuck them away forever. That's what was considered prudent investing and one has to confess it's not a bad definition. The world didn't get the idea that bad companies are often too cheap and good companies often too expensive. Most investors in those days predicted the future by assuming companies maintained a constant return on their retained earnings. The ROE is never constant, however. It's always changing. There is a systematic tendency for high returns to fall and low returns to rise, in both cases slowly regressing toward the typical corporate return. Our research showed that high-return companies had ended up on average with an earnings growth rate little in excess of low-return companies.

David Morse's dividend discount model incorporated mean reversion. His model assumed that the returns for every company regressed to the market average at the same rate over a seven-year period. Our basic research at Batterymarch in 1972 had revealed that the regression of corporate earnings was actually much quicker than expected. We would take 50 large and 50 small companies over

---

* Up to 2009, when I exited this type of analysis to concentrate on very big picture analysis, every rebalancing process, index or otherwise, added value. Even the value indices themselves added value. The rapid movers would graduate to the growth universe and the fallen growth stocks would move to the value index. This rebalancing, as long as the world was at least slightly mean reverting, added value.

a five-year time period and look at the profitability of high and low return groups *using hard copy data and hand calculations*. Over weeks of sampling and errors, we worked out a pretty good rate at which profits appeared to be regressing toward the average. At GMO we tested what the actual regression rate was on average. At first we did that by hand using an elaborate sample. When we finally got our mini-computer going, we found that our old data had been much more accurate than expected. For every company, we calculated its regression rate and stepped it through time. We found that the rate of mean reversion was not identical for every company. Some regressed more quickly than others.

Later we took a giant step forward by isolating those factors that appeared to accelerate or decelerate the rate of regression. Not surprisingly, we found that anything that looked or smelt like a monopoly was key to slowing mean reversion. Monopolies are characterized by very high and very stable returns. Firms can only achieve this if they are price-setters with a dominant market position, thanks to patent protection, an amazing brand or whatever. Otherwise, an abnormally high return would suck in competition and bring returns down. These sticky high returns are characteristic of what we called quality companies. At the other end of the spectrum, there are companies in cyclical industries. When a mining stock has a high return, you had better believe the rate of regression is fast. The miner goes from one year's handsome 24% return against its long-term average of 11% and two years later it's at −5%.

We also noticed that having debt speeds up the regression rate. High leverage makes profits more volatile. This is not surprising. If you take two companies with similar characteristics, the profits of the more leveraged company are going to drop much faster when things turn bad. It turned out that having no debt at all slowed regression. We saw this as kind of the icing on the cake for monopoly businesses.

Monopolies don't need to futz around with debt. They can make as much money as they think reasonable. Debt is an unnecessary risk. Why do the only thing that might upset the apple cart? That is to take on a lot of debt and then run into a crisis that takes you down with it. Quality companies don't need debt and in those days on the whole they didn't have much.

We found that we could improve the model by giving debits for debt and credits for no debt in terms of the regression rate. The model was designed so that the regression rate varied with the company's quality. Companies that had high and stable profits got extra credit. Cyclical companies, like U.S. Steel, would regress more rapidly. Because I had always had a bit of a bee in my bonnet about quality, we rigged the model to take as much quality as we could get without paying through the nose. We ended up with a value portfolio with about the same quality as the S&P 500, whereas a typical "dopey value" portfolio, based on P/B, had much lower quality. This was key because Eugene Fama and Kenneth French, the two finance economists whose later research on factor investing garnered a lot of attention, got something right in describing P/B as a risk factor. Our alpha was genuine rather than a reasonable extra return for taking more risk.*

---

* For example, the top decile of our present value model simulated over 50 years added around 4% per year over the S&P 500 with the same quality as the benchmark (although after costs we only delivered about 2.5% for two decades). This was absolutely not the case for P/B, P/E or small cap, all of which had much lower quality. A respectable, high-quality dividend discount model proved that the market was inefficient, as did the performance of high-quality stocks on their own. These lower-risk stocks should have underperformed by, say, 1% per year, like everyone knew the AAA bonds did, but instead outperformed by about 1.5% per year.

THE MICROSOFT EFFECT

Our improved dividend discount model worked better than P/B. But in its first years not by much. The disappointing thing was how well simple-minded P/B and P/E did in the era up to about 1990. Dick's attitude was if book and earnings are so easily accessible and doing just as well, why bother with this elaborate model from Chris and Jeremy? He was quite understandably irritated by the constant steady equal performance of the traditional value factors.

The payoff only came in the mid- and late 1990s, when our high-quality form of value outperformed the traditional forms of value that competitors were using. From around 1994, P/B started to act rather badly and continued to perform badly for several years. Our present value model did a whole lot better. This was due to what we called the "Microsoft effect" because it was by far the best example, although there were many others less spectacular. The software company turned out to be the sweet spot in our model. The day that Microsoft went public, it appeared to us to be in the most attractive value segment. It had a heroically high and utterly stable ROE, no debt, and, of course, an unassailable monopoly. Our model said that any company with a high return that's hardly regressing at all should be worth mathematically many times book.

Throughout the 1990s, Microsoft continued to score in the cheapest decile of value in our dividend discount model. Even at 7x book, it was still seen as cheap. We were probably the only value managers in the world who honestly believed that Microsoft was cheap. Deep into the tech blowout, we continued buying. Although the stock handsomely outperformed almost everything on the planet, it stayed in our top decile of value until July 1999. At which point we committed to take it out of the portfolio, slice by slice, over the following 12 months (which is how we traded value, moving in and out of stocks with 12 monthly slices). By the summer of 2000 the entire position had been sold. Only later that year did the share price peak and then crash. That was a very nice escape.

MOMENTUM

Now that we were in the quant business, we needed something to offset the volatility of value. Momentum is the name given to selecting stocks based on their recent price performance. David Morse had presented us with both earnings momentum and price momentum data at Batterymarch. We did not use it in those days but we could see that momentum worked pretty darn well. It turns out the stock market has its own version of Newton's First Law: bodies in motion tend to stay in motion. Earnings and stock prices with great yearly momentum tend to keep moving in the same direction, at least for a while. Stocks that did well last year tend to continue outperforming.

When you buy a stock with momentum, the number one rule is value does not matter. It's irrelevant. You can buy the most overpriced damn stock on the planet when it has momentum. Momentum and value are the opposite sides of the same coin: the former carries the price away from fair value and the latter drags it back toward fair value. They are negatively correlated with each other. If you added them together, however, momentum usually turned out to be heroic when valuation was dreadful. We ran a few tests and saw that three-quarters of the time when value was doing badly, momentum did well and vice versa. They balanced each other very nicely. We ran an efficient frontier and chose to use 60% value and 40% momentum, at first divided evenly between earnings and price momentum. We would buy the best performing decile of momentum stocks and hope they would continue their run for a while. The momentum signal burned much more quickly than value so we didn't want to hold a momentum stock for long: we'd buy it and then sell it in slices over the following nine months. Only if the stock remained in the top momentum decile, which was rare, would we hold on to it.

After a while we gave up on earnings momentum because it wasn't adding anything to the other. In the interest of simplicity, we stuck with price momentum and value. Price momentum was so powerful and simple in those days that you made money if you said, "Hands up for those stocks that outperformed last year." We spent decades modeling momentum and value. We tried to improve the model, racking our brains, working with top PhDs in particle physics but in the end we found no lasting improvements. The moral of that story is that sometimes you do better by keeping things really simple. We never made a change that did not make sense and was not tested. And we made many changes. But overall, the earlier, simpler models did at least as well.

Back in the early GMO days, we always viewed value as the senior parameter and momentum as the junior. You can understand completely the logic of why value works. It has the additional benefit that it can be measured. You look at the value range and can see when it is particularly underpriced. Then you know that you're bleeding for a good cause. The opportunity set is getting better and better. I like to say we never made tons of money without taking painful losses beforehand. You need to have the confidence to hold your position when it moves in against you and to increase your weighting as it gets more attractive. Value gives you that confidence.

Although momentum beat the market, I never quite trusted it. Momentum does not have to work. In fact, there have been disturbingly long periods when it's gone flat and the odd year or so when it dropped quite badly. But it always came back. I have no compelling answer as to why momentum worked other than that markets are made up of human beings and human nature doesn't change that much or that fast. In the end, it's just a behavioral twitch, dependent on investors under-reacting and over-reacting to new information. Momentum is just blind trend following. There was always a little voice in the back of my head suggesting that one day it wouldn't come back. If momentum ceased to function, it would just fail and you wouldn't be sure that it had for years. This was a terrible, debilitating background thought. I believed we should own as little momentum as it took to get the job done. I saw myself as a pragmatist above all. Investors are in a street brawl and they must do what it takes to win. Even though I believed passionately that valuation brought order to the chaos in the universe, we embraced the Antichrist, momentum, because it helped when you needed it the most. And without that help you may lose the client, which does nobody a favor.

The fact that momentum worked reliably for long periods flatly contradicted modern finance theory. The main message of Malkiel's *A Random Walk Down Wall Street* was that there is no information in stock prices alone. Yet, if you took 20 years of data from that book's publication onwards and divided it into deciles of momentum, you'd find that the top decile handsomely outperformed the market and that all 10 deciles were in the correct order with the lowest-momentum decile 10 doing easily the worst. This finding kills even the weak form of market efficiency, in my opinion. Academics finally started to look at this and accepted in the 2000s that there was a momentum factor. GMO got there two decades earlier. We were possibly the first investment firm, certainly one of the first handful, to combine value and momentum in a portfolio. Later, other investors did the same, realizing that the yin of momentum and yang of value worked nicely together.

NEGLECT

We were always looking for new parameters and eventually we found one that we called neglect. Our idea was that a stock's popularity and visibility were correlated with excess returns. There were several ways of measuring neglect: the number of analysts following the stock – the fewer, the better; information flow – the less the better; and low beta, above all, was a measure of how little interest there was in the stock. We modeled the lack of interest in stocks and found that it worked with moderately greater power than either value or momentum. Adding neglect appeared to increase the quality and lower the risk of the portfolio.

This seemed like a truly free lunch. We had about 25 years of data and it was so straight and smooth it would break your heart. But the moment we put neglect in the model it stopped working. Eventually, after about six years, we gave it up, whereupon it resuscitated moderately but never became convincing as an independent parameter. Why neglect chose to stop just then I put down to gremlins. Neglect turns out to be very closely related to low beta. Whether neglected stocks outperform or not depends on their value, just like everything else. There was no law of nature that said it should work. From 1994 onwards, when neglect stopped working, the risky end of the spectrum – high beta stocks – did better, the entrails of the great bubble were apparent as early as then.

Still, for a while we ran with three parameters – value, momentum and neglect – and we built a model that looked like a cube with 1,000 boxes, and you could refer to any company by its number – say, 732, which referred to the seventh decile of value, third decile of momentum and second decile of neglect. There were some pretty empty boxes, some very crowded boxes and a lot of noise. Chris, being a champion mathematician, came up with a cube smoother in three-dimensional space, in which all of your neighbors acquired some of your characteristics to smooth out the data in a three-dimensional way. For a terrible moment there, we added another dimension with four parameters and four-dimensional smoothing, which boggles the mind. At the time it was all clever stuff. It was elegant and looked good but didn't work very well, in fact much less well than our original much simpler model, because one of the parameters had decided to drop off the edge of the world.

Gradually we built up a small team of quants. Alexis Belash, who had worked at Batterymarch and was an old buddy of Dean's, joined us. We hired another quant, Michael Kagan, straight out of Harvard. Michael was a computer junkie and his reputation was already well known. Chris was really hot to hire him. He ended up with two job offers, one from us and the other at this tech start-up in Seattle. He was going to be Microsoft employee number 25. Chris and I sat down with this guy and I said, "Michael, come on, don't tell us you want to work for some flaky little tech company. You want to come work with us where we have just spent $110,000 on a prime mainframe and are doing some serious research." Michael came to work for us. That decision actually cost him hundreds of millions because he was going to get Microsoft stock. Unfortunately, it didn't work out that well for him at GMO. He stayed a few years and then left for business school.

Our quant approach was somewhat unusual in that Chris and I started quant after a fairly long, intensive time doing traditional research of the tire-kicking variety. This was not commonly the case. Most quants come out of university with PhDs in mathematics or physics and go straight into the investment business. They have very little background. I like to say about quants that they like to prove their discipline by, on occasion, marching off the edge of a cliff like the Zulu impi is said to have done long ago on the command of the great chief Shaka Zulu.

Their other failing has to do with intellectual elegance. I voted for a sign to be put on every quant's office wall saying "There are no points for elegance!" because quants can really fall in love with the elegance of the math. In the end, investment is a pragmatic business. It's about what works, it's about strange humans who don't fit into models that well. In our U.S. quant effort we had more people and resources and were operating in a more sophisticated market. As a result, we had a greater tendency to tweak the model. Whereas in our international products, where we had fewer resources and less data, we tended to stay a little behind the curve of what we were doing in the U.S. and actually made quite a bit more money. The lesson is that the model doesn't have to be elegant. As long as it works, it can be as simple as hell.

At Batterymarch and in GMO's first years we had a monopoly of hand-cranked data extracted from the library stacks. Later, we were among the very first to apply technology – bulky, expensive computers – to investing in stocks. When we started quant there hadn't been a lot of work done on this front by other firms. I sensed that we were probably further ahead at the beginning of the computer age than we had ever been. Other people were simply not ready to do this kind of dirty, assumption-driven, sample-ridden, rough and ready research. We were moving fast and doing new things that hadn't been done before. The passage of time revealed what worked and what didn't work.

The great returns of our early years show the advantage of being a step ahead of the competition. In time, however, all good investment ideas are arbitraged away. The arrival of computers at other investment firms did us huge damage. That wasn't bad luck. It was inevitable. Although GMO was a quant pioneer, we would have been much better off had the computer never been invented. In the hand-cranked era, using very small but well selected samples, we knew more than anyone, for hand-cranking masses of data and using your brains was a very unpopular and unfashionable approach. And for a while longer when we were one of the few using computers, we still had a data-cranking edge. But when everyone had powerful computers, we had to find other edges, which was not nearly as easy.

One of the irritating things about the quant business is that our very first *serious* model for the IMF (conveniently forgetting our short-lived simplistic effort), still prehistoric as it was, dating back to 1982, would have beaten the pants off the more sophisticated quant models we developed later. That's just the way it turned out. We made perhaps 100 or so changes, including a handful of major ones, over the next 20 years or so, and each one was rigorously tested and seemed to make sense based on our understanding of the market. Each change was agonized over and really seemed better in terms of risk and return. But the simpler model still very inconveniently won. It was easy enough to develop a dividend discount model to beat P/B; and relatively easy to improve on the simple momentum of "hands up which stocks did best last year." But it was impossible to have the fancier versions fit together as effectively as the primitive versions did. So, in a way, we wasted 10 years or more of very serious research.

CHAPTER 4

The Sausage Factory

With our first two quant accounts, we won each of the first three years by a modest 2.5% a year. Although off the pace from our U.S. stock-picking product, it was entirely satisfactory. We soon found richer pickings for our quant models in foreign stocks. It's hard to know how lucky we've been at GMO but on occasion we have been exceptionally lucky. The reason we got into international stocks is not that we thought it was going to be the greatest thing since sliced bread; that investor interest in the asset class would explode, as it did over the next two decades; or that these markets were dreadfully inefficient and offered us the opportunity to make huge amounts of money, as they did. The truth is we got into international because we were desperate to find something for Eijk to do.

At GMO's start, Dick managed the fund with me and, later, Chris Darnell. Eijk was fidgeting around, increasingly frustrated that he was not part of the process. Dick and I had had eight tough years working together at Batterymarch to settle most of our differences. Eijk was clearly not going to settle in with us easily, and that potentially was going to rock our finally smooth-sailing boat. It was straightforward for us to say to clients, this is the team that at Batterymarch generated consistently good performance over the years, six wins, a draw and one loss, with 6% a year added value, and we're continuing with the same portfolio. Eijk wanted us somehow to incorporate him and change things. Quite sensibly, we would not agree to that. Eijk had had some international investing experience with his two insurance companies, so having him run the new international division would kill two birds with one stone.

In any case, Chris and I believed inefficiencies in foreign stock markets offered a potential opportunity. We started to look into the possibility of launching an international fund and asked ourselves the question as to whether value investing would work as well in international markets as it had in the U.S. We launched a huge research effort, aided by Jody Shuman, who had joined us straight from Dartmouth, to answer that question. First, we needed some data. At the time, the only provider of statistics on international stocks was Capital International (now MSCI), which later provided the standard index for Europe, Asia and the Far East, comprising 21 developed markets and more than 1,000 public companies. The firm put out a monthly report, Capital International Perspective, which contained data going back to 1968. We called their head office in Geneva but the person guarding the data was an autocratic administrator who was strangely reluctant to release it.

As luck would have it, Jay Light at the Harvard Business School had recently donated hard copies of Capital International reports to the school's library. We sent Jody along to the stacks, where she spent week after week photocopying the quarterly and monthly books at the cost of a nickel a page. The data had to be cleaned up and input into the computer, which was all done by hand. It took a year and a half to collect and refine the data before testing could begin.

At last, we had a machine-readable database of international stocks, the first in the world. Can you believe that? The competition allowed a tiny new firm to get there first. Oh, the joys of being alive in the investment industry in those days. We ran simple tests of P/B, dividend yield and price-to-sales and even price momentum and eventually one or two other things that took a little calculating to see how they worked. To our delight, they worked even better than in the U.S., which was still doing handsomely well. Traditional value measures in the U.S. such as P/B and P/E had been adding about three points a year for decades. For international stocks, those same measures earned roughly five points a year.

In 1981 we launched the new fund, International Active, with Eijk as the boss. Chris and I pumped the data and ran tests for the first few months as Eijk built his own team. For each country we ran a fairly straightforward value model that worked beautifully, to which Eijk's team began to add sensible judgment and deeper fundamental analysis. We were the first team anywhere, I believe, to demonstrate that there was a return to value and small caps in the international markets. Academics didn't write about it until nearly 20 years later. This gave us a huge head start on the rest of the industry.

Leading U.S. institutions at the time had very little foreign exposure, perhaps 5% of their total investments. Cambridge Associates and the leading pension funds, however, had decided that international was going to be the new hot area. There must have been a score of other international managers – Capital Guardian in Los Angeles and the rest mostly in Britain. All of them employed a traditional fundamental approach and exhibited a bias toward growth and large cap stocks. None applied quantitative techniques. Our database at first contained only equal-weighted data. It wasn't until later that we figured out how to handle market-cap weighted data. This gave our international stock selection a small cap bias, which worked out just fine.

We had an effective monopoly: institutional investors venturing into international stocks would pick a growth manager and a value manager because that was the style. They'd pick one of the 20 growth managers and then they'd pick us because no one else was doing international value. We were also the only ones buying cheap small caps apart from John Templeton, who had an identical-looking portfolio. Templeton did well but thankfully he was only selling to private individuals through his mutual fund and ignored the institutional business. Our first international client was Amherst. Other clients soon signed up, including 3M, the World Bank, the Common Fund, Phillips Exeter and Swarthmore. We scooped up nearly every account we went after.

PRESENTATION SKILLS

I made all the early international presentations, though Dick and Eijk often came along. When I made a presentation, I didn't try to pitch in any conventional sense. Instead, I explained how we managed money and tried to persuade potential clients as to why it was a good idea. If I could get into the mindset, which I could almost always, of conveying data and ideas, not pitching them to give us business but persuading them that this or that made sense and why it made sense, I had pretty much won. That's how I have done it throughout my life – I would get into teaching mode, and I did have a great deal of current and historical data in my head. Looking back I would say I was obsessed by this stuff. My memory of what had happened in individual years was very strong. It turns out that trying desperately hard to convey what you truly believe is a pretty good selling technique.

Our first 22 presentations for foreign equities landed 23 accounts. How is that possible? We were turned down once, but another presentation delivered three accounts. When we went before the investment committee of the Harvard-Yenching Institute, Walter

Cabot, the head of the endowment, was immediately hooked. He suggested we should present to the Harvard Committee. Then, someone at the table said this is also the Harvard Committee, and Cabot looked around and said, "Oh, yes, I suppose it is." The Boston brahmin also happened to be the chairman of the investment committee at Wellesley College. Without a further presentation we were hired there, too. With one shot, we won Harvard, Wellesley and the Yenching Institute. That was efficient. The one account we lost was at the famous Sierra Club. The competition was a blind woman with a guide dog. When Dick and I saw her in the waiting room, we looked at each other and made the sign that our throats were cut. What chance did we have against a blind woman at the Sierra Club? Anyway, she won.

The fund's early performance was outstanding. In its first year, International Active beat its EAFE benchmark by nearly seven points. The following year it added 4.3% alpha. In 1983 the fund was up 32%, eight points above the benchmark. What's more, our performance turned out to be negatively correlated with other fund managers. After four years, International Active reached its asset target of $550 million and was closed to new investors. As the international markets exploded in size and the number of companies listed increased, we would take a couple of new accounts each year, but not for the first few years. In the year International Active closed, Eijk hired Peg McGetrick. Peg had previously worked for the Common Fund, a nonprofit that provides investment services to educational endowments and foundations. Peg later took much of the responsibility for managing International Active and much later, after a very successful hedge fund career elsewhere, served a stint as GMO's interim chief executive.

In 1986, we launched our first quant product for foreign stocks. The fund used simple valuation tools, such as P/E and dividend yields to select stocks. A number of existing clients signed up, including the World Bank, the IMF and Bell Atlantic. By our standards, the international developed markets were still back in the cowboy days. They were gloriously inefficient. Contrary thinking was undeveloped. Groupthink prevailed, especially in Japan. Simple investment disciplines continued to work well in foreign markets, whereas at home those disciplines increasingly resembled trying to get blood out of a stone.

It made sense, therefore, for investors to gain exposure to foreign markets through what I called "modified indexing," namely, by owning half the market cap but the cheapest half. A modified index portfolio also tilted toward the least efficient markets. It was around this time that I published my paper "You Can't Fool All of the People All of the Time."* I pointed out that the cost of indexing outside the U.S. was considerably higher. I wrote that our "approach has many of the advantages of an index in implementation [namely, low costs and diversification] but would still add considerable value for a few years until foreign markets improve." The performance of the fund lived up to this promise.

Our research found that small cap stocks moved separately in each developed market, which offered good opportunities for diversification. Years later, my colleague Forrest Berkley produced a famous exhibit that showed the ebb and flow of small caps across various countries. The lines, marked in different colors, looked just like strands of spaghetti. There was no uniform tendency. Our international quant fund was able to exploit this opportunity. Markets being what they are, more or less the minute after Forrest showed this exhibit the various developed markets started to morph slowly into a sine curve and began to move in tandem.

---

* Published in *The Journal of Portfolio Management*, Winter 1986.

THE OCTOBER 1987 CRASH

Over the course of 1987, Dick and I had become increasingly fearful of the latest new investment fad known as portfolio insurance. This strategy simulated the purchase of a put on the S&P 500. As the market rose, the portfolio insurers bought stocks and, as it fell, they sold and increased their cash holdings. In my view, portfolio managers had become insurance salesmen. Unfortunately, the analogy with home insurance wasn't enlightening: when a home burns down it does so on its own. When the stock market goes down it can be like the whole of California falling into the sea. This strategy of selling insurance belonged to that group of techniques known as Gambler's Ruin because it created a very small chance of total wipeout.

Everyone who knew anything was well aware that portfolio insurance was dangerous. It was academic in the sense that it hadn't been stress-tested in the marketplace. Trendy institutions with an interest in appearing avant-garde were signing up all over the place. A couple of firms, led by academics, raced around selling the idea that you could be fully invested but by selling at a given rate, you could duplicate the effect of having puts protect your portfolio. They said you wouldn't lose your hedge when the market declined. Quite a few of us thought and talked about it at the time: wouldn't there be rather a rush to the door? Would market liquidity be able to keep up with it?

As we got into September, the ground began to shake. We could see the market getting nervous and twitchy, with big up and down spikes. Dick and I considered the prospect that an unprecedented sharp decline was not unlikely and took a large bond position in the U.S. fund. In mid-October, I attended the Contrary Opinion Forum, which met at Lake Champlain, Vermont, along with Ned Johnson of Fidelity and the technical investment strategist Robert

Prechter. My comments were written up by Eric Miller, a strategist for Donaldson, Lufkin & Jenrette, a broker known at the time for its high-quality research. I expressed a concern that too many market professionals were exhibiting a "stay in the pack mentality." Bond yields had climbed sharply and U.S. stocks were no longer as cheap as they'd been a few years earlier. As the forum was breaking up, I was asked a convenient question that gave me a chance to reply with another question: "After the greatest equity bull market in history, are not U.S. Treasury bonds yielding 10% about as close as we can get to a free lunch?"

A week before the 1987 crash, GMO moved into new offices in Rowes Wharf on Boston Harbor. On the Thursday of that week, I had to drive out to a local college, which was one of our favorite accounts. We would go there three or four times a year and chat to a very interested, attentive investment committee. En route from Boston I drove into a terrible thunderstorm. My car had just reached the top of a hill. It was night-time. There was no one around. Suddenly, there was this blue light all around the car and a deafening noise. My hair prickled like mad from static. I used to get a bit depressed in my thirties and forties, nothing concerning, but a few weeks here and there, and I was depressed at that moment. As the lightning hit my car, my depression disappeared. I was on a notorious high for about two weeks after that.

The meeting started at 8.30 the next morning. I told them that I thought the market was about to collapse. This started a terrible argument between the old fogies, who sided with me, and the young Turks who sided with the chairman of the committee. The next thing we knew, it was almost noontime. We'd been there for hours and had begun to shout at each other. They kicked me out and after another hour of shouting they got to a vote. The good guys won this one and decided they would put on a short position in S&P

futures equal to 30% of their portfolio. The chairman, a very rich and very bright private equity financier, resigned on the spot. The committee gave its instruction to the treasurer. This poor guy was about to trade when he saw the Dow was down 100 points, which at the time seemed enormous, so he decided he'd wait till Monday. The trade never was put on.

When the market opened on Monday it was like a bottomless pit. Futures were selling at huge discounts to stocks and all manner of incredible things were happening. Seeing the future contracts selling at an impossibly low price, Chris, our chief quant, went long futures against stocks in his own account. But the market fell so quickly he couldn't deliver the collateral in time. The broker just sold him out. He was doing the right thing and should have made a fortune, but the market played some funny games and marked him out. At the start of the week, our U.S. fund was down about four points relative to the market. But with over 20% of our theoretically 100% equity fund in Treasuries and bonds enjoying their biggest up day in decades, we were now a bit up on the year having lost over 5% less than the market in two days. It was a wonderful break for us.

A journalist at *Businessweek* had seen my comments at the Contrary Opinion Forum and jumped on the telephone to ask me, "You appeared to see this coming. What happens now?" I told him that bonds were no longer as attractive and stocks were much more attractive. Of course, I noted that after such an extreme market move you had to rebalance: it was time to sell bonds and buy stocks. I soon learned Dick was pissed off with me for talking to the press, claiming the limelight, as he would say, "once again." He also felt we should stick to our new ultra conservative position and, because he was the portfolio manager, he had me call *Businessweek* back and tell them we were not going to make the trade. Afterwards, the market rallied over the next couple of months and our big bond position handed us our first down year.

Up to this point, Dick and I had enjoyed a great run: we won six out of eight years at Batterymarch with one draw and one loss and then won the first nine years in a row at GMO – in 17 years we'd had only one loss. In those nine years at GMO, we won by eight points a year, which meant we doubled the money of our clients against the benchmark, and the benchmark itself had doubled, so that quadrupled our assets – the market move plus outperformance. After my unfortunate call with *Businessweek*, we had the mother of all rows, the result of which was that I stopped spending half my time helping Dick in our U.S. Active Fund and ended up with one job, working with Chris on our growing quant business.

I understand Dick's position. The two of us had a great track record picking U.S. stocks. Then this irritating partner – me – works to complicate a simple, very successful relationship by insisting on starting yet another division, quant, with a highfalutin math approach led by Chris. He wanted us to stick to our successful knitting while I liked the novelty of quant. So, we fell out on that topic, but I completely get his point and sympathize. I felt I had no choice. You only live once and you had better try everything new and interesting you can. From this moment GMO became, in effect, three separate investment boutiques: Dick in U.S. Active, Eijk in International Active and me in quant.

Not only were our fund management processes separate, but each of the three divisions had its own billing systems, record-keeping and back offices. This provided a stable structure going forward. Our loose structure minimized bureaucracy, infighting and office politics. We had not planned it that way, but anyone inside or outside the firm could see what a blindingly lucky decision it was. The move enabled the three founding partners, who from time to time were barely on speaking terms with each other and who were incredibly different on every parameter, to do things somewhat their own way in three more or less independent operations. This was a survival strategy that worked better than we could have hoped. It was only later that we came to realize and value the few important things we had in common: don't run the firm to maximize profits, but really look after your clients' well-being; always level with them – if you disagree with your clients, tell them; and, of course, maintain a remorseless value bias.

THE SAUSAGE FACTORY

Our early stock-picking funds, both U.S. and foreign, were very size limited. By industry standards, we deliberately grew slowly when we could have grown very fast indeed. Our quant division, however, was designed to have no tight limits on assets under management. Chris and I hunkered down. I didn't worry too much about how fast our business expanded. Pretty quickly, U.S. quant had more than Dick and foreign quant had more than Eijk. We had many ideas that we were testing out and needed computing power to make headway and, of course, someone who could program. We were lucky when Rob Soucy joined in 1987. With his programming capabilities, we were suddenly able to move at warp speed – he could practically program our ideas in real time, which moved us forward dramatically.

MUTUAL FUNDS

When we launched quant, Chris and I badgered Dick into agreeing to have us start a mutual fund. We couldn't hope to do separate accounts – we just didn't have enough people. Our early investors in our first quant product, U.S. Core, the IMF and Corning Glass, were pension funds and were able to go into a bank-pooled trust so we could have one account to manage. But endowments, a big part of our business thanks to Cambridge Associates, could not do that. We also wanted to be able to mix endowment and pension fund assets together in the interest of operating simplicity. Only a mutual fund structure could do that. Our U.S. Core strategy was just about the first mutual fund anyone had offered to institutions. The word on the street was that you couldn't get institutions to pool. We proved that wrong. Our strength was necessity: if they didn't want to pool, we couldn't take their business. We just did not want an army of operators doing what three or four could do in a single account. We may have lost one or two accounts, but basically 95% of our clients accepted the mutual fund structure.

This turned out to be completely significant for our firm because mutual funds offered an enormous increment of efficiency. It was the only way our small staff could handle all aspects of managing a score of institutional accounts. The mutual fund structure also led to fewer errors than had we been running an army of individual accounts. By pooling assets, the firm could deliver uniform results for all our clients. It also reduced costs for custodial and other new back-office functions. Another advantage was that inflows could be used to shift investments and cover withdrawals without extra transaction costs. Total savings for clients were up to 100 basis points a year for investors in the less liquid international markets; transaction costs back then were horrific.

Pooling also enabled us to start more funds than we could have dreamt about on a separate account basis. The SEC wasn't quite as neurotic then as it is now, with good reason, I might add. GMO evolved into what a Harvard Business School professor called the

"Sausage Factory" because we applied a uniform set of techniques to manage many new and different types of investment products. We used the same simple quant model to crank out a variety of sausages. In 1987, we launched International Core (later International Intrinsic Value) using quant techniques developed for the U.S. In 1989, Forrest Berkley took over management of this fund. When he stepped down as portfolio manager in 1994, its assets had grown to nearly $3 billion, then about a quarter of the firm's total assets. Over the course of the 1980s, the quant division expanded its products to a full line of U.S. equity (core, value, growth, small cap value and growth), together with international and, later, emerging equities. By the end of the 1990s, GMO was operating nearly 20 quant equity strategies.

Half the things we did had never been done by mortal man. As early as 1979, with the IMF account we started to trade our entire portfolio by handing the whole trade over to Goldman Sachs or Solomon. We designed an incentive program to prevent them from ripping us off – no mean feat, by the way. If one could beat the other side, we would share the profits. So, that incentivized them to beat up on their other customers because we were giving them a share of the loot. We could trade our whole portfolio in a couple of days. The technology wasn't polished like it is today – it was really creaky. At the time, no one was doing block trades.

GMO WOOLLEY

We also teamed up with Paul Woolley, who had left the IMF to set up a quant investment operation at Barings in London. GMO agreed to provide a budget for operational expenses of the new U.K. operation and to split the profits. Initial negotiations were fraught as both sides were nervous about legal aspects and liabilities. Having spent several fruitless, irritating hours going round and round in circles on the legal stuff, Paul and I found ourselves sitting on a bench in a little park on the Embankment by the Thames. Paul finally got up and stretched his legs, and said, "To heck with this. Why don't we just do it and work out the details later?" So, we shook on it and did exactly that. It worked out fine.

In early October 1987, GMO Woolley moved into a tiny basement office in a 1950s-style building in the City of London. When the stock market crashed two weeks later, they weren't able to follow the events of the day because they didn't have live electronic feeds. Instead, they relied on buying successive issues of the evening paper in order to follow the crash. For the first few years, Boston and London shared data to save money. Whenever someone from the London office traveled to Boston, they would return armed with computer diskettes. Surprisingly, these rudimentary arrangements turned out to be beneficial. The London quants discovered that getting their value data with a six-month lag actually enhanced performance, which gave us another interesting line of research. Who would have thought that for the previous 40 years or more if you stored away the recent value data and seasoned it for six months you would have better performance? But back then it was so and had been for decades.

COMPETITION

At the outset, there was little competition from other quantitative-based investment strategies. The only person we were aware of competing with was Barr Rosenberg, a well-known quant academic who'd started his own shop, Rosenberg Capital Management, based in California. Their marketing person was a handsome blonde woman, who became kind of notorious. She was very smart and very good-looking and represented their performance as very good. We told prospective clients that we aimed for two points of alpha, plus or minus four a year, whereas she said her firm aimed for four points, plus or minus four – in other words, twice the returns with the same amount of the volatility. Not surprisingly, we did not have great success marketing against her at first. But happily for us, in the third year of our competition, they hit a minus eight year, followed by another minus eight. It seems they had mis-specified their risk. We started to win a lot of business.

Rob Arnott was a rising star in quant investing. In the early 1980s, he co-wrote a paper with someone from Fidelity that was published in the *Financial Analysts Journal*. This sent Chris and me into a freak-out because they wrote about everything we were working on. We immediately invited the Fidelity guy out to lunch and it soon became clear that he'd had little to do with the article. It was all Rob. So, we knew that he was the man and he was hot on our tail. We figured we just had a slight edge – of course he might have been writing slightly archaic versions of his thinking, which would have been a perfectly sensible thing to do. We felt we didn't need to write papers for prestigious journals. In those days, we didn't write anything down. We felt everything we were doing was much too precious to give away. In meetings with prospective clients, I would hand out a few sheets of paper and collect them before they left the office. But Rob was working for a large firm; for him, visibility and status were worth a lot more than they were to us. Of course, we read everything he wrote, checking whether it offered an improvement to what we were already doing. If anything, he was giving away stuff to us, which we tried not to reciprocate. I later offered Rob a job at GMO but he turned me down.

INFORMAL ORGANIZATION

In its early years, GMO was a pretty loose organization. After 1987, the three founding partners ran their independent boutiques and didn't have much to do with each other. People didn't have set job descriptions. There were no formal committees. No internal legal counsel. No office manager. No formal shareholder services. No client relationship specialists. We didn't do much marketing. It was 18 years before we hired a dedicated salesperson. Imagine nearly 20 years without any sales team even though we were quite big. Until Alan Smith joined in 1997, no one was formally responsible for HR. Our vacation policy was "you may take as much vacation as your colleagues will allow you to." In our first 17 years only one investment professional left the firm.

We had a small staff to handle a rapidly growing number of assets and funds. It was somewhat chaotic, very lean and mean. Everyone mucked in. When Mason Smith came to work as a temp after the 1987 crash she started out on the reception desk and then joined the quant team, even though she was a history major. She sat at a desk near my office and on a typical day she'd be opening the mail, settling trades, working on performance, calling up clients, setting up some meetings and trying generally to keep us out of trouble. For many years I had no personal assistant. Then one day I was scheduled to be at three different client meetings in three different cities at the same time. So in 1993, Justine McGeary, who had also worked at reception, came to work as my assistant. She used to keep a packet of macaroons in her drawer, because she knew that if I didn't eat, I would crash. When I was about to crash, she would walk into my office and feed me a cookie.

For a number of years, our fairly casual approach to recruiting was based on who came to us rather than us seeking people out.

A candidate would meet different people each time they came to the office to interview. We never made or compared notes. In fact, I was never quite sure how we hired people. We didn't take many on the investment side. In retrospect, we ended up being somewhat understaffed. One of the downsides was that we were so desperate for people to fill empty positions that there was a tendency for GMO to Peter Principle, which is to say if someone could do one job well, we would give them twice the work and twice the responsibility and then four times until we found the level of their incompetence. Including me.

But this also meant there were glorious opportunities. People had an unprecedented opportunity to spread their wings, take risks, season themselves, make mistakes and become broad-based, dependable, self-reliant professionals. Anyone who wanted to take initiative, particularly in the first 15 years, could do so and their job would grow. Forrest became CEO-like because he had lots of initiative and we wouldn't stop him. Similarly, Mason was soon functioning as a COO. It was only as we became a little more bureaucratic that it began to be a little bit of a drawback. I have no executive skills. My definition of leadership was to be inspirational: get people thinking and set a high target that we needed to be the best. I would go around asking people what their idea was for that week. I expected at least one good idea every week. They were very nervous to start with but then they got into the spirit of the exercise. Anyone who had a half reasonable idea was able to do it. My style was to let everyone do what they wanted, to make sure we were moving fast, having ideas and being generally excited.

The founding partners were united in their belief that we should always put our clients' interest first. Whether that meant closing Dick's fund at $250 million or Eijk's fund at $550 million because we felt that having too many assets would affect performance. On one occasion, we put through a block trade on an IMF account with one of the tickers reversed. Instead of buying a moderately large position in Coca-Cola, we bought a ludicrously large position in Crompton & Knowles Loom Works, a textile company in Connecticut. We pushed the price up by almost 10%. After a day or two, we noticed our mistake and reversed the trade. Not surprisingly, this knocked Crompton & Knowles's share price back to where it had come from. We had lost, perhaps, $50,000. Anyway, we sent the IMF a check, with a brief explanation of what had gone wrong, and we didn't give it a second thought.

Well, the good side of GMO has been that we would always do that kind of thing. It didn't depend on whether we thought the client would notice what had gone wrong. If it was clearly a barefaced error, we would make good – as would our competitors, of course. But in this particular case, with hundreds of trades flying back and forth, it was glaringly obvious that the client would not have spotted our error and never would. Later Paul Woolley, who was working for the IMF then, told me this was the best purchase of goodwill in the history of the investment business, precisely because they could tell that it would never have been noticed.

GROWTH

The launch and subsequent winding down of our Growth Allocation Fund shows how we attempted to manage our clients' money in their best interests. As mentioned earlier, I have always maintained that there was no such thing as a value effect or small cap effect. There was only a cheap effect. In my view, the categories of value and growth had been mis-specified. The distinction should really be between stocks with fast growth and those with slow growth.

This may seem surprising to anyone who has cut their teeth at investing in recent years. But back in the late 1980s, fast-growing stocks had underperformed the market forever. This was almost certainly because growth had always sold at too high a premium relative to intrinsic value. There are solid behavioral reasons for this. Growth is pleasing, investors want to own it and are willing to pay up for it. So growth underperforms. By contrast, slow growth is unappealing because investors believe it to be riskier. It was, indeed, on average, lower quality. Investors priced the stocks accordingly. Historically, for at least the previous 70 years, slow growth had had a fairly steadfast excess return, beating the market by a couple of points on average every year and fast growth would generally underperform by a couple of points.

That was the way life normally was. Throughout the 1980s, however, the returns from growth had been particularly poor. In late 1988, I went on a trip to California to see Pomona College and others. I turned up at a meeting where they told me that on the agenda was the firing of a growth manager. This was the kind of stuff you could say to a value manager who was in good standing, whose performance was on a roll. By this date growth managers had bad one-year, three-year and ten-year numbers. They hid under the table at business lunches, just as value managers had at other times (like in 1973 or later in 1999), and shied away from the limelight. I went off to a second meeting in Southern California and commented, in the context of my reporting about the ebb and flow of growth and value, that the last client had firing its growth manager on the agenda. They laughed and said, "Well, we do too." I repeated the story at a third meeting, and they too had plans to fire their growth manager. Every one of these institutions had had it with growth. Each had reached the point of no return at the same time.

Not surprisingly, this occurred at exactly the moment when, on our measurements, growth had never been more reasonably priced. It was not handsomely cheap, just a bit below fair value based on our dividend discount model. Normally, these stocks sold at a 20% premium and now they were 10% cheap. Sure as eggs is eggs, I thought, this thing is going back to its normal premium. There was a 30% spread to play for. I returned to Boston fired up. We tested the subset of growth stocks in U.S. Core, of which we had always had plenty, and found that we had done a perfectly respectable job picking growth. This seemed like an opportunity. We decided to launch our first quant-based growth fund. Dick went ballistic because he was a value investor and didn't think I should be going around telling everyone to buy growth stocks. But he eventually agreed. So we went to clients and pointed out that we had a good record at picking growth stocks. We were going to use the same quant parameters, momentum and value, but with modestly more momentum and less value than we had used in the past.

To be conservative, we told clients we saw an opportunity for them to earn around 15% above the return of the S&P 500 over a two- to three-year period. Given growth was considered by us value investors to be the devil, we would certainly not recommend hanging around in a sector that had a long and inglorious history of underperforming. You didn't want to get stuck holding growth stocks, but here was an exception to the rule. The fund's offering memorandum explained:

> Growth stocks have had seven bad years in a row. However, our growth indicators are near the top of the favorable range for future performance. Growth stocks seem to be particularly cheap now... We will, of course, advise you when we feel growth stocks have had their run and that the time has come to reduce your exposure

to the group. This service is unlikely to be offered by a manager exclusively in growth stocks...

Almost all our clients liked the idea. They were impressed by our numbers, which showed how cheap growth was. They wanted to hedge their bets. So, they gave us half the money they got from firing their old growth managers. We sold the fund to all the usual suspects and to quite a few others. It sold like hot cakes at a time when U.S. Core was boring everyone to death in one of those periods where nothing was working. Within six months we had more clients than we had for any other product.

We launched the Growth Fund at the beginning of January 1989 and, after years of monstrous underperformance, growth stocks, without any great fanfare, had a modest outperformance of about three points for the year. Then in 1990, they outperformed by five or six points, and in 1991, they did pretty well and beat the benchmark by another seven points. Our timing was almost to the month perfect, for the first and only time in GMO's history. Usually we were a couple of years early with our bets and occasionally three years early. Anything less than a year was considered a victory, but this was just perfect. It had to happen sooner or later. This was very fortunate for our firm and had nice commercial implications for quant.

Of course, the clients who bought the fund didn't really believe we would tell them when to get out. But that is what we did. In March 1991, we called them and said, "The valuation gap has closed, growth stocks are now pretty close to normal. Now, we suggest you sell out of our fund." Of the 30 or so accounts, only three clients refused to budge. Having peaked at $1.2 billion, assets in the Growth Fund fell to a little over $200 million. After which, growth underperformed. If only our investing had always been so easy!

JAPAN: A ONCE IN A LIFETIME OVERRIDE

In the late 1980s we also ran into the biggest bubble in both the history of the stock market and the real estate market. Japan was the Real McCoy. We kind of gritted our teeth and made what I called at the time a once in a lifetime override. We took Japan to zero in our international equity funds at a time when it had a 40% to 45% benchmark weighting. In many ways, this was the biggest bet we had ever made or probably ever will make.

When we started International Quant in 1986 we were slightly underweight Japan. Then Japanese stocks went up and up, and we became more and more underweight. We had quite a bit until 1987 when the market reached a P/E in the 40s. The P/E had never been higher than 25, just like the U.S. market before that. At this point, we got entirely out of Japan. Independently, Eijk had also gone to zero in his actively managed foreign equities fund. Without any conversation between the teams. This was not only typical of the time, it also revealed our joint commitment to value. Nearly four decades later, Peg McGetrick assured me that Eijk's team beat us to the zero punch. But at the time they didn't tell us, which certainly speaks to the unusual independence of our decisions. We truly were a federation of independent boutiques.

Anyhow, it seemed prudent for any serious value investor to exit Japan. Of course, after we went to zero, Japanese stocks continued climbing and for three long years we underperformed painfully as the Japanese market went to 65x earnings. A year after getting out of Japan, Forrest and I went to Yale to explain to their investment committee why we owned no Japanese stocks. After I had made my presentation, a committee member commented, "We are very impressed with your analysis of the situation. All this data you have does make an incredibly powerful case that Japan is overvalued. But tell us, with Japan comprising more than 50% of the weight of the benchmark, are you concerned for the solidity of your firm if you are wrong?" I explained that GMO had three divisions, so was not dependent on this one bet (although as mentioned above, Eijk, unknown to me, was also betting big against Japan). "Besides," I added, "this is the bet we *should* make on behalf of our clients." I considered it fiduciarily irresponsible to own any Japan. David Swensen, Yale's chief investment officer, called Forrest the next day and said his phone has been ringing off the hook all day. His colleagues on the Yale Investment Committee had loved the presentation. And that was the beginning of our relationship with Yale.

One particular problem with Japan was that its weighting in the benchmark was overstated. In my 1990 essay, "The Dirty Secrets of International Investing,"* I pointed out how the poor construction of the foreign stock market index vastly overstated Japan's position in the EAFE benchmark. In those days many Japanese companies held shares in their trading partners. The index double-counted these cross-shareholdings, thereby pushing up Japan's overall weighting in the index. At the time, Japan was 62% of EAFE. Adjusted for cross-shareholdings this fell to 44%. We created our own benchmark, "EAFE-Lite," which had a lower Japan weight. I persuaded many of our clients to accept our bespoke benchmark. But it was a hard struggle. It took up an enormous amount of time and at the end of the day, even if it was right thing to do, it probably wasn't commercially sensible.

Even adjusting for the cross-shareholding complex, the valuation of Japan's stock market still looked like an amazing bubble. It

---

* Published in *Investing Worldwide*, Association for Investment Management and Research, 1990.

was hard also to miss the supreme silliness of the Tokyo real estate market. Real estate in Tokyo was selling at 3x the price of real estate in Manhattan. The ground under the emperor's palace was said to be worth as much as California at current rates. In disbelief, we spent quite a few hours researching this and, remarkably, it appeared to be about true. This reinforced our willingness to believe our own eyes when it came to the Japanese stock market. What we saw in Japan was, I believed, the biggest bubble in history, including the South Sea bubble. It really was supremely absurd.

Of course, we were told we didn't understand Eastern markets: the politics, the solidarity, the discipline, the accounting – the general zen of the whole business. In 1989, when the Nikkei was bumping up against 40,000, the "Brains Trust" from Solomon Brothers, one of the leading New York investment banks, toured the U.S., explaining why Japan at 65x earnings was actually cheap and should go to 120. Their reasoning was that interest rates were low and economic growth was high. In fact, between 1986 and 1990, when Japan's P/E ratio doubled, economic growth fell from 10% to 4% and interest rates were starting to rise sharply.

For three years we underperformed the EAFE index by about 10% a year. Yet we didn't lose any business – not a dollar or a yen's worth of business. We lost nothing for some very interesting, important reasons. First, the great Japanese land and stock bubble was utterly persuasive to everyone in Japan, but completely unpersuasive to almost all our clients. American investors had a nice distance from Japan. The U.S. market was ordinary during these years and it was easy for them to see the craziness in Japan for what it was and keep a cool head. Our clients believed us – that sooner or later things would work out badly and they were not willing to fire us.

Second, clients at the time hadn't made many international investments. Our underperformance was not really killing them.

International equities were only a small fraction of their total portfolio, perhaps 5% was typical. So, in 5% of their portfolio they were underperforming by 10% a year. Most of them had signed up a few years before and had enjoyed several years of very good performance, which were followed by three years of very bad relative performance. More to the point, during those three years when we were badly underperforming EAFE, international equities were still trashing the U.S. market – and they thought it was fine.

One client, however, said, "If you don't give us Japan, we're going to have to leave." We treated this one a bit differently because they'd been with us for several years. So, Forrest put together a Japan fund that was overweight small cap stocks which had lagged the market and were relatively cheap. This fund was not recommended to anyone else. Initially it did very well. The client formed a special attachment to it and against our advice put in more money. During its second year, however, the Japan Fund lagged the market by 11%. The client was notably upset with this underperformance and, in early 1989, took two-thirds of its money out of the account. The next year, small stocks experienced a sharp revival and the fund outperformed by 19%. It's not uncommon in our industry for funds to strongly outperform soon after disappointed investors have pulled their money out.

When the Nikkei finally peaked in December 1989, Japan was over 60% of the EAFE benchmark. Then Japanese stocks collapsed and we got all our previous underperformance back with a lot of interest. Ultimately, we made good money on the round trip. In 1990, Eijk's fund, International Active, beat its benchmark by 12.8% and our quant fund, International Intrinsic Value, won by 15.3%. Both funds outperformed their benchmark for five consecutive years. Not surprisingly, this turned out to be very good for business.

Our "once in a lifetime override" in Japan was the most important demonstration of our difference from mechanistic quants. From our perspective, Japan was a gigantic unmissable bubble which meant that owning any Japanese stocks was plain irresponsible. In contrast, any quant optimizer focusing on benchmark deviations would have treated such an extreme bet as too "risky" – even though in real life, of course, it reduced risk. As discussed in the next chapter, the main risk to most investment professionals in an uncertain world is the career and business risk of underperforming competitors. Going short in a rapidly rising market too soon is a particularly quick and painful way to do this. However, our big bet against the bubble in Japanese equities hadn't lost us clients. We weren't so fortunate when we took a similar position against the great U.S. bubble a decade later.

EMERGING MARKETS

For many years, GMO had a small exposure to emerging markets through Eijk's International Active fund, which allocated up to 5% of its assets to markets outside the developed markets. Eijk and I were naturally interested in the opportunities presented by expanding our respective capabilities into the emerging markets, which at the time represented approximately 12% of the market capitalization of non-U.S. equities. I felt the inefficiencies in the emerging markets offered significant opportunity for us to add value.

Our first attempt to enter emerging came to naught. In the mid-1980s, Eijk had come across Antoine van Agtmael, another Dutch aristocrat, who is credited with coining the term "emerging markets." We offered Agtmael a job and he agreed to join us. But shortly before he was due to arrive, he told us that Hilda Ochoa, who was then in charge of the pension fund at the World Bank, was starting her own enterprise to manage assets and had offered him a decent chunk of stock in the new firm in return for joining her. As a result, we lost a critical five years or so in getting into emerging equities until we located Arjun Divecha.

Arjun had a degree in aeronautical engineering from the Indian Institute of Technology and after completing an MBA had gone to the consulting firm Barra, where he'd become an expert in emerging market equities. Initially, Arjun proposed a three-way joint venture between GMO, Citibank and Barra, but in the end we decided against this. Instead, we suggested that Arjun come to work for GMO. Both Eijk and I had propositioned him separately, or rather counter-proposed. To me he replied, "I thought you'd never ask." Apparently, he said more or less the same thing to Eijk. GMO's emerging equities strategy was launched in December 1993. Over the previous couple of years, several markets in Latin America and Asia had been on fire. Institutional investors were keen to get some exposure. I called a few of our clients who had historically been interested in hearing from the firm about new and exotic opportunities. Columbia University agreed to invest $25 million to seed the fund. Stanford invested later that month and by the end of January, we had $150 million and a roster of seven or eight impressive clients invested.

Arjun came straight in without ever having run a dollar. My advice to him was to "beware the curse of creeping professionalism." Because he didn't have first-hand portfolio management experience, the events that would catch his attention would be the 3-sigma outliers – those very rare events that occur by chance only once every hundred years. In the investment world, however, 3-sigma events are much more frequent. "Pay attention to them and you will make money. But each day, as you become more and more of a professional, you may lose the ability to tell the difference between a 1-sigma event and a 3-sigma event and there's little money to be made in 1-sigma events."

Ours was the first quant fund to invest in emerging markets. No one had attempted that before given there was so little data available. Nobody believed it could be done. However, we believed that our model for developed markets would work even better in markets that were very inefficient. There were only a few years of data for emerging. But we had many years of data from developed markets that worked just fine. We didn't see why emerging should be any different. We downloaded our quant methodology and tested it and found that it worked brilliantly for the first 15 years, which in the investment world is an eternity for anything to work. Later, GMO became for a millisecond the largest manager anywhere for emerging market equities and debt which, when combined, came to about $30 billion.

GOLDMAN REBUFFED

As GMO fortunes waxed, we attracted a boatload of suitors. The first of them was the British merchant bank Guinness Peat, which in the mid-1980s offered to buy our developed markets stock-picking fund, International Active. At the very last minute, they decided they wanted my fledgling quant division as well. I couldn't agree to that. Early the following decade, the Swiss Banking Corporation showed an interest in buying GMO, but we felt our cultural differences were too great. Next was UBS, which in 1994 made an offer of $1.2 billion to buy us. But they appeared more interested in acquiring North American assets than in the potential to apply our quantitative investment techniques to their own portfolios, which would have been much more interesting to me.

Goldman turned up shortly after UBS. This was altogether the worst temptation that was ever dangled in front of me: they were a sexy firm. They were having a dreadful year in 1994 and had taken some huge losses. This made me feel that it was perhaps an opportune time to get a good deal done in terms of our relative strength versus theirs. The boss, Jon Corzine, liked the economies of scale provided by our quant approach: you crank out 40 products and your sales force goes out and sells them. That's the way to make money, he might have thought, reasonably enough. We had a much higher ratio of assets to people and profits to people than anybody. We were making more money per partner than Goldman, which in those days was the gold standard. "Those were the days, my friend. I thought they'd never end."

We came very close to an agreement. Goldman's offer was slightly less than UBS had offered, with a third in cash, a third in preferred stock and a third in partnership interest. Offering us a partnership stake was a relative rarity given Goldman's penchant for developing talent internally rather than acquiring other businesses. Had the deal gone ahead, at Goldman's public offering in 1998 our partnership stake would have been worth 12 times as much and the value of the preferred stock would have multiplied by eight. At the IPO, we would have been the largest selling partners in Goldman. We would have made tons of money.

We turned the deal down because at the signing dinner, Goldman's investment people showed their claws and made it clear what an uncomfortable mismatch of cultures it would be to have the relatively thoughtful, clients first, genteel pussycats from GMO being embedded in the Wall Street firm, where the culture was dog eat dog and slit anyone's throat who gets in your way. The culture shock would have been painful. We were pretending it wasn't as bad as it was, and they reminded us of our naïveté. Jon Corzine, who was charming as always, desperately wanted to go ahead. But his legs weren't long enough to kick his investment people on the shins, so he was spitting blood as his colleagues stomped all over us. When their man called up five years later in 1999 to rub it in how foolish we'd been to ruin Goldman's deal, I told him my consolation was that I would probably have been fired by then. "Oh, Jeremy," he said, "you would have been fired years ago." Of course, he was right. By then I had been fighting the greatest bull market in history for almost two years.

Goldman was obviously a very exciting organization and had the potential to grow our business, although at the time I thought the investment banking culture was too short term. I believed then, and still do, that patience has an enormous amount to do with good institutional investment management. Goldman was very well suited for trading and modestly well suited for some hedge fund work, but not necessarily well suited for long-term investment. Maintaining our independence turned out to be vital for us later in the decade, 1997 through 2000, when we were underperforming and losing clients rapidly. The stance we took during the great stock market bubble would have been impossible if we had been beholden to an owner demanding quick results. Our long-standing stance of closing winning strategies would also have been difficult. Dick and I were convinced that independence was in the best interests of the firm and our clients.

HBS CASE STUDY

In 1994, the Harvard Business School completed its first case study of GMO, which provides a good snapshot of how things stood at the time. The firm was on a roll. Since their launch and particularly during the previous year, all our major products had significantly outperformed their benchmarks. GMO was entering its 17th year in business. Having started out with a single U.S. equity portfolio, we now had 15 funds. The firm's total assets under management topped $14 billion, of which roughly half was in overseas investments.

Dick's fund, U.S. Active, which closed to new investors with $250 million in 1981, had grown organically – without taking in new accounts – to $1.7 billion. The assets of Eijk's fund, International Active, whose day-to-day operations were overseen by Peg McGetrick, exceeded $3 billion. Our three largest quant funds – U.S. Core, International Core and Value Allocation – together managed more than $6 billion. In London, GMO Woolley had grown to nearly £550 million in assets. The performance of GMO's family of funds had been consistently good. The traditional funds, U.S. Active and International Active, had added, respectively, 4.3% and 4.6% a year, net of fees, since inception. The annualized value added since inception by the quant division was: U.S. Core 1.2%; International Core 6.8%; Growth 7.5%; Value 2.5%; and Japan 4%. Best of all was our U.S. small cap fund (U.S. Core II Secondaries), which had delivered 13.3% of outperformance a year since its launch in late 1991.

We'd been very busy expanding our product range. Over the previous year we had launched our emerging equities strategy, an emerging debt strategy and an international bond fund. Asset allocation (described in the next chapter) accounted for a rapidly growing share of the firm's assets. In October 1992, GMO also entered the hedge fund business with a long/short position in U.K. equities. From inception through to the end of 1993, this "value arbitrage" strategy delivered a cumulative return of 54% above the U.K. stock market. Plans for a market neutral or hedged equity product were in the works.

By 1994, GMO had offices in four cities: Boston and London, and newly opened offices in Hong Kong and San Francisco (where Arjun ran the emerging equities strategy). "In general," the study reports,

"GMO found that good strategic insights developed in one market in one part of the world, often traveled easily and profitably to other markets, and the global transfer of quantitative investment strategies was a primary goal of the overall GMO organization." The idea being that Boston would export its tried and tested quant insights and, in turn, would receive new ideas from its satellite operations.

The business school authors note that we spent little time or effort attracting new assets, in part because many of our new clients were introduced to us by Cambridge Associates, Hunter Lewis's consulting firm. The study depicts us as being "very much a performance-driven firm." We were credited with never launching a product unless we believed it was in the clients' best interest and gently reproved for our high-handedness. GMO, the report states, "had been known to 'tell off' clients when they strongly disagreed with them, sometimes without the greatest tact. Most times, clients respected such candor. Sometimes, however, they did not."

Our three main principles were listed as being to:

- Keep assets under management reasonable in relation to the approach used to invest them;
- Avoid growth for growth's sake; and
- Pay careful attention to investment cycles – especially when introducing new products.

Elaborating on the third principle, the study notes that GMO believed that "offering a new product sends a signal (intended or not) that GMO thinks the product will outperform not only its specific benchmark but also the asset classes or subclasses from which the client will likely draw monies to fund it." Our investment policy is described as waiting for the fat pitch. We committed to make significant bets (or to encourage clients to do likewise) "only when objective valuation measures reach extreme levels. This policy has governed both the timing and magnitude of GMO's major strategic bets over the years, e.g. to underweight Japanese stocks from 1986 to the present; to overweight U.S. growth stocks from late 1988 to mid-1991."

By this date, we were facing more competition from other quant shops. These firms had the latest sure-fire computer model whose back tests demonstrated excellent performance. Happily, once applied to real markets, the competitors' models often faltered. We were one of the few quant shops that had not yet blown a tire. In part this was because we didn't have a black box. Essentially the same model – comprising a value component, momentum and neglect – was applied for all our quant equity products. The model was calibrated to market conditions – when value stocks were abnormally cheap, the value component was given more weight. "Over the years, GMO's base model had grown increasingly complex and sophisticated. Whereas it originally was based solely on value and price considerations it now weighed dozens of complex variables (including such items as seasonality)… In general, GMO believed that its models and strategic insights should constantly evolve in order to maintain a competitive 'edge' on the markets."

The study also describes haphazard piles of documents and computer printouts on my desk and scattered around my office in Rowes Wharf, which "attested to the fact that more ideas were generated over the course of 1993 than could ever be thoroughly studied." I am pictured gazing out over the boats in Boston Harbor, "pondering these new investment strategies, product concepts and ideas for whole new businesses… [and wondering] how to best channel the firm's energy and resources."

There was a danger, I thought, in developing ideas that were starved of attention and resources. Yet I also believed that to stand still in this business risked losing our competitive edge, which can happen surprisingly quickly. The study ends with me pondering GMO's future: "Should we attempt to enlarge and diversify our client base? With what new kinds of clients? With what new kinds of products? Are we well positioned for the coming bear market?" The coming bear market turned out to be six years away. What we weren't well positioned for was the great bull market that over the following years came dangerously close to pushing us out of business.

EVERYTHING I KNOW ABOUT THE MARKET IN 15 MINUTES

In November 1991, I delivered a talk to the Collins Associates Client Conference called "Everything I Know About the Market in 15 Minutes." It was originally published by *Barron's* and changed only a little over the following years. Some advice we have already encountered but it's worth printing the talk in its entirety. It's what passed for an accurate analysis of the market back in the good old days at the end of 1991.

1. Equity investors overpay for comfort.
2. Historically, equity investors have overpaid for excitement or sex appeal: growth, profitability, management skills, technological change and, most of all, acceleration in the above.
3. Bodies in motion tend to stay in motion (Newton's First Law). Earnings, and stock prices with great yearly momentum, tend to keep moving in the same direction for a while.
4. Everything concerning markets and economies (and everything else, for that matter) regresses from extremes toward normal, faster than people think. Factors that regress include sales

growth, profitability, management skill, investment styles and good fortune.

5. The key to investment management is balancing Newton (momentum, growth) and regression (value).
6. Growth companies seem impressive as well as exciting. They seem so reasonable to own that they carry little career risk. Accordingly, they have underperformed for the last 50 years by about 1.5% a year. [True at the time I delivered this talk.]
7. Value stocks, in contrast, belong to either boring, struggling or sub-average firms. Their continued poor performance seems, with hindsight, to have been predictable, and, therefore, when it happens, it carries serious career risk. To compensate for this career risk and lower fundamental quality, value stocks have outperformed by 1.5% a year. [Also true at the time.]
8. Real risk is not accurately measured by beta or volatility, which is compromised by a positive correlation with other characteristics, such as growth, excitement, liquidity and analyst coverage, which are valued as "goods" and reduce career risk. Real risk is a mix of career risk to the investor and fundamental risk (of bankruptcy) to the company. The good news is that they don't take Nobel Prizes back.
9. Ninety percent of what passes for brilliance or incompetence in investing is the ebb and flow of investment style (growth, value, small, quality). Or luck.
10. Since opportunities by style regress, a manager's past performance tends to be negatively correlated with future relative performance.
11. Therefore, managers are harder to pick than stocks. Clients have to choose between facts (past performance) and the conflicting marketing claims of several potential managers.

Practical clients will usually feel they have to go with the past facts. They therefore rotate into previously strong styles that regress, dooming most active clients to underperformance.

12. The stock market is approximately efficient and getting more so. Ninety-five percent or more of all market moves are unknowable noise and perhaps 5% are manageable (or predictable). Fortunately, this frightens away most first-rate scientific minds, leaving the field to us.
13. The investment management business creates no value, but it costs, in round numbers, 1% a year to play the game. In total, we are the market, and given the costs, we collectively must underperform. It is like a poker game in which the good player must inflict his costs and his profits on to a loser. To win by 2%, you must find a volunteer to lose by 4%. Every year.
14. Transaction costs are certain but anticipated outperformance is problematical.
15. Given the above, within single asset classes indexing is hard to beat, and relative passivity is not a vice.
16. Therefore, indexing must surely squeeze out active managers until it represents a substantial majority of the business. Remember, it is the worst players who drop out of the poker game to index. The standard of the remaining players, therefore, rises… and rises… but, fortunately, for us, beginners continue to join the game.
17. Indexing is held at bay only by the self-interest of the players or agents, as opposed to the real investors. The outside managers want fees, and the hired guns want a job that looks demanding.
18. There is no size or P/E effect, or stock vs bond effect, only a cheap effect. The current price tag is always more important than historical averages.

19. The stock market fluctuates many times more than would be suggested by its future stream of earnings and dividends or by the changes in GDP, both of which are historically remarkably stable: i.e. the market is driven by greed, fear and career risk, not economics.
20. The industry is moving to increased manager specialization, which reduces the arbitrage between different asset classes and types of stock. There is, in consequence, a growing dichotomy between what managers say and what they do (fully invested bears).
21. Size of assets under management is the ultimate barrier to successful investing. As assets grow, you are forced either to pick increasing numbers of decreasingly good stocks or to buy larger, indigestible positions of your original holdings. The investment business is the perfect example of the Peter Principle: do well with $500 million, and they'll give you $5 billion. [How quaint this reads in the era of trillion-dollar companies and a total market at 3x book compared to its wandering around 1x in the 1970 to 1997 period.]
22. Inflation is the primary influence on the general price level in the U.S. stock market, however illogical that may be for a real asset.
23. Therefore, stock markets tend to top when inflation and interest rates are low (and vice versa). But since inflation is probably mean reverting, and certainly unstable, buying when inflation and interest rates are low and P/Es are high will mostly be painful.
24. Foreign markets are less efficient than the U.S. market, but the process of investment is much more expensive.
25. Never underestimate the effectiveness of idiot savants vs conventionally bright people. If you want to make money, take knack over learned skill.

26. In the good old days, little talent came into the business as belief in efficient markets discouraged serious quants in particular. Now finance professors run quant shops and vastly more talent is drawn into the business, painfully increasing competition.
27. Quantitative investing is to traditional investing as the written word is to the spoken: you believe it more and can march confidently off the cliff.
28. Quants also find it irresistible to put in just one more variable and risk drowning in data mining.
29. Quants naturally prefer the mathematically neat to the rugged and simple. A sign on every quant's wall should read: "There are no points for elegance!"
30. For quants, the advantage lies in their ability to handle complexity with speed and consistency. Quants also never fall in love with a stock – just methodologies.
31. The most critical advantage for quants, though, is that they can build on the past, remember mistakes, and pass on all their accumulated knowledge.
32. Getting the big picture right is everything. One or two good ideas a year are enough. Very hard work does get in the way of thinking as you're so busy shoveling in new data you have little time to really think. I must say I like to be right so I try really hard not to miss the big ideas and reconcile myself to missing masses of the little ones. End of job description.

CHAPTER 5

Markets Can Remain Irrational Longer than You Can Remain Solvent

"Sit down. You've done a really bad job managing our money. Tell us why you are underperforming, and for God's sake don't give us any more of this nonsense about reversion to the mean." This torrent of angry words was hurled at me as I entered a meeting with one of our clients, a Boston hospital group. They were spoken by the investment committee's irate chairman. It was the crack of dawn one morning in late 1999, just months before the peak of the great technology bubble.

Of course, his words were offensive to me. I was somewhat flushed and looked down at my notepad, thinking. Responses were flicking up and rotating in my mind. What should I say? Tell him to screw himself and walk out of the room? Lick his boots, and say we'll try harder? These thoughts were flashing past me. Then I heard my voice, and it said, "Um, I'm afraid there is no way I can possibly explain to you where we've been and where we're going without talking about regression to the mean. I'm sorry about that, but that's the way it is."

That's what I said and it's exactly what I should have said. The U.S. stock market at the time was trading at its highest valuations in history – higher even than in 1929 before the market crashed. Because I wouldn't buy stocks at crazily inflated prices, our portfolios were lagging their benchmarks. And some of our clients were mad at us – and none madder than this particular client. So, I repeated our case, explaining why I thought it was critically important to hang tough, that history was quite clear that this bubble would break in the not-too-distant future and that it would be incredibly painful to be caught with an overweight in growth stocks, particularly in aggressive speculative growth stocks, and that cash was a safe haven or better yet, owning the cheapest stocks, some of which looked like they might actually make money.

I went over the pitch describing how cheap some of the nooks and crannies of the market were. How inflation-protected bonds (TIPS) yielded over 4% and how we were the second biggest holders of these newly issued securities. Regular bonds also yielded handsomely. Value was off the scale and as cheap as it had been in 1974, which I never thought I would see again in my life. Small cap value was a contender to make genuinely decent money. Real estate investment trusts (REITs) sold at a discount to the value of their properties and those properties sold at a discount to their building replacement cost. And they yielded 9% in dividends, though the growth guys belittled this by saying the dividend growth for the S&P 500 was higher. And they were right. The S&P dividend stream had grown just over 1% a year faster for the last 20 years. But it yielded nearly 7% a year less than REITs. That was the level of logic that prevailed in late 1999.

The prevailing idea then was that dividends were irrelevant. Growth was everything and growth was going to be superb. Just as we talk today about artificial intelligence, the internet was a new paradigm that was going to change everything. As Fed chairman Alan

Greenspan said, we were going to see new levels of profit margins. GDP would grow faster, productivity would go up. Why would we be interested in dopey 9% yielding REITs?

People were selling their real estate stocks and even sold their TIPS, in the sense that they didn't put money into them, to buy tech stocks. Investors were thinking, "Why take 4.3 real, a risk-free return guaranteed by the U.S. government, when I am going to make 10 times as much in a portfolio of dotcoms?" One can just about get one's brain around the argument. All it takes is faith in a new golden era. But the way I saw it, there was nothing unique going on here that we had not seen in 1929. It had been a long time since 1929 and between 1929 and 1999 there had been nothing like this. The entire market was buying into a new golden era. The irony here is that it did look as if the internet would change a lot of things. It would certainty stir up the balance of power in corporate America. But, my view at the time was that it would surely take quite a few years to settle out. In the meantime, just like the railroads before, the very real potential of the internet to change the world was sucking in money and producing one of the great bubbles in investment history.

After the meeting, as I was getting into the elevator, one of the investment committee members came out and apologized for the rude behavior of the boss, which is always a good sign. For the time being, we kept that account. But we lost many others. Well over half our book of business in Asset Allocation – the division I'd been running for the previous few years – walked out the door in just 15 months. For me and the firm this was a bitter outcome, far worse than anything I could ever have imagined.

STARTING OUT IN ASSET ALLOCATION

We got into the asset allocation business by accident. I'd been given a bit of credit for my timely call before the October 1987 crash that buying bonds was a no-brainer. Our decision to avoid Japanese equities in the late stages of the bubble had also paid off handsomely. Then, in early 1991, we surprised clients by recommending they get out of our Growth Fund, after it had delivered the excess returns we had promised. It was more than clients could believe that a money manager would advise them to redeem with no expectation of keeping the money. You can imagine that was not a winning play but, in fact, it turned out more to our advantage than we would ever have guessed.

What was really unusual, one might even say unique in my experience, is that those clients who redeemed basically told us, "Okay, you got us in and you've gotten us out. What should we do with the money now?" In other words, they treated that money as if it were ours to allocate. The strange business of getting them in and out of growth had created a mini franchise for us. This came from the trust we had inadvertently developed. So, to some clients we recommended small cap value and to others emerging, and so on. Then we got into the habit that whenever we visited a client, every quarter or half-year, we would come with some fun-sounding new products and they would nearly always buy one of them. We enjoyed a golden era of cross-selling, with clients getting in the habit of doing what we suggested. When we finally made the jump into fully-fledged asset allocation, which involves choosing what proportion of the portfolio to hold in equities, bonds and other investments, many clients had already been softened up.

Shortly after the success of the Growth Fund, I attended a quarterly meeting of the Princeton Investment Committee. This was a very august body of investment people that included Dick Fisher, the then boss of Morgan Stanley. At the meeting, one of the committee members said our investment recommendations weren't that useful because they were not in a position to do anything about them. The committee only met four times a year, and didn't normally shuffle assets around. But he said, as GMO seemed good at it, why didn't we take a piece of their portfolio and make those calls. I ducked. But they wouldn't take no for an answer. A few months later, they repeated insistently and I tried to duck again. They continued to badger me. Eventually, I threw in the towel.

That's how we found ourselves doing asset allocation. My thought was that getting in and out of asset classes was quite close to sector-tilting, which I'd been doing since the Batterymarch days. Dick and I had made successful bets on bonds in 1981 and again in 1987 in our U.S. equity fund. In the old days, it wasn't unusual for investment managers to make asset allocation decisions within their portfolios, but now they were more constrained by benchmarks with asset allocation done largely by consultants. For several years, we'd been helping a few clients with their allocation to global equities.

Asset allocation had a redeeming feature, as seen through my eyes, which was that it was extremely interesting. I had spent a lot of time digging around in U.S. stocks, and then slowly extending, if you will, upwards into comparing various asset classes. There was no important information in the daily paper that was not relevant to the job. When you've done 30 years of standard stock market stuff, it was a very agreeable change of pace and very entertaining to me, anyway, to spend my time working at this level.

In my view, the most important thing about markets was their tendency to revert to the mean. Asset prices are sometimes pushed away from trend but are eventually dragged back by the powerful logic of value. We had enjoyed a fair amount of success using mean reversion to pick individual stocks and bet on the ebb and flow of sectors, such as small cap, value and growth. At the asset allocation level, market inefficiencies appeared even more pronounced. As I wrote in my 1986 paper "You Can't Fool All of the People All of the Time":

> Allocating resources between asset classes is, I believe, intrinsically more rewarding than stock picking. The barriers between asset classes can be substantial and potential rewards much higher... Funds in each market are predominantly managed by specialists in each market. Neither they nor their clients are eager to risk reputations in macro decisions where errors are horribly obvious and where their experience may be very limited. Experienced asset allocators are rare and do not yet have an established role in our business. So, not surprisingly, the arbitrage mechanism among asset classes and countries is defective.

Although I understood the attractiveness of indexing, I never believed that a buy-and-hold investment approach made sense at all times. When markets are at extreme valuations, investors should expect lower than normal returns going forward. When we examined the returns of the S&P 500 from 1926 through to the early 1990s, we found that investors who had bought near bull-market peaks had done poorly. I was skeptical of academics who argued that investors should buy and hold the market regardless of valuation. If your investing time horizon is 15 years or less, which seems a reasonable definition of long term for most people, then the market's long-term average real return of 6% a year was by no means foreordained. It made obvious sense to seek out the cheapest markets and asset classes.

Initially, GMO Asset Allocation was a branch of quant that sat on the fourth floor of our Rowes Wharf office. I remained head of both groups. Later, Asset Allocation moved to the fifth floor and Chris Darnell took charge of quant. I had many projects to work on and needed help. David Swensen recommended that I hire a young Yale graduate, Ben Inker, who'd taken his investment course. Ben came in to see us but I didn't feel he was the right fit. Swensen called me back telling me what a mistake I had made. The conversation ended with Swensen, who was a big client of GMO, telling me to do it. To which I said, being at least in the last resort sensible, "Yes, boss." Ben turned out to be the boy wonder of his era. He later took over as head of Asset Allocation. But back then, he worked with me as a kind of trainee.

We decided against using an optimizer (a quantitative tool for constructing portfolios) for asset allocation because history suggested that it occasionally made ridiculous bets. It turned out that there wasn't enough information to put into an optimizer. Instead, we used a rule of thumb. And the kluge was that we viewed every asset on a range between the most attractive and least attractive valuation. We weighted our bets according to where each asset was on the range. So, if we defined the maximum bet on emerging debt as plus or minus 10 points and found that emerging was two-thirds through its range, we'd have a 7.5-point bet. This approach was simple-minded. It was suboptimal, but it guaranteed we would not do anything crazy. This simple rule generated the kind of portfolio that a human being could feel comfortable with.

My view was that in the long run, assets that are absolutely cheap, and much cheaper than normal, should make more money. I guessed there would be the odd decade when something powerful and odd happened that might cause an aberration, but in general, this approach would work. Now, to do this you've got to have a decent valuation model. At first, we started out using the most basic measures, like dividend yield and P/B. We calculated a market's expected returns and ran deciles of valuation. Later, Ben and I developed a more sophisticated equity forecast that assumed profit margins and valuation multiples reverted to the mean over a 10-year period.

Asset allocation prompted yet another surge of new products because we constantly found that we wanted to do things for which we did not have the tools. Hiring Arjun Divecha to manage our emerging markets funds was pretty straightforward. Arjun got off to a good start, with a significant portion of his assets coming from Asset Allocation, which from 1994 onwards held an overweight position in emerging equities. Fixed income was a totally different matter. Princeton had dragged us kicking and screaming into global bonds. For me, fixed income was terra incognita. Our first foray into bonds was a kind of catch-all portfolio, called the Bond Allocation Fund. This fund reflected an equity specialist's view of fixed income. We started out making some fairly handsome bets on the shape of the yield curve and then ran straight into the great bond market bloodbath. Clearly we needed some bond specialists. We put out the buzz, at which point Tom Cooper and Bill Nemerever walked into our offices. The two had been billeted with a small firm in Boston that had not picked up enough business to be commercially viable. They had a very plausible story to tell and good experience. So, in October 1993 we hired them. The bond bets that we had made came storming back, which got them off to a wonderful start.

Tom's genius for emerging market debt played an important role in Asset Allocation's early success. At the time this was a little-known asset class. In early 1994, emerging country debt had one of its many great conniption fits along with the other fixed income markets. After Mexico devalued the peso, emerging bonds went to a 14-point spread yield over U.S. Treasuries. Bill and Tom believed this was a fantastic opportunity. In April 1994 they launched our

Emerging Country Debt Fund. As there were no other significant asset class bets to be made at the time, we took an eight-point position in emerging debt in all Asset Allocation accounts. Emerging debt came roaring back. Tom knocked the lights out, adding huge alpha against the benchmark. Three years after its launch in 1994, the GMO Emerging Country Debt Fund was the best performing U.S. mutual fund *of any kind*. For Asset Allocation clients, our overweight position in emerging debt generated a win of 58% relative to the returns of the S&P 500 over this period.

Ben and I did some pretty interesting and totally non-traditional thinking on asset allocation in those early years. We did a lot of thinking about questions like, "What should you get paid for taking on more risk? How do you get paid in an asset class? How can you determine if you are likely to get paid what you should?" This culminated in the worst-received speech of our collective lives, called "How to Lose Your Job in Asset Allocation."

One of the reasons I'd been initially reluctant to take up Princeton's offer was because the asset allocation business seemed risky. The basic problem was that there weren't a huge number of bets to be made. And if you make only one bet a year and this is your practice most of the time, you are still likely to have prolonged periods of poor performance. Our paper showed investment decisions for asset allocation in the shape of a pyramid. At the bottom of the pyramid were thousands of little stock bets spread around the world. By our reckoning, we expected to win those bets around 55% of the time. Given there were so many stock bets, our investment edge would be evident. Higher up the pyramid, there were fewer bets to be made on countries, industries, sectors, currencies and so on. At the top there was just the single decision as to whether to be in or out of stocks. Assuming the same hit rate, there simply weren't enough bets at this level to prove you had any skill. It would take decades to make a statistician happy that you knew what you were doing. And it was certain you would hit a period when you would lose one or two of those big bets in a row. When that happened the clients would run out of patience. You would not survive in the asset allocation business.

In those days, we were helped by the fact that GMO funds reliably outperformed. If we had a bad year in allocating assets, the funds' outperformance saved our bacon. But it was easy to imagine that one day the funds' returns would be average. Then the big bet on stocks versus bonds was likely to sink us, even if it delivered a decent long-term record. The intermissions would kill you. That was obvious. We made this presentation to a large group of CFA types at a conference in Bermuda and were met with the most extensive set of yawns I've ever encountered. They were totally unimpressed with the concept, and yet it seemed to me then, and still seems, a pretty interesting idea.

Our hybrid model, part quantitative and part judgmental, worked reasonably well. We were winning against the benchmark by around 1.5 points a year by having the right allocation and another couple of points from the outperformance from all the specialized funds that made up the portfolio, like Emerging Country Debt and U.S. small caps. Furthermore, we did that by taking less risk because we avoided overpriced assets which, by definition, are more risky. Our Sharpe Ratio (which measures returns relative to volatility) was high. But in those days clients didn't care about volatility-adjusted returns even though it is a good indicator of investment efficiency.

GTE STRATEGIC RELATIONSHIP

In 1995 we were hired along with three other managers to do asset allocation for one of the Baby Bells, GTE (now Verizon). The strategic global asset allocation relationship, as it was called, was designed by GTE's chief investment officer, Britt Harris. The other managers were Goldman, J.P. Morgan and Morgan Stanley. I joked that along with GMO these were the "Big Four" of the investment world. In fact, although we were tiny compared to the others, we had more hands-on experience because we had already run dozens of accounts along similar lines while the others had not.

We started a contest in which every quarter we would get together and once a year we'd have dinner and review all the details. I was always unnerved at our jamborees where I'd be sitting at the big boys' table with three or four Verizon bigwigs and the bosses of the other contestants. Morgan Stanley's Barton Biggs was always very complimentary about me. He once described me as "a seeker of truth" and as someone who didn't care what the world thinks. At our meetings Barton would always turn to me and say, "Well, what does Jeremy think?" He was one of the very few people I ever came across who made more fuss over me than I thought I deserved. That's a very high hurdle. We had a good deal of flexibility to make asset allocation bets. For the first few years everything went well. By September 1997, we were dead-heat second place with Morgan Stanley. Goldman was in first place but they did not have any fixed income in their initial benchmark, which was not adjusted for. J.P. Morgan was stuck in fourth place.

THE BUBBLE INFLATES

As it turned out, 1997 was the high point for GMO's asset allocation in its early years. We had enjoyed a strong record since inception and accounted for over 40% of the firm's assets, then around $26 billion. For several years, U.S. stocks has been trading at historically high prices relative to earnings and historically low dividend yields. In August 1995, I had given an interview to the *Washington Post* in which I stated that "Our most heroic bet is against U.S. equities. We think they are dramatically overpriced." I noted that over the past eight years, profits for U.S. companies had been consistently and uniquely high by historical standards. Dividend yields had fallen further. Over the previous decade, U.S. stocks had delivered 12% real. We did not expect that to continue. Yet in 1996, the S&P 500 was up 23% after rising 36.7% the year before. In December 1996, Alan Greenspan delivered his famous "irrational exuberance" speech. "How do we know," the Fed chairman asked, "when irrational exuberance has unduly escalated asset values, which then become subject to unexpected and prolonged contractions as they have in Japan over the past decade?"

Unlike Greenspan, we had no trouble identifying a bubble. We defined the bubble as a 2-sigma event. Because we live in a mean-reverting world, we reasoned, when asset classes move two standard deviations from trend, which should occur only once every 44 years, that was a bubble. With increasing anxiety, we re-examined and re-re-examined the data to see how well the pieces really held up. We started with the obvious data, but as the bull market went on and on we had an unexpected amount of time and incentive to do more and more research. Back then I realized that under stress I would hide in research. When times were good, I tended to go out and talk to clients and do all such agreeable things. When times were bad, I did more and more research and as little client begging as possible.

Our belief in mean reversion at the asset class level was very high. And the more research we did, the higher it got. We searched the databases for historic bubbles, knocking off asset class by asset class until we had done everything for which there was machine-readable data that we could find. The old joke was that someone

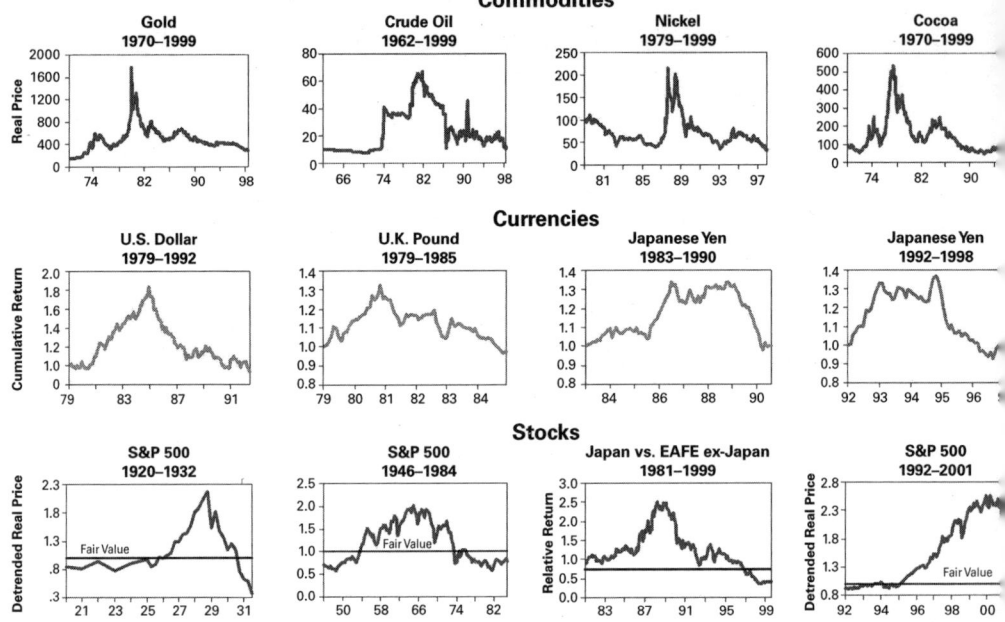

All bubbles burst. A selection from GMO's internet-bubble era study of historic major bubbles across asset classes, showing how unprecedented valuation gains across assets have tended to fully mean-revert. Data from GMO, 2001

was jumping around in the corridor saying he had a data series on Prussian rye going back to 1694. We never included that in our viable tests, but we looked at pretty much everything else – currencies, commodities, bond markets and stock markets – from all around the world. We had prices, we had trends, we had volatility and we had 2-sigma events.

We plowed through the historical data and we eventually came up with 27 major bubbles, excluding real estate, in commodities, bonds and stocks. All the major ones had broken. It was nice to see that history confirmed my suspicions that humans in general are given to extreme waves of optimism and pessimism.

GMO'S UNDERPERFORMANCE

After years of what I can now see as our walking on water phase, in which more than two-thirds of our funds were winning in any given year, our fortunes began to shift in 1996. At that time, our funds started to underperform. This was when our valuation models showed equities to be overvalued at home and abroad. Speculative sentiment was evident by the high volume of IPOs and equity issuance. Beginning in 1997, the market started to accelerate. It veered toward growth stocks, becoming more and more focused until they were rising rapidly and value stocks were giving ground. This produced one of the worst – if not the worst – relative performance of value, which ran from late 1997 through March 2000, ever seen in the history books. (The current cycle, in mid-2025, is now also a contender.) Not only did we have a strong value bias across the entire firm, but it also completely informed our Asset Allocation division.

By late 1997, the U.S. market went through the highest P/E ratio in history – right through the 1929 peak of 21x earnings. We were still swinging for the fences and making good money. We were still a player as the exceptional performance of some of our smaller specialized funds kept our aggregate performance in the game. It was only in 1998 when U.S. stocks entered previously unknown territory that we started to reduce our stock exposure steadily. Updating clients in June of that year I noted that:

> In the second quarter, contrarian value failed as badly as in any period for which we have data. Every cheap asset class underperformed, while the overvalued U.S. and European equity markets became more expensive... over the past few years, we have underestimated the ability of investors' attitudes to drive values far away from underlying fundamentals.

The S&P 500 ended the year up 28.6%. Meanwhile our bets on emerging market equities and debt were upended by the Asian crisis and Russia's debt default. Value was also suffering. Asset Allocation suffered its worst year ever, lagging its benchmark by nearly 16%. The rising U.S. market, and especially U.S. growth stocks, handsomely outperformed all our bets: fixed income, small cap stocks, REITs, emerging equities. It was a bloodbath. In my opening remarks at our client conference in the fall of 1998 I posed the question:

> How do you tell the difference between a severe but normal run of bad luck and being slipped some faulty dice? Or, if you prefer, how do you tell if the rules have been changed? I conclude you never know for sure – you must depend on judgment and research and more research. I believe the results of our research show that we are suffering from an extreme case, a very unlikely string of events, but one that follows the old rules.

I drew on my own investing experience in small cap stocks in the post-Nifty Fifty era and the Japan bubble of the late 1980s. The U.S. market was undoubtedly a bubble, I told clients.

At the conference, I also addressed the difficulty of market timing in speculative bubbles, citing MIT economist Paul Samuelson's observation that, "Although economic science knows much about bubbles upward and downward, it has no useful theorems about their duration and amplitude." The fair value of any tangible asset, I pointed out, is its replacement cost. Very gradually, things work their way back to fair value.

Careful estimates based on value usually treat you well, but timing often kills you. Sensible value-based investors always sell too early in bubbles and buy too early in busts. If the timing were knowable, it would be an arbitrageable situation: if you knew what would happen and when, then, like a *Star Trek* "paradox," it would be anticipated and, therefore, could never occur. Market timing, in my view, was a disparaging tag used by some buy-and-hold investors to put down anything that involves using your brain. These are the same people who watch the locomotive coming down the tracks and, in the name of discipline, get run down.

People used to ask me what is going to happen next year, and I'd say I hadn't the faintest idea. In general, the short term is unknowable and in an uncertain world, it should be unknowable. Then they'd ask me how I could be so certain of some event occurring in the long-term future when I admitted I was not certain about the short term. It bamboozled me until I came up with the analogy of standing on a high building in Miami with a bag of feathers in the middle of a hurricane. If you throw the feathers up in the air, one of them will hit the ground a block away in a few seconds and another one may end up in Maine after seven or eight days, the way some poor unfortunate canaries get swept along by storms. But you know one thing about all those feathers with absolute certainty: at some future time, every single one of them will hit the ground. That is really the analogy with value. You are not sure of the time horizon, but it is like a gravitational pull. Although value is a weak force in any single year, it becomes a monster over several years. Like gravity, it slowly wears down the opposition. Eventually valuations hit fair value or replacement cost. You may, though, have different clients by then. Or no clients at all.

CLIENT EXODUS

In the meantime, we started to lose business, which was a novel experience for us. In our first 18 years, as far as I could tell, we had never lost more than a couple of points of assets per year from redemptions and had these modest withdrawals for the usual reasons, like unexpectedly high payouts in pension funds. This was a truly enviable record. Over the years, however, we had become a large fraction of many of our clients' portfolios. Some fairly decent-sized institutions had over 40% of their assets with us, which was not the norm. In a world looking for an excuse to scale us back, we delivered some pretty good ammunition.

Some products that were making very hard-nosed value bets – like those in International Quant – underperformed very badly over a number of years, particularly in 1998 and 1999. Asset Allocation was a massacre, but in an interesting sense. We did not lose money in absolute terms or against prior expectations. Clients would budget for 6% returns and we were delivering 10% or more. But the benchmark was up 15% and Fred up the road was delivering 21%. There's always someone up the road who's delivering 21% when you don't need it. For two and a half years, we kept on losing on a relative basis. Two and a half years is, generally speaking, not long enough to get fired on a wholesale basis, but this cycle had a particularly interesting spin. We were identified as non-believers in the new world order. We were seen as stuck in the past while the world had changed dramatically. The word on the street was that we had "lost our way."

The client exodus began as a trickle in 1997 but by mid-1998 the clients were telling us, "Hey, guys, you're underperforming big time. Six points a year, in total." Because the clients were playing golf with people who were making fortunes, their patience wore incredibly thin. It is often said that managers should avoid underperforming in a bear market like the plague, but it's simply not true. In a bear market clients are paralyzed. They make very few moves and wait until it's all over to adjust their portfolios. In contrast, in a great bull market they become hypercompetitive and resentful of rivals beating them. They become fearful for their jobs, too, as their committees also become excited and impatient. So, they shoot you quickly. We really started losing accounts in 1998. And then 1999 became a waterfall. They fired us en masse – billions of dollars flowed out the door. Assets in International Intrinsic Value went from the 1996 peak of nearly $3 billion to a low point of $578 million. In two and a half years, GMO lost 45% of its book of business, which was a catatonic shock. In Asset Allocation we lost perhaps 60% of our hitherto rapidly growing business. In total, our assets under management fell from $30 billion in 1997 to $20 billion at the market peak in early 2000 when other equivalent-sized firms would have grown from $30 to $50 or $60 billion. This was a decline in market share of such scale and speed that you would indeed have thought we were trying to do it on purpose, as suggested by the indignant investment committee boss of the local Boston hospital that infamous morning.

The experience rammed home the problem about clients' patience, especially when it came to investment committees. Sometimes a client would call and say, "We've had a committee change and the new people just can't stick with it." Or, a consultant would say, "I've been fighting and fighting for GMO on this, but I just can't convince the committee to stay with you." A hired gun who worked for one client called me up one day begging, "Jeremy, give me something. I know you're right but give me something. The committee is killing me." I gave him some tidbit and he came back to me, "Yeah, yeah, I think they bought that." Two quarters later he returned, "Look, I'm really sorry. I know you're right, but it's either your job or mine." He sacked us. It was perfectly understandable. As he said, it was his job or mine. But saving his job cost that retirement fund a lot of money: when they fired us they almost never chose another value manager. They hired an extra growth manager, which in 1999 was destined to be a brutally expensive mistake.

CAREER RISK

I used to think financial markets were approximately efficient and getting more so. I was touchingly naïve. In the old days there were the gentlemanly hand-holders from Morgan Guaranty Trust. They'd been replaced by CFAs and MBAs – well-educated young tigers. I thought the net effect would inevitably be behavior that was more sensible, more logical and more closely approximating rational Economic Man. Well, it hadn't happened. Far from the markets becoming more efficient, the market was darned inefficient, and if anything, getting less efficient every day. (I am willing to hear the case for similar stocks in the same industry becoming more efficiently priced relative to each other, but industries seemed to be moderately more inefficient. At the top level – asset classes – the bets were so obvious, and hence the career risk so severe, that they had become much less efficient as witnessed by the record mispricings of the 2000 Tech Bubble, at 35x earnings; the Global Financial Crisis of 2008; and the highest priced market ever in the early 2020s.)

When I had started in the investment business it consisted of 35% professionals and 65% amateurs running their own money. By the late 1990s, it was the other way around. When you put money into the hands of professionals, the focus gets transferred from real risk to benchmark risk. Risk is not accurately measured by volatility as the finance professors claim. Real risk is mainly career and business risk, which together shape our industry. Everyone's ultimate job description becomes "keep your job." As a professional, you can afford to pick some stocks and be wrong about a few of them. But you cannot take the risk of being seen to be wrong about the "big picture" for very long. Thus, it makes no commercial sense at all for asset managers to attempt to warn clients of impending doom. It is terrible business to blow the whistle on a major bull market. If you are a commercial enterprise, you make your money by having the bubble continue.

By the late 1990s our industry had reached the point where career risk and business risk dominated the investment process. You could no longer manage money with a view to absolute risk, the way you would in your personal account. Efforts to reduce career risk were leading to herding, momentum and extrapolation, which together are the main causes of mispricing. As my friend the economic consultant Andrew Smithers wrote at the time, fund managers were said to be like lemmings running off a cliff, but it was not their fault, it was the clients' fault. The fund managers knew very well that if they didn't get on the lemming team they'd be fired. So, they bought momentum stocks. The moral of the story was simple, according to Andrew: if you wanted to invest, don't be rational. And if you wanted to be rational don't invest. And that sums things up pretty well.

Clients had lost the idea that the main event is to protect your capital. At GMO, we had a client base with a longer time horizon than most. But that didn't mean that when you got a 2-standard deviation event, they were not full of misgivings. They wished like mad that they didn't have so much money with a value manager and a contrarian one at that. Concerned with the risk of underperforming their benchmark, managers were tailoring their portfolios to track the index, plus or minus a bit. As the benchmarking grip tightened, the market's arbitrage mechanism weakened. Large cap managers buying small caps were accused of "style drift" – and quickly got shot. Equity managers could no longer buy fixed income instruments. That meant longer and bigger deviations from trend and greater career risk for those trying to take advantage of the opportunities that were opening up – until you had truly legendary opportunities that no one dared accept.

JOHN MAYNARD KEYNES

My hero, John Maynard Keynes, understood better than anyone else that the only thing that really matters in life in the institutional investment business is career risk. Keynes was an accomplished investor who managed his college's endowment and was chairman of a City insurance company. In Chapter 12 ("The State of Long-Term Expectations") of his *General Theory*, he provides a wonderful, polished view of career risk as the dominant factor in investing. He wrote that it was better to fail conventionally than to succeed unconventionally. "Never, ever be wrong on your own" was the message. Even being right on your own was a little dangerous. They might pat you on the head while you are in the room, but they describe you as a dangerous eccentric the moment you leave.

Once you've got that idea in your head, you pretty well know what's cooking. Chapter 12 was way ahead of the market in 1936. And it still hasn't caught up. Keynes understood the perils of long-term investing. "It is the long-term investor," he wrote, "he who most promotes the public interest, who will in practice come in for most criticism, wherever investment funds are managed by committees or boards or banks. For it is in the essence of his behaviour that he should be eccentric, unconventional and rash in the eyes of average opinion… if he is successful, that will confirm the general belief in his rashness; and if, in the short run, he is unsuccessful, which is very likely, he will not receive much mercy." Anyone who attempts long-term investing, Keynes wrote, "must surely lead much more laborious days and run greater risks than he who tries to guess better than the crowd how the crowd will behave… Life is not long enough. There is a peculiar zest in making money quickly."

His point is that if you want to make money, just look around and see what everyone else is doing and beat them on the draw. Just be a little quicker and slicker. If you do that, it will create herding and momentum. He also got into extrapolation, and how to deal with making a forecast. Making a forecast about the future, Keynes said, is incredibly dangerous, full of career risk. Instead, the convention we adopt to deal with an uncertain future is to assume that the past will continue – extrapolation – even though we know from personal experience that that is not the case. In my opinion, this is the major inefficiency in the stock market. There are many inefficiencies, perhaps hundreds. Investment is a very inefficient enterprise, but by far the biggest inefficiency is momentum. It exists in every asset class that I have ever studied.

From 1998 to 1999 we ran an experiment that tested Keynes's theory. We had the temerity to forecast – declaiming greatly about the coming breaking of the bubble. We urged clients that it was on the edge of fiduciary irresponsibility to buy overpriced growth stocks. We took a long-term view. We stood out from the crowd. And we suffered, as Keynes predicted. Clients lined up to shoot us. Our Asset Allocation division lost more than half its book of business in two and a half years – a faster rate of firing than anything that I have ever discovered in our business where there was no actual cheating involved. We did not cheat; all we did was invest rationally in an irrational world.

INSIDE GMO

The fact that we were independent counted for a great deal. GMO was able to stand its ground when other value investors fled. The three founding partners agreed on nothing except that we were a value shop and we would buy cheap stocks and we would treat our clients well. Those were the things we agreed on. Everything else we disagreed on. But it turned out that the things we agreed on were much more important than we realized at the time. We had more in common than we thought. Eijk retired in 1996, just before things started to get exciting. But Dick remained a value investor to his core.

Within the firm I made a huge effort to keep up morale. Our very small marketing team, recently formed in the late 1990s, thought we were crazy and were unnecessarily pushing our luck. There were also some investment colleagues who clearly didn't believe we should push our value bet so hard. They made the odd comment. On the investment side, all GMO's individual funds were value-based so they were also suffering. Asset Allocation was merely suffering more. Because of the nature of the pyramid that I described, the top decision in asset allocation is equities versus cash. The value versus growth decision made by equity managers can be very painful but is nothing like the pain of cash versus equities.

I made it clear that my personal investments were consistent with what I was recommending for clients, so my own interests were completely aligned with those of the firm. One day, I asked the quants who crunched the numbers that showed our assets were cheaper than the market's favorites how they wanted to proceed, letting them know that if their analysis was proved correct all would be well for the firm. If, however, we were incorrect in our analysis, the ramifications would be severe for GMO's book of business, even in the longer term. I also made the group aware that being right and losing business was also a distinct possibility because client patience might not endure the length of the bubble. When I put the decision to a vote as to how the quant team should proceed, every single hand in the room was a vote to continue, unchanged, with our strategy. The data was absolutely clear to the quants that these were the bets we should be taking for clients and no one in the room wanted to change that.

For our first 15 years, GMO had been run without a single person whose job description included client service. Our focus was on investing. We were all too busy doing portfolio management and research and everything else. Two of our three divisions were closed to new clients. Performance was good. Clients were loyal. We were operating in an industry where good firms would lose 7% of their clients per year and historically we had lost not more than 1% per year. Besides, in our early days there were relatively few clients. On a Friday afternoon I would often speak with some of them on the telephone and chat about the markets. Every fall, many came to Boston to our conference where we explained our strategies.

Over time the client base had grown to around 400. Then, as our performance suffered in 1998, clients started to leave. It was an incredible eye-opener to all us investors that client service was a big deal. Right around the time someone rang a bell and fortune moved against us, Jon Hagler joined GMO, having worked in the investment business for more than 30 years, to help with organizational issues. Jon was the first person to tell us we could not run a business this way. He moved quickly to build up our client servicing capacity. Jody Shuman and Mason Smith were given the job of handling our biggest accounts. They immediately got down to firefighting and dealing with the most difficult clients, which was extremely stressful.

A few years later Tony Ryan joined from State Street to head up our client service and marketing effort. I'd given us 10 years to get to average in working with clients and doing marketing, because, as I like to say, other firms had people who'd been sitting in the bathtub on a Saturday morning obsessing about marketing and all we had was a group of people doing the same about investment, and that kind of gap was not easily closed. But Tony was able to bring in sufficient talent so that within five years we were average and later probably a bit above average. Unfortunately, he later left for Washington where he worked for Treasury Secretary Hank Paulson.

PROPAGANDA OFFENSIVE

In my first three decades as an investor I'd kept a pretty low profile. I thought we had so many secrets, so many investing advantages – why talk about them? There was a general view at GMO that we would not go public on much – occasionally we might be invited to give a talk to investors by some trade organization. We would speak to a client audience when asked, but we'd not volunteer anything. We published almost nothing. As the bubble progressed and we started to bleed business, however, I changed my position.

My view then, which I still think is correct, was in for a penny in for a pound. The firm was paying such a high price for our sensible value-based investment decisions that I decided to drum up some publicity. As I've said, the commercial imperative of the investment business is to be a bull all the time. That makes sense. The only way you can ever make sense out of being a bear, in terms of a broad investment firm like ours, is to absolutely capitalize on the rareness of the position, spin the reasons for doing it effectively and make sure everybody knows that you called the bear market and why you did. *You must be seen to be right.* To be right and invisible is to take the pain and not get that much glory. So I upped the ante and started to talk to everybody publicly and debated everybody who showed up for the job. I debated just about all the famous bulls, of whom there were plenty. I got a lot of visibility for a little company. By the end of the bull market, everybody on the planet, or at least in the U.S. investment community, knew that we were the Crazy Bears.

Everyone knew that we were predicting doom and gloom. So when it occurred, we received a lot of free publicity.

My most popular debates were with Jeremy Siegel of the Wharton Business School. He'd published a widely read book called *Stocks for the Long Run*, which came out in 1998 and epitomized the prevailing view that stocks always won out over bonds. The book can be summarized in one line for an intelligent layman as "Price does not matter!" Just tuck stocks away and you will do well. His book was ceaselessly quoted as a cause to relax as P/E ratios rose on to new high ground. His work, and others like it, brought out a good quote from a serious economist (you can rightly deduce that I believe there are many of the non-serious variety). Siegel's old PhD teacher, Paul Samuelson, designated interestingly by *Forbes* as "also an astute investor," was quoted in that magazine on June 16, 1997 as saying, "I have students of mine – PhDs – going around the country telling people it's a sure thing to be 100% invested in equities, if only you will sit out the temporary declines. It makes me cringe." Me too.

Siegel's book, more than any other semi-serious book (this means ignoring the more farcical, indeed "criminal" *Dow 36,000* type), delivered what the typical investor wanted to hear. It also echoed a remarkably similar book from the 1920s that did precisely the same thing. In 1924, Edgar Smith wrote *Common Stocks as Long-Term Investments*. This book, serious enough to be positively reviewed by Irving Fisher, the infamous believer in the "new high plateau" for stocks, had as its central idea that stocks not only had much higher returns, but were also less risky than bonds. Fisher's respect for this idea was so great that in February 1930 in his book *The Great Crash and After* he produced the remarkable sentence, "It was only a few years ago that stocks were considered more risky than bonds!" Such a thought could not have resurfaced for several decades after February 1930, but it certainly resurfaced in Siegel's book.

Keynes was also impressed by the results shown in Smith's book and seemed almost willing to accept the idea that stocks had the lower risk. Though he added a typically Keynesian killer thought: "It is dangerous, however, to apply to the future arguments based on past experience, unless one can distinguish the broad reasons why past experience was what it was." This quote should be Siegel's epitaph. The 7% historical real return he reports from stocks – so superior in the past to bonds – was observed in a world where Siegel and others confirm that the average P/E ratio was only 14, or the earnings ratio (E/P) was 7 (100/14). In other words, the market had been on average priced to return 7% real. To suggest that this large and very superior return applies at any P/E ratio is to ignore Keynes's warning. (If the market were priced at 10 P/E, you should expect 10% a year, but if priced à la Japan at over 50x, you might be lucky to get 2%.)

Our debates became the music hall event of the bubble era. Come and see SIEGEL and GRANTHAM punching it out. The drum rolled as we were introduced: in the blue corner weighing in at 205 pounds, Professor Siegel, "the Permabull." And in the red corner, weighing in at a sprightly 150 pounds, "The never-wrong-but-often-early Jeremy Grantham." We did nine debates in all, I think. One was held at the huge annual financial analysts bash in Los Angeles, with about 1,200 people in the audience. The reason I finally quit after nine bouts was that Siegel would not answer my question about the inconsistency of his position. He was publicly claiming that stock investors got the inverse of the P/E. So, when the market was selling at its historic average of 14x, they got around 7% real annual returns. I had no argument with that. Then he maintained that you still got 7%, even when the market was selling at 29, 30, 31, 32, 33x earnings in early 2000. And we debated how come you don't get 3%, which was my position and appeared to me a mathematical necessity. His responses were evasive. In debate after debate, he refused to answer that paradox. I just noticed that he was being inconsistent.

Siegel helped investors walk confidently off the cliff in 2000. His follow-up work in journals and the press can be summarized as, "Whoops, price really does matter." But the damage had been done. Still, he seems to have been forgiven. Having laid the biggest investment egg one could possibly lay, Siegel rose to be the dean of Wharton. He succeeded, as Keynes would say, by failing conventionally.

Trying to debate these bulls (and most strategists at brokerage houses fell into this camp in the late 1990s) was like talking Swahili to a Russian. We believers in value and mean reversion talked exclusively about adjustments and fair value and they talked about productivity and GDP growth. Our research, however, showed that there was no stable relationship between economic growth and stock returns.* Besides, despite all the ballyhoo, the performance of the U.S. economy at the time was decidedly mediocre. Merrill Lynch replaced its chief economist with this hairy-chested bull, Bruce Steinberg, who went around claiming that the 1990s were the greatest decade in the history of economics. In fact, the 1920s was the greatest decade for U.S. economic growth in the 20th century by a large margin. In 1929, inflation was zero and productivity growth was 5% a year. (And we know what that got us.) In second place, albeit far behind, was the 1960s. In a very respectable third place came the 1990s.

I debated the most famous of the Wall Street cheerleaders, Goldman's strategist Abby Joseph Cohen. It was set up so that

---

* If you have a 10% GDP growth rate in, say, Malaysia and corporations earn a 9% return on equity (ROE), you're not going to grow earnings per share (EPS) as fast as the U.S. would with a 3% growth rate and, say, 18% ROE. In Malaysia, faster growth would be accompanied by much more stock dilution and slower growth in the U.S. by stock buybacks.

she gave her pitch on a screen while I gave mine from the podium. That's not really a fair debate. Her argument was that the market's level was reasonable and earnings would be up a bit next year. And if you adjusted for this and that, the true P/E was lower. It was truly half-baked stuff. Genuinely unintellectual. I'm not saying she didn't know a lot better. She might be as smart as hell, for all I know. She certainly understood the business imperative to be bullish. Being bullish sells. Clients will not easily hear honest advice when it is bearish. Goldman Sachs has to make money. If you want to make partner there, you had better make them money. If you want to make money, you had better be bullish. QED. I also went nose to nose with Jeffrey Applegate, who was Lehman Brothers' equivalent and very bullish. None of them had a satisfactory argument. At least I never heard one, and I would remember if I had. But I'm sure the bosses thought they were doing the right thing. And, yes, Abby Cohen duly made partner.

WHAT THE INVESTMENT PROFESSIONALS KNEW BUT DIDN'T SAY

Jeremy Siegel was not the only inconsistent market bull out there. At the start of my debate with him in Los Angeles in late 1999, with those 1,200 financial analysts in attendance, I was asked whether I'd like to go first. And I said I would. So, I went first, which I always do when I want to pull some weaselly trick, but this was a very weaselly trick that I had planned just for that occasion.

I asked the assembled audience, "How many of you consider yourselves to be full-time equity professionals?" About 400 hands went up, an estimate made by a colleague and me, counting as best we could. Addressing only the 400 professionals, I asked, "How many of you think that if the market goes back to 17x earnings from today's level of 33x at any time in the next 10 years, it will guarantee a major bear market. Does anyone disagree?" No, 100% agreed. It was a mathematical necessity. If the P/E halves any time in the next 10 years, it was going to guarantee a major bear market. You could make the case, I suppose, that if it took fully 10 years, it would only be a minor bear market because of the earnings growth in between.

The second and more important question was, "How many of you think it will go back to 17x earnings? I think we know if it does, it guarantees a major bear market. How many of you think it will go back to 17x?" And all the hands except two went up. What does this mean, I thought? I was so surprised that I said, "No, let's make sure we got this right." So, I rephrased the question, reversing it because I just couldn't believe the answer. I said, "Let's put it this way. How many of you think it will never go back to 17x earnings again in the next 10 years?" And, indeed, there were only two votes. This is the sad truth about the peak of 1999: over 99% of fully-fledged equity professionals – the investment engine room, if you will – believed in data that guaranteed a major bear market. Right. But the spokespeople for the firms that employed them were at the podium with me saying that nothing bad would happen. What a demonstration of hard-boiled cynicism from the investment community. The spokespeople saying everything would be fine. And 99% of the engine room believing in data that guaranteed a major bear market!

I repeated this survey at every investment conference I attended during the late bubble period, which would typically have a large percentage of fully-fledged investment professionals. Sometimes there was one person in the room who believed the market wouldn't revert toward its historic average valuation over the next decade. But that was all. I asked another question. I didn't get to put it to many groups because I started to ask it too late in the cycle.

Profit margins have averaged 5% of sales. They peaked in the 1960s at 7.2%, just as they peaked in 1997 at 7.2%. And since then are coming down a bit. My question is: who believes that in the next 10 years, the profit margin on sales – in effect, under the power of the most efficient competitive market ever recorded – is not going to come down to, at best, 6%?

The average historic profit margin was 5%. I used 6% out of the kindness of my heart. And 100% of professionals, maybe with one exception, agreed with me. I asked at least seven different groups this question. And I'd gotten only a single dissenting vote – one. The clear message was it's not good for business for them to tell their clients what they think. But that was the view that investment professionals had. It was quite a shock – because the vast majority of non-professionals at the time believed that the market view was quite mixed among us professionals. That simply was not the case. And it was not even a case of incentive-caused bias. Their knowledge was clear.

So, they were generally not lying. It was just that they refused to talk about it – because it was so shockingly bad for business. Even when I talked about it I got a lot of grief. It was genuinely not good for business, a point I conceded completely. And I didn't blame them for keeping quiet. But I was sorry for the general public who believed in the nitwittery that got passed around by the bulls and was so well promoted in the press. From the press, you'd have thought that the professional community was three-quarters bulls and one-quarter bears – when in reality, professionals were, when you got down to it, overwhelmingly bearish. Most of the bulls who got quoted in the financial press weren't professionals at all – like the *Dow 36,000* folks. They were just propaganda merchants. Before taking advice, particularly in bull markets, you should always remind yourselves of the industry's bullish slant and vested interest and always ask yourselves who are the foxes and who are the chickens.

In GMO's Asset Allocation team we were assuming a fair value P/E of 17.5x and a profit margin of 6% for the U.S. stock market. Incidentally we also assumed sales growth share of 4% a year. The long-term trend up to then had only been 1.8%. We put in 4% only because the clients couldn't stand anything less. During the previous 10 years of this incredible progress we'd gone through – the ineffable productivity "miracle" of the New Paradigm period – sales growth per share had been a mere 1%, actually slightly below trend. In order to deliver 7% real returns – the sum of dividend return plus share price gains minus inflation – with a profit margin of 6%, sales growth would need to average 12.8% a year. That was not impossible but statistically this would have been a 12-standard-deviation event – a probability that was certainly less than the chance of you or me personally being hit by a meteorite.

Now if you plugged those numbers into our 10-year forecast model, together with the then current dividend yield of 1.2%, the S&P 500 was set to generate negative 1.9% annually over the next decade. If the P/E reverted to 17.5x overnight, the market would be down almost 50%. At the same time, emerging equities were forecast to deliver nearly 8% annually, REITs over 10%, TIPS over 4% and emerging debt nearly 6% (excluding any alpha). I challenged anyone to tell me with a straight face that I was using seriously bearish assumptions – because I definitely was not.

There was such a profound gap between what the professionals knew the data to be saying and the bullshit that floated around in the ether. That's the nature of the beast – a lot of ignorant people, as Keynes said, believing and behaving on very little information like a pack of hysterical sheep and the vested interests piping out good news, good news, however overstated it must be. My final question to the investment professionals was: "Imagine the archangel Gabriel comes down to Earth and tells you that there is a 70% probability that cash will outperform equities over the next year. What will you do?" Those same managers said they'd keep their fund 100% invested in equities. Because nobody in this business, or almost nobody, was willing to bet their career on a 30% chance of failure. Of course, they'd keep a ton of cash in their own personal account. Virtually every one of them expected a substantial bear market. But saying so would mean committing hara-kiri business-wise, because if they didn't tell the clients what they wanted to hear, the clients would go to any of the myriad who did. Therefore, they didn't. I can't say I blame them.

The only people who may have believed the bull market nonsense were on the investment committees. Thirty years ago, these committees were models of prudence. But from about 1995, they metamorphosed into a bunch of gunslingers. You had private equity guys who, because they knew something about private equity and had made a fortune, thought they knew everything about everything. The venture capital guys were just as bad. Add the hedge fund guys who knew everything about next week and nothing about what came after. In general, they were the worst members on the committees. They always wanted to get into growth stocks. Maybe they were clever enough to do what Keynes said – to be quicker and slicker than the other guy, just beat them on the draw, play the game till the last minute and jump off before it's too late. But a vanishingly small fraction can actually pull that off.

SHORTING THE S&P

In May 1999, I gave an interview to *Forbes*. I was a bit woozy from borderline pneumonia but, as the magazine commented, I "may just as well be suffering from bubble sickness, the dizzying impact of trying to apply well-honed reason to the stock market." At the time, the earnings yield on the S&P 500 index, meaning the composite earnings per share divided by the index price, was 2.8%. That was a good deal less than you could earn on a Treasury bill. I was quoted as saying, "The miracle is how loony it is and how few will say the emperor has no clothes." I mentioned that our performance record had been consistently exceptional up until the last two years, when we'd turned bearish too soon. I was unrepentant: "We're right, just early."

Forbes printed that our forecast for real total returns on the S&P 500 over the next decade was minus 1.5% a year. I arrived at this figure by combining normal real earnings gains, a meager dividend yield and a steady unraveling of P/E ratios. I was comparatively bullish about small company shares – which, I believed, should earn a real 3% per year over the next decade. My own personal portfolio then was short U.S. big-company stocks and long emerging market stocks and bonds, REITs, Treasuries and timber. Treasury bonds were yielding 5.5%. I liked the inflation-indexed Treasuries even more. The one due in 2029 had been issued on April 15 to yield 3.9% (real return) to maturity. From this strange mix, I expected an annual return of 7% after inflation over the next decade.

In truth, my personal short position in the S&P was becoming a source of great discomfort. We used to joke that it was the size of a small institutional bet. In fact, it was probably around $10 million. In any case, it was a big position compared to my net worth. When I put this bet on I had reckoned that if the stock market continued climbing, at least my income from GMO earned from fees collected on assets under management would rise in tandem. So, my day job provided a natural hedge to being short the market. Whereas it turned out to be the opposite of a hedge. My income fell as clients fled the firm and the margin calls on my short position increased.

I was forced to liquidate anything I could get my hands on. All my cash and earnings and everything else was poured into keeping this position. I was dangerously close to running out of cash at some points. But I was not going to be squeezed out of my position. The experience was a bit of a nightmare because it stressed me separately and independently of everything else, which was incredibly stressful anyway, and was the exact opposite of what I had planned for it to do, which was to stabilize my income and therefore my nerves. I just didn't think it through. I didn't realize the clients would move so quickly or, to be honest, that we could underperform by so much so quickly.

EXPLAINING P/E

The bulls argued that high stock prices were justified by low inflation and falling bond yields. To my mind this was complete nonsense. The economist Franco Modigliani of MIT, another hero of mine, had famously said at a Boston investment lunch in 1982 when inflation was roaring that the stock market was ridiculously cheap, inflation was a pass-through, corporations were a real asset with real factories – and the market then selling below half its book value was at half fair value. He returned to Boston in early 2000 at the top of the Great Bubble for a talk to a society of quants, sadly so old and frail he had to sit to talk. He basically said it was ridiculous for the market to be selling at 35x earnings and over 2x book and that it should be half the price. "Of course, low inflation has nothing to do with the evaluation of stocks in serious economic terms any more than it did the other way around with high inflation. And, of course, the market is hugely overpriced," Modigliani told the assembled investors. On both occasions he was quickly proved right. I think

I was the only person at both meetings. Unlike the nitwitted efficient market Nobel Prize winners, he knew the market was capable of crazy bubbles and equally crazy busts.

That's not to say that inflation didn't affect investors' willingness to hold stocks. I had this hunch that the market's P/E could be explained by factors related to comfort and confidence. I asked Ben to test various macro factors that might explain changes in the market's valuation. I thought that inflation was likely one of the significant factors and left him to think through what the other drivers might possibly be. Then I went on a trip. On my return I found that Ben had come up with a model, done and dusted. He'd tried a dozen things that had a mild correlation with P/E and anything to do with comfort. Ben's model determined that three factors drove everything else out:

- First is inflation. Investors like low inflation. We live in a real economy, of course. These are real companies. And of course they pass through inflation, as Modigliani had said. However, investors have felt uncomfortable during periods of higher inflation. They like low inflation, à la 1999.
- Second, unsurprisingly, they like high real profit margins, also high in 1999. They don't care about sales growth – which was fortunate given the sales growth of the last 10 years had been below average.
- Way down in third place, they like the stability of GDP. Investors don't care about the GDP growth rate. It has no correlation with P/E, despite what everyone expects. They care about stability. And it had never been more stable on a five-year moving average basis than it had been in the period up to the late 1990s.

In short, investors care about profit margins, stability and low inflation. Inflation appeared the most important of the three factors. The low and stable inflation of the Goldilocks economy – neither too hot nor too cold, around 2% – led people to believe they were living in a New Era, just as they'd done in the late 1920s. We'd been going through a period of low inflation and high profit margins, and GDP growth was pretty stable, not as volatile as normal. All three factors were working to make the typical portfolio manager feel comfortable. The market should have been expected to trade at a much higher than average P/E. Our model said that a new world record valuation of 26x earnings could be explained by these favorable facts. The market did indeed go to a record. In fact, it roared up to 35x cyclically adjusted earnings. The model couldn't explain that. It was pure irrational exuberance!

Abby Cohen at Goldman used a comfort model to justify the market's high P/E. But there is a world of difference between justifying and explaining. Our comfort model *explained* why P/Es were high, *but it didn't justify it*. It was clear that investors extrapolate today's conditions forever: when inflation is low, they assume it will be low forever. The trouble with comfort, like everything else in life, is that it's mean reverting. Stability is followed by instability. And high profit margins are followed by lower profit margins. After all, that's what capitalism does. If you buy when people are most comfortable, you earn a real return of 1% per year. In contrast, if you buy when people are most uncomfortable, you earn 11%. That's the nature of the game.

Not only were investors betting that benign economic conditions would continue indefinitely, they were also putting a record high price earnings multiple on the highest profit margins ever recorded. To me this seemed like the most barbaric double-counting. A rational market would do the opposite. In a rational market, profit margins

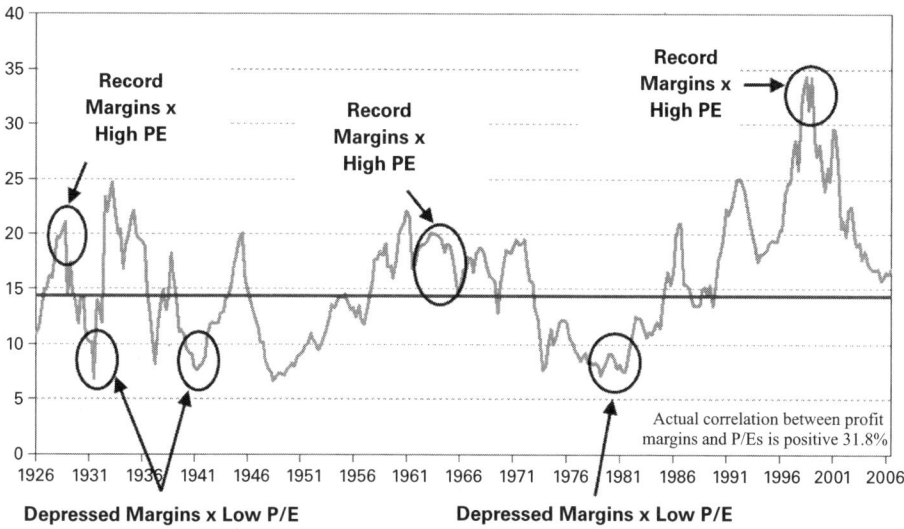

The barbaric double counting of profitability. The trailing 1-year price-to-earnings ratio for the US stock market from 1926 to 2006, indicating that high profitability and high valuations go hand in hand, even though profitability has historically been mean-reverting. Data from GMO, 2012

and valuation multiples would move inversely.* The investment industry was simply not adjusting for profit margins, which up until that time had been the most provably mean-reverting series in the whole of finance. If profit margins did not mean revert, I used

---

* That's to say, when profit margins are above average, valuations would be below average and the market trades in line with its replacement cost. With a correlation of −1 between profits and valuation, the market would be boringly stable. Looking at the historical correlation between profits and P/E, it was clear the market couldn't even get the sign right. We had record profit margins on a then record P/E in 1929 and record profit margins again in 1965, with the P/E equal to 21x earnings on an annualized basis. Then, in 1974, profit margins were almost half normal, times the market trading at a half normal P/E of 7x. If you multiply twice normal profits by twice normal P/E, the market will trade at 4x replacement cost; and if you take half the normal P/E on depressed profit margins, the market will trade at a quarter or a third of replacement cost.

to argue, then capitalism was broken. (Later, we will arrive in an era when capitalism does indeed become a bit broken and profits remained high, at least for a while. A pretty extended while.)

The growth rate of the U.S. economy had been remarkably stable over time. I liked to call it "battleship GDP" because it sailed through thick and thin. The Great Depression bounced off, without changing its long-term course. The Yale economist Robert Shiller showed that starting in 1906, a long-term stream of future dividends was also an incredibly stable series. If the underlying GDP is stable and you have a smooth long-term discount rate, the true discounted value of the market does not change much. By dint of double-counting and overstating growth in good times and understating it in bad times, however, the market is nearly 20 times more volatile than is justified by the underlying stable data to a long-term stockholder. This is not impressive. This is not efficient. I had spent 30 years being extremely irritated listening to the intellectual torturing of logic to explain that it is, in fact, a rational market.

THE GREAT BULL MARKET CONSPIRACY

In fact, profits were not as high as were officially recorded at the time. And we knew it. Management of U.S. companies was being lavishly compensated with stock options. This form of compensation didn't threaten to make senior managers rich. It threatened to make them disgustingly rich. Hundreds of millions of dollars, even billions of dollars, were being transferred from shareholders to the top management. And those options were incorrectly accounted for – accountants had tried to account for them correctly, but corporations lobbied against them and it was not allowed.

The cost of options was not deducted from earnings at the correct value – which is the fair value at transfer – but the cost was deducted at full value from taxes. Stock options, as Warren Buffett pointed out, produced an enormous incentive to overstate earnings and manage them to the nth degree – which is exactly what was occurring. The biggest overstatement was the failure to account for stock options. The second biggest were so-called "recurring, nonrecurring charges" – which amounted to about 11% of earnings.

People have a hard time understanding vested interests. I concluded we were in the middle of a "great bull market conspiracy" that was much bigger than ever before because of stock options. Politicians also wanted the stock market to be high. They wanted to be held responsible for a bull market. And whenever given a chance, they engaged in an orgy of self-congratulation. The Federal Reserve under Alan Greenspan was the great bandleader, a little bit of this, a little bit of that, and plenty of moral hazard: "It is my duty to prevent a bubble from breaking, causing damage to the U.S. economy," he said (paraphrasing), "but of course it is not my responsibility to interfere with the bubble." If that doesn't make us feel that speculation is underwritten, nothing will.

And then there were the vested interests of the investment industry. Andrew Smithers, a little more cruel than me, referred to "stockbroker economics" – that is to say, everything written about economics by people who have a vested interest in bullishness and keeping the market rolling and everyone optimistic. As I've said before, the big houses on Wall Street had a vested interest not to tell the unvarnished truth – because, very simply, a bull market was good for business. It was a time when, as the inimitable Jim Grant of *Grant's Interest Rate Observer* put it, "Buy and hold" had replaced "I love you" as the three most popular words in the English language. And I was one of the few professionals saying "sell," which in this context meant, "I hate you."

STARTING THE QUARTERLY LETTER

If you're going to stick your neck out and fight a bubble, as I've said, you need to be seen. So in April 1999, I published my first quarterly letter to explain how dangerous the bubble was. I had always had trouble putting my thoughts down on paper. I write like I talk. And I talk easily. But I don't find it easy to write. In fact, I have always had writer's block. At school, essay writing was torture. Maybe I was a little dyslexic. When I have to write something I always find an excuse for not doing the initial work. I will even read a damn fashion magazine. Anything, you know, to avoid sitting down and doing what I have to do.

Although my writing may sometimes look easy, I had to go through draft after draft of my quarterly letter, seven or eight times, before I was satisfied. Then the final draft would go to Cheryl Wakeham (as indeed this book has done), who'd make sure my facts were accurate, the punctuation correct and the lawyers happy that I hadn't libeled anyone. Based on the number of people who claim to have been reading my letters for a long time, they had a decent readership initially. In those days, it was quite rare for professional investors to put their letters out to the public and therefore there wasn't that much competition. It was like free insight into one person's view of what was going on in the marketplace. I suspect within the trade we built up quite a decent readership pretty quickly.

In my inaugural letter, I observed how the continuing stock market rise depended on a handful of growth stocks:

> The performance of the markets in the first quarter was very much "business as usual," that is, a continuation of the trend favoring a highly concentrated group of large cap names and increasingly speculative behavior in internet stocks. Just five stocks were

responsible for more than 50% of the return of the S&P 500 and, with the exception of a small group, nearly every stock in the index declined...

Our research showed that in the 18 months ahead of a bubble bursting, the market becomes spectacularly narrow. At GMO, we developed a "bubble detector," which measured the percentage of stocks that had underperformed the whole market by more than 10% over the previous 12 months. By April 1999, this bubble detector had climbed to more than 70% of all U.S. stocks – the only time in more than three decades it had gone this high. In September 1929 and again in June 1973 the bubble detector peaked at just under 70%, ahead of major market collapses.

The Standard & Poor's Low Price index, comprising very fallen industrial angels – a wonderful index, which unfortunately they gave up – had gone up, I think, by more than 80% in 1928. It started falling from the beginning of 1929 and by the day before the crash was down about 40%. I call that the biggest primal scream from the stomach of the stock market in history, while the S&P was plowing upwards to brilliant new highs and 21x earnings, the highest ever then recorded. And the fallen angels that had led the market in the previous few years were down badly. And nothing like that happened again until 1972 and nothing after 1972 until 2000. So, it's a very scary indicator. But it had been accurate and warned you every time there would be trouble ahead.

Within the firm we were hurting badly back in early 2000. Clients continued to give up on us. The World Bank, one of our earliest clients, finally lost patience. The chief investment officer of Schering-Plough, the pharma company, who really liked us and had stuck with us, called up very apologetically to tell us they were firing us. He said his investment committee told him either you fire

GMO or we'll fire you. There was another client who forbade me to come to speak to the investment committee on the grounds that I was dangerously persuasive and totally wrong.

So, it was just a complete nightmare for the client service team. Jody Shuman, who looked after some of our biggest clients, was out there getting beaten up every day. It was really terrible. She began to suffer physically from all the stress. To be fired by a client or to underperform is terribly stressful for most client service people and the more you care about their well-being, the worse it hurts. Jody took it personally when a client with whom she'd had a close relationship for many years fired us. On Friday afternoons she would come to my office to swap war stories, looking pale and worn, and I'd joke that I'd have to give her a blood transfusion.

In February 2000, minutes from the peak but with things looking as bleak as they could for GMO, Jody came with me to the Appalachian Mountain Club on Beacon Hill. With nothing to lose, I told them it was on the borderline of fiduciary irresponsibility (my favorite phrase at the time) to move out of value stocks after so much pain when value was so cheap. To move into growth stocks, which were so legendarily overpriced, would massively increase the risk and massively reduce the long-term potential return, which is like an ironclad law: if you buy something expensive, it must return less. One or two lucky stocks might grow very fast. But for the portfolio, there is no hope. And that we were witnessing something that had been repeated through history, time after time. But this one was a doozy. It was 1929 revisited. Anyway, I laid it on the line, absolutely as thick as possible, expecting to be shot in the head with interest.

As we walked out, they were all growling at us. In the end, I'd said just enough that they just didn't feel comfortable and hedged their bet and fired us for half the account. What was almost unique was that we managed 100% of their money. They shot us for half and put the money into a growth fund. And I remember the numbers very clearly: 21 months later the half that they'd taken away was worth half of our half. In under two years they had managed to wipe out a quarter of their endowment with a single decision.

In my year-end letter to investors I noted how in many respects 1999 had been a repeat of 1998. In the U.S., stocks rose more than 20%, growth beat value and technology stocks again soared more than 70%. Despite impressive gains, U.S. equities were not the best performing asset class in the world. That distinction went to emerging equities, which rebounded 54%. "The resurrection of emerging equities," I wrote, "was a powerful demonstration of mean-reverting action both by markets and by economies."

I pounded the table for our preferred asset classes: emerging equities, still incredibly cheap despite their recent recovery; REITs with their 8.5% dividend; TIPS, yielding 4.5%; and small value stocks, both in the U.S. and the rest of the world, that were especially undervalued and had a real return potential of 5% annually. "Despite our bearishness about the outlook for the U.S. stock market and economy," I concluded, "we believe that there are opportunities in today's markets for reasonable absolute returns and excellent relative returns."

There was no let-up in early 2000. If you looked at the history books, the P/E average was 14x and ranged from 7x to 21x. It had maxed out at 21x in 1929 and at the same level in 1965. This time it completely shattered that range and went to 36x. That was like a Himalayan peak coming out of the plain. You didn't have to be clever to see it. You had to be blind not to see it. In my next letter, I described how the spread between value and growth was at least as wide as it had been during the Nifty Fifty era of the early 1970s, and on some measures the spread had reached the highest levels *ever* recorded. By GMO's calculation, beaten down value stocks could look forward to a rally of more than 80% to get back to trend. By now, however, value managers were fast becoming a rare species – as I wrote in the letter:

> The first quarter was brutal for investors who paid attention to things like company fundamentals, P/E ratios, book value, dividend yields, indeed, any of the basic yardsticks that have been used historically to provide a measure of value. All an investor needed to invest profitably in the 2000 first quarter was optimism.
>
> The first part of 2000 has been remarkable in that some of the country's – no, the world's – most prominent value investors threw in the towel and quit the business. This illustrious group included George Vanderheiden (Fidelity), Gary Brinson (Brinson/UBS), Tony Dye (Phillips and Drew) and, most recently, Julian Robertson (Tiger) who, having been significantly underweight in technology stocks, finally closed his remaining hedge funds.

Brinson, whose advice in 1998 and 1999 was excellent (i.e. agreed with mine), was shot by UBS less than a month from the market peak. He was a tough nut and, if anyone could get away with unpopular advice, he could. His failure made me believe that no large, public enterprise with quarterly responsibilities to shareholders can withstand the pain of a substantial short-term loss of business in these situations. A few years later he complained to me that he had not been fired but had decided to retire. Yet he left in the same week or so that Tony Dye was definitely fired from Phillips & Drew, another division of UBS.

THE GROUND BEGINS TO SHAKE

The U.S. equity market continued on the path it had been going. Technology stocks completely dominated all other sectors of the market, with euphoria spreading to smaller, more speculative issues and reaching levels probably never seen before. The market's extreme narrowness continued. By March 1, 2000, tech stocks trading on the Nasdaq had climbed $3.1 trillion in 12 months. Over the same time the total value of *all* U.S. stocks – including Nasdaq shares – rose by only $2.1 trillion.

One of my partners, Kingsley Durant, had been fortunate five years earlier in acquiring 140,000 shares in a venture start-up, Puma Technology, at 25¢ a share. As it came public he gave the stock in trust to his children – a generous gift that was worth $200,000 in July 1999. It was the most advanced stock of 1999, which was a good year to be the most advanced stock. At its peak worth of $14 billion on $24 million in sales, the stock represented to me the epitome of the greatest speculative market in U.S. history. By early March the stake was worth an improbable $6.2 million at $41 per share (great generosity indeed!), and an even more improbable $102 per share by mid-March.

There was a day in February 2000 when the Nasdaq went down 11% by noon. Yet it closed down less than 1%. On that day, Pumatech went down 40% by lunchtime and closed down less than 5%, having rallied almost 60% in the afternoon to get back – on no news at all. Such extreme volatility was a symptom that people had no idea of the underlying value. They weren't buying because a company had certain attributes. They were buying because the stock price was rising, and selling when it fell. Day trading had obviously exaggerated the problem.

As a value investor, when you've seen these kinds of moves, you don't celebrate the first few days when the market goes down because you're still braced for the market to recover. What made that seem unlikely was the speed with which the dotcoms went down when they tanked in March. They were down 30%, 40%, 50% very quickly. It made me think, well, that's clearly the beginning of the end. As I wrote in my letter, "the ground certainly feels like it is beginning to shake."

In the fall of 1999 I had traveled out to California to meet with clients and consultants and received what essentially amounted to a hostile reception. I begged people to stand their ground. A handful of people from big pension fund consulting firms showed up and there were wall to wall nasty questions with bad implications. The tone was gruesome. Yet by March 2000, when I returned to the West Coast, sentiment had shifted in our favor, much to my surprise.

People who had been fully skeptical of our bearish approach, who completely or partially had bought into the new golden era that Abby Cohen and Greenspan had talked about so effectively for a couple of years, had begun to have doubts. They knew or felt the bubble was unlikely to continue. And because I was a well-known bear, they were suddenly interested in what I had to say. I went out there ready for hell and the turnout was two or three times greater than before. Everyone asked serious questions and listened very carefully to my responses. I was puzzled at first, and then increasingly shocked. I arrived home talking about it as a phenomenon – it was so completely unexpected. With hindsight, it turned out to be a brilliant last-minute warning that the bubble was about to burst.

CHAPTER 6

Vindication

In June 2000, *Forbes* published my debate with Merrill Lynch's notorious internet analyst Henry Blodget, the great advocate for Amazon and the dotcoms. The discussion had taken place a couple of months earlier. On the cover *Forbes* billed it as "a super-heavyweight bout between representatives of the Old and New Economy." I was hoping for blood and guts. But Blodget was polite and friendly and deferential. He was much too gentlemanly for the task.

At the end of February, the combined market valuation of the internet sector was $1.2 trillion against a negative $2.5 billion in earnings. Some of the internet companies would turn out to be good, I suggested, but most would soon cease to exist. Blodget pointed out that despite the recent brutal market pull-back, the Nasdaq was still up 40% over the past year. To which I replied that we basically believed that, sooner or later, the S&P 500 would decline 50% and the Nasdaq 70% from their highs. Our Nasdaq forecast was also published in *The Economist*. The actual magnitude of the decline necessary for Nasdaq to reach fair value had been 75% but we had rounded that down to 70% to be friendly.

As it turned out, our seemingly aggressive forecast for a Nasdaq decline turned out to be conservative. A year after the forecast went public, the technology index was down 67.5%. Its largest component,

Cisco Systems, which for just a day or two in March 2000 was the world's most valuable company, worth $550 billion, suffered a share price collapse of 84%. My selection for the quintessential "flake" stock of the Tech Bubble, Pumatech, which had peaked at $102 per share in mid-March, at which point the company was worth $4 billion on $24 million in sales, hit a low of 17¢ in October 2002. A month earlier, the Nasdaq bottomed, down more than 80%. It didn't regain its peak for another 15 years and 9 months.

For years, we had complained of the wind blowing in our faces. By the end of the third quarter of 2000, however, the wind was finally at our backs. Over the previous three months, value had beaten growth, small beat large and bonds beat stocks, as technology and telecom stocks fell around the world and global markets slowly declined. Small cap value stocks in the U.S. recorded their strongest-ever performance. Our bet on REITs paid off brilliantly as did our bond positions in TIPS and emerging country debt. Across the board, cheaper asset classes, as designated by our 10-year forecast, outperformed more expensive asset classes, with the exception of emerging market equities, whose time was yet to come. Over the course of the year, of the 52 products GMO offered to clients, 51 beat their benchmarks. The bubble experience had been extraordinarily painful for our clients and us but was now, finally, beginning to pay off.

It wasn't until after the financial crisis that the accuracy of our asset class forecasts was fully demonstrated. We had forecast on December 31, 1999 that the egregiously overpriced S&P would underperform cash and everything else over the next decade – what should you expect with the market valued at over 30x earnings? In addition, we had assumed that emerging equities would do extremely well despite having a 0.7 correlation with the S&P, because they were cheap. The December 1999 forecast had U.S.

REITs at the top of the list followed by emerging market equities and the S&P 500 at the bottom. In the end, emerging market equities did best, returning 8.1% a year after inflation (the forecast was 7.8%), REITs were third with 7.4% (10.0%) and the S&P was last with −3.5% (−1.9%). The ranking of the assets in between was almost spot on. The probability of getting that right by chance was 1 in 550,000, according to my calculations. Normality is what we had assumed in our then 10-year forecasts (today they are seven-year forecasts). It's an awfully normal world we inhabit in the long term. It's only the short- and intermediate-term zigs and zags that drive us all crazy.

Asset Class	Estimated Rank	GMO 10-Yr Forecast Dec-31-99 (% Real Return/Yr)	Actual 10-Yr Return*	Actual Rank
U.S. REITs	1	10.0	7.4	3
Emerging Market Equities	2	7.8	8.1	1
Emerging Country Debt	3	6.1	7.5	2
U.S. TIPS	4	4.3	4.9	4
Barclays Capital U.S. Gov't. Debt	5	3.8	3.5	6
International Small Cap	6	3.4	3.5	7
Foreign Bonds	7	3.0	3.9	5
U.S. Small	8	2.5	2.3	8
U.S. T-Bills	9	2.1	0.3	9
EAFE	10	0.4	-1.4	10
S&P 500	11	-1.9	-3.5	11
Correlation of rank order: 93.6%					
Probability of picking same or better rank order randomly: 1 in 550,000				

The vindication of value. This exhibit, from December 2009, compares GMO's asset class return forecasts from ten years prior — near the peak of the internet bubble, at the most difficult point in GMO's history — to the actual realized returns over those ten years. Ultimately GMO's forecasts were remarkably accurate. Data from GMO, 2010

ENRON

In late 2000, we were at the early stages of a long-term market correction in favor of fundamental value. Every week, corporate earnings were edging down. Investors were becoming more discriminating. They were now beginning to take notice of the quality of earnings and sales growth instead of myopically focusing on earnings per share growth. Accounting gimmickry, a hallmark of the bull market, had become one of the market's greatest vulnerabilities.

As the smoke cleared, it became clear we had not been living through a new era after all. In the late 1920s, there were some spectacular cases of embezzlement, but there was not the breadth of weaseling that was going on at this time. "Weaseling" covers the shaving of ethical standards, the pushing of reasonable accounting boundaries, massive overcompensation of management and outright cheating. As J.K. Galbraith pointed out in his book, *The Great Crash*, the size of the "bezzle" as he called it (to describe all cheating and embezzlement) grows on the upside of an investment bubble and shrinks on the downside; this time the "bezzle" got to be pretty big – far bigger than any of us had expected.

Significant corporate scandals surfaced at Enron, Tyco and WorldCom. Enron, the poster child for dodgy accounting, went bust in August 2001. This turned out to be a win for the quants over some large traditional investors, who had famously owned big positions in the company. Even if you had believed Enron's own lying inputs for earnings, its stock peaked at close to five times the average value of an already overpriced market on our particular value model (and probably all other quant models) and had never made it into our value stream. Many traditional investors, in contrast, not only believed the imaginary data, but also much of the hype for Enron's future, none of which was believed by any quant model.

Quant models get at least a measure of protection against the typical overconfidence that behavioralists tell us typifies our species, not least the investment branch of it.

THE GREATEST VALUE RALLY IN HISTORY

Enron's collapse occurred in the midst of the greatest value rally relative to growth in history. In March 2000, value had never been cheaper relative to growth. It was the all-time, world-record low – by a wide margin. The second-place candidate was at the end of the Nifty Fifty period in December 1974. In 1974 the relative performance of value stocks hit bottom, and from 1974 to 1983 value outperformed growth by more than 100 percentage points. Value stocks went from incredibly cheap to quite expensive, and small stocks did the same. Now, in the space of a single year, 80% of the four-year downward move in value stocks was retraced, mainly because growth stocks (especially tech stocks) had collapsed.

As the market fell from its March 2000 high, owning small cap value stocks cushioned all the pain. The very probable cause for this outperformance was that small stocks were very cheap indeed relative to the rest of the market. In fact, Ben Inker and I took more grief in our forecasts for favoring small caps than anything else. "If you're so gloomy on the market and particularly Nasdaq, how on earth can you recommend small caps as a haven?" would be a close approximation of the standard objection. Our answer was that yes, in the past, small caps had, on average, underperformed in market declines, but when we divided all bear market periods into four quartiles (based on how cheap this group was relative to the S&P), we found that when they were in the cheapest quartile they in fact outperformed in bear periods. In March 2000 they were at the very top of the best quartile of value.

Curiously, at the moment of its great triumph, things started to go wrong with value. In the past, value had always earned investors three or four points a year from rebalancing the portfolio, selling winners and buying losers. Then in 2000 rebalancing a portfolio of value stocks suddenly stopped working. And the same happened the following year and the next. By the time we had had our huge value rally, which kind of fizzled out about 2005, it was clear that value was around 20 points behind where it theoretically should have been based on its behavior in the previous 70 years or so. From 2000, value should have had a theoretical rally of over 80% but ended up with, say, about a 65-point gain. Now, a 65% gain was more than enough to make us look like heroes, but it should have been a great deal more.

For most investors, 2001 was a terrible year but it was a good year for GMO. Despite our two major markets, EAFE and the S&P 500, being down 21.4% and 11.9%, respectively, we finished the year with more dollars under management than when we had started – 85% of our funds beat their respective benchmarks. We were out of the things that absolutely collapsed. We were generally in the things that went up and the things we were in that went down did so much less than the market. I told *Global Investor* magazine that "We can and did take bigger bets in many of our funds. Others were constrained by business and career risk." A couple of months later, Dick Mayo announced he was leaving GMO to join his son, who was running an independent hedge fund. As I wrote in my year-end letter: "Dick and I had worked together for 33 years. He was a passionate, hard-working professional who shared my obsession with winning. And he did win more than his fair share partly because he was also tough enough to make some big, unfashionable bets and hold them."

Our emerging bet was finally paying off. Arjun Divecha's Emerging Markets Fund finished the year first out of almost 200 competing mutual funds (and in September, GMO was ranked the best-performing mutual fund family in the U.S. by Morningstar). Even at the end of 2001, emerging equities were still incredibly cheap relative to the U.S. market. Over the course of the third killer year of the bear market, 2002, the S&P went down 22% while emerging, with its beta of 1.3 to the S&P, fell just 2%. Further proof, if needed, that valuation, not volatility, is the true measure of investment risk.

In Asset Allocation, we made money in 2000, we made decent money in 2001 and eked out half a percent in 2002 – which, because everyone else was losing money, was a marvelous result. In my second 2002 quarterly letter I castigated the academic exponents of the Efficient Market Hypothesis (EMH) who had led so many investors over the cliff. At the time, GMO's funds had beaten their benchmarks in 68% of all product years, with an average outperformance (net of fees) of 3%. "For our firm, I believe this is the best 2.25 years' performance I will ever see, even if my 'eat less and live forever' diet works," I wrote. The chance of getting a 68% hit rate across our product line was about 1 in 300,000.

By now we were well ahead of the competition in our GTE/Verizon strategic relationship. In 1999, we had performed dreadfully and at the start of 2000 were in last place among the four investment firms. Barton Biggs, head of Morgan Stanley Asset Management, was unbelievably complimentary about us in his book *Hedge-Hogging*. He wrote that he'd known that GMO was better positioned than Morgan Stanley for a bear market, but during the event we came past him so fast it felt like he'd been stuck in reverse. We just shot past them all, going from last place to first place in 12 months – not just for the year but since inception. As the market imploded and our asset allocation started to work, they felt we were almost cheating.

And in a way we were, for being a private partnership we could take substantially more career or business risk than they ever would. We had more freedom to make or break our business. Britt Harris, the chief pension officer at GTE/Verizon, had been skeptical about our bearish stance in the late 1990s. To his credit, he had stuck with us. "Well, Jeremy," Britt said to me in mid-2001, "I have to give it to you. You were right and I was wrong."

BNP OFFER FOR GMO

As GMO's fortunes recovered, suitors came sniffing around again. In 2001, Banque Nationale de Paris (BNP) got in touch with us about acquiring the firm and we replied that we might sell a minority interest in return for a flow of business from them. Then, after a few weeks of talking, they disappeared without a trace. Several months went by and our portfolios were roaring ahead. Running into 2002, we were rapidly restoring our credibility and beginning to get new business to replace the market losses. Then BNP came back. Apparently, they'd been off sweet-talking somebody else who, as we had done many times in the past, had gotten cold feet the night before the wedding and called it off.

So, we started discussions again. Months went on as our business boomed. BNP then sent a squad of fairly heavy-booted people to do the due diligence, stomping around despite my warnings of the sensitivities of quants and investment managers; in general, they created a very bad impression. I was, however, very impressed with the head people and I thought the deal might have a lot of risk-reducing potential. I could also see, though, this deal was going to diminish the joy of the business. But it would also diminish the threat if the market had another leg down, as I believed likely. Forrest put in the hard work and eventually, after what felt like billions of hours of negotiation and trivia as well as a hobnailed boot inspection of our operations, we had a deal on the table.

By this time, however, our business was roaring and our confidence was back up again. Naturally, my junior partners could not imagine the threats I was talking about protecting them from. They were on a roll, so why would they be conservative? And why would we accept the constraints of partnering with an outside investor? The nail in the coffin was Ben Inker getting up on behalf of his significant junior partners and saying, "Let us put it this way. If you, Jeremy and Forrest, are right, and five years from now we have an income 25% higher than we would otherwise have, we would rather not do the deal." It was a terrific line of argument. It went straight to my heart because I knew the French, although charming, were going to be difficult. The deal was off.

As it happened, our business exploded from around $20 billion at the time we decided not to do the deal to $165 billion four and a half years later. It was one of the more remarkable jumps in the industry. The junior partners had probably been right to rebuff the BNP offer, and they certainly saved a lot of senior people a whole lot of headaches. It was during this period that Forrest turned his tremendous energy to doing finals presentations, winning a remarkable 46 of his first 48 pitches. Beginning in August 2002 until his retirement a few years later, Forrest did a total of 140 finals presentations, canvassing the country and developing first-name relationships with the American Airlines crew serving the end-of-the-day Boston to L.A. flight. He won 90% of his pitches. As far as I know, this is an unprecedented feat in the institutional business.

Yet of the clients that fired us, not one came back. We had done the right thing for the right reasons and won. They had done the wrong thing for the wrong reasons and lost. Nobody came back. It is just the nature of the beast and career risk. They were not going to underline the terrible error they had made by returning. It's like selling a stock at 4 and buying it back at 17. A machine can do that but it can't be done by many humans. You can change the management and the new hired guns can do it. Quite a few clients we did business with later had formerly fired us. But it was always a different guy and a different product. No one who'd fired us for Asset Allocation came back.

A few years later, I was asked at a Boston Security Analysts Society forum what the secret was to our rapid growth of assets (*sic transit gloria*). I replied, "We were simply willing to lose more business than the other guys." By this I meant that we were prepared to make very big bets on those relatively rare occasions when we had very high confidence. I repeated my point that career and business risk – the fear of losing clients – dominated our business and were so hard to sidestep that the big bets would always be available and always be career-threatening. And that is the turf we staked out: make the "near certain" bets as large as we could, sweat out the timing problems and pray for patient clients. Or, because you couldn't find them in the investment business, pray for relatively patient clients.

By 2003, GMO had long outgrown its origins as a value equities shop. By this time, we were running several billion dollars across eight hedge funds and one fund of funds, $2 billion in emerging markets debt, $3 billion in emerging-markets equities and $300 million in timber assets. Around four-fifths of the firm's assets were invested in stocks, with the rest in fixed income and cash. After a torrent of inflows into our emerging equities and debt strategies we decided to close both to new investors. As I wrote in my year-end letter:

I believe that every professional investor knows that it is an ironclad law that size reduces outperformance, but I also understand the investment guild's vested financial interest in muddying the water. The basic truth is that as you add assets, you have three disagreeable alternatives. You can either add more stocks or buy more of the original list, or both. As you extend your list, you dilute the one or two brilliant stock ideas that many good professionals have every now and then and you dilute the dozen or so good ideas. You are quickly into your "B team" stocks, and eventually you are forced to buy anything that is merely acceptable. If the "merely acceptable" beat or even equal your highest confidence bets, then you have a very eccentric talent.

For at least 25 years I have had some apparently contradictory beliefs. First, I believed it was an exciting challenge to help build a large and profitable firm. Second, I believed the main characteristic of a good money manager was reasonably steady outperformance. Third, I knew that my partners and I wanted above all to be seen as good money managers for, to repeat my own axiom, "There is nothing more supremely useless than a mediocre money manager." But fourth, my partners and I shared the belief that size impacts performance. The way to reconcile or compromise with the conflicts was to have a very broad product line, doing everything we thought we could do that did not compete with our other products, and to close each product down at an appropriate size.

Dick Mayo and I, along with Chris Darnell, closed our first product, U.S. Active, at $250 million in 1981 and closed it about as "hard" as could be done, taking no money from anyone… The closing of the two emerging products (equities and debt) continues this tradition.

FURTHER THOUGHTS ON BUBBLES

I spent much of my time during the bear market pondering about who was to be held responsible for the mess of the unprecedented bubble forming and then fully breaking. I felt like kicking the enemy when he was down, which was very un-English of me, but irresistible. Naturally, I laid part of the blame on finance academics who had promoted the concept that the market was either efficient or at least guaranteed by divine right to outperform bonds over any decently long period, regardless of price. The increasingly accepted wisdom regarding market efficiency probably guaranteed a more extended bubble than ever before.

Earlier spectacular bubbles, such as the 1720 South Sea Bubble in England, had been accompanied by considerable cynicism to the effect that investors were inherently greedy, gullible and prone to group hysteria. The 1995–2000 bubble was the first one to be built on a remarkably different belief: that the market was efficient. In an efficient market, an individual can always rest assured that prices are an accurate reflection of reality and that there can never, in fact, be a bubble. This belief had become completely dominant in academic circles, and had steadily impacted the views held by the investment world as well-regarded investment people promoted the idea that it was a losing proposition to try to outguess the market. (I called this idea the "watch the locomotive coming effect" or, alternatively, the "step off the cliff with considerable discipline effect.")

The EMH can be viewed as a branch of new classical macroeconomics in which economic forces are assumed to be driven exclusively by the drive to maximize profits for firms and utility for individuals. The theory comes in several consistencies, from soft to hard. In general, it assumes that investors are well and speedily informed about all knowable data; that they have the skills and wisdom to process the data accurately and sensibly, and the psychological make-up not to mess it all up. Most critically, their motivation is economically driven – to maximize their returns at prudent risk. This collective wisdom is deemed to be embedded in the market so effectively that no meaningful number of players can beat the market after costs (although perhaps an insignificant handful may succeed). It has always seemed to me to be self-evidently wrong in almost all particulars as well as completely missing the overall flavor: that the market is a behavioral jungle.

From around 1975 or so, doing serious work on market inefficiencies was academically dangerous for one's health, and a fairly strong efficiency case came to dominate at most business schools. The academic finance establishment, whose membership included Bill Sharpe, Robert Merton, Eugene Fama, Ken French and others of that ilk, was so powerfully and monolithically behind the EMH that interesting contradictory work had usually been kept out of journals and generally marginalized; career advancement was threatened for the heretics. "Heretics" is in fact a good word, for there was a religious, faith-based quality to the belief in market efficiency. It was based on axioms – some dating back decades to Von Neumann and Morgenstern – which, for example, proposed that adequate quantitative tools were available and used by all investors to process the available data effectively. Like many other economic axioms, this one had not been established as a fact and flew in the face of a growing number of behavioral studies claiming that this was precisely not the case. Axioms, though, are hard to struggle with, and new proofs of inefficiency were incorporated as merely another risk factor that had been missed in the original formulation, a process that could presumably go on forever.

A useful theory should not only do its best to fit the facts but be capable of being proved wrong by the right data. The theory of efficient markets failed both tests. The intensity of the religious belief in efficiency was attested to by a comment by Robert Haugen in his book *The New Finance: The Case Against Efficient Markets* (1995). Haugen claimed that while speaking at a conference, Eugene Fama had become so enraged with his long list of probable inefficiencies that he called out from the crowd, "You're a criminal." According to Haugen, Fama added that, "God knows that the market is efficient." Shades of Einstein's "God doesn't play at dice." There has always been a need for scientists and wannabes to believe in order, neatness and, above all, elegance. Confronted with Fama rather than Einstein, I believe Heisenberg would have said, "Stop telling God what to believe."

Among the other bubble culprits, investment houses had been carried along by their self-interest, as were boards of directors and top management. Stock options and corporate greed had provided the fuel. The media, relatively blameless in my opinion, did what they were paid to do: give the public what it wants. The general public was left on its own, with dangerous brainwashing and perhaps a predisposition to want to play with the crowd and believe good news. Still, I believed that the facts and common sense indicated that the single largest contributor to the calamity was the Federal Reserve chairman, Alan Greenspan.

In my view, the chief job of the Fed should be the maintenance of general economic stability. Major stock market bubbles are one of the most dangerous things that can happen to an economy. They cause wasteful overinvestment and, through the vast paper wealth they create, substantially increase the amount of greed that is in any case in plentiful supply in a vigorous capitalist system. This, in turn, increases outright corruption a little and unethical behavior a lot.

Bubbles redistribute wealth. Much of that wealth goes temporarily to stockholders and is later given back. But while it is there, the unexpected wealth changes people's behavior. They consume more, which further boosts corporate profits and share prices. By the same token, the bubble reduces the flow of funds into retirement plans, which seem to be doing so well from capital gains that they need no further help from incremental savings. When the market tide recedes, past savings are revealed as inadequate. The loss of this fools' paradise causes resentment. Most of the redistribution of wealth ends up in the hands of corporate managers. In the latest cycle, stock-based compensation had not been effectively tied to good performance, and most was awarded by precisely those companies, such as Enron, where shareholders had been most hurt.

GREENSPAN'S RESPONSIBILITY

The downside of the great bull markets always proves to be a paradise for the operation of Murphy's Law: whatever can go wrong will. The overinvestment caused by excessive stock prices and excessive lending is followed by a capital spending bust. For all these reasons, in my view, bubbles should be avoided at any reasonable cost. The stability of the U.S. economy can only be protected against the real dangers of a bubble breaking by the Fed and its chairman being willing, at rare intervals, to intervene beforehand. They must attempt to identify and moderate major stock bubbles and be prepared to bear some consequences. If they are not prepared to do this, then the risk level of the economy rises substantially.

It was easy to brush aside Greenspan's argument that bubbles were hard to detect in advance, for the stakes were just too high not to try; in any case, great bubbles are like mountains sticking out of the plain. Comparing the stock market on 36x earnings in 2000 to its previous 1929 high of 21x and a 75-year average of 14x did not take particularly sharp analytical skills. Greenspan could have raised rates a little back in 1996 and added a lot of jawboning about his determination to prevent an asset price bubble. Most obviously, perhaps, he could have increased margin requirements. Had he been prepared to use all the tools available to him, it almost certainly would have cut the last substantial piece off the upswing and offsetting downswing in the U.S. equity market. In addition, it would have reduced the overinvestment, greed and corruption that go with a truly major bubble.

While I was marshaling my thoughts on the Greenspan fiasco, the maestro himself overtook my efforts with a breathtakingly shameless denial of responsibility for the bubble at Jackson Hole in late August 2002. According to Greenspan, jawboning the market "would have been ineffective unless backed by action." I could agree on that one. He claimed that the belief that "well-timed incremental tightening" of rates could have succeeded against "the late 1990s bubble is almost surely an illusion." Even more controversially, he argued that increasing the margin requirement would have had little effect. He asked rhetorically whether the size of the bubble could be limited by policy and replied, "From the evidence to date, the answer appears to be no." But given he did not try any of the above, there was precious little evidence that his case was valid.

Besides, Greenspan had known more than he let on. Paul Krugman in *The New York Times* pointed out the Fed chairman's remarkable September 1996 statement to fellow members of the Federal Open Market Committee: "I recognize that there is a stock market bubble problem at this point. We do have the possibility of increasing margin requirements. I guarantee that if you want to get rid of the bubble, whatever it is, that will do it." This was only one of several smoking guns. So, despite believing that bubbles were dangerous and delay potentially ruinous, despite knowing that he had the tools to break it and despite sensing back in 1996 – probably with perfect timing – that then was the time to act, he did not act, leaving us to face the painful consequences. One of the worst of which was being forced to listen to his excuses and to see so many acolytes nodding agreement and licking his boots whenever possible.

Why did Greenspan not follow through after his "irrational exuberance" warning? J.K. Galbraith probably had it nailed. In his account of the 1929 Crash, Galbraith concluded that the Fed did indeed have the tools to prevent a major bubble; but that such tools would never be used. As he said, no one wants to be caught "holding the pin." No central banker looks forward to taking a lot of political heat and we know that Greenspan took a good deal because of his "irrational exuberance" speech. Hesitating under pressure is reasonable, but hesitation in dealing with a bubble is like waiting to jump off a London bus as it accelerates. It is at first an unpleasant proposition, but delay any longer and it becomes just plain dangerous.

At such times, wishful thinking becomes an appealing proposition, and Greenspan seemed genuinely to have been deep into wishful thinking. As a believer in the new era, only a few sell-side strategists such as Goldman Sachs' Abby Cohen and Lehman Brothers' Jeff Applegate ran him a close second for relentless and increasing enthusiasm for the New Economy, its new high plateau of productivity, profitability and growth and its justification for higher stock prices. The Fed chairman, though, was not selling shares and yet he seemed to have believed more completely in this new era nonsense by March 2000 than anyone else.

It is worth reminding ourselves of the extravagance of some of his statements. In January 2000, for example, he claimed that "the American economy was experiencing a once-in-a-century acceleration of innovation, which propelled forward productivity, output, corporate profits and stock prices at a pace not seen in generations, if ever." Phew! The internet, which he claimed had "pushed back the fog of uncertainty" for corporations, was his particular pet. "Lofty equity prices," he said, "have reduced the cost of capital. The result has been a veritable explosion of spending on high-tech equipment… And I see nothing to suggest that these opportunities will peter out anytime soon… Indeed many argue that the pace of innovation will continue to quicken… to exploit the still largely untapped potential for e-commerce, especially the business-to-business arena." All this within one week of the peak from which the Nasdaq's "lofty prices" declined by more than 75% and the business-to-business dotcom stocks fell 95%.

The economic basis for his enthusiasm always looked shaky. As I have pointed out, the U.S. economy was not doing particularly well in the late 1990s. Things simply were not as good as Greenspan believed. Besides, much of the productivity gains we had seen came from an unsustainable boom in capital equipment. At the time, it seemed to many of us that the case for a permanent and significant improvement in economic performance was possible, but absolutely not proven, and the degree of improvement was never likely to rival Greenspan's vision.

Whatever the Fed chairman's motives for voicing his enthusiasm for the New Economy, we know what its effect was. It removed reasonable doubt for most investors. The *Financial Times*, which incidentally received from me the award for least boot-licking of the major papers regarding Greenspan's performance, pointed out that his "increasingly bullish observations… may well have contributed to the explosion of exuberance in the late 1990s." Morgan Stanley's economist, Stephen Roach, went further, arguing that Greenspan's outspoken belief in the unique features of this cycle – rapid growth yet low inflationary pressure – removed the need to raise interest rates. "That was the buy signal every investor and speculator dreamed of," said Roach.

As for Greenspan's post-bubble defense, what could we expect? That he would repent his lack of character? That he would admit even partial fault? His complete denial of responsibility brought to mind an incident in the Profumo sex scandal of the 1960s in England. One of the women involved, Mandy Rice-Davies, on hearing that one of the politicians had denied having sex with her, replied with the immortal words, "Well he would say that, wouldn't he?" Sometimes the blindingly obvious is funny. This time the equally predictable denial of responsibility and the apparent credulousness of many opinion makers (but, encouragingly, not all of them) in accepting his argument was merely irritating. Irritating or not, it must be conceded that in terms of avoiding widespread blame, Greenspan appeared to have gotten away with it. You can indeed "fool most of the people all of the time."

LESSONS

In my second quarterly letter of 2003, I added an appendix entitled "Lessons from the Great Bubble." (N.B.: time references and tenses have been left in the original form. Additional thoughts to the original piece are in square brackets.)

Lesson 1: Do not believe the consensus and particularly the bullish propaganda.

It is a natural human tendency to believe that "they" are right, that the experts know what they are doing. Remember that most of what you read and hear in a bull market is propaganda. Ask yourself about the probable motive of the speakers. Are they trying to sell stocks? It is many times easier selling stocks in bullish times with optimistic clients. Are they like Greenspan, trying to keep congressmen happy? Witness how fast he backed off his beautifully timed advice on "irrational exuberance." Recognize that the government has a vested interest in bull market revenues. Recognize that, especially in this recent cycle, corporate officers have a huge, vested interest in talking their stocks up and exaggerating their earnings because of their excessive, sloppily issued stock options. Recognize that corporate accountants want to keep their jobs by providing the answers that CEOs want. Most importantly, in recognizing propaganda, recognize that the media's job description is to attract viewers and sell copies. This means, in general, delivering what makes readers feel good. If raining on the parade reduces sales, why would they do it?

When all these factors are in sync, they create an enormous brainwashing capability and your first job as an investor – as we have all painfully relearned – is resisting this pressure. "They" are usually wrong. You must dare to be independent. Contrarian impulses are usually better. They are always better in major bubbles and busts.

Lesson 2: The market is inefficient.

The dominant academic group in stock market research has held, since about 1970, that the market is efficient. The Efficient Market Hypothesis (EMH) assumes that investors are well and speedily informed about all knowable data and that they have the skills and wisdom to process the data accurately, and the psychological make-up not to mess it all up. The reality, I believe, is that investors are fallible and emotional and have neither the mathematical nor the psychic means to process data accurately, nor in the case of professionals, whose main job is protecting their careers, the incentive.

We have just had the type of bubble that should occur by chance in an efficient market every 60 years. It has been followed immediately by the type of downward move that should occur every 40 years. This immediate connection should occur regularly every 1 in 60 times 1 in 40 years, or every 2,400 years! Yet every major bubble since before the South Sea Bubble in 1720 and including the 1929 Crash and Japan in 1990 has had exactly that configuration.

One of the many traits of human behavior that causes inefficient markets is wishful thinking, and this, ironically, has been shared by the academic establishment. They wished investors to be rational. They wished investors not to be biased by wishful thinking. They wished the "heretical" data proving market inefficiency to be inaccurate. They wished the study of markets to be as serious as physics. They wished the evidence of irrational crowd behavior that typified all historical market cycles would simply go away. But their wishing has not made it so. The market is enormously inefficient and getting more so. This mismatch between the EMH and reality has been described by Larry Summers, President of Harvard University and former U.S. Secretary of the Treasury, as the most remarkable error in the history of economic theory.

Lesson 3: The market is driven by behavioralism.

Individual investors not only want to believe that "they" are right, but also that good news is better than bad. They are also good at suppressing dissonant information, so that bearish input easily bounces off those who have decided to be bulls. They also disproportionately prefer markets, situations, stocks and so on, that make them feel comfortable. Worst of all, they adopt the convention for dealing with the future (that Keynes pointed out in 1936) that the current situation will continue. In this way, they extrapolated the unprecedented fat profit margins, low inflation and low interest rates of the late 1990s into the indefinite future, just as they had extrapolated the 13% inflation and low profit margins of 1982.

Lesson 4: The real, cruel world regresses to the mean, and the current bear market [that of 2000–03] is a great example.

Unfortunately, the world record profit margins of 2000 were fated to regress back to average. That is, after all, how capitalism works. If exceptional profit margins do not attract assets and increased competition, until we drown in, say, fiber optic cable, then the capitalistic system is broken. So, investor comfort and good times are coincident indicators, and as inflation and rates rise and margins fall, so investors' discomfort drives down P/Es. Perversely, therefore, 1982 with terrible inflation, 15% government bonds, a recession, an oil crisis and destroyed profit margins also had a low P/E. Similarly, March 2000 had perfect comfort factors and the highest P/E ever. All of which were doomed to regress painfully. For the record, all 27 of the bubbles in all asset classes that we have identified in the last 100 years went all the way back to the pre-existing trend. There were NO NEW ERAS, despite Irving Fisher's "new high plateau" belief in 1929; despite the belief in "Japan Inc." in 1989; despite Greenspan's belief that the internet and new technology had caused higher productivity that in general probably justified higher stock prices. "This time" is never different.

The bubbles that reached their biggest peaks in March 2000 have all regressed back toward normal once again. Growth stocks were at the highest premium ever to value stocks, and in the last three years the gap has completely closed. In the process, value stocks saved enormous pain. Large cap stocks had the second largest gap over small caps and are now back to normal. The S&P 500 had retreated 80% of the way back to normal. These bubbles have all behaved perfectly. Regression to the mean is alive and well.

["This time is never different" is always claimed, and in the long sweep of history there are indeed empires that fall and revolutions that occur. But by 2003 you could look back at market bubbles and reasonably conclude that they had never been different in one important sense: they all broke. At the sector level it had been the same. Regression to the mean in 2002 was, indeed, very much alive and well.]

Lesson 5: Regression may be near certain, but the timing of regression to the mean is very uncertain and therefore playing it is dangerous to your career health.

Risk for investors is not primarily the volatility of the asset prices. Risk for practitioners is mainly career and business risk of being wrong in the short term. For individual investors, risk is primarily the chance of losing money. The timing uncertainty, though, creates enormous risk. No fund manager would build up a lot of cash even if he knew the probabilities were 70% in favor of cash outperforming and only 30% for equities. No professional would take a 30% chance of losing his career. If he did, he would have a 2.4 year life expectancy.

[Relative loss – underperforming the benchmark or your rivals and competitors – is far more dangerous to you than simply losing money. Thus, professionals are often prevented from doing what they know is in the clients' best interest because of timing uncertainty.]

With more specializations like small cap value and emerging countries, few managers can move across boundaries so that the arbitrage mechanism between categories is weakened and inefficiencies become larger, but also riskier to play *for benchmarked professionals*. These great opportunities will therefore always exist and always be dangerous to careers.

Lesson 6: Great bubbles are not like ordinary bull markets.

Major bubbles and busts are the only very important events in investing. The rest of the time, you show up for work, do a competent job, keep your nose clean and everything works out okay because nothing much is happening. In a major bubble everything changes; stock picking fades into relative insignificance and asset and sector mix dominates completely. A major bubble is the kind that occurs every 40 years or so (statistically, a 2-sigma event), and there are only three important ones in equities prior to the current one [the Tech Bubble of 2000]: 1929 and 1965 in the U.S. and 1990 in Japan.

The major error in analyzing bear markets is to apply rules derived from ordinary bull and bear markets. "After three interest rate cuts, the market on average is up 21% a year later." "Six months before the end of a recession, the market turns up and on average is up 26% two years later." Many more than three interest rate cuts did not stop the Japanese decline or the 2000 U.S. decline. After the first recession in Japan and the U.S., the market continued to decline. Different rules apply to major bubbles, and the most important difference is that when major bubbles break, moves to stimulate the economy seem to get much reduced traction.

Lesson 7: Great bear markets take their time and almost always overrun on the downside.

Great bubbles usually take about the same time period, or a bit less, to get back to trend as they took to rise above it. This market should therefore have been expected to hit trend (680 ±10% on the S&P 500) by about the fall of this year [2002]. Typically, the overrun below trend will also take several years. Remember, all asset classes spend half their time below trend, much of it following the bursting of bubbles. Following the 1929 Crash, it took over 20 years from early 1931 for the stock market to get back to trend and stay there. After the 1965 peak, it took 13 years from when the trend was crossed in early 1974 to get back above trend. Japan, following its bust in 1990, took seven years on its way down to trend and is now five years below trend and counting and counting.

This information was all available in March 2000, but by far the most common opinion given by the investment industry was that the bear market would be mild and quick and last no more than a year. Such a short decline after a major bubble would have been unique in history.

There are no "new eras." The behaviorally driven, inefficient market is full of minor distortions that can usually be helped a lot by governmental action, and a few, very much more important major bubbles and busts in which the rules change and the usual governmental moves are of little or much reduced help. Only price matters and can be depended on in the long run, but sometimes it can be painfully long before rational pricing is restored.

[Although unique events do occur, it is usually a bad idea to bet on them. "New eras" are as rare as hen's teeth. A return to roughly normal is always a good bet because there are a few ironclad laws. If you double the price of an asset, you will halve its return. But sometimes the return to normalcy will take a very long time, outlasting your career. This is why you seldom get good long-term advice: an efficient capitalist enterprise will feel it must feed you what you want to hear and stay with the pack. This guarantees that in the few exceptional bubbles we will almost all walk off the cliff together.]

CHAPTER 7

The Greatest Sucker Rally in History

Because I felt that mean reversion was all I knew, the success of our 1999–2000 era forecasts was very gratifying for me. Still, I was troubled by the fact that the U.S. stock market in 2000 never quite reverted to trend. Full trend reversal had happened in all the earlier 27 bubbles that we'd studied and I sat patiently waiting for the 28th bubble, the S&P 500, to do likewise. Previous bubbles had always overcorrected, but the retreat from the technology bubble between 2000 and 2002 fell well short of the average retrenchment. In September 2002, the stock market fell to within 10% of long-term trend, the level likely to give investors the historical average 6% average real return. That was close but still no cigar.

From this low point in late 2002 the stock market took off. New bull markets typically start after the great bubbles have broken badly and overcorrected so that stocks become very cheap for roughly half the time. After this bubble burst, however, the S&P fell to 19x earnings, which was down from its peak of 36x, but still barely below the peaks of the two previous great U.S. bubble markets. (To be fair, on original reported earnings the market appeared to be less expensive, but over the following years aggregate earnings were revised down several times.) Bull markets also typically start with a different leadership. Yet in the substantial rallies that occurred in 2000, 2001 and 2002, technology and growth stocks led the way, particularly flaky little companies, including my old friend Pumatech. The rally continued into 2003 with the substantial outperformance of low-quality stocks. Investor confidence quickly bounced into top quartile levels and newsletter confidence rebounded to 1999 levels. Cash holdings in equity funds were also way below normal.

The scope of the speculation and the leadership of tech and the surviving internet stocks were just not typical of a new bull market. At least we old men remembered what a real bear market was like, and the young ones hadn't a clue. To my mind, this had all the indicators of a bear market rally. Except bear market rallies typically don't have legs. In the U.S. none had ever lasted more than a year. Except this one. As I told *Barron's* in November 2003: "The simple story is the market is overpriced… Currently, the market is around 24x trailing earnings, on a fairly generous earnings estimate. This is not just a bear market rally but the greatest sucker rally in history."

PRESIDENTIAL CYCLE

By now we were in the third year of the U.S. presidential cycle. This cycle had interested me since my Batterymarch days. The third year of a president's term had always been used by the administration to attempt to stimulate the economy by creating a favorable environment for re-election. For me, the presidential cycle started in 1932. Before then, the whole idea of stimulus hadn't sunk in. Keynes explained the concept and in Franklin Delano Roosevelt he found a very interested listener. From then on, administrations have understood it was a good idea to stimulate the economy in year three of the presidency, so that in year four, unemployment – and this is key – is dropping. It's fine to have a strong economy, but it is unemployment that really drives the vote, our research showed. The third year in a presidential cycle is not just a bull market year, but one with a bubbly zing to it in which growth wins over value.

Since 1932, in years one and two of the presidential term, the market had delivered 4.5 points *below* average, but in year three its return was eight points *above* average. What we found, too, is that the third year is fairly indifferent to value. Years one, two and four are reasonably sensitive to value. In year three, it doesn't matter whether the market is cheap, expensive or in between: the market seems to go up regardless. On cue, 2003 turned out to be a classic third year in the presidential cycle. The S&P climbed nearly 29%. Growth outperformed value, small cap did twice as well as usual, because it had the added kicker that small caps always do very well in the months following a low in the economy (and low-quality or junk does spectacularly).

This was all helped by the fact that the Fed was holding down interest rates at 40-year lows and strongly negative in real terms. Greenspan was promising to keep rates low for a long time. Investors realized they could leverage portfolios without too much risk. So determined was the language and action of the Fed that Stephen Roach at Morgan Stanley suggested that Greenspan was producing "chain-linked bubbles" (a mixed metaphor if ever there was one, but one that still worked beautifully). The result was that by late 2003 we were faced with substantially the worst investment prospects of my 35-year career. There were no longer any large asset classes to hide in, unlike March 2000, which offered up REITs, bonds (especially TIPS), small cap value everywhere and emerging country equities. Of that list, only emerging equities, despite their huge move, remained cheap, and only slightly cheap at that.

In my *Barron's* interview, I fretted about the debt problem. Normally, debt rises in bad times and falls in recoveries. What was unique to this cycle was that debt had not declined. It had, in fact, risen dramatically at the government level, quite dramatically at the corporate level and very substantially at the consumer level. I warned of painful years ahead, of a financial "black hole." I explained, "There is debt everywhere, and there are problems that have not been addressed, only postponed, by this administration and the Federal Reserve. In addition, we have a horrifically overpriced market. It is the third most expensive year ever recorded." Real estate, I said, had been like a cat with nine lives, escaping the last downturn unscathed. But now housing prices had risen to a multiple of incomes that appeared dangerously high.

QUALITY STOCKS

I was asked by *Barron's* in November 2003 whether I was still anti-blue chip stocks. To which I replied:

> I'm anti-blue chips in terms of absolute return. In terms of relative return, one of the places to hide in the U.S. market will be quality stocks. Quality stocks, whether large cap, or small or mid cap, provide noncontroversial, straightforward return on equity, stability of profits and balance sheet strength. Meat and potatoes. Those characteristics have underperformed continuously all year. This has been a junk year by every parameter.
>
> The net effect is that quality is already pretty cheap. If this bear market rally continues for quite a long time, then quality will become about as cheap or cheaper than it has ever been. In the event the market goes another leg down, accompanied perhaps

by some measures aimed at the overleverage in the system, quality could be a terrific defense against huge declines. Quality stocks will still go down, unfortunately. But they will provide real resistance to big declines.

Since my Batterymarch days, the investment attributes of companies with strong business models and high barriers to entry had entranced me. Quality was not a factor we had discovered. Moody's and Standard & Poor's had been ranking companies by quality for decades. But no one took any notice of them. Investors took a lot of notice of their bond ratings, but no notice of their stock ratings. Our great insight – a simple-minded insight but way ahead of the curve – was that a stable high return means profits regress very slowly. If you have no debt and a high and stable return, you are a price-setter. Why would your competitive advantage necessarily go away? It may go away very, very slowly, but surely. High quality moderates the rate of regression; low debt also moderates the rate of regression.

Both modern portfolio theory and common sense strongly suggest that quality stocks should be priced at a premium and return a little less than ordinary stocks. Theoretically, in return for accepting lower returns, clients get to own the most obviously successful companies in their portfolios. In the event of another 1932, these are the names that survive, as many did in fact survive the Great Depression. Yet in our dividend discount model, back in the day, quality averaged a little cheap most of the time, other than during the Nifty Fifty, which is a period so aberrant as to boggle the mind. It meant that quality stocks had slightly outperformed the market over at least the previous 40 years, beating the S&P index by nearly one percentage point a year. All of this outperformance came in months when the market was down. In other words, quality had a lower beta on the way down than it did on the way up. And investors didn't have to pay up for this protection.

This seemed to me perhaps the greatest inefficiency in the marketplace. Obviously, quality is like an investment-grade bond. If you buy a triple A bond, you expect to get a point less than if you buy a B bond. So how was it possible that when you bought a triple A-rated stock you outperformed? To needle the efficient market guys, I joked that quality as represented by the likes of Coca-Cola and Johnson & Johnson must be a hidden risk factor! In truth, I believed that quality outperformed due to behavioral factors, namely the willingness of investors to overpay for the rapid but volatile growth of lower-quality companies. In the end, growth is sexy. Cheap is also pretty sexy, at least to some of us. The great quality companies are rather staid in comparison. They are a bit dopey and boring and boring sells at a discount in the real world. Coca-Cola is boring. Pumatech is exciting. People overpay for excitement. Growth dazzles. So, investors have historically underpaid for boring old high-quality companies. Yet, they say the market is efficient. Beats me.

As I have mentioned, our early dividend discount model had a strong bias toward quality, which we defined as businesses with higher, more stable profits and less debt. Our aim was to identify the monopolies that wouldn't mean revert – the Microsofts of this world, which in the late 1990s we estimated to be worth 15x its book value. While conventional measures of value, based on P/B and P/E, favored junkier companies, our early model was dripping with quality. Its top decile of value had roughly the same quality as the S&P, which is a blue chip index. If you could find companies that have a really high return on capital and a low payout ratio, those companies are magic. Our back tests showed that this approach worked better than the rating agencies, whose models suffered from inertia and sometimes ranked businesses as triple A, such as Xerox, that were clearly in terminal decline.

By late 2003 I considered the creditworthiness of the secondary companies in America as almost terminally bad. My view was that if you had to be invested, quality was the best place to hide for the next market leg down. Because a lot of our funds were tied to benchmarks, there was a limit to how much they could tilt toward quality. So, in early 2004, GMO introduced its U.S. Quality Fund. The new fund owned no stocks with material debt and no small caps. Its largest positions were pretty obvious companies with global franchises.

In Asset Allocation we took initial small positions in the Quality Fund. The idea was to use quality to armor-plate our portfolios. Having less debt in this cycle appeared more important than it normally was. Typically, low debt is a distant third criterion, after high and stable profits. But in this credit-driven cycle we wanted to be more careful about debt levels. As I wrote in early 2004, quality "comes with absolutely no exposure to credit problems and consequently in any credit crisis will likely accrue a scarcity premium. In a severe market decline, the strategy should be a relative haven for those of us who have to invest in U.S. equities." Later, we implemented an override, excluding several banks from our list of quality stocks. Whether the clients liked it or not, I believed that we had to treat banks separately.

Equally important at the time was the fact that quality stocks were usefully cheaper than average after the great value rally that started in 2000. Quality was cheaper than it had been for 95% of the time since 1965. In all our funds, including emerging markets, we tried to increase the exposure to quality. We also ran a long quality/short junk bet in several of our hedge funds. This bet was the focus of the Tactical Opportunities Fund, run by Chuck Joyce; Yale was one of the first investors. In Asset Allocation we implemented the same bet, on a smaller scale, in our Mean Reversion Fund. This bet paid off handsomely in the market rout of 2008, when Tactical Opportunities and Mean Reversion returned over 36% and 18%, respectively.

By 2004, several of GMO's strategies were underperforming, once again. However, emerging and small cap international had brilliant returns over two years, and Asset Allocation enjoyed its fifth consecutive good year. This was atypical and in a sense, lucky. Every time I went out to talk to the brokers, I had to tell them, dudes, do not count on us doing this. Our value stance meant we expected to win in a falling market and lose on a rising one. I said this over and over again, but they never listened. The fact that we were winning steadily in a bull market was a minor miracle.

We were taking less risk than competitors but not eschewing risk entirely. The purist's investment position was clear: when the market is overpriced investors should duck. The problem with this position, as we had painfully learned over and over again, is that an overpriced market can really run, and this overpriced market had quite a lot going for it in the near term. The pragmatic position, which I hoped was not too greedy, was that because moral hazard was still out there, careful and balanced risk-taking was the percentage shot.

HOUSING BUBBLES

The essence of the Fed's moral hazard was to create an environment conducive to debt expansion, with the unspoken promise that there would be no negative consequence from more debt, at least for the "foreseeable future." Easy credit and low rates were designed to offset the negative effects on the economy of the bubble breaking. Probably the most effective component of the program was the enormous increase in mortgage refinancings. An incipient housing bubble was evident to all, except perhaps the denizens of the Federal Reserve. On Friday, April 16, 2004, *The New York Times* reported that the price of Manhattan apartments was up a stunning 35% year on year.

Our research showed that house prices mean revert around a trend multiple of household income. Our London quants reviewed the data and found, to my mild surprise, that for the previous 45 years there had been no clear upward trend in this ratio. By 2004, U.S. median home prices as a multiple of household income had risen from their long-term average to more than two standard deviations above the mean, which by our normal definition meant it was already in bubble territory. In my third quarterly letter that year, I warned that there had never been a more broadly overpriced mix of assets. "The housing market," I wrote, "is also clearly overstimulated through prolonged easy and cheap credit and contains a real threat to consumption when home prices finally fall off even a little. A major potential risk is that a combination of price weakness in financial assets and price weakness in housing, both resulting from overpricing, will coincide with some financial crisis, even a minor one."

Early the following year, I traveled around the world for the first time – 19 flights in 35 days – mostly on business, and I could not help noticing a few things. First, you should travel east to west. Yes, it's 10 or 12 hours longer flying time, but jet lag kicks in at around 6 p.m. at your new location when nobody cares if you're whacked. Traveling the other way, I found myself continually trying to talk to a group of analysts or clients at 4:15 a.m. on my internal clock. And as soon as I had adjusted, I moved on again. The other thing I couldn't avoid noticing was the attention given to house prices in the three main English-speaking countries that I visited. New Zealand residential real estate was up over 20% in the last two years, and it was rumored that Sydney had pushed San Francisco out of the champion's spot in the "Who's got the lowest return for renting the house?" contest. I was quoted in *The Australian Financial Review* commenting that the Australian residential real estate market could be the canary in the coal mine – that is, a harbinger of bad things to come for a lot of us. Sydney house prices had risen earlier, faster and further than any other. This was not a topic that Australians were happy to discuss. Tell a Brit you think they're in a housing bubble, and you'll have a discussion. Tell an Australian, and you'll have World War III. They hate you. They will hate you for years!

Increasing paper wealth from rising house prices had more than offset the negative wealth effect from the stock market declines of 2000 through 2002. Alan Greenspan may have been impressed by the increases in household financial strength caused by higher house prices, but any believer in replacement value could not be, and I was certainly one of them. When the price of a chemical company's stock doubles, I always urge people to focus on its more or less unchanged replacement value and not the change in its paper value. How much easier it was to see this effect with changes in house valuations: the price of my house in Boston might have tripled in the previous 10 years, but the flow of actual services that it offered me was clearly unchanged. It still protected me from the wind and the rain as before, in fact, slightly less well because it was now older.

My best guess at the time was that U.S. house prices would peak over the coming year. By early 2005, it was clear that several cities that had appreciated the most on the way up were now flat to down on a rolling month-to-month basis. And more cities were showing rising inventories of unsold houses. In both September and November, U.S. median home prices, seasonally adjusted, started to fall. This peak was six months earlier than I had predicted at the beginning of the previous year.

My concern was that housing prices would eventually retreat to trend, and this would cause the credit expansion to stop and quite possibly to reverse. By this date, the credit cycle was also turning down as interest rates had been raised, although they remained far lower than normal and were therefore still stimulative. Moral hazard was being removed equally carefully as evidenced by the sprinkling of a few cautious comments from the Fed's interest-setting committee, which warned that sustained easy money "might be" encouraging "potentially excessive risk taking" and pushing up asset prices (they noticed!).

In my quarterly letter of October 2005, I reversed FDR's famous exhortation, warning clients: "You Have Nothing to Fear but the Lack of Fear." By this time, even Greenspan was shocked and awed by the lowest premiums on risky assets recorded in modern times. "History," he had recently commented, "cautions that extended periods of low concern about credit risk have been invariably followed by reversal, with an attendant fall in the prices of risky assets." Given, in my opinion, the Fed chairman had produced most of the fuel for the credit boom and thrown it on the fire himself, his newfound concerns got him my Chutzpah Award for 2005.

In January 2006, after 18 interminable years, Alan Greenspan finally retired as Fed chairman. There was no cause for celebration. In fact, for those of us who feared the long-term consequences of moral hazard and believed that a greater degree of concern with major asset class bubbles was warranted, the news was entirely bleak. His replacement, Ben Bernanke, appeared to be an unreconstructed Greenspan, in spades. In his academic career, Bernanke had become an expert on the early 1930s. For me, however, he was a guy who had studied the Great Depression and drew all the wrong conclusions, because he showed no interest at all in the speculative bubbles in real estate and stocks that preceded the economic collapse.

Known as "Helicopter Ben" for his 2002 comments about dropping money by helicopter if necessary, Bernanke did not get his nickname by sounding like he would remove all traces of moral hazard. "For the Fed to interfere with security speculation," he had said in 2004, "is neither desirable nor feasible," but "if a sudden correction in asset prices does occur, the Fed's first responsibility is to protect... to provide ample liquidity until the crisis has passed." This was as pure a statement of moral hazard as you could have. As for the real estate bubble, Bernanke sounded utterly complacent. At least Greenspan, toward the end of his tenure, had warned about "the enormous increase in housing prices." Bernanke, by contrast, declared in late 2005 that high real estate prices merely "reflect strong economic fundamentals." At the time the average U.S. house price as a multiple of family income was over two standard deviations overpriced. Nor was Bernanke any more sympathetic to the view that low risk premiums posed a danger to risk assets, commenting a few months earlier that "Risk premiums [on U.S. stocks] look quite normal." As the former head of the Princeton economics department ascended to the Fed throne, I wrote "The Bernanke put is alive and well. And where it leads no one can tell." In fact, within GMO we were beginning to have a strong conviction as to where it was leading. And it was nowhere good.

Going into 2006, my investment recommendations were to be as underweight as possible in U.S. equities and to shift money into cash, plus anything that might do a little bit better than cash, including conservative hedge funds. In the first quarter, we started to trim our big bet on emerging equities, reducing the position down by one-third after our emerging fund had delivered 40% over the previous 12 months. To a degree I had never seen before, the U.S. equity market appeared completely unimpressed with the growing list of negatives, among them: steadily rising interest rates, soaring oil prices, decreasing global liquidity and an apparent topping out of the Anglo-Saxon housing markets. In the past, a rapid surge in oil price alone had been a horrifically accurate warning of impending weakness in the economy.

In the Looney Tunes cartoons, the admirably persistent assailant, Wile E. Coyote, is still racing off the end of the road, over the cliff and halfway out across the chasm as Road Runner hides behind a tree. But however narrow the chasm, the coyote never makes it more than halfway across before he looks down and realizes the ugly truth and, losing heart, falls like a stone. This is what the market in early 2006 felt like to me, although it lacked Wile E.'s frenzy. It was as if the coyote this time was strolling out across the bottomless pit without a care in the world, whistling and looking up at the birds.

The only good news, as far as I could see, were soaring profit margins. Profits had benefited in the U.S. from a phase of rapid outsourcing. Initially, outsourcing had had a large positive effect on margins as the first outsourcer to, say, China, pocketed some of the reduction in costs as extra profits and displaced domestic workers helped keep labor costs down. Most importantly, the last 20 years had been uniquely favorable to financial profits, which had expanded thanks to a stable economy, easy money and moral hazard. Banks were enjoying close to zero write-downs for bad debts. In total, the financial sector's share of corporate profits had risen from about 15% in 1980 to over 30% in 2006. Not bad for a sector that makes not a single widget, and in the case of our own sub-sector – money management – in aggregate delivers zero value-added even before counting management fees and transaction costs.

LET'S ALL LOOK LIKE YALE

My advice to clients in early 2006 was to diversify across all asset classes, insofar as was possible. "The conventional view on this," I wrote, "can be summed up basically as 'don't put all your eggs in one basket.' The academic view comes to the same conclusion, albeit with a lot more math." But diversification had itself become caught up in the risk bubble.

Like most in our business, I was an admirer of David Swensen, the Chief Investment Officer of Yale University. David was also a good friend to GMO. His 2005 book, *Unconventional Success*, raked through the rather thick layer of muck at the bottom of the money management industry in great detail. To my mind, Swensen revealed the truth, the whole truth and the very ugly truth. He had enjoyed great investment success over the years by diversifying the endowment across illiquid and liquid asset classes. The trouble was that too many investors were now imitating the Yale model.

By this date, the top U.S. university endowments – of which Yale's was the most celebrated – had outperformed the average pension fund during the previous decade or so by an astounding 5% a year. That outperformance set off a stampede to copy them. Because it was hard to copy Yale's resources, talent and independence, the copying focused on increasing diversification. Remarkably, 15 years earlier, endowments invested about 85% of their money in U.S. blue chips and bonds. In fact, starting in 1980, we had sold almost all the Ivy League endowments their very first specialized foreign equity funds. It is hard to imagine their prior level of conservatism. In contrast, by 2006 they had become the cutting edge of investment management, led, it seemed, by Swensen's example at Yale. On average, they now had less than 30% in these "old-fashioned" assets. Instead, their money was flowing into newer and more exotic asset classes, like emerging equity, forestry and, above all, "alternative investments," notably private equity, venture capital and hedge funds.

The change in the style of portfolio management ran straight into the comparative illiquidity of many of these new asset classes. Even more troubling was the fact that when everyone imitated Yale, using leverage, the price of every asset was driven too high. The formerly large gap between the yields on alternatives and traditional assets had declined. Indeed, in some cases like private equity, it seemed to have produced extreme overpricing. Investors had forgotten that all these fashionable, repackaged assets were still part of a zero-sum game and their higher fees must, in aggregate, deliver lower returns for the investment community as a whole. Throughout 2006, however, flows into non-traditional areas showed no sign of abating despite their ridiculously small risk premia. As I wrote in my October letter ("Let's All Look Like Yale"): "With bad luck, it will help produce a major credit and asset pricing crisis. Bravery will most definitely be called for in our new world. Caution would be a good idea too."

THE WORLD'S FIRST TRULY GLOBAL BUBBLE

The two necessary conditions for a bubble to form are quite simple. First, fundamental economic conditions must look at least excellent – and near perfect is better. Second, liquidity must be generous in quantity and cost: it must be easy and cheap to leverage. If these two conditions had ever been present without causing a bubble it has escaped my attention. Bubbles, of course, are based on human behavior, and the mechanism is surprisingly simple: perfect conditions create very strong "animal spirits," which are reflected statistically in a low risk premium. It may be superfluous to add that if we find ourselves in near-perfect conditions, history tells us that we extrapolate those conditions forever. This will get us to the same point.

Widely available cheap credit offers investors the opportunity to act on their optimism. Sustained strong fundamentals and sustained easy credit go one better; they allow for continued reinforcement: the more leverage you take, the better you do; the better you do, the more leverage you take. A critical part of a bubble is the reinforcement you get for your optimistic view from those around you. And, of course, this is helped along by the finance industry, broadly defined, that makes more money when optimism and activity are high. Hence, it has every incentive to support rising markets.

Low interest rates were contributing to a reduction in economic and financial volatility. Investors responded to these new conditions by increasing their risk exposure. To my mind this was mistaken. In the investment world, the most accepted definition of risk is volatility. We can all agree that the degree to which a stock or asset class bounces around its long-term trend is an important part of risk. Some of us, however, think this is an incomplete definition as it ignores both valuation and liquidity. The most popular technique for measuring risk in the run-up to the financial crisis was called value at risk (VAR). This measure purported to come up with a precise estimate of the probability of portfolio losses, based on historical price trends and volatilities. But those using a VAR model were driven to consider the stock market over time as having the same risk regardless of price. So, the U.S. stock market selling at 8x earnings in 1982 was deemed to have the same risk as when it sold at over 30x earnings in 2000.

In my view, the problem with using volatility as a complete measure of risk is that it exaggerates the market's usual tendency to extrapolate present conditions rather than to assume current conditions will tend to regress to normal. Thus, the extremely low volatility during the so-called "Great Moderation" of the early 2000s was seen as predicting that the market would have low risk into the indefinite future. Because volatility was very low, portfolios that in the past would have been considered very risky were considered acceptable.

Hyman Minsky, the sadly neglected economist, had said famously that "stability is unstable." What he meant was that long periods of stability, like the run-up to 2008, cause leverage and other risk-taking to grow until investors use up all the risk units freed up by the greater stability. This process can go on and on until finally something goes badly wrong and all the excessive risk-taking is revealed. The boss of a Midwestern pension fund echoed this attitude in 2005 when he was quoted in *The Wall Street Journal* as saying that he was reaching for risk because it was getting hard for him to use up all his available risk units in what he saw as a decreasingly risky environment. In my January 2006 letter, I pointed out that:

> Since we have never had such a long, drawn-out period of falling inflation, falling interest rates, rising market prices in all three great asset classes, and above all, explicit moral hazard delivered in person by the Fed's boss, we are looking at possibly the greatest opportunity to test Hyman Minsky's theory: we have had an unprecedented long period of good and stable times and we have responded by taking out unprecedented levels of debt leverage. The good news is we are engaged in an exciting real-life experiment for which there is no clear precedent. Guinea pigs of the world, unite! We have nothing to lose but our shirts!

This time, everyone, everywhere was reinforcing one another. My April 2007 letter was entitled, "It's Everywhere, In Everything: The First Truly Global Bubble." I wrote, "From Indian antiquities to modern Chinese art; from land in Panama to Mayfair; from forestry, infrastructure and the junkiest bonds to mundane blue chips; it's bubble time!" Wherever I traveled I heard it confirmed that "they don't make any more land," and that "with these growth rates and low interest rates, equity markets must keep rising," and "private equity will continue to drive the markets."

To say the least, there had never ever been anything like the uniformity of this reinforcement. Not a single country anywhere – emerging or developed – out of 42 listed by *The Economist* was growing its GDP by less than Switzerland's 2.2%. This amazingly uniform strength was yet another sign of how globalized and correlated fundamentals had become, as well as the financial markets that reflected them. The results were quite predictable and consistent: all three major asset classes – real estate, stocks and bonds – were expensive compared with their histories and compared with replacement cost wherever it could be calculated. The risk premium had reached a historic low everywhere.

In modern portfolio theory, the efficient frontier describes a set of investments that provide the highest return for a given level of risk. This is typically presented in chart form, with the assets' expected return (based on historic average) shown on the vertical axis and risk (as measured by annualized volatility) on the horizontal

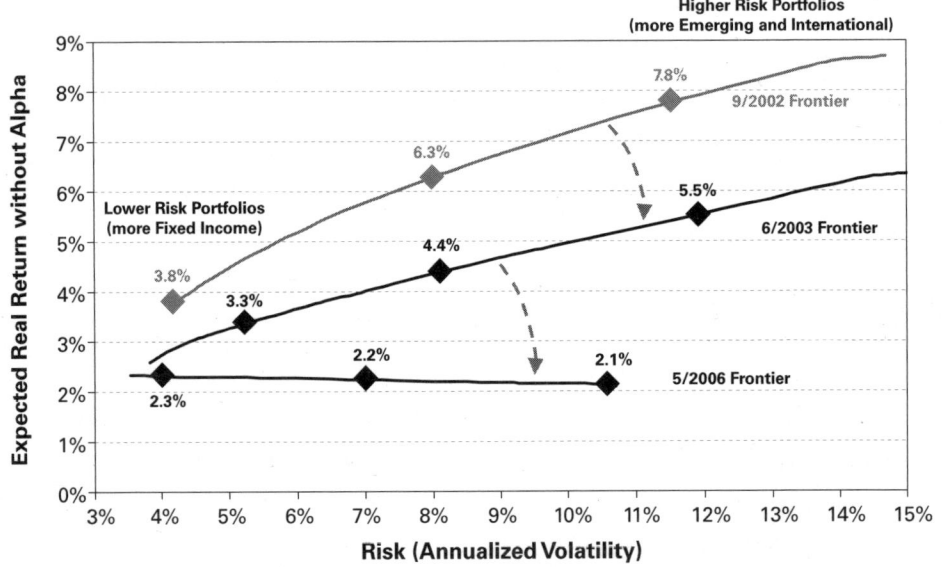

2006's inverted risk curve. GMO's housing-bubble era exhibit, published in our April 2007 quarterly letter, showing how forecast forward-looking returns across financial assets had fallen over the previous four years, with the forecasts for the riskiest assets falling the most – to such an extent that by mid-2006 riskier assets were generally lower-returning than safer assets. This was another indication, along with house prices, of irrational investor behavior and a risk bubble spanning asset classes. Data from GMO, 2006 axis. An upward-sloping curve links the various asset classes, from low-risk cash at the bottom left of the chart to higher-risk assets, such as corporate bonds and equities, at the top right. At GMO, we constructed a novel efficient frontier by substituting our own seven-year asset class forecasts for historic returns. The gap between our low- and high-risk portfolios on our seven-year forecast in September 2002 was 6.4% points and by May 2006 it was down to a paltry 0.8%. If we were correct (as indeed we were soon shown to be), then investors were actually paying for the privilege of taking risk. "If you believed this data," I wrote that September, "you should, of course, put all your money in cash."

In summary, I pointed out that global credit was more extended and more complicated than ever before and that no one could be sure where all the increased risk had ended up. But every bubble had always burst and this one would be no different:

> The bursting of the bubble will be across all countries and all assets, with the probable exception of high grade bonds. Risk premiums in particular will widen. Since no similar global event has occurred before, the stresses to the system are likely to be unexpected. All of this is likely to depress confidence and lower economic activity. Naturally the Fed and Fed equivalents overseas will move to contain the economic damage as the Fed did last time after the 2000 break.

Up to this time no areas of this unprecedented global bubble had yet gone hyperbolic, as the internet and tech stocks did in 1999. By summer, however, the growth rate of leveraged loans that were used to finance buyouts was running 60% up on the previous year. That number rang a painful bell as it was about the same percentage rise year over year as the internet and tech stocks delivered in 1999. Just as press coverage in 1999 had been dominated by news and gossip about internet and tech companies and the leaders who ran them, now the news was full of stories about private equity heroes and particularly the vast wealth they had acquired and the low taxes they paid, but also the splendid parties they gave. The nice coincidence of some very visible public offerings, notably that of Blackstone, the leading buyout firm, underlined the immense scale of the new wealth. All this appeared to me as an important watershed event, a defining moment of the global financial bubble.

I had the feeling of watching a very slow-motion train wreck. By the summer of 2007, the subprime disease – best characterized as the questioning of the market's previously blind faith – was gradually spreading, with a little widening of the junk bond spread here and a little tightening of private equity credit there. Still, the equity market seemed totally unaffected with volatile and risky stocks still making the running. I likened the situation to a brontosaurus that had been bitten on the tail, but the message has not yet reached its tiny brain, but instead was proceeding up the long backbone, one vertebra at a time. Steadily increasing mortgage defaults were making it harder for house prices to stabilize. The inventory of unsold houses was growing. Yet we were told on all sides, even by the Secretary of the Treasury, that the problems in the subprime market were "contained." My response, in my July letter was: "We have to wonder if the container, in this case, will turn out to be Pandora's."

I remained guardedly optimistic that the worst-case outcome could still be avoided, writing that:

> The global financial market seems like a giant suspension bridge with complicated engineering. Thousands of bolts hold it together. Today a few of them have fractures and one or two seem to have failed completely. The bridge, however, with typical redundancy

built in, can take a few failed bolts, perhaps quite a few. And only with bad luck will some of them line up in a dangerous enough sequence to bring a major strut down. This global financial structure is far too large and has far too many interlocking pieces for weakening U.S. house prices and a few subprime issues to bring it down. No, what we have to worry about is whether we are reaching a broad-based level of financial metal fatigue in which bolt after bolt will fail with ultimately disastrous consequences. The scary part is that this global financial structure is faith-based, held together by unprecedented amounts of animal spirits. If the faith starts to fail it is, "*sauve qui peut*" (the old cry as a ship foundered), or "every man for himself."

As it turned out, I was far too optimistic.

THREE NEAR CERTAINTIES

In my July 7 letter, I also predicted that within five years at least one major bank (broadly defined) would fail. This comment was widely cited in the press. Two months later, in September 2007, *Fortune* magazine ran a comment by me in which I described the three near certainties that I anticipated were about to hit the financial markets. First, house prices were in genuine bubble territory in the U.S., Britain and elsewhere. "From these high levels," I wrote, "prices are guaranteed to fall. In doing so, they will reduce consumer borrowing and spending power. They will also increase mortgage defaults, most of which lie ahead, and lower financial profits and confidence." Second, I noted that profit margins, then at record levels around the world, would certainly fall, as profits reverted to the mean. Third, and most important, I predicted that risk would soon be repriced.

But the market was not interested in bad news. In August 2007, the S&P and Nasdaq indexes climbed to new post-2000 highs after the Fed announced a big rate cut. Around that time I read in the *Financial Times* that corporate profit margins were taking a hit from the economic slowdown. This sent me into a rare panic because a decline in profit margins is typically a powerful confidence killer. On hearing this news, I barged into our offices on the Boston waterfront totally agitated, as though the firm had only minutes to shift our assets around before a market blow-up. But nothing happened. Two or three days, nothing. A month, nothing. I was embarrassed in front of our younger troops and felt like an idiot. As I took a break on the beaches of Mexico with my family over the Christmas holidays, the markets digested all the dire economic data coming in and finally began to convulse. The stock market brontosaurus that had happily ignored the several stings on its tail over the last year from real estate and structured debt and the sharp bite on its tail from collapsing profit margins finally let out a loud "Ouch!"

QUANTS IN TROUBLE

For once we had nailed the major issues (my three near certainties) in a year. You might have thought, therefore, that GMO had a brilliant year. But this was not the case. In general, we had a poor year. In our desire to have more of our fixed income team's enviable alpha in Asset Allocation, we had reached for too much of it and found that our holdings of asset-backed securities showed growing losses, at least on a mark-to-market basis.

Quants everywhere were in trouble. The good old days of the domination of the first generation quant models, where you simply showed up with three concepts – value, momentum and discipline – were over. Ten years earlier the investment world had been dominated by traditional stock pickers. Now multiples of the quant assets and talent of those years (perhaps 20 or 30 times) fought for an edge. It had never been easy to find quantitative edges. There are simply not that many. Quant investors were now crowded into a handful of variables with predictable results: outperformance had gotten a lot tougher.

GMO's equity strategies hit several headwinds. First, we were predominantly value managers and "value" by early 2007 had overrun its normal range, not surprisingly after seven consecutive strong years. Second, there were the difficult shivers that ran through many quant portfolios in the summer, caused by the rise in volatility and the overcrowded quant turf. This affected us, albeit less than most. But, even more critically, there had been a need for a judgmental override of traditional investment discipline when faced with a rare macro event.

Optimal investing seems to be a mix of a few important judgmental overrides interspersed with long periods of cold, disciplined blocking and tackling. But who was to do this? Overriders like to "use their brains" all the time, even on small issues, which can be a weakness. But quants tend to shrug off outliers. They like to argue that overriding their models to deal with outliers sets a bad precedent and that in the long run they are better off sticking with their disciplines. After all, they've been optimized with over 40 years of data. But occasionally something very big and important hasn't happened in the period contained in their models.

If an unforeseen, outlying event takes place – a "Black Swan," as Nassim Taleb's best-selling book termed it – the vaunted model often does not know how to react. The banking crisis was one of those outliers. Quant models had not calculated how to deal with a housing decline of 25% to 30%, for instance, or a credit crisis of global proportions. As I had often said, quants like to show off their discipline by marching off the cliff in rows. During 2007 the quants and their mathematical trading models were humiliated in dramatic fashion.

January 2008 turned out to be one of the more exciting months in my investing career. By some measures, I had never seen the likes of it. In this business, I was in constant dread of being bored to death. So, for me, the credit crunch was intellectually challenging and exciting. If you liked to have real problems, this was absolute heaven. The experience was a little bit like *Alien*, my favorite horror movie: in equal measures terrifying and thrilling, as the enemy threat is never truly exterminated. Every minute is something you have to watch through your fingers.

I started getting a lot of attention in the media for my prescient warnings. A French newspaper described me as "*la légende de Wall Street qui a prévu la crise.*" Yet my insights were not original. As I said at the time, the financial crisis was the most widely predicted surprise in finance. Almost everyone we dealt with at GMO saw it coming. In fact, my own super-bearish views turned out to be insufficiently pessimistic. My "very slow motion train wreck" was misjudged: "Train hits end of track at full speed" would have been more like it, perhaps with the sub-heading, "Several killed and hundreds hurt, but survivors showered with government aid."

In the first week of the year, quality stocks leapt into battle, opening up a 3.5% lead over the S&P. As I'd expected, many players were caught with risk levels far above their desired level and were now forced to cut back on leverage and risk in general. The Minsky Meltdown had finally arrived, and as one shoe after another of the market centipede dropped on to the floor, we waited for many more. As I wrote in January 2008: "This is the most important U.S. financial crisis since World War II: it is of course far more global than previous crises, with tentacles reaching everywhere, and it coincides with a broad overpricing of assets." Having predicted a major bank would fail within four or five years, we only had to wait six months for Bear Stearns, the fifth largest investment bank in the U.S., to be rescued from the financial abyss by the U.S. Federal Reserve and J.P. Morgan. Goldman Sachs was now predicting that bank write-downs could amount to $500 billion. Knowing Goldman's conservatism, I decided to double that figure, anticipating that "by the end of this credit crisis, perhaps better defined as a sloppy-debt-issuing crisis, we will be lucky if the amount of write-downs does not start with a 'T.'" Again, I couldn't claim clairvoyance. All I knew was that in previous banking crises, major banks had failed, and this crisis seemed likely, to us semi-pros, to be worse than most. So, I studied previous crises in broad strokes and armchaired that I should up the ante. I got lucky in an area in which I was not a real expert.

ABANDON SHIP

My investment advice remained unchanged: take as little risk as possible. If you had to take any risk, I recommended holding U.S. quality stocks and also some emerging equities. The previous year, we had sold a third of our emerging stocks. I still believed that emerging markets had the potential to trade at a premium to the developed markets because they had less debt and better growth prospects. At the time, emerging was expensive, but less so than anything else, and the fundamentals appeared to me so much superior to the rest of the world. I ventured that emerging was likely to form the next bubble.

That summer I changed my mind. In early July, a Scottish economist for an Asian broker, Jim Walker, visited our Boston offices. Walker reminded me of an old-fashioned Presbyterian preacher, with his wild beard and doom-laden intonations. He was predicting the end of the world and laid out the 13 reasons why we should avoid emerging. Bang, bang, bang, bang, bang, bang. I had already considered many of these 13 reasons, and a few others, but had done so on an individual basis. As I sat there listening to this litany of woes I realized that having them all occur *together* was so much worse. In a flash, I understood that I had been making a little allowance here and there for emerging, and had accumulated far more allowance than was justified. I had felt that although we were the bears, we should not have to be 100% bearish. And emerging equities was our single bullish bet. Now, it dawned on me that their situation was substantially worse than I had been representing. Economically, most emerging countries really looked to have decoupled for the past 18 months as the U.S. slowed. But in a global recession no one decouples. Now was the time to batten down the hatches.

On July 15, I sent out a quarterly letter to clients. We had been against taking risk for quite a while, I wrote, but we had advised that if you had an itch to be invested, do it in emerging. We now recanted completely. It was time to abandon ship. Things were going to be a lot worse than we thought they were:

> There is, though, one important change in our outlook for emerging market equities… I now realize that in an unexpectedly bad global economy, the combination of rising inflation, commodity dependence and particularly high export ratios leave them more vulnerable than I had thought… To this end, we have done an about-face and lowered our weightings in emerging equities to neutral or just below. To critics of this change, I would cite the quote attributed to Keynes, caught in the same predicament: "When the facts change, I change my mind – what do you do, sir?"… for those who can keep some of their powder dry, there

are likely to be much better investment opportunities in a year or two (or three) than we have seen for 20 years. Our motto should be: Don't be brave, run away. Live to fight another day.

A week or so later I get a call from the people at Singapore's sovereign wealth fund, GIC, an important client of ours. They're all on the telephone and we talk for a couple of hours, and they end up in an intractable disagreement: they were caught between their own overexposure to risk, on the one hand, and the danger of "market-timing," or overreaction to bad news, on the other. Later, they told me that they had gone to the chairman, Lee Kuan Yew, the father of modern Singapore, whose official role at the time was Minister Mentor. They had never before gone to the boss for advice. He was seen as far above usual investment concerns. But he was technically the head of GIC and had a great reputation for wisdom. And they were stuck. So, on this unique occasion they asked him for advice. He listened to the story and said words (to the effect), "I'm not an expert. Obviously, this is important because you've never sought my advice before and now you have. And my perception is you are not asking to do something risky. Quite the reverse. You're asking to do something unusually conservative. So you should do it." And they did. They reduced their market exposure and their investment leader later told me by his back-of-the-envelope calculation they avoided some $17 billion of potential losses. A year or so later, I was invited to GIC's 25th anniversary celebration, along with Ray Dalio and a couple of Wall Street economists. They gave us each a silver replica of a $100 Singapore bill with a piece of paper saying it was legal tender, which was cool.

By the summer of 2008, the fundamentals were turning out worse than I had anticipated. "I am officially scared," I told the assembled investment professionals at the Morningstar Conference in Chicago toward the end of July. When asked by a money manager what I would buy now, I suggested "long mattresses" to store cash. More seriously, I advised, "Put money into something incredibly safe, like a high-quality hedge fund." I confessed to the group that I had bought my first gold the previous week, and I had always hated gold. It doesn't pay a dividend. I would only buy it if I were desperate. And believe me, by this date, I was quite desperate. On a much bigger scale I adopted the best anti-risk bet I could think of – namely, short British pounds and long Japanese yen, the reverse of the popular "carry trades" that had proliferated in recent years.

"Reaping the Whirlwind" was the title of my October letter, published a few weeks after Lehman's demise:

> The combination of favorable conditions and irrationally exuberant encouragement from the authorities produced a poisonous bubble in risk-taking itself… The icing on the cake as far as the bust is concerned has been provided by Buffett's "financial weapons of mass destruction" – the new sliced and diced packages of loan material so complicated that, shall we say, few understood them. The uncertainties and doubts generated by their complexities were impressive. Trust and confidence are the keys to our elaborate financial structure, which is ultimately faith-based. The current hugely increased doubt is a potential lethal blow to the system and must be addressed at any cost as fast as possible. Concern about moral hazard is secondary and must be put into abeyance for the time being.

The greatest sucker rally in history was finally over. The only market bubble of 28 tracked by GMO that had not broken all the way back to pre-existing trend lines had mean reverted. By our calculation, the fair value on the S&P index was about 1025. In my October letter, I wrote: "We can say that, with the S&P at 900, stocks are cheap in the U.S. and cheaper still overseas. We will therefore be steady buyers at these prices. Not necessarily rapid buyers, in fact probably not, but steady buyers. But we have no illusions. Timing is difficult and is apparently not usually our skill set, although we got desperately and atypically lucky moving rapidly to an underweight in emerging equities three months ago."

I predicted at the time that the S&P would likely bottom out in the 600 to 800 range within the next two years. "All too easily," I wrote, "we forget that you can compound wealth rapidly only by having cheap assets. For those with a long horizon, it is always better to have assets fall in price so that the compounding returns are higher. For an unparalleled 20 years, global equities, especially U.S. equities, had been overpriced. Now, finally, they are cheap and likely to get cheaper. Likely, I believe, to set up a once-in-a-lifetime investing opportunity (or maybe twice in a long career). It was time to use some of our dry powder.... After all, if stocks are attractive and you don't buy and they run away, you don't just look like an idiot, you are an idiot." It was around this date that we started repurchasing those emerging stocks at roughly half the price we had sold them only a few months earlier.

REINVESTING WHEN TERRIFIED

Most investment strategists had been more or less "permabulls" over the previous decade. By contrast, I had often been accused of being a permabear. Of course, we so-called "permabears" are criticized because negativity is off-putting to most investors. Sometimes the accusation became downright abusive. Back in the spring of 2004, the investor Kenneth Fisher wrote a rousing bullish article in *Forbes* that the bull market would not end until some notorious bears like Bill Gross and me took some public abuse. My first thought was that it was comforting to be tarred with the same brush as Pimco's Bond King. My second, which I put into my quarterly letter, was that I didn't think the bear market that began in March 2000 would end until one or two of the notorious public bulls claimed to have predicted this long, two-legged bear market all along.

Yet when the Global Financial Crisis arrived, ironically for a permabear, it turned out I had underestimated in almost every way how badly economic and financial fundamentals would deteriorate. Our 10-year forecast for the S&P 500 from September 1998 was a lowly −1.1% real return from U.S. equities, which was an extreme outlier among forecasts. At the end of September 2008 the real 10-year return came to exactly zero. But it only took three days in October to hit our −1.1% forecast on the nose! After which the market continued falling. In fact, we overestimated the returns for global equities, except for emerging, where we were more or less spot on.

I took immense pleasure in highlighting the successful outcome of our forecasts from the bubble era. As Zero Mostel says in Mel Brooks's film *The Producers* as he looks down at the yellow Rolls-Royce parked outside his office: "That's the way, baby. When you've got it, flaunt it!" It also gave me ammunition to use against the "notorious bear" label that a journalist had recently given me. The truth is I didn't want to be seen as a bear or a "perma" anything. Rather, I am contrarian by nature and professional inclination and had always taken pleasure in telling it differently. I'm also a stickler when it comes to avoiding overpriced stocks. And that meant I could be wildly bullish at times – as I had been in 1982 at the start of the great bull market or when raving about real estate and emerging markets in 2002. After 14 years of an overpriced S&P, I felt like a permabear just as I had felt like a permabull as the underpricing of the market started to end in the early 1980s.

I had said as far back as 1999, while suffering from selling too soon, that my next big mistake would be buying too soon. This probably sounded ridiculous given my bearish reputation, but I meant it. After Lehman's bankruptcy, I believed that the crisis would take longer than normal to play out. But I also believed that equity prices were starting to overreact to bad news. U.S. house prices, the trigger for our present woes, had fallen back in line with their long-term trend. In February, GMO lifted its Global Balanced Fund weighting in equities from 40% to 55%. Our intention was to move slowly to a neutral weighting of 65% by the summer if stock prices stayed slightly cheap. Over the course of that month, however, the market fell like a rock. On March 4, 2009, with the S&P benchmark trading below 700, I sent a one-page letter to the *Wall Street Journal* entitled "Reinvesting When Terrified." The newspaper sat on my letter for three long business days. Feeling that time was precious, and encouraged by my PR advisor, Tucker Hewes, we pulled the letter and posted it on our website. It was one of only two letters I have ever written that was not an official "quarterly." Below is the full text:

> It was psychologically painful in 1999 to give up making money on the way up and to expose yourself to the career risk that comes with looking like an old fuddy-duddy. Similarly today, it is both painful and career risky to part with your increasingly beloved cash, particularly because cash has been so hard to raise in this market of unprecedented illiquidity. As this crisis climaxes, formerly reasonable people will start to predict the end of the world, armed with plenty of terrifying and accurate data that will serve to reinforce the wisdom of your caution. Every decline will enhance the beauty of cash until, as some of us experienced in

1974, "terminal paralysis" sets in. Those who were over invested will be catatonic and just sit and pray. Those few who look brilliant, oozing cash, will not want to easily give up their brilliance. So almost everyone is watching and waiting with their inertia beginning to set like concrete. Typically, those with a lot of cash will miss a very large chunk of the market recovery.

There is only one cure for terminal paralysis: you absolutely must have a battle plan for reinvestment and stick to it. Because every action must overcome paralysis, what I recommend is a few large steps, not many small ones. A single giant step at the low would be nice, but without holding a signed contract with the devil, several big moves would be safer. This is what we have been doing at GMO. We made one very large reinvestment move in October, taking us to about halfway between neutral and minimum equities, and we have a schedule for further moves contingent on future market declines. It is particularly important to have a clear definition of what it will take for you to be fully invested. Without a similar program, be prepared for your committee's enthusiasm to invest (and your own for that matter) to fall with the market. You must get them to agree now – quickly before rigor mortis sets in – for we are entering that zone as I write. *Remember that you will never catch the low.* Sensible value-based investors will always sell too early in bubbles and buy too early in busts. But in return, you may make some important extra money on the roundtrip as well as lowering the average risk exposure.

For the record, we now believe the S&P is worth 900 at fair value or 30% above today's price. Global equities are even cheaper. (Our estimates of current value are based on the assumption of normal P/Es being applied to normal profit margins.) Our 7-year estimated returns for the various equity categories are in the +10 to +13% range after inflation based on an assumption of a 7-year move from today's environment back to normal conditions. This compares to a year ago when they were all negative! Unfortunately it also compares to a +15% forecast at the 1974 low, and because of that our guess is that there is still a 50/50 chance of crossing 600 on the S&P 500.

Life is simple: if you invest too much too soon you will regret it; "How could you have done this with the economy so bad, the market in free fall, and the history books screaming about over-runs?" On the other hand, if you invest too little after talking about handsome potential returns and the market rallies, you deserve to be shot. We have tried to model these competing costs and regrets. You should try to do the same. If you can't, a simple clear battle plan – even if it comes directly from your stomach – will be far better in a meltdown than none at all. Perversely, seeking for optimality is a snare and delusion; it will merely serve to increase your paralysis. Investors must respond to rapidly falling prices for events can change fast. In June 1933, long before all the banks had failed or unemployment had peaked, the S&P rallied 105% in six months. Similarly, in 1974 it rallied 148% in five months in the U.K.! How would you have felt then with your large and beloved cash reserves? Finally, be aware that the market does not turn when it sees light at the end of the tunnel. It turns when all looks black, but just a subtle shade less black than the day before.

This accidental delay led to the letter being published on March 9, the exact day of the infamous market low, when the market troughed at the devil's special, 666. The drawdown from the market high in October 2007 to the March low in 2009 was 56.8%, the largest since World War II.

CHAPTER 8

Lessons Not Learned

By 2008, we had spent 20 years or more digging our deep hole. We had slowly and steadily lowered our financial standards and increased our debt leverage and our general risk-taking in the ways predicted by the late Hyman Minsky, who was belatedly rediscovered and feted during the financial crisis. We and many others had commented quite bitterly on this long slide in financial strength. But what remained underanalyzed, to my mind, was the proximate cause – the thing that really tipped us into the manure: namely, a remarkable unwillingness of the authorities and financial leadership to believe that asset bubbles, however arrived at, always revert to normal. Instead, we had lashings of immoral hazard.

When asked by *Barron's* on October 13, 2008 what we would learn from the crisis, I quipped that "We will learn an enormous amount in a very short time, quite a bit in the medium term and absolutely nothing in the long term." That would be the historical precedent. We had had a bloated financial industry feeding off the real world, and a breach of the social contract with the increasing maldistribution of income (encouraged by tax changes) in favor of the very rich at the expense of ordinary people. We also had unnecessary flaunting of this new great wealth. To cap it off, we had blinkered, narrow-minded leadership by the government and financial corporations. Well, much of this appeared to be ending. Some undesirable elements, I believed, would disappear for a long time and some would just be moderated, but, in my view, it was truly the end of an era and a rather disgusting one in my opinion, speaking as a thrifty Yorkshireman.

High up my list of silver linings and lessons learned was the Fed's apparent change of heart on the topic of bubbles. The breaking of the Tech Bubble set up the excess stimulus of 2001 to 2003, which in turn created the housing bubble as surely as if a law had been passed that all house prices had to be marked up 50%. And now at last, there were signs of hope: signs that Bernanke was reconsidering, finally realizing as he put it that: "Obviously, the last decade has shown that bursting bubbles can be an extraordinarily dangerous and costly phenomenon for the economy and there is no doubt that, as we emerge from the financial crisis, we will all be looking at that issue and what can be done about it." So all the unnecessary suffering inflicted on us by short-sighted policies dictated by academic economists was not entirely in vain.

However, as I wrote in my October 2008 letter, it was definitely not a done deal. Few academics ever change their minds, and few scientific theories founder on the simple facts. "Science advances one funeral at a time" is how the German physicist Max Planck expressed his belief in academic inflexibility, but a suggestion that we use firing squads to speed up the process would seem mean-spirited. Already, Fed members were making the obvious point that interfering with investment bubbles by using the "blunt instrument" of raising rates would likely "in the short run curtail some economic growth." Unfortunately, this viewpoint informed monetary policy over the course of the post-bubble decade and beyond.

I viewed the banking collapse as a Global Competence Crisis. The bigwig bankers at Merrill, Citi, Lehman, Bear Stearns, et al.

could never have behaved the way they did had they understood the size of the likely drop in housing values. I had always thought it was the Bear Stearns of the world who really knew what was going on, and that when the music stopped, the financial junk would be safely (from our point of view) in the hands of, say, Taiwanese banks. How did the guys who put the dead rats in the pot end up eating some of their own stew? To be charitable, perhaps the head chefs did not realize that the kitchen staff were throwing in the odd rat to increase their Christmas bonuses.

Career risk is why all those bank CEOs, entrusted with our money, were still dancing late into the game. So late that the clock had already struck midnight and they had already turned back into pumpkins or rats, but just didn't know it. It's what I called the Goldman Sachs Effect: Goldman increases its leverage and its profit margins shoot into the stratosphere. Eager to keep up, other banks, with less talent and energy than Goldman, copy them with ultimately disastrous consequences. And woe betide the CEO who misses the game and looks like an old fuddy-duddy. The board would simply kick him out, in the name of protecting the stockholders' future profits, and hire in more of a gunslinger from, say, Credit Suisse.

CEOs are picked for their left-brain skills – focus, hard work, decisiveness, persuasiveness, political skills, and, if you are lucky, analytical skills and charisma. As I discovered at HBS, the "Great American Executives" are not picked for patience. Indeed, if they could even spell the word they would be fired. They are not paid to put their feet up or waste time thinking about history and the long-term future; they are paid to be decisive and to act now. The type of people who saw these problems unfolding, on the other hand, had much less career risk or none at all. We knew literally dozens of these people. In fact, almost all the people who had good historical data and were thoughtful had given us good advice, often years before the troubles arrived. They all had the patience of Job. They were also all right-brained: more intuitive, more given to developing odd theories, wallowing in historical data and taking their time. They were almost universally interested – even obsessed – with outlier events, and unique, new and different combinations of factors. These ruminations took up a good chunk of their time. Do such thoughts take more than a few seconds of time for the great CEOs who, to the man, missed everything that was new and different? Unfortunately for all of us, it was the new and different this time that just happened to be vital.

Their failure to understand outliers was only half the problem. By degrees over the recent years, we had fostered a culture in which the people in power never admit to their mistakes. Almost none of the CEOs who brought companies to their knees – or graves – accepted blame clearly and emphatically. Honchos at Lehman and Bear Stearns were victims, it seems, rather than incompetents. Hundreds of billions of stockholders' money was obliterated without clear apologies. Government agencies that nearly ruined us all also admitted no mistakes. And yes, perhaps subprime instruments did need to be regulated, and banks could not be depended on to be wise enough to limit risk on their own. These unadmitted mistakes brought the global financial system to its knees. It was claimed that no one – neither the Fed nor the Treasury – had the legal authority to save Lehman. But such excuses were given only after it appeared to have been a disastrous decision. When you make mistakes, or even when the people you are responsible for make serious mistakes, you should surely admit it, at least once in a while. In cases of extreme error, of which we had just had an unprecedented number, someone might even offer to resign. Not a prayer. In Iceland (population 390,000), God bless them, 20-odd financial types went to jail, justifiably in my opinion. In the U.S., population nearly a thousand times bigger, where the crisis really began, no one went to jail – not one!

A GIANT BLOODSUCKER

It is not often one gets the opportunity to debate a Nobel Prize winner, but Richard Bookstaber and I went to Wall Street in late 2009 to debate Myron Scholes and Robert Reynolds (Putnam's CEO) on a very topical topic: "Financial Innovation Boosts Economic Growth." Bookstaber is an experienced quant who, despite that, wrote an excellent book, *A Demon of Our Own Design: Markets, Hedge Funds, and the Perils of Financial Innovation* – a title so superb you might think it unnecessary to read the book. There are no prizes for guessing which side opposed the proposition.

For my part I argued that our economy suffered from a painfully overdeveloped financial sector. Take the investment business. As I had long argued, it should be obvious to everyone who thought about it for more than a minute that it's a zero-sum game. Investors, I added, collectively add nothing but costs. They produce no widgets; they merely shuffle the existing value of all stocks and all bonds in a cosmic poker game. And those costs have steadily grown. As our industry's assets grew 10-fold from 1989 to 2007, despite huge economies of scale, the fees per dollar also grew. There was no fee competition, contrary to theory. Why?

1. Agency problems – we manage the other guy's money, and
2. Asymmetric information – the agent has much more information than the client.

Clients can't easily distinguish talent from luck or risk taking. It's an unfair contest, nothing like the fair fight assumed by standard economics. As we added new products, options, futures, CDOs, hedge funds and private equity, aggregate fees per dollar rose. And as the layers of fees and layers of agents increased, so too products became more complicated and opaque, causing clients to need us more. As total fees grew, we agents basically reached into the clients' balance sheets, and turned it into income. Magic! But in doing so, we lowered the savings and investment rate by the same amount. So, we got a short-term GDP kick at the expense of lower long-term growth.

This is true with the whole financial system. Let us say that by 1965 – the middle of one of the best decades in U.S. history – we had perfectly adequate financial services. Of course, adequate tools are vital. Finance was 3% of GDP in 1965; after the financial crisis it was 7.5%. So the real economy was carrying an extra 4.5% load. The financial system was overfeeding on the real economy. It's like running with a large, heavy, and growing bloodsucker on your back. It slows you down. From society's point of view, this additional finance burden works like looting or an earthquake. Both increase short-term GDP through the money spent on replacing or restoring property but chew up capital. All of the extra financial workers might as well be retirees or children, in that they are supported by the rest of the workforce, but they are much, much more expensive.

My contribution to the debate concluded with the following warning:

1. Beware the financial-industrial complex: they are eating your lunch. (And to be honest, I've eaten more than my fair share. It was a good lunch.)
2. The client world pays up precisely in proportion to how bamboozled it is by unnecessary complexity and this, among other negatives, is what the fancy new instruments were offering: confusion, doubt and bamboozlement.
3. As for our opponents: academics so badly want their theories to be right that they assume them to be so, and with no proof.

They assume not only that market participants are efficient and well-informed, but also that they are good and worthy citizens. But they're all self-serving, and many are slightly wicked. As for mutual funds: they need complexity coupled with a client's lack of confidence, or more clients would invest on their own. So, for them, the status quo is just fine.

I would have mentioned Paul Volcker's opinion that the only financial innovation useful to the country in the last 50 years was the ATM, but at the time he hadn't made that compelling point. My partner and I won the debate handsomely. At the start the audience of around 300 financial types, who'd paid good money to attend the conference in Manhattan, voted 80 to 20 in favor of the motion. By the end, they had switched by the same margin against financial innovation. Scholes, who incidentally was one of the two Nobel economists involved in the hedge fund fiasco at Long-Term Capital Management, looked like he had chewed glass.

My experience of managing money in 1999 and 2000 and later in 2007 and 2008 confirmed my view that what really matters in investing are the bubbles and the busts. Benoit Mandelbrot, one of my economist heroes, weighed in on this point with his book *The (Mis)Behavior of Markets*, which contains one of my favorite quotes: "Economics… has not truly come to grips with the main difficulty, which is the inordinate practical importance of a few extreme events." Bubbles are extreme events. Any value manager worth his salt should be able to identify a large bubble and has a duty to avoid it. A failure to avoid the bubble reveals either intellectual laziness or pure chickenry.

Finally, the financial crisis revealed how Wall Street's ethics had deteriorated over the years. We found out that bankers had deliberately designed toxic products and then traded like mad against their own clients. In fact, you might say they didn't have clients anymore. They just had patsies. If you did business on Wall Street, you had to be braced for the possibility that they'd tear your eyes out. Back in the day, Goldman would not trade against its clients. Goldman didn't deal in stocks. It sold them for its clients. The Senate report on the crisis quoted me, to my extreme satisfaction, on this very topic of ethics.[*]

The quote was taken from my pleadings in late 2009 for Wall Street firms to get out of proprietary trading, which I believed to be unethical, unnecessary, a conflict of interest and an added cost to institutions, including our clients, amounting to a ton of dough. "Proprietary trading by banks," I was cited as saying, "has become by degrees over recent years an egregious conflict of interest with their clients. Most if not all banks that prop trade now gather information from their institutional clients and exploit it. In complete contrast, 30 years ago, Goldman Sachs, for example, would never, ever have traded against its clients. How quaint that scrupulousness now seems. Indeed, from, say, 1935 to 1980, any banker who suggested such behavior would have been fired as both unprincipled and a threat to the partners' money."

THE FED LEARNS NO LESSONS!

Because the authorities couldn't bring themselves to admit to their past mistakes, they learned nothing from the financial debacle.

---

[*] "Wall Street and the Financial Crisis: Anatomy of a Financial Collapse," United States Senate Permanent Subcommittee on Investigations, April 13, 2011, page 637. The quotation was taken from my quarterly letter, "Lesson Not Learned: On Redesigning Our Current Financial System," GMO Newsletter Special Topic, October 2009.

Banks Too Big to Fail? We adopted a particularly simple and comprehensible policy: make them bigger! Over-bonused financial types induced to take excessive risks with other people's money? A year after the crisis, Goldman reported huge "profits," two-thirds of which went for bonuses – the largest-ever dollar amount. Even outside the financial system, there were many painfully obvious unjust deserts in the form of top management rewards. And most of the excessive rewards came out of the pockets of our clients and other stockholders, which was particularly galling. Excessive moral hazard? Our financial leaders so overstimulated the risk-taking environment that junky, weak, marginal companies and zombie banks produced a record outperformance – the best since 1933 – of junk over the great blue chips (which were GMO's largest equities position!). Easy money fueling speculative bubbles? Bernanke's response was to take the Fed Funds rate to near zero – the lowest level in history – this time with the extra gasoline provided by hundreds of billions of dollars of securities purchases.

In my January 2010 letter I listed the lessons that should have been learned from the past decade:

- The Fed wields even more financial influence than we thought.
- Low rates have a more powerful effect on driving financial assets than on driving the economy.
- The Fed is capable of being extremely out of touch with the real world – "What housing bubble?" – plus more doctrinaire – "No, the low rates had no effect on housing." – than anyone could have imagined.
- Congress is nearly dysfunctional, primarily controlled by large corporations, and hamstrung by the supermajority now routinely required in the Senate.

- Government administrations can be incompetent for long periods.
- Poor leadership can really damage a country's hard-won reputation in a mere 10 years.
- Obama is not a miracle worker!
- The leadership of major corporations can be very lacking in insight and competence on a fairly routine basis.
- The Fed learns no lessons!

CHAPTER 9

Spaceship Earth

My love affair with timber began in 1990 when I was offered the chance to purchase 800 acres of woodland in Vermont. The cost of the land, at $400 per acre, was less than half the value of the standing timber on the property. Not surprisingly, I was taken aback by the seemingly low valuation of the parcel relative to its intrinsic worth. That spurred my interest in understanding the dynamics of the forestry business. Timber, as I soon discovered, was at least for a few years the only low-risk, high-return asset class in existence.

Since 1910, timber prices had compounded pretty steadily at around 3% per year in real terms, which was 1.5 times the real annual increase in the S&P's earnings per share. Furthermore, it was the only reliable negatively correlated asset class when you really needed one. Stumpage prices held up during the Great Depression and in the bear market of the 1970s. One reason for that is if you find the price of lumber is no good, you don't have to cut. Not only is there no cost of storage, but the tree continues growing and gets more valuable over time. That is a very nice feature. Timber also has the great virtue of making people think long term. That's another reason I liked it.

But investors were not familiar with it. And what they are not familiar with they avoid. Most investors then (and now) were not built for the long term. They hated the idea that timber returns come in decades, not day trades. They also tended to exaggerate the risk from fire and pests, which was only 0.5% annually. When you added the illiquidity premium to the non-traditionality premium, we were talking a seriously mispriced, wonderful asset class. As far as I could tell at the time, forests when well-managed, carefully bought and held for 10 years could reasonably be expected to return 7 or 8% annually after inflation in the U.S., and 1.5 points more than that in wild and woolly unsafe places, like New Zealand, Tasmania and Chile.

I started to talk about timber quite a bit in public and bored our clients waxing on and on about it. Finally, one of them had had enough and told me to meet with some forestry friends of his, which I did. In 1997, we went into business with Eva Greger and Eric Oddleifson from UBS and launched the GMO Renewable Resources division. The first investment was a scenic Glenburn, New Zealand timber plantation boasting 15,000 acres of land with 11 miles of coastline.

Back then, institutions had very little invested in forestry. Not long after we launched our forestry business, I gave an interview in which I predicted that investors' thinking about timber was set for a paradigm shift: "One day, 20 years from now," I told investment writer Larry Siegel in July 1998, "timber is going to be a perfectly accepted junior asset class. Its discount rate will be lower… and [when] you start lowering the discount rate, you do wonderful things to the price. At the end of the time, you will make a ton of dough." And so it turned out. In early 2000, we were forecasting that timber would deliver 7% real over the next decade at a time when we were expecting negative real returns from U.S. stocks. During the dotcom bust, timber performed its accustomed role as a bear market diversifier. Over the following years, institutional investors increased their timber exposure by perhaps fourfold.

During the 1990s, the Grantham family – me, Hanne and our three kids – had a series of fairly epic vacations in the tropical rainforests. Our first trip was up the Amazon and involved taking dugout canoes up rivers in pouring rain with my four-year-old daughter, Isabel, hiding under my poncho. The next one was to Rwanda, during a pause in the civil war, and from there on to Tanzania. The final one was to Borneo, where we sailed up a river to the middle of nowhere, staying in longhouses that typically had only one visitor a year. This exposed us to the masses of clear-cut forests and the interminable piles of logs lying along the sides of the rivers. It also exposed us to the dark interiors of forests; to leeches on our legs with socks full of blood; and walking through giant caverns as several million bats flew over our heads, then spiraled upwards to break mysteriously into smaller clouds heading to all points of the compass as the sun set. Indelible memories.

Our trips to the rainforests changed everything. The whole family, all five of us, came out as environmentalists. We just kind of experienced this transformation rather than talked about it. It was not an intellectual concept: it was visceral. In the beginning my interest in forestry had been entirely commercial. Now, it began to morph into "This is a decent investment, *plus* look at some of the real and very practical environmental benefits from forestry." After all, new and protected forests store carbon and preserve wildlife and water sources. I found myself investing in attempts to do sustainable tropical forestry. Our eldest son Oliver got his first job working on one project in Paraguay. Our other son Rupert studied forestry management at college. When Isabel graduated, she spent five years at the Environmental Defense Fund and the Conservation League of Massachusetts. All these life decisions were arrived at independently. We all seemed to get religion, as it were, at about the same time. Perhaps Oliver was a little ahead of the rest of us.

It was pretty clear, though, who the teacher had been: those rivers, forests and bat caves.

Until this point in my career, making our clients – and myself – wealthy had filled my working days. For the first few years, money was important to me, like counters in a competitive game. I would cross Boston Common on my way to work, and say to myself, "Holy cow, I'm going to make $175,000 this year." Back in the day, I had made $50,000, which was a lot of money, but now I was making multiples. And then it went from, "Holy cow, I'm going to make half a million this year," to, "Holy cow, I'm going to make over a million." That was important to me in the sense of "Oh, what a clever boy I am. I'm making more than most of my classmates at HBS." By then I had entered a phase where I was making more money than I had ever thought about, and it was accumulating. I worried about how to invest it, but only as an investment professional with some competitive feeling that I was supposed to do it well. Beyond that, personal wealth didn't matter that much to me. We certainly didn't need or use much of it. Only as time went by did we come to realize just how lucky we were to have the luxury not to really have to think about money.

I still retained the frugality of my Quaker and Yorkshire roots. Our lifestyle changed for the better. I enjoyed a reasonable fat-cat existence. But it was more like I was a decently paid mutual fund manager at Putnam, not the boss of a firm whose assets had gone through the roof with profit margins at 85%. I owned a 10-year-old Volvo station wagon, a 40-year-old Boston Whaler motorboat that I'd bought from Eijk and a country home near the ocean in Westport, Massachusetts – a farmhouse that had been made semi-derelict by some college students, who had let the radiators burst in winter. Hanne and I started collecting textiles in the 1970s and later collected Asian art. But these acquisitions didn't make much of a dent in my growing income. At first, I started giving money away to the usual suspects, like Harvard Business School – at one moment, I was the second biggest donor in my class – and we were making fairly generous gifts to the local museums.

After our environmental epiphany, Hanne and I decided that we should give money to green organizations. From the mid-1990s, we started giving to the World Wildlife Fund and The Nature Conservancy. We were just feeling our way, knowing that we knew nothing. We had a series of lunches once or twice a year with the most senior person we could get access to. In the case of The Nature Conservancy, which is by far the biggest environmental group in the world, we would take the boss of the Massachusetts chapter, Carter Roberts, out to lunch.

Carter became a friend and later rose to be the head of the World Wildlife Fund, which has the biggest brand in the business. At the end of every lunch with Carter and others we would ask them where would they give money other than to their own organization. This was a more powerful idea than we reckoned at the time and constituted 100% of our research effort. After a year or two they would come prepared with a list of four or five suggestions. Then we would ask about the competition and who was doing well or badly in their opinion. And after we had three or four of these lunches, we were getting cross-references as to who in the environmental world was dependable.

At which point, we hit on the idea of starting our own foundation. One of the great reasons for doing this was that it would give us a way of ducking all those pesky fundraisers. The Grantham Foundation for the Protection of the Environment was established in 1997. Initially, I funded it with around half my year's income. We then discovered that if we established a public trust, we could deduct more from taxes. So, in 2005, we created The Jeremy and Hannelore

Grantham Environmental Trust. Within a few years, we became much more fanatical and put in much more than half my income.

The growing urgency to fund our foundation meant that rather late in life it suddenly became very important to me to make a lot of money: everything other than what we needed for living went into the foundation. A couple of decades after establishing the foundation, I committed publicly to giving away 95% of my wealth. They still call me a billionaire. But I am only a billionaire by a strange construction, and that is if you count the money I have given away, which is a pretty whimsical way of calculating someone's net worth. In terms of what I actually could go out and spend, I'm well over an order of magnitude short of that.

MY NEW JOB DESCRIPTION

After the financial crisis, I stepped back from my active investment role at GMO. After 40 years at the job, it was about time. I was 70 years old and had been doing asset allocation for the past 15 years. I had spent on average 15 years on each of the earlier three phases of my investment career, as a U.S. value manager, quant investor and asset allocator, with a five-year overlap between each phase. My new job description was really to be a propagandist – to produce an interesting or useful quarterly letter. In their early years my letters had focused on what I saw as growing investment problems, such as the Tech Bubble of the late 1990s and the risk bubble that followed it. Along the way though, starting in 2007, I began to filter in sections on resource limitations, agricultural problems, climate change and the general and impressive deficiencies of capitalism. By around 2012, it dawned on me that all my growing concerns could be characterized as neglected but very important longer-term problems.

Trying to keep abreast of all these topics was a full-time job for me, as some of them were changing very rapidly indeed. But it was extraordinarily interesting and diverse. Just as I was beginning to feel a little "been there, done that" about finance, these new areas gave me more to work on. Further, as the next few years passed, our foundation became much more aggressive in both grant making and green investing. The information challenges seemed an almost bottomless pit but as exciting as anything I could imagine.

I had always had a much more interesting job than average in the investment business, with an enviably large chunk of my time free to examine whatever I chose. Nevertheless, there was quite a bit of boring maintenance work needed to support the brainstorming time. Now, I had an ideal job in which almost no maintenance work was required. I had no routine day-to-day responsibilities and was consequently free to obsess about anything that seemed to me both relevant and interesting. My curiosity led me to consider bigger issues that circle around outside the narrow confines of investment and how they interrelated. When you do that, your familiarity expands outwards. And if you're curious enough, you keep on going. Obviously, the things that really matter are bottomless pits. You'll never know too much. You keep on trying but you still only know a tiny fraction of the problem. I like to keep my focus on the central idea, which in the stock market is patience and value and mean reversion. Now my direction shifted toward environmental issues and the deficiencies of capitalism. That was, and still is, plenty to go on.

The financial crash had revealed a chronic weakness in establishment economic theory, whose trust in the efficiency of capital markets had encouraged deregulation and helped land us in deep trouble. Bubbles and crises are debilitating, in my view, but they would not bring us to our knees. There were some other problems, though, that surfaced on rare occasions in the post-crisis economic discussions that seemed to me likely to do so. Environmental research came to overshadow my earlier interest in bubbles. To focus solely on investment at a time when mankind and the planet faced several existential threats seemed like fiddling while Rome burned. In my view, it was surely more important to obsess about such threats, which we often prefer to ignore. Good news, in contrast, usually looks after itself.

It was absolutely shocking to me how little interest at that time my fellow investment peers had in issues upon which our long-term well-being absolutely depended. I find the parallels between how some investors refuse to recognize trends, and our reaction to some of our environmental challenges, very powerful. There was the same unwillingness to process unpleasant data. In a bull market you want to believe good news. You don't want to hear that the market is going to go off a cliff. It was surprising because some of them are unbelievably smart and yet missing whatever it is. I don't know if it's wisdom or peripheral vision, but they just weren't interested. It was enough for them to become expert in fiddling and diddling with finance and making a lot of money. In my investment life, I'd always been a contrarian, but it is one thing in a herding marketplace; in science, however, contrarians can easily produce a smoking-doesn't-cause-cancer or the-climate's-future-can't-possibly-be-that-bad perspective.

Wishful thinking and denial of unpleasant facts are simply not survival characteristics.

The lack of public interest in environmental matters was even more disturbing to me. The older I've gotten the more aware I've become of how little information the average guy processes. Most people are concerned with making a living, paying the rent. They are bombarded by political views, particularly in the world of social media. One reason people ignore environmental matters is because of myopia. We have a shockingly short horizon when it comes to investing, as I witnessed during the internet bubble. But, we also have a shockingly short horizon about social and environmental problems, where all we want to hear is how rapid economic growth will be. Humans, in general, suffer from risk myopia, a complete aversion to unpleasantness, which is a particular form of cognitive dissonance. The level of processed information, of what passes for the hardest facts, is so little appreciated. It reminds me of the famous quote from Churchill: "The best argument against democracy is a five-minute conversation with the average voter."

GETTING GREEN ISSUES OUT TO THE PUBLIC

By 2008 I'd been writing my letters for nine years, so I was kind of well established and had a good following. It was a way to get a lot of publicity for GMO. When we started putting out my quarterlies I'd always wanted to make the content available and comprehensible to the average Joe with some interest in investing. This was not the most appealing idea to our marketing department, but I was persistent. I tried to be useful to the small investor as well as our institutional clients. Now, I saw my mission as not just researching environmental issues but getting them out to the wider public, to stand on my soapbox. I guess in some ways I'm a natural propagandist. In my new role, I worked closely with my research assistant Jamie Lee, first at GMO and later as an employee of the Grantham Foundation. So closely, in fact, that it became impossible to say who originated our big ideas, me or him.

More recently, I've done many more podcasts, which usually reach a wider audience and are much less effort for someone like me who sweats blood when writing. Of course, most people are interested only in my investment views. So I try to filter in important issues, like climate change, every time I talk about the stock market – rather like short commercial breaks. This isn't hard given my view that climate change and resource shortages would dominate the investment portfolios of the future. Still, there's a huge disparity in the public's interest. Not long ago I did an interview for Consuelo Mack's Wealthtrack podcast, which she put out in two parts – one on bubbles and the other called "investing for climate change." The segment on bubbles attracted around a quarter of a million listeners to the YouTube version, much more than average, while the climate change section got less than a tenth of that number! How is that possible? They were both done at the same time in the same place with the same people. The green discussion wasn't at all bad and was focused on green investing topics. Afterwards, my nephew called up and said it was one of the best I'd ever done. It was not my delivery – apparently, I gave off the impression of clearly being more excited about the environment than investing. It was the topic. People simply don't want to hear unpleasant news and they're always interested in the stock market. I had already known that trying to sell the importance of critical, even existential issues, was an uphill struggle, but this semi-controlled experiment was a real reminder of just how hard it was going to be – a real smack on the nose.

THE TYRANNY OF THE DISCOUNT RATE

Capitalism does millions of things better than the alternatives. It balances supply and demand in an elegant way that central planning has never come close to. However, it is totally ill-equipped to deal with a small handful of issues. Unfortunately, they are the issues that are absolutely central to our long-term well-being and even survival.

Over the centuries, the economic system has tuned itself to rapid growth at almost any cost. Circumstances such as the fossil fuels revolution and the ensuing population explosion have allowed for both high growth and high profit margins.

Sustained high returns have in turn trained capitalists – or corporate executives if you prefer – to set high hurdles for all investments. The 14% hurdle for discount rates that was considered a minimum in the late 1990s, for example, halves the future value of a dollar every five years, so that in 10 years, today's dollar is worth 25¢; in 20 years 6¢; and in 50 years $1/10$ of 1¢. It is hardly surprising that any event that far out is ignored. This very high discount rate structure prevents economic agents from taking a long-term view. For a typical corporation, anything 30 years ahead literally doesn't matter. For example, let's say that a firm's current actions are going to cost society at large a billion dollars' worth of harm in 50 years. Further, let's agree that all the costs will definitely be imposed on the company. The company would feel that pain today as equivalent to a mere $1 million hit to earnings. Why should they care? Or, as I like to say: the tyranny of the discount rate means your grandchildren have no value. Capitalists usually act as if that were true, even though I'm sure they are actually very kind to their own grandchildren.

The tyranny of the discount rate also puts an absurdly low cost on the depletion of scarce essential resources. My favorite thought experiment involves a contract between the farmer and the devil. The devil says to the farmer, "Sign this 40-year contract and I'll triple your farm's profits." But there are 25 footnotes, as there always are with the devil. Footnote 22 says that 1% of your soil will be eroded each year, which is horrifyingly close to the real average over the past half-century. The farmer signs and makes a fortune on this contract. And his son then signs up for the next 40-year contract and makes another fortune. And his grandson in turn signs up for the third and final contract. He still does very well, and in the final 20 years the family has accumulated enormous wealth, but the soil has completely gone. It's the same story for all his neighboring farms and everyone is out of business. My sick joke is that at least the farmers will die rich when the starving hordes arrive from Chicago. Every graduate who takes Econ 101 would probably sign that contract. There is no single theory that is used in economics that considers the finite nature of resources. It really is shocking.

WEAKNESSES OF GDP MEASUREMENT

The failure to consider depleting resources is reflected in our measurement of economic output. GDP is a mishmash of costs and outputs of "goods" and "bads" indiscriminately jumbled up. Put more of your unemployed in prison and the GDP rises. Raise your legal or consulting fees and the GDP rises. Hire more lawyers to sue and cover that risk with more insurance and the GDP rises. (Japan has only $1/16$ of our lawyers per capita, 1 in 4,000 to our 1 in 250.) Fight more wars, build more tanks and have them blown up and the GDP rises. You get the point.

As currently done, our measurement of GDP most closely describes labor costs in any single year. Because this is a very far cry from the sum of "goods" and goodly (or beneficial) services that we often imagine it to be, it motivates us in perverse ways, mainly toward growth at any price and regardless of its true costs. With incredibly good fortune we have inherited a remarkable, but finite, stock of resources and an amazing biodiversity. All free. This is our capital account, yet as we run our assets down we are not accounting for the losses. Free clean water becomes expensive recycled water. Free fish and free trees become expensive fish farms and tree farms.

A free mountainous watershed area in China becomes a deforested invitation to ruinously expensive flooding.

True accounting after Sir John Hicks, the great English economist (who, as I mentioned, graded my finals papers in economic theory), defines growth or income as the amount that can be withdrawn (or paid out) without affecting the ability to produce the same amount next year. That's how corporate accounting works by subtracting annual depreciation and amortization from reported profits. Yet when we deplete copper and anthracite mines there is no allowance for replenishing these resources, at least for mankind as a whole. The full replacement cost of our resources is somewhere between very expensive and impossible. So our measurement system simplifies this complicated issue by ignoring it completely. And just as we run down our irreplaceable metals, we have ruined our soils, polluted our waters and started to warm the atmosphere and the oceans. But the GDP reflects none of this. If it did we might have reported negative growth for the last several decades. The sooner we adopt a more complete accounting that comes closer to measuring true utility, the sooner we might start to protect our collective long-term well-being.

THE HYDROCARBON REVOLUTION

It has been remarked before that modern economics is a belief in a perpetual motion machine. There's capital and labor, but no mention of energy. Yet without energy the whole thing grinds to a halt and the whole theory is demonstrated to be totally false. The burning of fossil fuels has played a very central role in the development of modern civilization. The Industrial Revolution was not really based on the steam engine, it was based on the coal that ran steam engines. Without coal, we would have very quickly run through all our timber supplies, and we would have ended up with what I think of as the great timber wars of the late 19th century. The demand for wood would have quickly denuded all the great forests of the world.

Over the past 150 years, oil and natural gas have supplemented coal as the essential fuels for economic growth. A gallon of gasoline has over 400 hours of labor equivalent. This means that ordinary middle-class people today have the power that only kings used to enjoy in the distant past. And that incredible gift of accumulated energy over millions of years has catapulted us forward in terms of civilization, in terms of culture and science. The long-term correlation between energy use and GDP growth is over 0.95. That is the equivalent of saying that since the Industrial Revolution, almost all our gains have been dependent on increased resource use.

Yet the stock of fossil fuels is being depleted. We are constantly pumping those wonderfully cheap, irreplaceable barrels of Saudi oil from their great oil fields (the likes of which have never been discovered since the 1970s or, one could argue, the 1950s) – oil that begged to leap out of the ground with an extraction cost of only a handful of dollars. In their place, to maintain oil production we have squeezed oil from Canadian tar sands, bulldozing and heating and polluting at a scale previously undreamt of. Yet the "good" that comes out is the same good that came out of the Saudi fields – one barrel of nearly identical oil – but instead of say $10 per barrel lifting cost the bill is multiples more, all of which will be accounted for as Canadian GDP! So, the more you torture the planet to produce oil, digging up tar sands and baking the oil to dribble it out, the higher the economic output. The greater our collective pain, the greater our measured benefits appear to be. What a counter-productive mess!

Without new sources of effective energy, cheap and in vast quantities, there would have been very little science, and very little productivity. And without productivity, little capital would have been created, and labor without capital would have remained as near useless by modern standards as it was in the early 18th century, with just a few windmills and canals. There are millions of years of stored energy from the sun, in the form of coal, oil and natural gas. It's in our bank account. And we've been draining down the bank account without any real regard for what we're doing – in effect, we are treating capital as if it were income. It's our inheritance and we're running through it.

Another of my few economic heroes is the British-born economist Kenneth Boulding who, at 22, got a paper into Keynes's *Economic Journal* and later emigrated to America. At the age of about 50 he appeared to realize that economics was not taking its job seriously, that it was not interested in utility, in real serious improvement in the world, but was increasingly dominated by elegant mathematical theories that were good for the economists' careers but not useful in the real world. Boulding declared that the only people who believed you can have compound growth in a finite world were either madmen or economists. Economics is a very soft science, but it has delusions of hardness or what has been called physics envy. Boulding summed this up nicely: "Mathematics," he said, "has brought rigor to economics. Unfortunately, it also brought mortis." My view of economics, particularly in finance, is that we have spent our whole time arguing about models and assumptions, not real life. The orthodox view is that real life is merely an irritating special case. I am, however, very attached to real life.

The economists' blinkered attitude to resource limitations was described by Boulding as "cowboy economics." Driven by the spirit of the limitless frontier, their approach has been to shoot (or drill) first and ask about the consequences later. In my view, the American genius was well suited to the era of the Industrial Revolution. As the Confederate General Forrest said, victory goes to those who get there first with the most. An age of resource limitations is more like the "Tragedy of the Commons," where uncontrolled and uncooperative access to the common land resulted in sheep destroying grazing pastures. The American hard-driving way has historically been to get the most darned sheep on the common first.

THE IMPOSSIBILITY OF COMPOUND GROWTH

When considering the impossibility of sustained compound growth, I like to present people with a thought experiment. Take the longest civilization in history – ancient Egypt, which had the same religion, the same culture, the same language for 3,000 years – and imagine what would have happened if they had started with a cubic meter of physical possessions and managed to achieve 4.5% growth over three millennia? I once asked a roomful of New York University PhDs in math this question and refused to go on with my talk until they made a guess. Eventually they agreed that those possessions would be miles deep around the earth. Then someone said, "No, it will be much bigger than that. Those possessions will stretch beyond the moon." But even that was far off the mark. The correct answer is that the physical possessions would eventually fill a billion of our solar systems. How about a lowly 1% compound growth in population (which is far less than the growth rate of the world's population in my lifetime)? Egypt's starting population of about 3 million would have increased by over 9 trillion times. People don't get it. We're just not programmed to have a feel for compounding – what Einstein is said to have called the eighth wonder of the world.

Before the Reverend Thomas Malthus wrote his famous *Essay on the Principle of Population,* for several hundred thousand years our species, like every other species on the planet, including rats, had run with its noses pushed up against the supply of food. Have a great harvest and the population expands. After a series of bad years, it falls back. Ironically, as Malthus wrote with this principle in mind in 1798, a profound change was taking place. The Industrial Revolution, or what should really be called the hydrocarbon revolution, was starting up. It was able to create a window of about 250 years for our species to expand.

Boulding was a modern Malthusian. He put forward the idea of Spaceship Earth, hurtling through space carrying only very finite resources and with no space depots or stations at which to refuel, resupply and fix problems. As every science fiction fan knows, the first requirement of a multigenerational trip to a distant star system is that the regenerative gardens are precisely limited to the exact number of crew members and their families. Of course, the spaceship's population can't grow endlessly either. It must be meticulously calculated at optimal replacement level, which requires everyone to stick to the rules. Well, folks, whether you like it or not, we are on just such a spaceship and we have been breaking those rules.

Our natural habitat is incredibly complex but almost perfectly suited to our species. It is, though, extremely sensitive to misuse and has been substantially damaged. Spaceship Earth, like every spaceship, has a limited carrying capacity for resources and also the people using them. A particular challenge to our spaceship is that on our bridge there is no commander and there are no rules. Our species, as it has learned to survive over millennia, has adopted a style of "Get what you need now by any means possible!" There has been no incentive to worry about the distant future, and so we don't.

Of all the technical weaknesses of capitalism the most dangerous, in my opinion, is its absolute inability to process the finiteness of resources and the mathematical impossibility of maintaining rapid growth in physical output. You can have steady increases in the quality of goods and services and, I hope, the quality of life, but you can't have indefinite growth in physical output. You can have "growth" for now, or you can have "sustainable" forever, but not both. This is the message delivered by the laws of compounding and the laws of nature. But many, given a choice between growth and sustainability, select "growth, and to hell with the consequences." Alternatively, they adopt a hear-no-evil approach and listen exclusively to good news.

The superficial good news for such people is that there are always a few optimistic experts lacking in long-horizon vision or whose cooperation has been rented, like industry "expert" witnesses at a tobacco trial, who can be dragged out to say that smoking is harmless. (One famous professor, who liked to be photographed while puffing a cigarette, went seamlessly from saying tobacco was just fine to saying that continuously pumping out greenhouse gases was also without consequences.) The optimists offer as evidence that we will always be in the best of all possible worlds; they don't refer to our species' tough million or so years of trial and painful error, but only the last 250 years, when hydrocarbons and other resources have given us a temporary reprieve. This reprieve does not make the finite magically infinite, but the 250 years of the hydrocarbon intermission can feel like forever for a short-lived species like ours.

Capitalists certainly act as if they believe that rapid growth in physical wealth can go on forever. They appear to be hooked on high growth and avoid any suggestion that it might be slowed down by limits. Thus, they exhibit horror at the thought (and occasional reality) of a declining population when in fact such a decline is an absolute necessity in order for us to end up gracefully, rather than painfully, at a fully sustainable world economy. Similarly with natural resources, capitalists want to eat into these precious, limited resources at an accelerating rate with the subtext that everyone on the planet has the right to live like the wasteful, polluting, developed countries do today. You don't have to be a mathematician to work out that if the average Chinese or Indian consumer were to catch up with (the theoretically moving target of) the average American, then our planet's goose is cooked, along with most other things. Indeed, scientists calculate that if they caught up, we would need at least three planets to be fully sustainable.

Do you know how many economic theories treat resources as if they are finite? Well, the researchers at the Organisation for Economic Co-operation and Development say "none" – that no such theory exists. Economic theory either ignores this little problem or assumes you reach out and take the needed resources given the normal workings of supply and demand, and you can do so indefinitely. I like to joke that the only thing that unites Austrian economists (like Friedrich Hayek) and Keynesians is their complete disregard for the limitations imposed by Spaceship Earth. But this failure in economic thinking – ignoring natural limits – risks far more dangerous outcomes than any temporary financial crash. Libertarians are a particular menace when it comes to environmental problems. They believe that any government interference is bad. Anyone with a brain knows that climate change requires governmental leadership, and the libertarians can tell this is bad news for their philosophy. Their ideology is so strongly held that, dangerously, it overcomes the facts.

CLIMATE CHANGE ADVOCACY

Not only are fossil fuels in limited supply on Spaceship Earth, their greenhouse gas emissions also destroy its living conditions. When we launched the Grantham Foundation I was initially most interested in alleviating damage to local environmental hotspots. Accordingly, some of our very first donations went to attempting to preserve bird migration routes through Costa Rica and Panama. The climate question wasn't there for me at that time. But within a few years it became at least half of the focus for the Foundation, for the penny dropped: what use would there be in protecting chunks of nature if we can't stop climate change? All our other efforts would be wasted. Sadly, the same argument applies to most philanthropy – a well-maintained museum or ballet company will not help if civilization fails through climate collapse.

In 2007, we gave money to Imperial College, London, after we heard they were on the cusp of starting a center for climate change research. We met with them and they gave us the full-court press with everyone from the top dog down promising all manner of incredible efforts and attention. We decided to do a 10-year contract with them, putting in a couple of million dollars a year. The following year, we helped set up The Grantham Research Institute on Climate Change and the Environment at the London School of Economics (LSE). The 10-year commitment was very similar to Imperial's: $2 million a year with five years' warning if we decided to get out.

The LSE connection brought us into contact with Nick Stern of the acclaimed *Stern Review*. His lengthy report, commissioned by the U.K. government and published in late 2006, described the biggest failure ever in economic theory as its inability to account for environmental and climate damage. It also estimated that the potential financial costs of climate change were much greater in terms of lost economic output than the probable costs of heading off serious consequences by appropriate and timely action. Nick had a pit bull at the LSE, Bob Ward, a PR expert, who became infamous in climate denial circles for combatting the false claims put out by the bad guys. We also financed two other research institutes: together with my GMO colleague Arjun Divecha, we supported the Divecha Centre for Climate Change at the Indian Institute of

Technology, Bangalore (in 2009) and another at my alma mater, Sheffield University (in 2014), aimed at addressing sustainability, which in the final analysis is probably the core of our problems. We are living beyond our means: excess pollution, including CO_2 and methane, are just a symptom, as is the steady degradation of farmland, biodiversity and all of nature.

Hanne and I also wanted to get environmental concerns in front of the general public. In collaboration with the Metcalf Institute in 2006 we launched an annual journalism award, The Grantham Prize, to recognize exemplary reporting on the environment. This was discontinued after a few years as we recognized the sad truth that serious newspaper coverage of environmental affairs had diminished to almost nothing as print journalism imploded in the age of the internet and nature coverage was at the bottom of their totem pole. In October 2008 the Foundation was a major funder of a two-hour PBS Frontline documentary, *Heat*, which examined what big business was — and mostly wasn't — doing to reduce its carbon footprint and mitigate the threat of climate change. It was brilliant, but it had little or no impact. To our disappointment, TV turns out to be a cost-ineffective medium for airing environmental concerns.

We later helped finance another climate documentary, "Years of Living Dangerously," which was produced by James Cameron of *Titanic* and *Avatar* fame and Jerry Weintraub (former head of film studio United Artists), and presented by Matt Damon, Harrison Ford and Arnold Schwarzenegger. The idea was simple: rather than using the film stars to record voice-overs, as in most documentaries, they would be sent around the world to witness first-hand the devastating impact of climate-related weather events and how individuals, communities, companies and governments were trying to cope. The reason I wanted to fund this was because Cameron was such a good propagandist in *Avatar* that he had the audience cheering for the blue creatures against what appeared to be red-blooded GIs simply following their orders. That's an amazing thing to do. So, I figured, if anyone can help influence this issue and set the tone, he could. This program, too, seemed well executed and yet it also registered little lasting impact.

We also funded political lobbying for green issues, which required spending my own taxed income, rather than the Foundation's resources – what the Internal Revenue Service classifies as C4 money. This type of funding is in high demand from environmental institutions as they can spend it on almost anything they want. In 2010, we helped get the Cap and Trade climate bill through the House – I personally put up $8 million because this type of donation is said to be political and therefore off limits to foundations. Unfortunately, it came to nothing. The recession more or less ruled it out. Unemployment and interest in environmental issues move inversely. President Obama was a complete no-show. He was using up all his political capital on Obamacare, which, in my view, still left America with the worst health care system in the developed world. It might have been less bad than it was at the start, but it was still the worst in the developed world by a wide margin. What Obama gave up in that precious two-year window when the Democrats controlled both the House and Senate was a chance for the U.S. to take a leadership role on the most important issues of this era. We will never know what difference it might have made.

I used my bully pulpit at GMO – quarterly letters, speeches and press interviews – to highlight climate change. Asked by *The Spectator* magazine in February 2007 whether I had strong views on the topic, I replied: "Goddam right I do. It's going to be the biggest investment issue of the next 20 to 30 years. We're going to get bored to death with it." But if you believed, as I do, that climate change is so severe that it was an actual question of the survival of our species and the

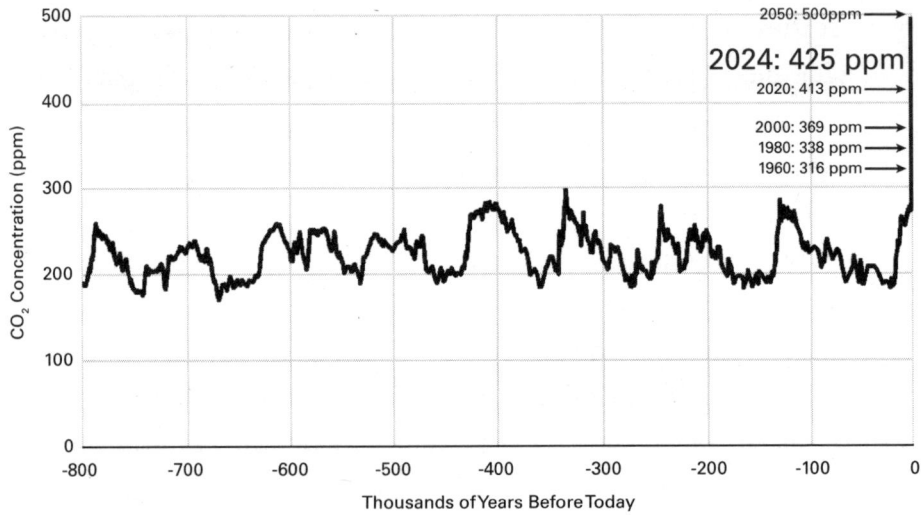

CO_2 levels go off the scale. Atmospheric carbon dioxide concentrations over the past 800 thousand years, taken from Antarctic ice cores. The current surge in greenhouse gas levels is completely unprecedented in its speed and magnitude over all of mankind's evolutionary history. Data from NOAA and GMO, 2024

future of the planet, then you had to take it extremely seriously even if that meant boring people to death. Simply put, climate change is the most important problem we face in the long term. If we fail in this, everything else we achieve will be for nothing.

Over the following years, I continued writing, speaking and giving interviews on climate change and what I called the "carbon bubble," because our use of hydrocarbons is unsustainable and like all bubbles must break. And I talked about the very powerful parallels between how some investors refuse to recognize unsustainable trends and our reaction to some environmental challenges. As ever, I found there was an unwillingness to process unpleasant data.

I summarized my thoughts on the topic in a quarterly letter, called "Everything You Need to Know About Global Warming in 5 Minutes" (published July 2010), which, being brief, I reprint in full:

1. The amount of carbon dioxide (CO_2) in the atmosphere, after at least several hundred thousand years of remaining within a constant range, started to rise with the advent of the Industrial Revolution. It has increased by almost 40% and is rising each year. This is certain and straightforward.
2. One of the properties of CO_2 is that it creates a greenhouse effect and, all other things being equal, an increase in its concentration in the atmosphere causes the Earth's temperature to rise. This is just physics. (The amount of other greenhouse gases in the atmosphere, such as methane, has also risen steeply since industrialization, which has added to the impact of higher CO_2 levels.)
3. Several other factors, like changes in solar output, have major influences on climate over millennia, but these effects have been observed and measured. They alone cannot explain the rise in the global temperature over the past 50 years.
4. The uncertainties arise when it comes to the interaction between greenhouse gases and other factors in the complicated climate system. It is impossible to be sure exactly how quickly or how much the temperature will rise. But, the past can be measured. The temperature has indeed steadily risen over the past century while greenhouse gas levels have increased. But the forecasts still range very widely for what will happen in the future, ranging from a small but still potentially harmful rise of 1 to 2 degrees Fahrenheit to a potentially disastrous level of +6 to +10 degrees Fahrenheit within this century. A warmer atmosphere melts glaciers and ice sheets, and causes global sea levels to rise. A warmer atmosphere also contains more energy and holds more water, changing the global occurrences of storms, floods and other extreme weather events.
5. Skeptics argue that this wide range of uncertainty about future temperature changes lowers the need to act: "Why spend

money when you're not certain?" But because the penalties can rise at an accelerating rate at the tail, a wider range implies a greater risk (and a greater expected value of the costs). This is logically and mathematically rigorous and yet is still argued.

6. Pascal asks the question: What is the expected value of a very small chance of an infinite loss? And, he answers, "Infinite." In this example, what is the cost of lowering CO_2 output and having the long-term effect of increasing CO_2 turn out to be nominal? The cost appears to be equal to forgoing, once in your life, six months' to one year's global growth – 2% to 4% or less. The benefits, even with no warming, include: energy independence from the Middle East; more jobs, given wind and solar power and increased efficiency are more labor-intensive than another coal-fired power plant; less pollution of streams and air; and an early leadership role for the U.S. in industries that will inevitably become important. Conversely, what are the costs of not acting on prevention when the results turn out to be serious: costs that may dwarf those for prevention; and probable political destabilization from droughts, famine, mass migrations and even war. And, to Pascal's real point, what might be the cost at the very extreme end of the distribution: definitely life-changing, possibly life-threatening.

7. The biggest cost of all from global warming is likely to be the accumulated loss of biodiversity. This features nowhere in economic cost-benefit analysis because, not surprisingly, it is hard to put a price on that which is priceless.

8. A special word on the right-leaning think tanks: As libertarians, they abhor the need for government spending or even governmental leadership, which in their opinion is best left to private enterprise. In general, this may be an excellent idea. But global warming is a classic tragedy of the commons – seeking

your own individual advantage, for once, does not lead to the common good, and the problem desperately needs government leadership and regulation. Sensing this, these think tanks have allowed their drive for desirable policy to trump science. Not a good idea.

9. Also, I should make a brief note to my own group – diehard contrarians. Dear fellow contrarians, I know the majority is usually wrong in the behavioral jungle of the stock market. And heaven knows I have seen the soft scientists who lead finance theory attempts to bully their way to a uniform acceptance of the bankrupt theory of rational expectations and market efficiency. But climate warming involves hard science. The two most prestigious bastions of hard science are the National Academy in the U.S. and the Royal Society in the U.K., to which Isaac Newton and the rest of that huge 17th century cohort of brilliant scientists belonged. The presidents of both societies wrote a note recently, emphasizing the seriousness of the climate problem and that it was manmade. (Both societies have also made full reports on behalf of their membership stating the same.) Do we believe the whole elite of science is in a conspiracy? At some point in the development of a scientific truth, contrarians risk becoming flat earthers.

10. Conspiracy theorists claim to believe that global warming is a carefully constructed hoax driven by scientists desperate for… what? Being needled by non-scientific newspaper reports, by blogs and by right-wing politicians and think tanks? Most hard scientists hate themselves or their colleagues being in the news. Being a climate scientist spokesman has already become a hindrance to an academic career, including tenure. I have a much simpler but plausible "conspiracy theory": that fossil energy companies, driven by the need to protect hundreds

of billions of dollars of profits, encourage obfuscation of the inconvenient scientific results.
11. Why are we arguing the issue? Challenging vested interests as powerful as the oil and coal lobbies was never going to be easy. Scientists are not naturally aggressive defenders of arguments. In short, they are conservatives by training: never, ever risk overstating your ideas. The skeptics are far, far more determined and expert propagandists to boot. They are also well funded. That smoking caused cancer was obfuscated deliberately and effectively for 20 years at a cost of hundreds of thousands of extra deaths. We know that for certain now, yet those who caused this fatal delay have never been held accountable. The profits of the oil and coal industry make tobacco's resources look like a rounding error. In some notable cases, the obfuscators of global warming actually use the same "experts" as the tobacco industry did! The obfuscators' simple and direct motivation – making money in the near term, which anyone can relate to – combined with their resources and, as it turns out, propaganda talents, have meant that we are arguing the science long after it has been nailed down. I, for one, admire them for their PR skills, while wondering, as always: "Have they no grandchildren?"
12. Almost no one wants to change. The long-established status quo is very comfortable, and we are used to its deficiencies. But for this problem we must change. This is never easy.
13. Almost everyone wants to hear good news. They want to believe that dangerous global warming is a hoax. They, therefore, desperately want to believe the skeptics. This is a problem for all of us.

On an icy morning in February 2013, I traveled by train to Washington D.C., with a load of environmentalists, including my daughter Isabel, who were planning to handcuff themselves to the gates of the White House in protest at the building of the Keystone XL 3,500km oil pipeline from Canada to the Gulf of Mexico. "What we are trying to do is buy time," I told reporters. "Buy time for the world to wake up." I was committed to getting arrested. But the day before the protest, Hanne checked with our lawyer, who said, "Don't do that!" It turned out that being arrested would have given me serious problems. So, I ran for cover on the third police warning and watched as my daughter was proudly taken off in handcuffs with *Splash* star Daryl Hannah, and a few others.

TIME TO WAKE UP

Until 2011, occasional references to green issues and other long-term problems in my quarterly letters didn't spark great interest from my readership, which, as I have said, was more interested in my thoughts on the investment climate than the actual climate. This changed in April of that year, when Jamie and I had our first breakout hit with a piece entitled, "Time to Wake Up: Days of Abundant Resources and Falling Prices Are Over Forever."

The letter pointed out that since 1800, the world's population had surged from 800 million to 7 billion, on its way to an estimated 8 billion, at minimum. This rise in population, the 10-fold increase in wealth in developed countries and the explosive growth in developing countries – notably, the utterly unprecedented 50-fold increase in China's GDP over 40 years – were eating rapidly into our finite resources of hydrocarbons, ores, fertilizer, available land and water. It was evident this was having a huge impact on commodity prices. In the 100 years until 2002, the prices of all important commodities, except oil, had declined by an average of 70%. Yet after 2002, this entire decline had been erased by a bigger surge in commodity prices than occurred during World War II. "Mrs. Market," I wrote, "is sending us the mother of all price signals."

The price of oil had undergone a "paradigm shift" during the OPEC oil embargo of the 1970s. Studying the data, it looked as if oil had undergone a second paradigm shift from around 2003. It was this shift that caused my formerly impregnable faith in mean reversion to break. I had always admitted that paradigm shifts were theoretically possible, but with oil I had finally met one nose to nose. It did two things. First, it set me to thinking about why this paradigm shift felt so different to those false ones claimed in the past. Second, it opened my eyes to the probability that other paradigm shifts would likely come along sooner or later. If we were running out of low-cost oil, I asked myself, why should we not run out of other finite resources?

By 2011, a whole range of basic materials and agricultural products – from copper to zinc – were trading not just 2-sigma, but many sigmas off the scale expensive. I described this as the "Great Paradigm Shift." With regards to metals, I observed that Ivan Glasenberg, head of the mining giant, Glencore, had recently been quoted in the *Financial Times* describing how his firm operated in the Congo and Zambia. "We took the nice, simple, easy stuff first from Australia, we took it from the U.S., we went to South America… Now we have to go to the more remote places." That seemed to me like a pretty good description of an industry exiting the easy phase and entering the rising slope of permanently higher prices and higher operational risks.

I predicted that price pressure, shortage of resources and recurrent supply bottlenecks would be a permanent feature of our lives. And that this would increasingly slow down the growth rate of the developed and developing world and put a severe burden on poor countries. However, I added a crucial caveat: "If China stumbles or if the weather is better than expected, a probability I would put at, say, 80%, then commodity prices will decline a lot. But if both events occur together, it will very probably break the market en masse. Not unlike the financial collapse." In the end, China did stumble. Its demand for iron ore didn't just slow from 12 to 10, 8, 6% growth, over a number of years, as normally happens. Demand growth went from 12 to 0 in one year! After which, for three years Chinese demand for almost every commodity stagnated. The price of basic materials crashed. To cap it all, the weather then changed to be very favorable for grain for almost three years (although, not so for almonds, etc. in California). I had warned that an abrupt change to favorable weather following the increased land use would cause us to "drown in grain, rather than rain." That's what happened. But the main point of the paper was not to deal with the short-term changes in supply and demand that the market, naturally enough, obsesses about. It was to make the point that something long term and important had changed. The inevitable consequence of finite resources being challenged by compound growth had led to a new era in which scarcity would finally dominate. In future, commodity prices would no longer be driven downwards by technology improvements as had happened in the past. If this were so, it would be one of the most consequential changes in economic history.

The trouble is that commodities are very much oriented to short-term supply and demand. People don't ask what the outlook is for the next 10 years in the commodity business. Price moves are fabulous, extreme and rapid. And so they were. But soon enough the prices of these things began to recover. By 2022, food prices, inflation-adjusted, as measured by the UN, were back at a new high, the price of oil had rallied and the price of half of the commodities were at highs and the other half had recovered a heck of a long way. If you redrew the curve of commodity prices, you could see how far away it was from the old trend. Looking back, nearly 15 years later, I still believe this "mother of all paradigm shifts" has occurred even though it may still take a while for this to be absolutely clear. There's still every sign that we're beginning to run out of key commodities. This is particularly the case when you look at the resources needed for the energy transition – copper, lithium, cobalt, nickel and graphite – that

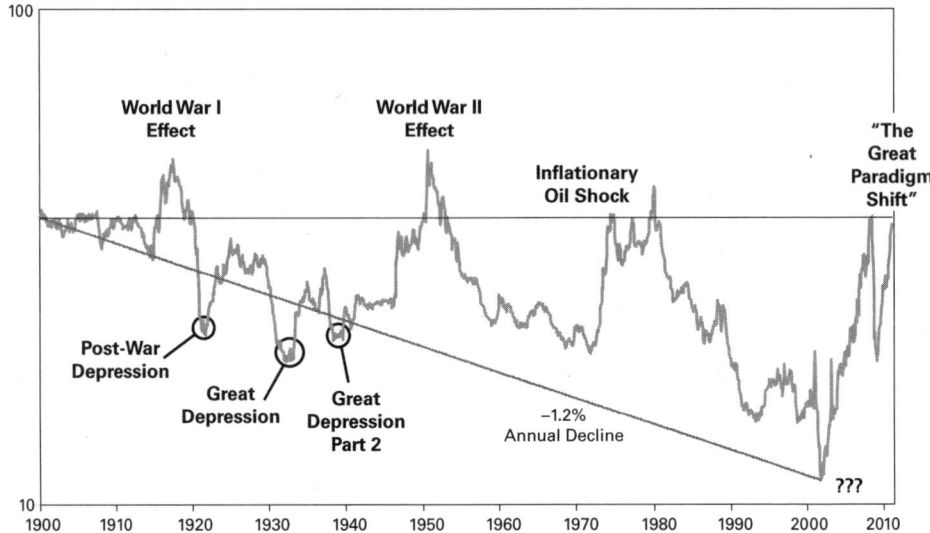

The great paradigm shift in commodity prices. GMO's Commodity Index, which I featured in my April 2011 quarterly letter, is comprised of the 33 leading traded commodities, equally weighted. It illustrates a) the clear downwards trend in commodity prices over time, as should be expected given technological progress, and b) the extraordinary and historically anomalous extent of the 2000s commodities rally – the biggest gain in aggregate commodity prices in recorded history, exceeding even World War II and the 1970s oil shock. It was becoming clear by the early 2010s that technological progress could no longer keep up with the massive expansion of demand from globalization and economic development, especially from China, against the backdrop of a finite world with limited resources. Despite a significant decline after China slowed down in the mid-2010s, aggregate commodity prices never again returned to their early 2000s low. Chart is on a log scale. Data from Global Financial Data and GMO, 2011 go into wind turbines and electric vehicles. There isn't even a quarter or sometimes a tenth of what is needed with current technology, given our objective to reach carbon neutrality in 2050.

Although from an investment perspective "Time to Wake Up" was mistimed, it was my first piece of writing on environmental matters to reach a broad audience. It was, in fact, our one and only scoop. No one else had made a clear claim that the resources game had changed forever. The paper took on a life of its own and helped to put these issues on to the institutional agenda. It was downloaded several million times and widely written up in the financial press, including *The Economist*, *Barron's* and *Business Insider*, as well as in the non-financial press, such as *The New York Times* and *The Guardian*.

The paper also led to a lot of wining and dining for Hanne and me. Shortly after it appeared, I was invited to attend a conference of OECD environment ministers at the organization's grand headquarters in Paris. At the end of my talk, the secretary general, a delightful guy named Angel Gurria, was standing at the back of the seats lobbing me these softball questions. At the close of the summit the next morning, the secretary general asked me to give my closing opinions. The only thing I remember was telling the ministers that they were going to find a lot of pushback and would have to use all their influence with finance ministers and prime ministers to try and keep them focused on the real risks of climate change and resource limitations. If you get outmaneuvered, I said, make sure at least you resign emphatically. Most political leaders, at the time, were not interested in climate change. You must make them suffer for that and make it public, I advised.

After that I was asked to deliver a talk at the European Union in Brussels. I told the EU gathering that over the past five years I had become a Malthusian, how I'd been won over by the data and by the logic of the math: "There's no such thing as sustainable growth,"

I said. "You have to make a pick. You can have sustainability or you can have growth, but you can't have both." In the same few months we were invited to a conference on the environment at Oxford, arranged by Lord Rothschild and attended by President Clinton and the TV naturalist David Attenborough, along with several military VIPs. The military appeared to take potential resource problems and climate change far more seriously than the financial and economic establishment.

The Prince of Wales (now King Charles) noticed our resources paper shortly after it appeared and saw its relevance to his own project on accounting for sustainability. The paper also featured the threat to agriculture from soil erosion, another of his keen interests. The prince was admirably early and determined on biodiversity and climate change. And stuck to his position despite widespread mocking from the Establishment, including countless cartoons of him speaking to flowers. I was invited to his official residence, St James's Palace, to address a collection of British capitalists on environmental accounting. Later, I had a couple of further meetings with the future king, including a splendid dinner at the palace, at which Hanne sat next to the prince while I sat next to his "man." I got to look at them through these incredible gold-plated candelabra designed by the great silversmith himself, Paul de Lamerie, the pride and joy of the Huguenot refugees who dominated 18th-century silver making, with Hanne and Prince Charles yakking away the whole time. Hanne made nothing of it, but I was impressed. Meanwhile, his man and I chatted about boring, down-to-earth topics. Hanne and I later had coffee with the future king at Birkhall, the Scottish property he'd inherited from his grandmother.

It was during the period when my interests were mostly directed toward environmental matters that I started to receive, for the first time in my life, a certain amount of public acclaim. In 2011, I was

Hanne and I being feted by the future King Charles (and his personal secretary, far right) at St James' Palace in 2012

Celebrating my election to the American Academy of Arts and Sciences in 2014 with (from left to right) my son-in-law John Rapaport, my daughter Isabel Grantham, my son Oliver Grantham, Hanne, my son Rupert Grantham and my daughter-in-law Jen Grantham named one of the Top 50 Most Influential People in Finance by Bloomberg and a couple of years later the British current affairs magazine *Prospect* ranked me in its list of the top "World Thinkers." In 2014, I was elected a member of the American Academy of Arts and Sciences for my contributions to "leadership, policy and communications." I later received the Carnegie Medal for Philanthropy and an HBS outstanding achievement award. I welcomed all this recognition as good propaganda for the cause. In November 2016, I was made a Commander of the British Empire, a step shy from a knighthood, for "exceptional services to climate change research." I was handed a medal at Buckingham Palace by Prince William. I asked him whether his dad had attempted to brainwash him about climate change and he replied with a grin, "You had better believe it."

As a final twitch to the recognition of our paper, I was invited to talk to the Nobel Prize winners at their annual bash in Kyoto, where for a couple of days they hold a series of panel discussions on various topics. A Nobel Prize winner sits on each panel, even though he or she may know nothing about what's being discussed. The proposition appears to be that somehow getting a Nobel Prize means you're smart on every topic, and boy, in my opinion, is that far off the mark, particularly in economics. On our little panel, we had a Nobel laureate from Harvard in physics, which everyone has to admit is top drawer, as far as these things go. And we had the boss of a science museum from Lisbon. We were being fed Japanese tea in a side room to calm our nerves before our presentation and this arrogant pig of a Nobel Prize winner says to the charming gentleman from Lisbon, "Do you know how long CO_2 stays in the atmosphere?" The museum man says, deferentially, that he didn't really get into that kind of stuff. So, our physicist browbeats him by pointing out that it stays up there for thousands of years. Then, if you can believe it, a few minutes later he repeats the question. Not able to stand this any longer, I snap at the physicist, "I'll tell you what, why don't you ask him again? Perhaps then he'll know." He looked like he'd seen a ghost. He could not believe what I had said. He was literally speechless. It was wonderful.

I gave my usual talk about the climate. But I was annoyed with my fellow panelist, the Nobel laureate, and seriously pissed off because I discovered that I had not been invited because of the merits of our paper on resources but because I was a fat cat who might be dunned to give them some money. This was not amusing to me. I thought, I haven't come all the way to Kyoto just to be propositioned. So my talk became a harangue against science and the establishment. At the end of the talk, which was very well received despite being venomous, an editor of *Nature*, who was there, asked if I'd write a commentary for his journal.

The title of my piece, published in November 2012, was "Be persuasive. Be brave. Be arrested (if necessary)." My argument was that scientists needed to get much more serious when writing up climate change. I'd have dinner with these guys and after a couple of glasses of wine, they would all say how worried they were, how rapidly things were deteriorating. But this did not show up in their writing. There was no urgency being shared. I understood the dignity of science. Normally, in science, overstating things is dangerous but with climate change understating the issue is dangerous. Get out there, I pleaded, and say what you honestly think. My piece ended with the comment:

> It is crucial that scientists take more career risks and sound a more realistic, more desperate, note on the global-warming problem. Younger scientists are obsessed by thoughts of tenure, so it is probably up to older, senior and retired scientists to do the heavy lifting. Be arrested if necessary. This is not only the

crisis of your lives – it is also the crisis of our species' existence.

I implore you to be brave.

That was my one and only pseudo-academic article in one of the oldest and probably the most prestigious of science journals. It got 54 citations, which is not bad for an amateur's first-time effort. And it created a decent stir in the climate community because half of them felt it was very accurate and the other half thought who the hell does Grantham think he is telling us what to do? When Donald Trump assumed the U.S. presidency a few years later, the scientists began to think, well, we're screwed anyway, so let's go down with the ship. They started to be much, much better. Even the UN's Intergovernmental Panel on Climate Change changed the tone of their language so that it was suddenly more appropriate to their data, with a tinge of desperation, as in "we are not winning this battle," rather than merely academic.

CHAPTER 10

The Race of Our Lives

The collapse of civilizations is a gripping and resonant topic for many of us and one that has attracted many scholars over the years. They see many possible contributing factors to the collapse of previous civilizations, the evidence pieced together shard by shard from civilizations that often left few records. But some themes recur in the scholars' work: geographic locations that had misfortune in the availability of useful animal and vegetable life, soil, water and a source of energy; mismanagement in the overuse and depletion of resources, especially forests, soil and water; the lack of a safety margin or storage against inevitable droughts and famines; overexpansion and costly unnecessary wars; sometimes a failure of moral spirit as the pioneering toughness and willingness to sacrifice gave way to softer and more cynical ways; the increasing complexity of a growing empire that became by degree too expensive in human costs and in the use of limited resources to justify the effort, until the taxes and other demands on ordinary citizens became unbearable so that an empire, pushed beyond sustainable limits, became vulnerable to even modest shocks that could in earlier days have been easily withstood.

Probably the greatest agreement among scholars, though, is that failing civilizations suffered from growing hubris and overconfidence: the belief that their capabilities after many earlier tests would always rise to the occasion and that growing signs of weakness could be ignored as pessimistic. After all, after 200 or even 500 years, many other dangers had been warned of yet always they had persevered. Until finally they did not. One of these scholars, William Ophuls, provides a straightforward summary and synthesis of all the ways to fail in 70 brief pages, yet with extensive notes and references. *Immoderate Greatness* (a quote from Gibbon's *The History of the Decline and Fall of the Roman Empire*), with the subtitle *Why Civilizations Fail* appeared in 2012. It is written in remarkably accessible, simple language and divides the causes of failure into six categories: Ecological Exhaustion, Exponential Growth, Expedited Entropy, Excessive Complexity, Moral Decay and Practical Failure.

Unfortunately, to my mind, all six seem to apply to us today in varying degrees. I have already described how we are running out of cheap and abundant resources and of the impossibility of exponential growth in a finite world. And also how energy is becoming more costly to extract (which is roughly what Ophuls means by expedited entropy). The excessive complexity and moral decay of our civilization was revealed by the Global Financial Crisis with its mind-bogglingly complicated subprime derivatives, marketed by Wall Street bankers, who should have known better, in fact did know better, but went ahead anyhow.

Where one of these factors that push a civilization toward collapse might be manageable – although often that has not been the case – Ophuls makes the chances of our managing all six seem slight. His conclusion is that we will not resist the impressive list of erosive factors and that, in fact, we are in the fairly late stages of our current civilization's race for the cliff edge with nothing much to head us off. His study of history led him to believe that civilizations are actually hard-wired to self-destruct: programmed to be overconfident, to keep on pushing for growth until limits are overstepped and risks accumulate to the breaking point. His meager good news is that after the New Dark Ages, when civilization again rears its head, presumably with a much smaller population, we will have acquired the good sense to be less overreaching, less hubristic, a lot humbler about growth and our use of resources and more determined to live in balance with the natural energy we receive from the sun and the heat, food and water with which we can sustainably be provided.

I found Ophuls's argument well reasoned. Although I acknowledge the strong possibility of a very negative outcome, I felt it was too pessimistic (which, sadly, is a rare occurrence for me on this topic). Yes, we are taking extreme risks with resource depletion and with the environment, especially concerning climate damage and ocean acidification. Yet I believe the case for the near certainty of our running off the cliff misses the existence of two extraordinarily lucky (and, one could argue, undeserved) gifts that were not available to any prior stressed civilization.

Unexpectedly, and for the first time in human history, our species has apparently decided to have steadily fewer children, so that on its current flight path, global population will drop, reducing the pressure on several of our overshoot problems. Our second unprecedented advantage that was available to no other civilization is that we are now technologically capable of developing cheap green energy sources that are effectively infinite. These two spectacular advantages may arrive like the U.S. Cavalry, just in time to turn us away from the cliff's edge. But the extent of the threats are so severe that at best, as Wellington is famously paraphrased as saying about the Battle of Waterloo, it will be a "damn closely run thing." It will be the Race of Our Lives.

SLOWING POPULATION GROWTH

Jamie and I put out a paper with this title in April 2013, in which we examined the two incredibly fortunate factors that might enable our current world to avoid at least partial collapse. The first was declining fertility. As we have seen, Malthus correctly analyzed the main problem of our history up until around 1800: population had always kept up with food supply, leaving even successful societies only a few bad growing seasons away from starvation. He predicted that this would always be the case but he was wrong on two counts.

The first is a short-term factor – only existing for 200 or 300 years and therefore irrelevant for the longer-term future of our species – and that is the increased ability to extract previously stored energy in the form of fossil fuels. This hydrocarbon interlude will end either when the share of hydrocarbons that can be extracted economically is used up, or more likely when the second law of thermodynamics imposes its tyrannous will: enough of the higher forms of convenient compact energy like coal and oil will have been converted into heat, waste and especially carbon dioxide to ruin our climate and our environment.

Malthus, however, completely missed declining fertility, a potentially very long-term and hence much more critical factor to the survival of our species. Neither he nor anyone else until recently even dreamed that we would voluntarily decide to have fewer children even as we became richer. In his day and until the early 20th century, rich families in many parts of the world routinely had eight or more children. Ironically, it has turned out that the same instincts that bring us the problems of excessive consumption and unnecessarily rapid resource depletion have also brought us the attitude that children are inconvenient and desperately expensive. Improved medical services that further allowed populations to explode now give people the confidence to have smaller families. Improved farm technology lowers the significance of the labor from many children. The most obvious drivers of lower birth rates, though, are the improved education of women and advances in birth control methods. The net effect of these factors is a change so profound that just a hundred years ago it was not even guessed at, and indeed population growth and fertility continued to rise until about 1962 – just the other day.

In the larger and wealthier countries, fertility has fallen below replacement. There has also been a remarkable drop in the richer East Asian countries, including China, with almost a fifth of the world's population. There are a number of important and sometimes spectacularly unexpected examples of slowing population growth. At the top of the unexpected list is Iran, which has dropped from a fertility rate of seven children per woman in 1960 to an almost unbelievable 1.69 in 2021. Another remarkable example of a large Islamic country is Bangladesh, which has also fallen from seven in 1960 to below two. This is extraordinary given the country's extreme poverty. The particularly important case is India, with its 1.4 billion people, which has fallen from six to around two. There are several serious disappointments in regions where the rates have dropped, but populations are still growing rapidly and most of them have intermittent food problems already. They are almost all in Africa, and even there, at current rates of decline, fertility is likely to reach replacement level of 2.1 in a few decades.

FALLING SPERM COUNTS

This remarkable decline in fertility is our best hope, both from our civilization's point of view as well as for the well-being of all the life on our planet. A much smaller population would be a great help in

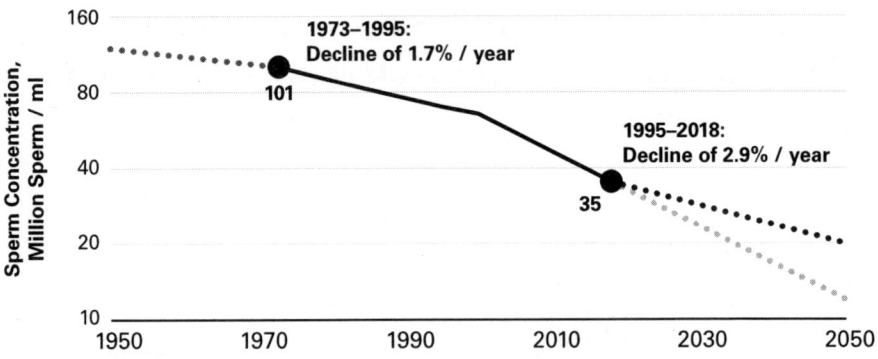

Sperm counts are down two-thirds. The conclusions, in graphical form, of Levine et al.'s definitive study, with my extrapolation into the past and future. Data from GMO and Levine et al. 2017

reducing stress on nature, climate, resources, toxicity and agriculture. However, there's a troubling aspect to the story. Our research showed that we, too, are part of the biodiversity that is threatened: in the developed world there's been over a 50% loss of sperm count over the last half century. The definitive meta-study on the topic of decline in sperm count concluded (from the largest and most rigorous studies selected from over 7,500 abstracts) that sperm concentration in the developed world had fallen from 99 units in 1973 to 47 in 2011.[*] This is a compound rate of decline of 1.9% a year, a rate sure to threaten the viability of our species unless action is taken.

Prior to this paper there had been concerns about falling sperm counts for more than 40 years, but the various studies had individually been considered too local or too small, and even the earlier meta-studies had been found unconvincing by a critical mass of influential academics. This study, though, removed almost all doubts,

---

[*] Hagai Levine et al, "Temporal Trends in Sperm Count: A Systematic Review and Meta-regression Analysis", *Human Reproduction Update*, Volume 23, Issue 6, November-December 2017

to a degree unusual in scientific circles. One Danish study said that healthy young men in Copenhagen today have lower sperm quality than men visiting infertility clinics 70 years ago! In China, coming from way behind us, they have had a 25% loss in the last 20 years. And no one is concerned! The decline in sperm count is probably contributing already to the declining fertility rate of the Western world, along with delayed marriage.

The more we obsessed about this data the more threatening it appeared to be. If the decline in sperm count were to continue, surely it would render the average couple infertile in a few more decades. This line of thought led us to get to know Shanna Swan, co-author of the sperm count meta-study, quite well. She had written a very direct book, *Count Down* (2021), laying out the data in a very straightforward way that made the argument compelling. We were sufficiently impressed to help fund the publicity campaign for the book, despite it being off our topic of climate change. Next we funded a follow-up study, whose objectives were to update the meta-study to the present day and include data from developing countries. That update was published in 2023 and showed that the decline in sperm count had, if anything, accelerated since 2000, and that developing countries showed similar declines.

In March 2021, I penned an op-ed for the *Financial Times* in which I suggested that the 50% decline in sperm count since the early 1970s and an equally rapid increase in age-adjusted miscarriage rates was most likely caused by endocrine disruption, which is the hijacking of our body's hormonal system by environmental toxicants. "The tens of thousands of artificial organic chemical compounds," I wrote, "that we use in everyday life are undoubtedly contributing to these effects. The detrimental health effects of some, such as bisphenol A, phthalates and perfluorinated compounds, are already well known. More research is needed to discover other culprits."

Widespread toxicity from these industrial compounds is causing, even, an apparent drop in human libido, on top of reducing sperm counts and increasing miscarriage rates. This is reflected in the steady decline in measured testosterone. And every study across the world is measuring a rapid decline in sexual activity, in all age groups. In Japan, for example, in a rare peer-reviewed study of 8,000 people between 20 and 49 years old, 45% of both men and women – and 55% of young men from 20 to 29 – had not had sex of any kind in a year – as John McEnroe would say, "you cannot be serious!"

We have created a toxic stew of very many dangerous chemicals. None has ever been tested together with other chemicals by the Environmental Protection Agency, although we know from academic work that in combination their danger levels can rise very materially. A great majority of chemicals have in fact never been tested at all, even on their own. Fertility loss is not the only problem. There are in fact indications that health and longevity in the U.S. are already being affected by high levels of toxicity. The U.S. has the worst numbers in the developed world for life expectancy and is also by far the most profligate country in chemical use. It uses the most per capita and has the least regulation.

Toxicity harms human health in many ways beyond fertility. Obesity rates, as is well known, have exploded globally in the petrochemical era of the last 60 years and there is conclusive evidence, based on controlled experiments in animals, that some specific industrial chemical exposures *in utero* can lead to lifelong weight gain.* The autism epidemic – the 200-fold increase in the rate of autism diagnoses in the past 50 years – is also now widely remarked

---

* The tome on this topic is *The Obesogen Effect* by UC Irvine professor Bruce Blumberg.

upon and still unexplained. There is building evidence that exposure to environmental toxicants causes neurodevelopmental damage that manifests as autism. Parkinson's – the world's fastest growing brain disorder – is now held to be primarily driven by toxic exposures. A very recent paper suggests that the risk of Parkinson's increases by around 150% if you live within a mile of a U.S. golf course, which are typically pesticide-ridden. (An intelligent crow would tell me that I'm proofing this chapter exactly 0.7 miles from our local course.)*

Another shocking paper that came out of the *New England Journal of Medicine* shows that heart disease patients whose arterial plaques contained nanoplastics had a 4.5 times higher risk of subsequent heart attack, stroke or death in the next few years than those who did not.†

From an environmental perspective, a smaller population is exactly what the climate and biosphere need. However, we must still fully decarbonize global industrial systems and reduce CO_2 in the atmosphere to its pre-industrial level of 280 parts per million from its probable future peak of more than 550 parts. Achieving this will require every biological and mechanical innovation of which we are capable. Unfortunately, lower economic growth caused by a

---

* James R Roberts et al., "Children's Low-Level Pesticide Exposure and Associations with Autism and ADHD: A Review," *Pediatric Research* vol. 85, No. 2, 2019; Amy E Kalkbrenner et al., "Environmental Chemical Exposures and Autism Spectrum Disorders: A Review of the Epidemiological Evidence," *Current Problems in Pediatric and Adolescent Health Care* vol. 44, No. 10, 2014; E Ray Dorsey and Bastiaan R Bloem, "Parkinson's Disease Is Predominantly an Environmental Disease," *Journal of Parkinson's Disease* vol. 14, No. 3, 2024; Brittany Krzyzanowski et al., "Proximity to Golf Courses and Risk of Parkinson Disease", *JAMA Network Open* (2025)

† Raffaele Marfella et al., "Microplastics and Nanoplastics in Atheromas and Cardiovascular Events," *The New England Journal of Medicine*, Vol. 390, No. 10, 2024.

shrinking and aging population may weaken not only the necessary innovation and investment but also the resolve to do it. Sustained disappointing growth seems to so easily lead to a frustrated and resentful public. That in turn makes public spending for even the most valuable long-term benefits seem unappealing.

In the worst-affected countries, such as Japan and South Korea, birth rates are already at such low levels that, if maintained for just four generations, these countries will be out of business. In South Korea's future, every eight grandparents will have to share a single grandchild! Try and imagine a society where one grandchild has that kind of burden. And birth rates are still falling. What are the likely outcomes for capitalism and society from a rapidly falling global population of babies and young workers, and an equally rapid increase in the number of unproductive old? In the short and intermediate periods, say up to 50 years, none of the likely outcomes are good. Top-line revenues continually shrink. It is undeniably much harder to manage an economy downwards: as 40 restaurants in the town become 20 and all 40 suffer in the process; and as highway and rail systems become too big for their boots (as it were), how do you select which parts of the infrastructure to maintain? Ask the city management of Detroit. They will tell you it is a very tough management task.

Still, it is important not to lose sight of the fact that ultimately a much smaller population is what civilization needs for its long-term survival. The decline in world population growth and its potential reversal hold out the best hope of maintaining a reasonably stable global civilization and continuing to improve the quality of the average life. The ruinous alternative is to have an ever-growing population run off the cliff collectively.

AGRICULTURAL PROBLEMS

Even if we no longer produce even a single carbon dioxide molecule, ice caps, for example, will melt over the coming centuries and ocean levels will continue to rise by several feet. I don't worry too much about Miami or Boston being under water – that's just the kind of thing that capitalism tends to handle pretty well. The more serious problem posed by ocean level rise will be the loss of the great rice-producing deltas: the Nile, the Mekong, the Ganges and others, which produce about a fifth of all the rice grown in the world. Agriculture is in fact the real underlying problem produced by climate change.

With climate change, there are two separate effects on agriculture. One is immediate: increased droughts, increased floods and

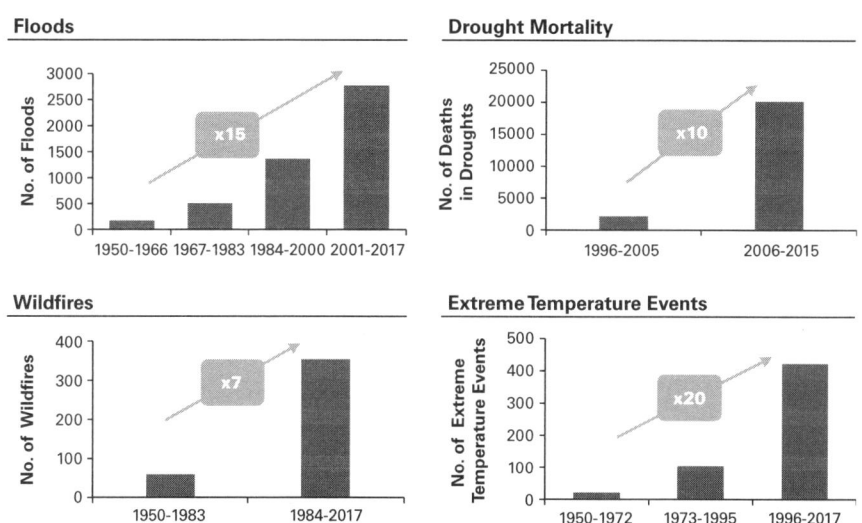

Climate change causes weather shocks. As we showed in "The Race of Our Lives Revisited" paper in 2018, the occurrence of extreme weather events has increased over time as measured by the EM-DAT database of international disasters. Data from GMO and EM-DAT, 2017.

increased temperature reduce quite measurably the productivity of a year's harvest. Then there's the long-term, permanent effect: the most dependable outcome of increased temperature is more water vapor in the atmosphere, currently up about 10% from the old normal. This has already led to a substantial increase in heavy downpours.

In August 2017, Hurricane Harvey dumped 10 inches of rain in a day in Houston, followed by 10 inches, followed by 10 inches. If you try to put a probability on that it just does not compute. Perhaps a 1-in-1,000-year event, perhaps almost impossible. It turns out that within the prior 18 months, Houston had already had a 1-in-200-year event. Within 18 months before that, a 50- to a 100-year event. In Japan in July 2018 almost 200 lives were lost and 2 million people were asked to evacuate because of a downpour that was so far off the scale that it made Harvey look like drizzle: 23 inches of rain in one single day. The number of floods is up by 15 times from 1950, deaths from drought up by 10 times, wildfires by seven times and extreme temperature events by 20 times.

It is precisely the heavy downpours that cause soil erosion. With regular rain, even heavy rain, farmers lose very little soil. It is the one or two great downpours every few years that cause the trouble. We're losing perhaps 1% of our collective global soil a year. We are losing about a half a percent of our arable land a year. Fortunately, it is the least productive half a percent. It is calculated that there are only 30 to 70 good harvest years left, depending on your location. In 80 years, current agriculture will be simply infeasible for lack of good soil. We must change our system completely to make it sustainable, which, critically, involves reducing erosion to almost zero by using no-till or low-till farming combined with cover crops. Because these are significant changes for a conservative community, it will take decades and we've barely started.

As we dug into these problems, we quickly discovered the giant seams that can run between different branches of science. Starting with erosion, we spoke to several soil scientists who specialized in erosion who were not aware that future climate change would materially affect erosion even though, as previously mentioned, the single most dependable feature of climate change is an increase in the very heavy downpours that do almost all the erosion damage – with 5- to 10-foot gullies sometimes appearing overnight after the great storms in Iowa and Kansas.

One of my horror show exhibits illustrates the loss of topsoil. It features a particular farming county in Iowa. In 1850, this county had 14 inches of wonderful Midwestern topsoil. Ideally, you need only 4 inches and 3 will get you by. Fourteen inches is a luxury beyond belief for the rest of the world. But by 1900, it was 11.5 inches; by 1950, 9.5 inches; by 1975, 7 inches; by 2000, 5.5 inches. At considerable difficulty, we found the experts responsible for the data on soil in Iowa. We called them and asked what the number was for 2017. And they said, "Yes, erosion is recognized now as a major problem. People are trying much harder; the rate of erosion has come down by a lot, by nearly half." But by then local soil depth was just 4.8 inches. Just think about that: 14 inches down to 4.8 inches. Our safety margin has gone from 11 inches to 1 or 2 inches. Yet there are still no signs of panic that reach the public or, apparently, the politicians. That may not scare you, but it certainly scares me. (The devil must be pleased with how his contract with the farmers is proceeding.)

A report from the journal *Proceedings of the National Academy of Sciences* studies the effects that actual downpours, droughts and increasing temperatures had on agricultural productivity in America over the last 50 years, and calculated the effect by each specific grain in each specific area. They put all that data into their model so that they captured the increasing incidence of floods and droughts from climate change. The authors then extrapolated the midrange of climate models into the future, building in the expected increases in heavy floods and severe droughts out to 2040, when the temperature increases also begin to really hurt (having had little effect up to now, with some areas gaining and some losing). They concluded that by 2040, if nothing else changed, the impact of climate change would be to take grain productivity all the way back to where it was in 1980. If this is true, it is incredibly bad news.

When we called in the lead author, Dr. Liang, to ask him some questions, he seemed unaware that erosion had any important impact on the future of agriculture. It does seem to be a problem: climate scientists like him in one box and erosion scientists, with mud on their boots, in another, with very little communication or attempts to coordinate. It is a problem for most specialists – and one we can sympathize with – that to be on top of their fields they have to have a very tight focus.

Every species has its limits. Humans will never be 12 feet tall. Let me point out they've been breeding racehorses for thousands of years – the chief of the tribe always wanted to have the fastest horse – and they're still breeding them today. Yet Secretariat still has the record for one and a half miles on dirt, set in June 1972 at the Belmont Stakes. Horses haven't gotten materially faster for 50 years and they were barely getting faster for years before that. You can't get blood out of a stone. You can get the horses to break more legs, but you can't get them to run much faster because they are already close to their limit. Now grain, too, has diminishing returns. When looking for diminishing returns, go to the best grain producers on the planet per acre. (Not the U.S. The U.S. is the best per person, say, a 62-year-old farmer and his son and 6,000 acres.) If you want the best per acre, you go to rice in Japan and wheat in Germany, France and the U.K. Their grain yields were growing brilliantly forever – until the last 30 years, when their progress became very slow and erratic. It is what you should expect.

One of the reasons for this is that increased fertilizer use, the backbone of the Green Revolution, is also peaking out. You can use more in poor parts of the world, but the U.S. and China, the two biggest users, already use too much – so much, it begins to be counterproductive as well as damaging to the health of waterways from excessive run-off of phosphorus and nitrogen. The growth in agricultural productivity in the U.S. was chugging along at a nice 1.5% a year from the 1930s. In the Green Revolution of the fifties and sixties, we accelerated for 20 years to 3.5% a year. Quite remarkable – every three years there was a 10% increase in the amount of crops grown on the same land. After that, productivity growth dropped back, then started to drop to new modern lows. Our 2010–2030 estimate, based on talking to scientists, is that productivity per acre will still continue to grow, other things being even, but at a slowly diminishing rate as we approach limits.

We also have bug and pathogen immunities to consider. Do you know we lose as much of our crop to weeds, bugs and pathogens today, as a percentage, as we did in 1945 before we declared chemical war on these organisms? If we pull back from the chemicals now, the bugs and weeds, which have turned into super bugs and super weeds, will eat our breakfast, lunch and dinner. Had we never splurged on chemicals, we would be losing approximately the same amount as we are now but saving impressive amounts of money – approximately as much as for feed or fertilizer.

Before we finish on farming, I'd like to touch on the global distribution of phosphate reserves. We cannot grow any living thing without potassium (potash) and phosphorus (phosphate). We mine these elements, which are very, very finite. We dig these essential fertilizers out and because they are cheap we scatter them in excess around our farms (where the heavy rains often carry them off and pollute the streams and rivers). The problem is that 75% of all the high-grade phosphorus reserves in the world are in Morocco and Western Sahara (which Morocco controls). This share of reserves makes OPEC and Saudi Arabia look like absolute pikers, and phosphate is much more important even than oil. Phosphorus, the key ingredient in phosphate, is an element and cannot be made or substituted. We simply cannot manage for long under currently configured agriculture without Morocco's reserves – perhaps 40 to 50 years. With Morocco's reserves we have much longer, but the world's dependence on this key resource is frightening. If we are lucky we will have enough time to convert much of global agriculture to be sustainable and regenerative with much-reduced need for external fertilizer.

Then there is urban expansion, which is nearly always in fertile river plains, taking the best arable land and concreting it over – calculated to be about 2.5 million acres a year. Plus, there are water availability problems from hell. Reservoirs in South Africa, in Morocco, in Spain, in Nevada, are all shrinking, all suffering from the increased heat. We're depleting our aquifers: in heavily irrigated areas such as Las Vegas or the Central Valley of California, well water levels have fallen by hundreds of feet. In China, parts of Beijing are sinking by a few inches a year – that's how fast they're pumping out the water. Over half a billion people globally totally depend on underground, very finite aquifers for their water and food. For all these many reasons, agriculture is key to our future success or failure. It is also where climate change has its most consequential effects. But, sadly, it is not the only problem.

INSECT LOSS

Now, we come to the next piece of very bad news: the 75% loss of flying insects. This is from a report done by German insect fanatics, amateurs who love insects. They went out every year to take samples from 63 forests. They put out the same nets in the same places at the same time of year. They took all the bugs they caught and laid them out and counted them. Germans are unbeatable at this type of thing! And to everyone's shock and horror, over 27 years there had been more than a 75% decline in the total quantity of flying insects. These are our pollinators. They have just gone missing. Why isn't this a dramatic item in our news? One-third of all the food plants we eat need pollination, every flower needs a pollinator. What we've done is create a toxic world, which is apparently not conducive to life as we know it.

Toxicity together with climate change and population pressure form an unprecedented threat to biodiversity. We are, as you probably know by now, in the sixth great extinction. The first five were caused by meteorites and by great shifts in the climate caused by the sun. This sixth one is caused by us, the people. I think toxicity and the chemicals causing it will turn out to be a hotter button than climate change. Climate change is regrettably a bit like the story of boiling the frog in the pot. (Speaking of which, frogs are going extinct too – scientists say the total amphibian population is falling 4% every year.) Toxicity, sperm counts, insects going missing and birds and frogs going with them is something that I think can excite people to action. Europe has turned unexpectedly serious, for example, on the risks of plastics, banning some single-use plastics. The European Union has also banned three incredibly important neonicotinoids that are hyper-effective at killing honey bees. And very probably do, along with all other flying insects that come near them. This is the problem though: in the EU, if regulators have some doubt, a company must prove its chemical is clean. But in the U.S., the chemical company has the benefit of the doubt. The U.S. will take the side, at least for the next few years, of the chemical companies because there is a lot of uncertainty. This is a complicated soup we are dealing with – it is hard to impossible to positively prove which chemical is contributing precisely to what damage. Have we in the U.S., inadvertently or otherwise, adopted an ultra-corporate-friendly standard that will produce so toxic an environment before we act that the consequences – totally avoidable on paper – will be extreme? In any case in the U.S., the chemical companies will get the benefit of the doubt – not our sperm count or flying insects or life in general – at least until we are more obviously on the ropes. An interesting choice to make.

THE OPTIMIST'S SPIN

There's a cheerful professor at Harvard, Steven Pinker, who's come out with a couple of books saying how wonderful things are. On the data he uses, he's absolutely accurate. Yes, we do live longer. Yes, we have fewer wars, fewer murders and fewer this and fewer that. But what he doesn't account for is sustainability and toxicity: that we're using up our resources and threatening our biosphere. It's a bit like the guy who falls off the top of the Empire State Building, and as he passes each floor on the way down he is heard to say, "So far, so good." "14 inches of soil, life expectancy increases, so far, so good." "12 inches of soil, 8 inches, 4 inches, so far, so good." "80% of our sperm count, 50%, so far, so good." "80% of our flying insects, 50%, 25%, so far, so good." We're simply not accounting for the real underlying damage. Without that accounting, things can indeed be construed as looking pretty good. It's seductive. Right up to the moment the body hits the ground, most of the numbers look better and better and just a few look worse and worse. But how super critical those few worse numbers are.

"The Race of Our Lives," and its follow-up, "The Race of Our Lives Revisited" (August 2018) are our two most important papers of the post-crisis period. I got to present the second at Morningstar's annual bash. And for once, I bushwhacked them. They were totally not ready for it, and it was incredibly effective and they were wetting their pants. Normally it bounces off; it's like water off a duck's back. They don't care. But this one managed to hit the right tone at the right time. And I just nailed it and it caused a real stir for the people who were there – it sunk in that maybe they should start worrying. The paper also attracted the attention of Eric Schmidt, the former CEO of Google, who tweeted it to his 2 million followers, so that it got to echo around Silicon Valley. This and other publicity we received led us to decide that our highest and best purpose at the Grantham Foundation was probably in influencing wealthy individuals to recognize that they could have a real effect on some of the most important environmental problems. And alongside that effort, my aim was to continue the long uphill slog to nudge the corporate and finance worlds to recognize the critical investment importance of decarbonizing the economy and generally mitigating climate damage.

Going forward, I'd tell them, the types of problems we have to deal with include climate change, environmental pollution, toxicity, resource limitations and the deficiencies of capitalism. These problems require thinking that is both long term and puts the common good above corporate interests. Unfettered capitalism, however desirable in principle, can't provide the answers. It can never prevent over-grazing or over-fishing of common property, any more than it can handle over-carbonizing of our atmosphere. Whether the think tanks and libertarians like it or not, tragedies of the commons need enlightened government, cooperation and leadership.

People tend to wait until there's a crisis to do something. The problem with climate change is that it is irreversible. When you drive a creature out of business, it doesn't come back. And when you destroy a habitat, it typically doesn't come back. The language "It's too late" is very unsuitable for most environmental issues. It's too late for the dodo and for people who've starved to death already, but it's not too late to prevent an even bigger crisis. The sooner we act on the environment, the better. We're racing to not just protect our grandchildren, but also our species. If you do it, you will at least be able to look your children in the eyes.

ENERGY TRANSITION

Fossil fuels will either run out, destroy the planet or both. The only possible way to avoid this outcome is rapid and complete decarbonization of our economy. Needless to say, this is an extremely difficult thing to pull off. It needs the best of our talents and innovation, which almost miraculously, it may be getting. It also needs much better than normal long-term planning and leadership, which it most decidedly is not yet getting. *Homo sapiens* can easily handle this problem, in practice; it will be a closely run race. I like to say never underestimate technology and never underestimate the ability of *Homo sapiens* to screw it up.

This brings us to the second factor that might just save us from civilizational collapse. It involves a branch of the "cornucopian" optimism that I usually deplore: that the infinite human brain combined with technology will solve all problems. Yes, this is the same brain that brought us World War II and, before that, the collapse of many civilizations. An obvious generic weakness in this cornucopian argument is that it ignores our massive dependence on cheap energy. For the last 200 years or so, each new wave of technology – steam engines and railroads, electrification, automobiles and even the internet and AI – required a new wave of fossil energy. Yet now, finally, there is an example of a great technological leap that reduces our fossil energy use – the technologies of solar, wind power and other alternatives as well as electric grid efficiencies and improved energy storage. Backing up these established, though still improving, technologies are some vast potential future sources of green energy: fusion, which now seems feasible from a technological viewpoint, and geothermal, which (if we could just transfer a small fraction of the drilling experience and technology gained from fracking) could be massive.

For once, many of the innovations, corporate start-ups and risk taking – the best part of the capitalist system – are working to decrease our use of depleting hydrocarbons and therefore to increase our chance of stabilizing our civilization before the cliff edge is reached. There has been a truly remarkable decline in the cost of electricity from photovoltaic cells. The only thing to compare it to is the Moore's Law decline in the price of semiconductors. That would indeed be a happy comparison, for the perceived physical limits to semiconductor progress have been overcome time and time again. If the physical limits on photovoltaic efficiency, and hence its price, are similarly maneuvered in future decades, then the price of photovoltaic energy would guarantee us cheap and plentiful energy forever.

Wind power may also be vital in less sunny zones, but there the cost reductions have been impeded by the rising price of steel, cement and aluminum from which wind towers are built (and all of which are incredibly energy-intensive). In future, both solar and wind power are likely to be cheaper than coal. All these comparisons, of course, are made without charging coal for "externalities" – those ills that the coal industry inflicts that we the people have to pay for: mountain tops ripped off and mountain streams polluted, acid rain and particulate matter damaging health. Even more serious in the long run, the CO_2 that is released by burning coal results in the rising costs of more extreme weather-related events. Even without this litany of social costs, coal is likely to be a hopeless choice for electricity generation as the price for alternatives falls. Yet coal plants are still being built in China and India – both with plenty of coal reserves and little natural gas – even as they ramp up alternatives. So even if coal's days are numbered, there will be plenty more parts per million of CO_2 put out in this race.

We have the time, technology and money to completely replace non-renewable energy over the coming decades and, on average, in that time period such replacement will be economic (less so in the earlier years but by a wide margin later). As we do it, we will increasingly have much lower marginal costs, for what is often forgotten in these comparisons is that the high cost component in our two main alternatives, solar and wind, are up-front capital costs. Once constructed, the marginal costs of merely operating the wind and solar farms are far lower than the marginal costs of digging and shipping coal, even without those other health and environmental costs borne by the general public.

You should be aware that the required investment return (hurdle rate) for alternative energy investments in developing countries is often higher than for traditional corporate investments, partly because of unnecessary uncertainties still surrounding these projects: erratic government policies, rapidly changing technologies resulting in most projects having new features and general unfamiliarity to providers of capital. But what of the social benefits of these alternative energy projects? Solving our long-term energy problems may not only be the most critical economic problem, but it may also be one of the two most critical inputs into our future viability as a civilization.

A discount rate that reflected this significance should obviously, in a reasonable world, be far less than the 10% or 15% return typically needed by a corporation for such projects. I could make a case for a zero social return hurdle in this extreme case, but let us merely settle for a lower-than-average corporate hurdle rate – say, 5%. At a 5% real return (which, by the way, compares to an average delivered 7% real return on all corporate capital in the past), these wind and solar projects would have a much lower levelized cost of energy (the cost that reflects both operating and capital costs) than they would have at higher corporate rates – up to 40% lower. At those lower capital costs, typical wind power projects would be more economical than a typical coal-fired plant. The point to remember is that once the capital is found and the project is built, a wind or solar farm delivers far cheaper energy than a coal-fired utility plant, at around one-third of the marginal cost of coal. Large-scale wind farms in Australia now have levelized costs that are lower than recent coal plants even though coal is plentiful and cheap Down Under.

ENERGY STORAGE

Energy storage is the holy grail of environmental progress. The bad news is that progress in the past has been slow. The good news is that there are now scores, if not hundreds, of research teams working on this. Before wind and solar reach a large percentage of total electricity production, it is extremely likely in my opinion that some major breakthrough will be made in storage, especially at the retail level where a storage device, unlike a car battery, can be heavy, bulky and relatively inefficient as long as it is cheap. Cheapness would deliver to the household electric market the potential for grid independence. However, let it be admitted that a lack of progress in energy storage could materially slow down the rate at which alternative energy is adopted. It is therefore an area that particularly needs encouragement and good fortune.

Over several decades, modernizing the grid to allow much wider and more efficient transfer will dramatically reduce storage needs. Reaching into homes and using temporary electric car battery and refrigerator adjustments, etc. (all by agreement with the end user and for a discount) would also reduce the problem. Coal for electricity generation is just not necessary today in the U.S., and the last coal plants anywhere may be built in the next 20 years. Whether we can move fast enough on these fronts and at the same time reduce the output of greenhouse gases to avoid going off the cliff is simply not knowable for certain, but every minute saved and improvement made betters our odds. Let the race begin.

GREEN INVESTING

Given the vital role that new technologies have to play in saving the planet, it should be clear that green investing isn't just a way to make money. It's an existential necessity. In recent years there's been a move within the investment industry that prioritizes environmental issues, social issues and corporate governance (ESG). S and G are terrific – what's not to like about good behavior? But E is a matter of survival. And it's clear that if you ignore E you're likely to wake up and find that the biggest industry loss of value in history is behind you and you missed it. Arguably, the whole point of ESG investing is to help put a value on our grandchildren.

The interest in ESG didn't necessarily arise because of a sudden outbreak of virtue among the investing public. It could be just good business. In fact, there's quite a lot of work which suggests that firms that are early movers on good behavior are simply thinking more deeply about the future, how it will look, how things will play out over 10 or 15 years. A study by HBS concluded that, in the past, the companies that were good on ESG did exactly that, and they outperformed.

If you're a manufacturer of consumer goods and people become worried about the plastics in your product, or botulism in your food, you lose business. In "The Race of Our Lives Revisited" I drew attention to the risks to public health from the widespread use of chemicals whose effects were poorly understood. As it turned out – a complete coincidence – Monsanto was successfully sued a few weeks after that 2018 paper was published and, just 18 months later, three successful suits (with many thousands of claims still outstanding) caused Monsanto's parent company Bayer to lose market capitalization, relative to other chemical companies, approximately equal to the entire price – over $60 billion – that Bayer had paid for Monsanto just two years earlier! This loss of value was caused entirely by a relatively marginal cancer, non-Hodgkin's lymphoma.

Global warming will be the most important investment issue for the foreseeable future. Climate change poses many risks for investors. Carbon pricing, technological disruption in the energy, automobile and utilities industries and stranded assets (i.e. the risk that fossil fuel producers will be forced to leave reserves in the ground) are just a few examples of climate-related threats that loom large and must be considered. Oil companies face increased regulation and costly lawsuits. In other industries, such as tobacco, firms have been forced to pay up when found to have knowingly sold harmful products. The oil industry faces a similar reckoning. This is the first time that a major industry has been put on notice that it is going out of business, even if it may take a long time. Investors need to pay attention to this risk. A lead indicator of this threat of loss comes from China's automobile industry, the biggest and fastest growing in the world, that will likely exceed 55% of EVs sold in 2025; it's such rapid growth that Chinese oil demand – traditionally half of incremental global demand – will probably start to drop in the next few years.

In my view, investments that benefit from the greening of the economy – anything to do with renewable energy, the electrification of the system, electric cars, etc. – in the long run will do much better than the rest. These companies are set to have top-line revenues that dwarf the declining growth rate of the rest of the global economy. To take advantage of these opportunities, in April 2017 we launched the GMO Climate Change Fund, managed by Lucas White, which employs a value-oriented approach to select stocks involved in energy transition. As for GMO's other funds, our fiduciary responsibility made it impossible to manage clients' money exactly as I would manage my own money. But there's no rule saying I can't proselytize those factors I believe are most critical, and I do. If it influences them, brilliant. If it doesn't, tough luck – I do what I can with what I've been given.

VENTURE CAPITAL

I've had a freer rein with the Foundation's investments. Up to 2008 I was doing the same as I would have done running a GMO portfolio. And because I was running increasingly scared at the time, we had a big position in anti-risk. I'm happy to say that that exploded in our favor at the time of the Lehman crisis. After 2008, the Foundation was being advised by David Thurston, one of the most experienced and smartest advisors at Cambridge Associates. I had known David for a very long while. We had both sat on the investment committees of Shady Hill School and the Massachusetts Society for the Prevention of Cruelty to Children for almost 20 years. Under David's control, the MSPCC became the best-performing small institution in the U.S. And he was pushing hard for us to get into venture capital (VC).

Until that point, I'd dabbled in VC with little success. Not having any special skills in that field, I had operated with a simple rule of thumb. I would only do a deal if someone with a real reputation, such as the venture capitalist Vinod Khosla or Silicon Valley's Kleiner Perkins, was an investor, and then I'd co-invest on the same terms. I did a series of those, and they all went bust at $10 million a crack. No one told me that Khosla and Kleiner Perkins were going to run into a buzzsaw. What is infamously known as Climate Tech 1.0 turned into a bloodbath. Fortunately, I was saved from utter disaster by an investment in QuantumScape, a company that was developing a solid-state lithium battery. A nod to our friends at Capricorn who talked us into what for me was a ridiculously large investment that ultimately made 10 times our initial stake (see next chapter).

Anyhow, I had a lot of respect for David. And I certainly liked the idea. In 2009, Ramsay Ravenel joined the Foundation as its first full-time employee. Ramsay had a background in green investment. We decided to start a VC portfolio, and within five years we were investing 20% of our total capital in mission-driven projects. Over the following years our green VC position got larger and larger. We now have up to a third of the Foundation's endowment invested in early-stage VC funds chosen by Cambridge Associates. We have another third invested in green tech VC using our own team of six very smart and highly motivated investors. The remaining third of our capital is invested by Ramsay and me, which includes allocations to GMO's Resources Fund and its Climate Change Fund, but whose main requirement, given two-thirds of the Foundation's assets are in VC, is liquidity.

It's hard for me to separate my growing enthusiasm for VC from David's. His was very much based on the long-term performance as shown in their data at Cambridge Associates. Mine was very much based on my belief that venture capital is the pride and joy of American capitalism. It's far better to be in the U.S. for VC than anywhere else. We generate the best ideas. We have perhaps 15 of the world's 20 great research universities that are integral to the flow of ideas. We take risk better than any other group on the planet with maybe Australia close behind. We also attract the best and the brightest from all over the world. More than half of all founders of unicorns (start-ups worth more than $1 billion) were born outside the U.S.

All the best and brightest now come into VC, all starting their new firms, as they should. It's the most useful branch of capitalism and particularly in green tech, highly suited in every way you can think of as serious investing. Venture capital has the potential to change the world for the better and, at the same time, can make you a very handsome return. And, of course, I want absolutely to make as much money as possible for the Foundation because we can use it. The green tech world is unlike any other quadrant of capitalism. These people are genuinely and thoroughly concerned: it's a big part of their driving force that there is an existential risk that they're doing something about. This is really heartening. I joke that they may get drummed out of the capitalism club because they have all these altruistic attitudes.

When putting money into start-ups, the risk to each individual investment is clearly higher than any other group of investing. Only by investing in a large variety of funds can you be certain that nearly every brilliant new idea will be picked up. Basically, in round numbers for the last 30 years, every important new idea – Amazon, Snapchat, Facebook, Google, Tesla – have all come out of VC. They didn't come from spin-offs from companies like 3M, as they used to in the old days. Large American corporations used to throw plenty of capital at their own internal ventures. But they have pulled back steadily and very substantially over the years. They now rely on the VC industry to pick winners. Large public corporations buy the winners once their success is proven and they are running smoothly. What that does is it takes the volatility out of corporate earnings and turns R&D into a capital transaction. Of course, they give up some return, passing that on to the early-stage venture capitalists. But risk-adjusted, you could say, it's satisfactory for them.

People say, look at all the money going into VC, as it has over the last decade. I reply, "Dude, you are missing the big picture." The total amount of money going into start-ups and ventures of all kinds is way down. The total amount of VC done by the capitalist system has gone down. It's just that the amount done in Silicon Valley has gone up. The opportunities are still just as good, if not better, than they used to be. There's a shortage of R&D capital, and yet people don't see it. Money invested in new ventures is way down. For evidence of this trend, look at how many people are employed in America in companies that are one or two years old. It is half of what it was in the mid-1970s.

I believe that early-stage green VC has the potential to make more profit than any other area of venture capital, because the environment is moving in our favor – the real environment and the financial environment. There is a wall of global money coming to decarbonize the global economy. It will take trillions of dollars. And what will happen, in my opinion, is that there will be a bottleneck for the early-stage green companies. There will be more money trying to get into the best new ideas, and there are many new ideas, by the way, and they will really prosper. People are flocking in from around the world into green tech. But investing has always been a boom-and-bust business and the more important the theme – and decarbonizing the global economy is one of the most important in history – the more impressive these cycles of boom and bust will be. It will be profitable, I believe, but it will not be a smooth ride.

The mission component on some of our investments is often so on target that even if they fail to make money, they still deserve some of our non-profit-making grants. Our hope is that at least one of the several game-changing projects for CO_2-reducing technologies going forward will simultaneously make our Foundation a fortune. I've mentioned our investment in QuantumScape, which aims to double the power-to-weight ratio of lithium ion batteries, and we have multiple investments in improved lithium extraction technologies. In vehicle development, the biggest opportunity we see is ultra-light electric-powered people movers, suitable for commuting and shopping in developed countries. Better make hay soon, Tesla! But you never know. Venture investing is particularly full of disappointments.

Our Foundation team has also done more than 50 direct investment deals on carbon sequestration. And we think they'll be ingenious and terrific and get the cost of removing CO_2 from the atmosphere down to $50 a ton, a tenth of its current cost. When we scale this up, it should become brilliantly cheaper. One of my favorite down-to-earth little projects is a robot that runs slowly on its own across a field, gathering about half the corn stubble and converting it at a very high temperature into biochar. Biochar is wonderful for microorganisms, wonderful for water retention; it really improves the soil. The problem is that until now you've had to convert agricultural waste into biochar, then truck it to the farm and distribute it over the land. It's all horrifically energy-intensive and expensive. But this little machine takes the stubble right there and converts it to biochar on the spot. And it does it potentially very cheaply, incrementally at something close to $10 a ton or maybe zero because the value of the soil enhancement on its own is enough to justify the process. The carbon sequestration, which is very substantial, is a free good. So, that fits in what we call the too-good-to-be-true category, of which there are quite a few.

People are racing into research labs from all over the world with a vision of having their own green VC company and making a fortune. And we have a wicked advantage, which is that we go to the labs and ask, "Who's doing what?" And if we like it, we'll fund them. We call it grants to commercialization. We fund the research and if it goes ahead, we get to co-invest with whoever leads them forward. And in a couple of cases, we have been the lead. We're one of the more aggressive operators so we often know early on what's going on at top research universities.

And this meshes very well with our big effort in investing. For instance, one research idea is to replace fertilizer with bacteria that fixes nitrogen in the soil. Well, nitrogen-based fertilizer is very, very energy-intensive. About 2 or 3% of all CO_2 emissions are from the Haber-Bosch process. We need to change this. Currently, a lot of the nitrogen gets washed off the soil, especially if there's a storm. But the plants need it steadily when they're growing. So, farmers put on much more nitrogen than they need, which means even more gets washed away. But if you can get microbes to fix the nitrogen, they release it slowly. There's no waste. No pollution. It's a great idea. We have another investment in very early-stage research that might improve the productivity of wheat and rice by 10% or 15%. These are the kinds of things one wants to be doing.

To date, the Foundation has distributed more than $700 million of grants since inception. Our plan is to spend around a third of our distributions on grants to commercialization. Another third on what I call environmental propaganda – attacking the enemy. Everything else goes to the academic institutions and our legacy relationships with WWF, The Nature Conservancy, Environmental Defense Fund and the Rocky Mountain Institute. We fund the legacy group at a fairly steady level with a tighter and tighter focus on our kinds of projects. They are very influential, and it is useful to have an army of scientists cooperate with us. Four of their people sit as outside directors on the board of our public trust – a public trust has to have a majority of outside directors – and they are extremely encouraging in their support, perhaps because we are doing the sorts of things they would like to do if they were smaller.

FOUNDATION TEAM

We have put together a very good team of experienced people, a team of six or seven doing our own green investing. Ramsay is the Foundation's president and CIO, Michele Martin its CFO and the managing director is Kevin Tidwell, who leads a team of six doing our own green investing. Jamie Lee helps me with research and writing and a handful of other tasks. I could not have wished for more agreeable colleagues. They are also very well intentioned, and other things being equal, it is good to deal with people who are well intentioned. They know what mistakes to look for, and they recognize an important idea when they see one.

We have a battle plan, which, funnily enough, we share with Khosla. We will invest in nothing, even if it works, unless it is going to be very important – game-changing – for our mission. Making money is not enough. It has to be an important idea. I say all the time to my troops at the Foundation that we have captured the feeling of the early years of GMO, when everything was new and we tried everything we could think of, with nothing to lose. And the essence of that is when I sit down with Ramsay and two or three others once a month or more and say, "Tell me again, what are we trying to do?" We believe this is what separates us as an NGO from almost all the others. We're operating as if we're a hedge fund, as if time is urgent, as if time is money, as if we're trying to maximize our returns on everything and we have a completely open mind. And to rub in our advantages we are answerable to no one. We have no career risk, which is the curse of almost everyone's life. Well, to be fair, I should probably say I have none and I do my best to make sure my colleagues feel as little as possible.

CORNUCOPIANS VERSUS PESSIMISTS

With the environmental damage reports steadily coming in worse than expected, and with technology in alternatives steadily coming in better than forecast, the race of our lives remains undecided. The pessimists, aka the Malthusians, seem determined to believe that nothing can save us, and, to be fair, their case is disturbingly well reasoned. They point out that our complex economy is tuned to be energy-intensive and needs a very high return on energy expended to sustain itself. They brush off the claims of optimists as superficial, wishful thinking.

"Rubbish," say the optimists, aka the Cornucopians, who argue that technology and redesign are everything. Making homes and other buildings as energy-efficient as possible using existing technology, introducing new lightweight electric cars and reducing waste everywhere can reduce energy intensity by up to a half over the next 30 years from today's needs. Improvements in farming practices, such as no-till and regenerative agriculture, can reduce soil erosion, toxicity and agricultural energy use. New sources of cheap energy – including nuclear fusion and geothermal (in which the Foundation has some investments) – can wean humanity off its dependence on finite and polluting fossil fuels.

As I struggle to decide which of these two powerful opposing ideas is winning, I have begun to think that it comes down to two very different takes on us humans. The optimists are accurately describing what we are capable of if we put our best foot forward, and the pessimists are describing what to expect given what they see as our rather dismal record of rising and failing civilizations. I am, though, sustained by the hope that the pessimists are underestimating the degree to which we can scale back and bear deprivations as we did in WWII, as in the U.K., where even potatoes and bread were rationed by the end. Yet, the social system stayed intact and many people were happier than they had been, the result of being given an unavoidable collective challenge. I do think that when times get much tougher, most will rise to the occasion. And, you never know your luck – even Congress might pitch in. Will it be enough? For today, anyway, until I read something to convince me otherwise, I side with the optimists. But as I say, it is going to be a very close and painful race. (My pessimism has deepened several degrees since the current Trump administration has shown itself to be so virulently opposed to environmental issues.)

CHAPTER 11

Waiting for the Last Dance

The recovery for the U.S. stock market was 80% in 2009, second only to 1932, and the really speculative stocks were almost double the market, as they also were in 1932. But 1932 was far worse than our latest crisis. Back then, they deserved that kind of rally. A year after my "Reinvesting When Terrified," financial conditions had turned extraordinarily loose. My April 2010 letter described the change in the market's mood:

> It's spring, and this spring a young man's fancy lightly turns to thoughts of speculation. The Fed's promises look good and, as long as you're not a small business, you can borrow to invest or speculate at no cost. The market has had a near record rally, sprinting far past our estimated fair value of 875 for the S&P 500. Bernanke is, in fact, begging us to speculate, and is being mean only to conservative investors like pensioners who cannot make a penny on their cash. Collectively, we forgo hundreds of billions of potential interest, but at least we can feel noble because we are helping to restore the financial health of the banks and bankers, who under these conditions could not fail to make a fortune even if brain dead. Oh, for the good old days when we could just settle for a normal market-clearing rate of interest…

Investors used to be more pain-averse. It used to be "once bitten, twice shy." This time, surely it should be "twice bitten, once shy!" The key shift seems to be the confidence we now have in Bernanke's soldiering on with low rates and moral hazard to the bitter end, if necessary, cliff or no cliff. The concept of moral hazard has changed. It used to be a vague expression of intent: "If anything goes wrong, I will help you if I can." It seems to have been transmuted into a cast-iron commitment. The Fed seems to be pledging that it will bail us out after every flood. All that is lacking is a rainbow!

SEVEN LEAN YEARS

I was convinced that this strong market response occurred because stocks are far more sensitive to both low rates and the Fed's promises than the economy. The revised numbers showed that at the 2009 low we had had by far the biggest drawdown in GDP (−5.1%) since the Great Depression. The economy was limping back into action but faced some tough long-term headwinds. At the time, most businesspeople (and the Fed) assumed that economic growth would recover to its old rate. I did not. In May 2009, I wrote that although the economy was likely to pick up, I believed that the longer-term health of the economy would remain weaker than the old normal. While many people were predicting a rapid V-shaped recovery, I thought we were facing a VL-shaped recovery, as in a "very long" and drawn out period of slow economic growth, a biblical Seven Lean Years. I forecast that the developed world would probably need to settle for about 2% trendline GDP growth, down from the 3.5% to which we used to aspire.

GDP growth can be conveniently divided into population effects and everything else, loosely described as "productivity." The developed nations were getting older and their annual workforce growth was set at less than 0.5% a year and steadily declining going forward – down from 1.5% in the 1970s. The outlook for productivity growth was also poor. The massive bailout program stopped the meltdown of the financial system and engineered at least a temporary economic recovery. We knew the obvious cost of this bailout in terms of the unprecedented deterioration of the Federal Reserve's balance sheet. But what of the less obvious costs incurred by taking away the rewards of caution by saving the reckless and incompetent? Those weak enterprises, financial and others, which should have been gobbled up by the stronger, more prudent and more competent natural survivors, instead lingered on with a long-term cost of reduced productivity. Productivity gains were also reduced by the somewhat slower rate of introduction of new, more productive, factories and equipment warranted by lower workforce growth. (In subsequent years, as I began to obsess about population growth, I became convinced that crashing workforce growth must enormously sap Keynes's critically important animal spirits, as seen in Japan's lost decades; and that we were almost all following Japan into a severe population bust.)

The most frightening aspect of my seven-lean-years scenario was that although the credit crisis was caused by too much credit on too sloppy a basis, the presumed cure was to increase aggregate debt by flooding economies with government debt. The widespread belief among economists is that more debt boosts economic growth. My heretical view is that debt doesn't matter all that much to long-term growth rates. What I owe you, and you owe Fred and Fred owes me is not very important; on the positive side, all it can do is move demand forward and then give it back later. This is the paper world. It is, in an important sense, not the real world. In the real world, growth depends on real factors: the quality and quantity of education, work ethic, and population profile, the quality and quantity of existing plant and equipment, business organization, the quality of public leadership (especially from the Fed in the U.S.), and the quality (not quantity) of existing regulations and their enforcement. If you really want to worry about growth, you should be concerned about sliding educational standards, inadequate capital investment and R&D expenditures and, above all, falling birth rates and an aging population.

In the U.S. the 3.4% historic average trend line of what I called Battleship GDP had been intact for over 100 years, from 1880 to 1982, just about the longest such growth spurt in history. Yet over the following three decades from 1982, we tripled our debt and GDP growth slowed. And it slowed increasingly, especially after 2000 and even more after 2008. It is possible to argue that the decline in GDP might have been even worse if we had not been wallowing in debt. But to me, it suggests that there is no important long-term connection between debt and GDP growth. All the real power of debt, to my mind, is negative: it can gum up the works in a liquidity/solvency crisis and freeze the economy for quite a while, as it did in 2008. Therefore, artificially low interest rates are also likely to be of insignificant help to long-term growth, for their main role in stimulating growth is to encourage more debt. The debt expansion, though, was great for financial industry profits: more debt instruments to put together, to sell and to maintain. Thus, the role of finance continued to grow far beyond its point of usefulness, taking several more percentage points of GDP as a cost of doing business, which extra burden could not possibly fail to slow non-financial growth to some extent.

In November 2012, I updated my thoughts in a letter entitled "On the Road to Zero Growth," in which I predicted that going forward, GDP growth for the U.S. was likely to be about only 1.4% a year. This lowball estimate of future GDP growth attracted attention and plenty of opposition. Yet shortly after my letter was published, the Congressional Budget Office slashed its estimate of the U.S. long-term growth trend from 3.0% to 1.9%. Into this quiet world of creeping adjustment, an IMF paper released in early April 2015 acted as an unexpected jolt of excitement as, unusually, consensus estimates for U.S. growth tumbled all the way down to 1.5%.

INVESTING IN A LOW GROWTH WORLD

Where I broke ranks with other pessimists was my belief that theory and practice strongly indicated that lower GDP growth would not directly affect stock returns or corporate profitability. At least not in a major way. All corporate growth has to funnel through return on equity. The problem with growth companies is that they often expand faster than their returns on capital, which forces them to raise more capital. Investors grow rich not on earnings growth, but on growth in earnings per share (EPS). There was almost no evidence that faster-growing companies enjoyed higher margins and EPS growth. In fact, it was slightly the reverse.

The same faulty intuition applies to fast-growing countries. How appealing an assumption it is that their stock market returns should beat the slow pokes. But it just ain't so. And we at GMO had (somewhat reluctantly for competitive reasons) been talking about it for years. Our research showed a moderately negative correlation between GDP growth by country and market returns. We went back 100 years for some developed countries and looked at emerging country equity markets as well, and all had the same negative correlations. When I asked Ben Inker if this was for the same reason that growth companies underperform – that they are overpriced – Ben came up with another completely sufficient explanation (in about 10 seconds): the faster-growing countries had simply had more slowly growing EPS, which in turn was the result of having a lower average ROE.

FREAKISHLY HIGH PROFITS

On one part of the fundamentals my forecast turned out to be far off target. On the topic of potential problems, I had written in May 2009, "Not the least of these will be downward pressure on profit margins that for 20 years had benefited from rising asset prices sneaking through into margins." I had trouble understanding how the U.S. could have massive amounts of unused labor and industrial capacity, as was the case after the financial crisis, yet still have peak profit margins. This had never happened before. In fact, before Greenspan, there had been a powerful positive correlation between profit margins and capacity in the expected direction.

Freakishly high corporate profit margins did not seem to be connected to economic reality. After 2008, a sub-average economic recovery, threatening to become painfully sub-average, had not stopped corporate profits from quickly rising to a level that was about as high as they had ever gotten. A large part of the workforce was either unemployed or discouraged to look for work or forced to work only part-time. There never was – and perhaps, with luck, never will be again – such a terrible comparison between the economic well-being of corporations and their officers and the economic ill-being of their ordinary employees.

Our research showed that the single largest input to higher profit margins was the existence of much lower real interest rates since 1997. Had interest rates remained at normal levels, we calculated, profits would have been much closer to their pre-1977 average. This finding tempted me to say, "Well that's it then, these new higher margins are simply and exclusively the outcome of lower rates and higher leverage." But then I realized that there was a conundrum: in a world of reasonable competitiveness, higher margins from lower rates should have been competed away.

But they were not, and I believed this was due to other factors affecting the business world. In my view, an increase in monopolies and rising corporate political power had created a new stickiness in profits, allowing higher margins to be sustained for so much longer than the old normal. Globalization had no doubt increased the value of top brands, and the U.S. had much more than its fair share of both the old established brands of the Coca-Cola and J&J variety and new ones like Apple, Amazon and Facebook. Even much more modest

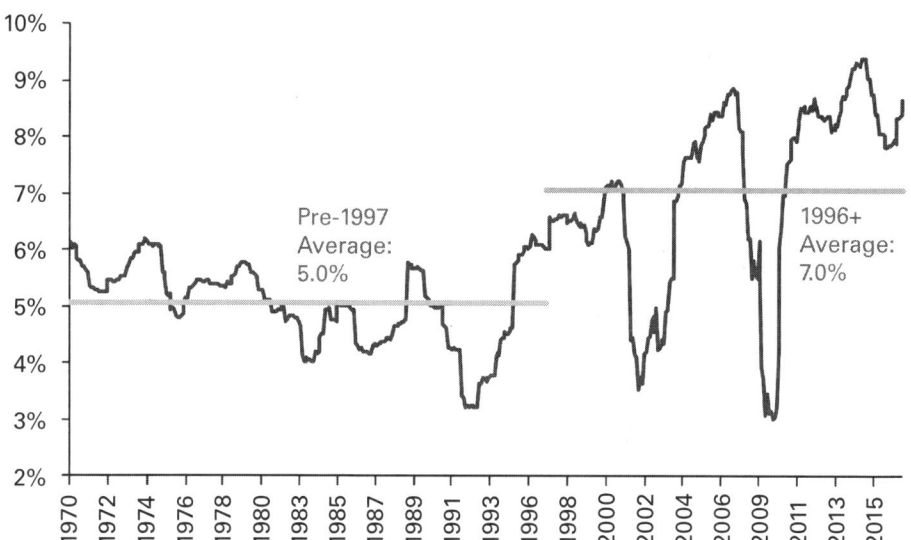

A new paradigm for S&P 500 profit margins. The profitability (as measured by profit margins compared to revenue) of US listed large caps from 1970 to 2017, showing that average profitability in the second half of the sample was much higher than in the first – in spite of far bigger, if short-lived, drops in profitability than had ever been seen before. Data from GMO, Compustat, 2017

domestic brands had handsomely improved returns by moving the capital-intensive production to China and retaining only the brand management in the U.S.

Steadily increasing corporate power over the previous decades has been, I think it's fair to say, the defining feature of U.S. politics in general. Antitrust enforcement was more or less moribund under Obama. This probably had a slight negative effect on GDP growth and job creation but was good for corporate profit margins. And not evenly so but skewed toward the larger and more politically savvy corporations. So, as new regulations proliferated, they have tended to protect the larger, established companies and hinder new entrants. Increased regulations cost all corporations money, but the very large can better afford to deal with them. Thus regulations, however necessary to the well-being of ordinary people, are in aggregate anti-competitive. They form a protective moat for large, established firms.

Corporate power really hinges on other things, especially the ease with which money can influence policy. In this, management was blessed by the Supreme Court, whose majority in the 2010 Citizens United decision put the seal of approval on corporate power over ordinary people. (Corporations were deemed worthy of human rights – even though, by the tenets of shareholder capitalism, they are unable to ever behave with the altruism sometimes demonstrated by real humans, lest they be sued by stockholders.) Low interest rates made it cheaper to consolidate industries, sparking a veritable explosion of mergers and acquisitions, to levels never seen before. It is hard to know if the lack of antitrust action from the Justice Department was related to the increased political power of corporations, but its increased inertia was clearly evident.

The general pattern described so far is entirely compatible with the increased monopoly power of U.S. corporations. What we would expect to see if they had materially more monopoly power was exactly what we did see: higher profit margins; reluctance to expand capacity; slight reductions in GDP growth and productivity; downward pressure on wages, unions and labor negotiations; and fewer new entrants into the corporate world. And because these factors affected the U.S. more than other developed countries, U.S. margins should have been higher than theirs, and they were. It is a global system and the U.S. out-monopolies the rest of the world and partly because of that it out-brands them too. These points played a huge role in the rise of the handful of giant U.S.-based global monopolies, later dubbed the Magnificent Seven (MAG 7).

Increasing corporate political power and bloated profit margins also went hand in hand with greater inequality across society. In February 2012, I wrote an op-ed for the *Financial Times* expressing sympathy for the Occupy Wall Street protesters:

> The Occupiers feel that capitalism and corporate-influenced governments have, for the time being, let them down. I believe they are right... For the time being, in the U.S. our corporate and governmental system backed surprisingly by the Supreme Court has become a plutocracy, designed to prolong, protect and intensify the wealth and influence of those who already have the wealth and influence. What the Occupy movement indicates is that a growing number of people have begun to recognize this in spite of the efficiency of capital's propaganda machines. Forty years of no pay increase in the U.S. after inflation for the average hour worked should, after all, have that effect... But the best propaganda of all is that the richest 400 people now have assets equal to the poorest 140 million. If that doesn't disturb you, you have a wallet for a heart.

But sadly, there was very little follow-through from "Occupy" and the dominance of big business has continued.

THIS TIME SEEMS DIFFERENT

Previously, margins in what appeared to be very healthy economies were competed down to produce a remarkably stable return – economists used to be amazed by this stability – driven by waves of capital spending just as industry peak profits appeared. I had always argued that if profit margins do not mean revert, then capitalism is broken. Sustained higher margins also meant that my most cherished investment belief – mean reversion at both the individual stock and market level – appeared broken. You get mean reversion if capitalism happens in the normal way. But profit margins weren't being allowed to mean revert. For more than two decades we had had abnormally high returns. Yet all the corporations were doing was buying back their own stock. They were trimming rather than boosting their capital spending. They weren't acting to expand the economy. They were running away from that in favor of caution and profitability, which protected managements' stock options.

Sir John Templeton famously said that the four most expensive words in the English language are "this time it's different." I was really lucky in that the first 30 years of my investment career were similar to the prior 30 years. In fact the market was extremely well behaved from 1935 until 2000. It was an orderly world in which to be a value manager because reversion worked reliably. If a value manager was patient, he was in heaven. The market outperformed when it was cheap, and when it got expensive, it cracked. But this turned out to be very bad preparation for what came next.

As I have said, profit margins used to be the most reliably mean-reverting data in finance. Yet over the last 25 years, margins have climbed to an unusually high level and stayed there. Margins since 2000 averaged fully 30% above the average of the 20th century. These higher margins were in turn multiplied by higher P/E ratios, fully 60% higher than the average of the pre-2000 era. In a mean-reverting world this was what I called "barbaric double-counting" and had always been followed by lower margins multiplied by much lower P/E ratios. But since about 1997 mean reversion had paused. Higher than average profits turned out to be unprecedentedly stable as did higher than average P/Es. The same applied in spades to the development of the MAG 7, these giant super-profitable instant global monopolies. To a financial historian this felt like mean reversion had ceased, at least for a long while, quite possibly because capitalism was at least partly broken. Broken mainly by the growth in political influence of the largest corporations and the consequent lack of anti-monopoly action; by abnormal reductions in interest rates and the cost of capital; and by abnormal reductions in taxes on capital, especially the favorable treatment of carried interest – all of which have also worked to relentlessly increase economic inequality.

You always need to be careful saying that things are never different but this time they were indeed different, at least for a long while. For after 2000, many old rules had changed. When such a rapid and unusual change in the rules occurs, value investors discover they have been overweighting the lessons of the past. The "value" approach to investment is simply a set of beliefs that previous behavior, psychological and economic, will continue into the future. But the changes this time were unusually powerful and persistent. Corporations had gotten more monopoly power. The Fed's continual easing represented a regime change. The discount rate structure had dropped by two percentage points. The yield on stocks was down by roughly the same amount. The stock market had adjusted upwards, reflecting low rates, low inflation and high profit margins.

During the post-crisis decade from 2009 to 2019, the valuation of the stock market remained high by historic standards and rose to the 2-sigma overvaluation level by 2018, our statistical definition of a bubble. If you'd been bullish since the crisis you'd been a hero, and if you'd been bearish you'd looked more than a little stupid. If you were a naturally conservative investor and still alive, you were doing pretty well. But to me, it didn't feel like a genuine bubble – it totally lacked the euphoria of 1929, of 1989 in Japan, of U.S. tech in 1999 and of the housing market in 2005. It was more like we had been climbing a wall of worry. From 2014 onwards, my GMO investment letters (which I ceased putting out every quarter) argued that although stock prices were far higher than their old averages, they still lacked the type of highly visible extreme speculative behavior that typically signifies a bubble on the verge of breaking.

As I mentioned earlier, in the late 1990s Ben Inker and I designed a simple model to explain the shifts in P/E levels of the S&P 500. Our model did not attempt to justify the P/E levels as logical or deserved, nor did it attempt to predict future prices. It just showed what tended to be the market's typical behavioral response over the years to major market factors. To recap, by far the two most important of these factors are profit margins, the higher the better, and inflation, where stable and lower is better, except not too low. Stocks, unlike bonds, are real assets, so inflation should not matter, and in the long run they clearly do pass inflation through. But in the short term investors hate the uncertainty it brings. A third behavioral factor, which still had explanatory power, although much less than the first two, is the volatility of GDP growth (not the growth rate of GDP, which has no explanatory power at all). Investment managers love stable GDP growth, and hate surprises, because they can feel more in control of their own forecasts. P/Es tend to be higher when GDP growth is stable, not when it is high. This is very far from a long-term dividend discount model, that in theory should explain the market level, but our "comfort model" – which captures what makes portfolio managers feel comfortable – had a much better record in the short term.

By 2017, global GDP volatility was at its lowest on record. Profits were high and inflation was quiescent. No wonder, said our comfort model, that stock valuations remained far above average. The speed of regression had clearly slowed way down and become sticky. This slowdown was because nearly all the factors causing it were themselves unlikely to change fast (although if we value an effective and efficient capitalist system, we should certainly hope they eventually mean revert, at least partially). Those factors included Fed policy and moral hazard, low interest rates, an aging population, slowing economic and productivity growth and increased political and monopoly power for corporations. My January 2017 letter showed how my own thoughts about mean reversion had evolved. It bore the title: "This Time Seems Very, Very Different." Or, as I now thought, *contra* Templeton, the five most expensive words in the English language were "this time is never different."

These comments caused quite a stir. The "permabear" Grantham no longer believed in mean reversion! After a few misquotes and misunderstandings by journalists I needed to reply. In an article for *Barron's* (June 30, 2017), I pointed out that the recent 20-year era of higher stock prices had been very severely stress-tested by the decline from the 2000 Tech Bubble and another steep decline in 2008–09, perhaps the biggest foul-up of the financial system in modern times. Yet neither spectacular event had proved enough, apparently, to jolt the market's valuation back to its former lower level. In a postscript, I added:

A fully-fledged bubble in the U.S. with full behavioral ecstasy can still occur. In today's changed environment, though, I think it would take a considerably higher level on the S&P 500. Now that's a seriously irritating thought! I suggest letting the evidence of bubble-type euphoria speak for itself, so when the TVs in the local lunch places [in Boston] are touting stocks and not Red Sox replays, as they did in 1999 and no doubt would have done by radio in 1929, I'll let you know.

Jim Grant, who writes the smart and amusing newsletter *Grant's Interest Rate Observer*, even called me an "apostate." I had spoken at a few of his famous conferences, at which the audiences worship value, including one poorly attended conference just before the tech crash of 2000 when the attendees including me all looked pale and worried. At that time I had been an uncompromising value proponent with no caveats. So by that standard I had indeed changed my spots. But "apostate" was a little steep so I complained and we ended up having a little debate at his next conference on the topic of "This Time Is Never Different" and I argued basically "what is not different this time for heaven's sake": margins, P/Es, interest rates, monopoly policy, Fed policies, etc., etc.

Historically, when dealing with real bubbles, being late has not been materially different in time and pain from being too early, but value managers only see one side of this. Value managers are typically painfully too early over and over again, as I knew better than most. For markets overpriced by historical standards quite often become very overpriced, and once in a while a superbubble appears, like Japan's in the 1980s, when the market became extraordinarily overpriced to a degree never seen before. Valuation alone no longer seemed to me, from long-suffering personal experience, to be a sufficient sign of an impending bubble break. Extreme overvaluation plays a huge role in the bubbles breaking. It is a necessary precondition. The more overvalued, the merrier. But, for judging the extent that bubbles will overrun fair value and for timing the break, valuation, sadly, is largely irrelevant. It is a necessary but absolutely not sufficient condition.

This brings up a related issue: if the market is way overpriced but still does not show the historically normal conditions of an impending bust, what is the prudent manager to do? For me it is pretty obvious that you should lower the risk exposure of portfolios, even if you feel it is unlikely that the market will break in the near term. Surely, skating on ice you know is very thin is absolutely not something you want to risk for your clients. But the alternative strategy of hanging on aggressively until the very end and then trying to time your jump is seductive, as Keynes pointed out, and quite possibly a better business strategy for investment managers.

Indicators of extremes of euphoria appear to me much more important than price. Ben Graham had said long ago that as far as he could see, no bubble had ever broken (by 1963) without being accompanied by signs of real excess such as those found in 1929. It must be admitted that I carried a lot of blame for exaggerating the significance of price alone as a bubble measure. After all, I helped pioneer the historical finding that previous bubbles have been separated from ordinary bull markets by passing through two standard deviations on their price series, a level that statistically should occur every 44 years in a random series. It had been a very useful assumption for our broad-based study of global bubbles across a variety of asset classes and it had, of course, a good historical record, because that's how we picked it.

But the 2-sigma boundary has its limits in usefulness. It said only that historically all 2-sigma equity bubbles in major equity markets had always, without exception, broken back to the previous trend, *sooner or later*. This does not speak to the pain of the "sooner or later," missing out on speculative gains as the 2-sigma bull market spends a year or two or three moving on to 2.5- or 3-sigma as it did in Japan (1989) and the Tech Bubble of the late 1990s. These were such long waiting times that, as we have seen, the latter became business threatening to GMO, but both eventually went all the way back to trend. As did the 3-sigma U.S. housing market of 2005, which in the end was very well behaved! One could argue that the rule of 2-sigma is a far better statistical measure than practical guide for investors. At the time of writing, in early 2025, we find ourselves in the fourth great divergent market in history. The U.S. stock market is statistically not as extreme as Japan or the U.S. housing market but more extreme on many measures than the Tech Bubble (and also the Nifty Fifty bubble of the 1970s). Its eventual reversion to trend, however, will not remove the pain of being too early any more than the previous ones did. Mean reversion is a useful and hitherto accurate rule but still a painful one. As I once wrote, "You will arrive back on trend eventually, but not necessarily with the same clients you left with."

On the topic of timing bubble peaks, a recent academic paper titled "Bubbles for Fama" concluded that in the U.S. and almost all global markets, the strongest indicator – stronger than pure pricing or value – is indeed price acceleration.* (This was perhaps the third time I have agreed with mainstream economists in the previous 50 years. I have a firm principle of generously quoting them when they agree with me.)

By January 2018, we had witnessed over the previous six months a modest pick-up in stock price appreciation, which I thought

---

* "Bubbles for Fama," by Robin Greenwood, Andrei Shleifer and Yang You, *Journal of Financial Economics*, Volume 131, Issue 1, January 2019.

might be the base camp for a possible final assault on the peak. I had previously defined a great bubble as "excellent fundamentals euphorically extrapolated." In general, the fundamentals of the post-crisis years had proved disappointing, but as the 10th anniversary of Lehman's failure approached, stock market fundamentals were at last improving. Other asset classes that were making impressive bubbly moves included real estate, where the average U.S. house price, as a multiple of family income, rose way higher than at any time before the great housing bubble of the early 2000s. Bitcoin's performance was dwarfing even the legendary South Sea Bubble! Having no clear fundamental value and operating in largely unregulated markets, coupled with a storyline conducive to delusions of grandeur, Bitcoin seemed the very essence of a bubble.

EXPECTING A MARKET MELT-UP

By this date, I thought there was a good chance the market's upturn would accelerate. My January 2018 letter was titled, "Bracing Yourself for a Possible Near-Term Melt-Up" in which I suggested that a melt-up or end phase of the bull market within the next six months to two years was likely. Once again my timing was poor. Over the rest of the year, the S&P index declined, but soon enough the market resumed its upward path but still without the appearance of acceleration and euphoria, reverting to a solid, boring advance.

What happened next was one of those unique events for which history is nearly useless: a brand new formidable virus, Covid-19 arrived, with what effects no one at the time could know. It gave me an opportunity to prove what I was good at and what I was lousy at. I threw myself at every rumor in early January 2020 and tried to trace back where they came from. I came to the conclusion that the virus was quite possibly going to be very serious medically and economically and it seemed likely that if it were serious, several countries, possibly including the U.S., would prove incompetent in their response, although I was encouraged by how high the U.S. and the U.K. were rated in their presumed ability to respond to a broad medical crisis.

On January 31, our Foundation made a substantial "Covid trade" to protect some of our portfolio. I get to brag here at how early this was compared to most. A while later I felt my rather insubstantial data and gut feel were enough to argue with my GMO colleagues to take it more seriously. The bad news was that when the smoke had cleared, our trade was so unlevered and so lacking in cleverness that we really might as well have done nothing. Hedge fund manager Bill Ackman, in contrast, made his Covid trade in March, over a month later, when you might have thought every day earlier was golden. However, according to Forbes, he made over $2.5 billion, 100 times what he risked, in options. What a reminder this was for me, as if I needed it that I am good at research and judgment, but left to my own devices sometimes mediocre at implementation. At the very least, it proved I needed good partners to maximize my best ideas, which quite often I had had. After "Reinvesting When Terrified" was published the day the market hit its low in March 2009, neither I nor our Foundation nor GMO came close to maximizing the potential rewards of such a highly confident call.

In the second quarter of 2020, Covid simultaneously caused supply and demand shocks unlike anything before. In March, the markets broke. But the Covid crash turned out to be quite different from those crashes associated with the end of a classic long bull market. As a sharp external effect, it was more like the 1987 technical crash caused by portfolio insurance: a short hit followed by a sharp recovery. Lockdown, not surprisingly, was also associated with the sharpest declines in GDP and unemployment since the Great Depression.

Within four months, however, the market came roaring back, with the S&P 500 index up 45% from the low. This was an acceleration nothing short of sensational. By the summer, I realized that what we were witnessing was the fourth "Real McCoy" bubble of my investment career. A market lost in one-sided optimism: it went up on good news and went up on bad news; as the general election loomed on the horizon, it could interpret a possible Trump victory as bullish and then seamlessly interpret a Biden victory as bullish. These are the typical characteristics of a bubble. The type where there was nothing much you could throw at it once it had gotten going.

By the fall of 2020, there was as much craziness as there had been in 1999 or 1929. It was bewildering, impressive and, for financial historians like me, exciting. The euphoria was completely understandable given the prospect of ultra-easy monetary policy for years to come and the spectacularly successful vaccines that were beginning to be approved by regulators. This was followed by the speed and size of President Biden's stimulus package. Trillions of dollars of government spending were bound to increase confidence. Investors were dripping in stimulus cash, bored to death and feeling trapped at home with nothing more exciting to do than learn to speculate. So they bought into every market setback and followed every one of the myriad tips floating around the ether.

Appearing on CNBC shortly after the November election, I warned of the dismal prospects facing long-term investors: "The one reality you can never change is that a higher-priced asset will always produce a lower return than a lower-priced asset. You can't have your cake and eat it. You can enjoy it now, or you can enjoy it steadily in the distant future, but not both. And the price we will pay for having this market go higher and higher is a lower and lower

10-year return from the peak." Those whose stocks were off to the moon did not want to hear this type of advice.

Stock market bubbles invariably attract a lot of new issuance. This time, however, the new issuance didn't come from IPOs but from mergers with blank-check public companies, known as Special Purpose Acquisition Companies, or SPACs. I considered them a reprehensible instrument, and very speculative by definition, due largely to their lack of listing requirements and regulation. The financial rewards were abnormally tilted toward the promoters, who were allowed by the authorities to get a large share of investors' money up front rather than a percentage of any eventual profits. Whether investors won or lost, they won. Not surprisingly, as long as there were suckers willing to accept this blatantly unfair deal there would be a supply of promoters, long on recognizability and short on ethics. There were more than enough of them. Over the course of 2020, more than 200 SPACs listed, raising tens of billions of dollars. The boom was symptomatic of the euphoria and cynicism one typically sees at bubble peaks, reminiscent of those hundreds of flaky companies that were floated in 1720 during the South Sea Bubble.

By complete accident, I turned out to be one of the prime beneficiaries of the SPAC craze. Seven years earlier, I had personally invested $12.5 million in a battery startup, spun out of Stanford University. This was one of a series of bets on early-stage green technology and by chance the biggest single investment I had ever made. QuantumScape, as the business was called, was still a research project. It had no sale or profits and freely admitted that it wouldn't be producing any batteries for years. Yet in September 2020, the firm announced it would come to the market via a SPAC merger at $10 a share, which represented a comfortable four times my original cost basis. The stock immediately shot up to $130 within months. For a minute, its market capitalization was bigger than General Motors or Panasonic. My own stake was valued for a glorious second in December 2020 at a sensational $625 million. But there was a snag: I was not allowed to sell for a six-month lockup period. At the time, I was pontificating to my young colleagues at the Foundation that this was the kind of stock that deserved to sell between $5 and $10. It was going to be a nerve-racking six months.

Those 18 months after the summer of 2020 had all the indications of a classic finale to a long bull market. There was peak overvaluation as measured by price to sales: the most expensive 10% of stocks on this measure were more highly priced than in the 2000 Tech Bubble. Margin debt was at a peak. The stock trading app Robinhood with its commission-free trading was enticing a surge of new investors who had no experience of past bubbles and busts. What they had, though, was money. It was by then calculated that the unprecedented Biden stimulus programs to offset Covid had left an extra $3 trillion in personal accounts.

Even by January 2021 the market was already building up such a head of steam that a reasonably near-term end to the cycle seemed to me to be extremely likely based on past experience. Accordingly, my January 2021 paper, "Waiting for the Last Dance," pronounced that "the market had finally turned into one of the great bubbles, along with the South Sea Bubble, 1929 and the Tech Bubble of 2000." I wrote "that the real problem… is that long slow-burning bull markets can spend many years above fair value and even two, three or four years far above. These events can easily outlast the patience of most clients. And when price rises are very rapid, impatience is followed by anxiety and envy. There is nothing more irritating than watching your neighbor get rich… I will tell you my definition of success for a bear market call. It is simply that sooner or later there will come a time when an investor will have saved money by being out… This definition of success absolutely does not include precise timing. Calling the week, month or quarter of the top is all but impossible." Clearly I should have added "year" to that last line.

The paper pointed out that the previously missing ingredients for a superbubble to break – "explosive price increases, frenzied issuance and hysterically speculative behavior" – had been added. What it missed, though, on this list was the strangest condition of all – when the previous high beta market leaders turn strongly down and yet the market led by blue chips continues strongly up. This very strange condition had only happened in 1929, 1972 and 2000 in the U.S. and never in between. And as of January 2021, this had clearly not happened yet.

The craze for meme stocks, or gambling on stocks that had no earnings simply because it was fun, appeared to me a nihilistic parody of actual investing. By June 2021, AMC Entertainment, a failing cinema chain, was up over 25x since January. GameStop, an equally challenged retailer of computer games, had gained over 10x. Cryptocurrencies were the most complete expression of this speculative nihilism. Dogecoin, which had been created as a joke to make fun of worthless cryptocurrencies, was up by about 50x from the start of the year. In fact, it was such a success that second-level joke cryptocurrencies making fun of Dogecoin sported multibillion-dollar valuations. Meanwhile, other cryptocurrencies enjoyed success purely on the basis of their scatological names. "This is it, guys," I told Bloomberg in late June 2021, "the biggest U.S. fantasy trip of all time."

SUPERBUBBLE DEFINITION

Other speculative indicators, such as call option volumes and the volume of individual trading in over-the-counter or penny stocks, were all at record highs. Individual participation as a percentage of trading had tripled in the previous 18 months. By historical standards this seemed indeed like the real McCoy. The scale of the folly was simply larger than anything I had seen before or read about in the history books. We were witnessing what I called a bubble trifecta: a euphoric equity market, a housing market that was racing upwards and a ludicrously overpriced bond market.

At GMO, as mentioned earlier, we defined a bubble for many years as a 2-sigma deviation from trend. But market extremes do not have to stop at precisely 2-sigma. A handful go on to become superbubbles of 3-sigma or greater – something that in theory randomly occurs once every 100 events but in real life is about twice as frequent. In 2021, the U.S. stock market broke through the 3-sigma barrier.

By my reckoning this was the fourth U.S. superbubble of the past century and the fifth globally. The others being in 1929 ahead of the Great Depression, the Tech Bubble in the late 1990s, the U.S. housing market in 2006 and the mother of all bubbles (until now) in Japan in 1989. Like all truly great bubbles, this one wasn't confined to the stock market but was also evident in real estate, where U.S. house prices as a multiple of family income were even higher than at the housing peak of 2006 although without the same euphoria as in 2005–06. We also had the highest-priced bond markets in the U.S. and most other countries around the world, and the lowest interest rates, of course that went with them, that history had ever seen.

Tyler Cowen, the well-known economist, asked me a series of difficult questions in a podcast I did with him in 2022, one of which highlighted the small number of previous data points on superbubbles. I granted that the fewer the data points the more significant the data has to be. But sometimes the data is so good that a single data point suffices. If a large meteorite approached of the scale that cost the Earth some 80% of all its life about 60 million years ago, I doubt even economists would belittle it on the grounds of there being one lousy data point.

"Ah," you will say, with some justification, "that is based on science, and the laws of physics do not change, even if our understanding of them does." I would reply that we have had several classic, gigantic bubbles, excluding our current, very worthy one, and human nature, on which they are based, presumably also does not change. In fact, it has probably changed less than our understanding of the laws of physics. My intellectual fallback, in any case, has always been the inescapable truth that if the price of an asset triples, its future expected returns are divided by three, and that fact alone may be enough to guarantee the miserable outcomes from those historic and dizzying market heights.

LET THE WILD RUMPUS BEGIN

What had been missing when I wrote "Waiting for the Last Dance" was the weird underperformance of super speculative stocks as the blue chips continued advancing. Finally in 2021 we got that in spades. Unfortunately, it started with my superstar stock QuantumScape, which fell from $131 in December 2020 to $25 a year later. By February 2021, the much-discussed ARKK fund of junior, mainly pre-profit super growth stocks, peaked at $152 and by the market high of year end 2021 was down to $94. The memes peaked throughout the year, GameStop in January and AMC in June. It was the same story for most aggressive growth stocks.

It was my personal misfortune that the confidence termites started by attacking QuantumScape, which was by very many multiples the largest holding I had ever had. The stock peaked in December 2020 and was about the first of the super specs to do so. Then over the course of January, other new issues began to peel off one by one. By spring, many of the meme stocks began to sag. And so it went on throughout the year. The pain for growth stocks with no earnings in 2021 was brutal – Goldman calculated they were down 50% or so for the year. QuantumScape had fallen 83%. I unloaded most of my position at $25 the day after the lockup ended. It was a sad opportunity loss. Our Foundation could have done marvelous things with the money. Still, I'd made over 10 times my money on what was the biggest single investment I had ever made. (The stock later traded down below $5 a share, half its flotation price.)

In complete contrast, at the year end 2021 the S&P 500 was up 27% even as speculative growth stocks were in ragged disarray. To repeat, nothing like this had ever happened – super high beta speculative stocks that had led the market up in the first place, being significantly down in a major market up move – except in 1929, 1972 and 2000. This divergence had always been followed, on each occasion, by a major market decline. Recognizing the significance of this rarest of rare conditions, my confidence in calling the bubble peak ratcheted up a lot and my January 2022 paper was titled "Let the Wild Rumpus Begin" – no longer "waiting."

I warned that the checklist for a superbubble running through its phases was now complete and the wild rumpus might begin at any time. I pointed out that a common feature of earlier superbubbles had been an acceleration in the rate of price advance toward the end to two or three times the average speed of the full bull market. This had happened in 1929 and in late 1999, and this time it had occurred in 2020 and early 2021 during which time the Nasdaq rose nearly 60%.

The hardest to define quality of a late-stage bubble, I wrote, lay in the touchy-feely characteristic of investor behavior. But over the previous two and a half years there could be no doubt that we had seen crazy investor behavior in spades – more even than in 2000 – especially in meme stocks and in electric vehicle-related stocks, in cryptocurrencies and in non-fungible tokens (a brief-lived fashion for digital art). I also tried to explain that strangest of all precursors to a bust, the massive divergence between blue chips and specs: people start to sense that things are not quite right and so they sell their specs and migrate to the blue chips. They are going to keep dancing, but they are darned if they are going over the edge in a speculative meme stock. They would prefer to run off the cliff holding a blue chip stock, like Coca-Cola or Walmart. That is how markets begging to break go: first the real flakes with no earnings are taken out and shot, then the small and extreme growth stocks buckle and so on.

By early 2022, we also had broadly overpriced, or above trend, commodities, including oil and most of the important metals. In addition, the UN's index of global food prices was around its all-time high. These high prices were starting to push up inflation and stress real incomes. The combination of still-rising commodity prices with a deflating asset price bubble was the ultimate pincer attack. As I wrote at the start of the year:

> We are in what I think of as the vampire phase of the bull market, where you throw everything you have at it: you stab it with Covid, you shoot it with the end of Quantitative Easing and the promise of higher rates and you poison it with unexpected inflation – which has always killed P/E ratios before, but quite uniquely, not this time yet – and still the creature lives. (Just as it staggered through the second half of 2007 as its mortgage and other financial wounds increased one by one.) Until, just as you're beginning to think the thing is completely immortal, it finally, and perhaps a little anticlimactically, keels over and dies.

The Inker-Grantham comfort model of explaining P/Es, described earlier, had had an incredible correlation with actual P/Es of over 0.9 since 1925. I would never have believed a correlation that high unless I had done the work myself. The factors had just not changed for almost 100 years, which is to say human nature had not changed. Inflation, especially unexpected inflation, of the kind we had starting in mid-2021, had always reduced animal spirits. The model had underestimated the major bull wave in 1999 but it had never got the sign wrong, as it did in the second half of 2021, when the model "explained" that P/Es would normally fall rapidly

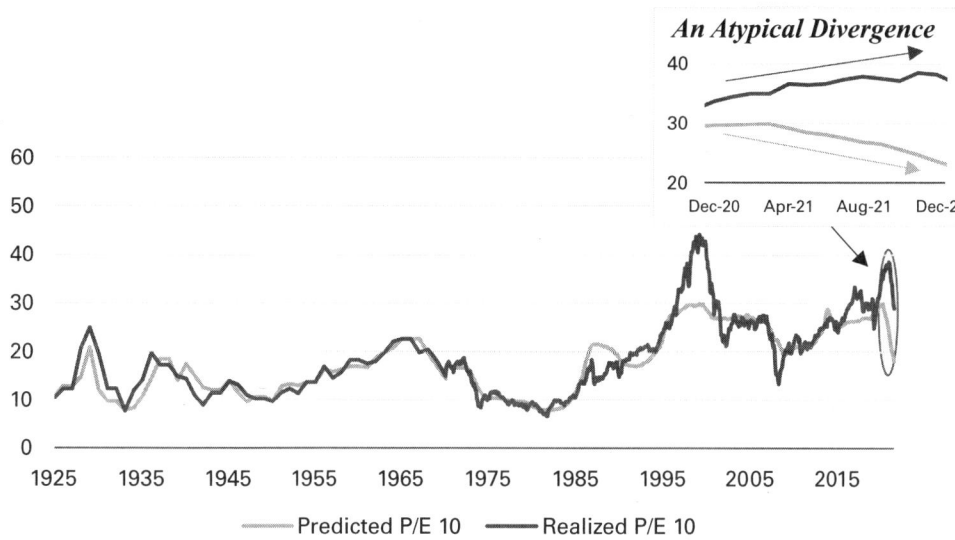

The Inker-Grantham comfort model for valuations. Our Inker-Grantham model for US equity valuations has had incredible correlation with actual valuations. There have been two major historic divergences between this model and reality. The first was in the internet bubble of the late 1990s, when very positive economic conditions justified a very high valuation and a speculative frenzy took the market to an insanely high valuation. The second started in the early 2020s and has continued up to the time of writing (2025), with inflation shocks justifying historically moderate valuations but stocks almost hanging on to their pre-inflation valuation peaks. Data from GMO, 2022 in the face of inflation. Instead they rose rapidly. My only guess, then and now, is that the confidence in easing and encouragement from both the Fed and government was so high, as was the belief that inflation would this time be "transient," where this favorable view had never before occurred. This unprecedented gap between actual and predicted valuations, from a model that had explained well from 1925 to 2019, is still evident in 2025.

There have been far too many boring years in my more than five-decade investing career but 2022 was not one of them. The S&P 500 dropped 25% to its October low. The global bond markets crashed, suffering their greatest losses since the modern bond markets opened for business with the advent of the British consols in 1753. At the beginning of 2022, in "Let the Wild Rumpus Begin," we had predicted that total losses across the three major asset classes of stocks, bonds and real estate could reach $35 trillion in the U.S. alone. Twelve months later, about half of the predicted losses had occurred. With real estate still making up its mind, losses in U.S. stocks had been over $10 trillion and in bonds over $5 trillion, in addition to an unexpectedly large loss of $2 trillion in cryptocurrency.

By late 2022 the first and easiest leg of the bursting of the bubble I'd called for in January was complete. While the most extreme froth had been wiped off the market, valuations were still nowhere near their long-term averages. At the start of the following year, stocks enjoyed a terrific January bounce. My QuantumScape went up 120%. Some of the meme stocks went up 50% to 100%. In my January letter, titled "Time Out Then Back to the Meat Grinder," I pointed to several factors that might pause or delay the bear market. We were entering the third year "sweet spot" of the under-recognized and powerful presidential cycle, when the stock market usually performs extremely well. Other factors included subsiding inflation, the ongoing strength of the labor market and the reopening of the Chinese economy.

The truth is that toward the end of the year I had been rather rattled by the enormous increase in pessimism and realism since my letters of a year and two years earlier. Equally disturbing, we were said to be facing the most widely predicted recession ever. It was all enough to make a God-fearing contrarian bear wake up in the night sweating. I was right to be worried. The widely predicted recession didn't come. Corporate profits held up. And the stock market decline was rudely interrupted in November 2022 by the launch of ChatGPT and consequent public awareness of a new transformative technology – AI, which seemed likely to be every bit as powerful and world-changing as the internet, and quite possibly much more so. This created an interesting conflict between the unusually widespread pessimism about the economy and, perhaps, life in general, and a rapidly growing enthusiasm for a handful of heroes that were very heavily investing in AI.

Over the course of 2023, the aggregate market capitalization of the MAG 7, seen by the market as AI beneficiaries, rose by some $5 trillion. If you took out those stocks, the U.S. stock market had hardly moved. To be sure, the MAG 7 deserved the name. These companies had the most remarkable and unusual leadership. Plus, they were giant monopolies that had been allowed to become so by the U.S. government. So, they'd had a wonderful environment in which to operate and had done an excellent job of capitalizing on that and moving very fast. They were some of the most profitable companies ever seen, whose profit margins were unprecedented and performance in the stock market even more unprecedented as each incremental dollar was valued more highly than the one before, as price earnings multiples rose far beyond the previous record. Yes, there had been similar crazy multiples before, but only for little speculative issues, never for a string of some of the largest companies in the world.

Now, what will happen next to the MAG 7 is a very interesting question. Will they continue to grow and become 70% of the entire world's market cap? Will they be attacked by governments? Will they attack each other, grow into each other's markets and break down their profit margins? Will new technologies arise that undermine their competitive positions? Who knows? As we have seen, one of the reasons that Nifty Fifty companies went to a 50% premium to the market in 1972 was that there had been no failures among this group for a long stretch. After 1972, however, they started to die like flies: Avon, Polaroid, Eastman Kodak, Xerox and others. The abject failure of a whole handful of former heroes pricked the bubble of invulnerability for the whole Nifty Fifty. They lost their magic and they lost their huge premium. And they underperformed badly for years.

Will that happen to the Nifty Seven? That is unanswerable. But we know that every technological revolution prior to AI – going back from the internet to telephones, railroads and canals – has been accompanied by early massive hype and a stock market bubble as investors focus on the ultimate possibilities of the technology, pricing most of the very long-term potential immediately into current market prices. Many such revolutions are in the end as transformative as those early investors could see and sometimes even more so – *but only after a substantial period of disappointment during which the initial bubble bursts*. The more important the new development is and the more massive its success is predicted to be, the more money is piled in regardless of price and the bigger the bust. For instance, during Britain's railroad bubble of the 1840s, six railroads were planned between Leeds and Manchester when only one or two were needed. The bubble breaking did not mean that eventually, out of the financial wreckage, railroads would not change the world, as they clearly did. During the internet bubble, Amazon led the speculative market, rising 21 times from the beginning of 1998 to its 1999 peak, only to decline by an almost inconceivable 92% from 2000 to 2002, before inheriting half the retail world!

So it is likely to be with the current AI bubble. But a new bubble within a bubble like this, even one limited to a handful of stocks, is totally unprecedented, so looking at history books may have its limits. Even though, I admit, there is no clear historical analogy to this strange new beast, my best guess is still that this second investment bubble – in AI – will at least temporarily deflate and probably facilitate a more normal ending to the original bubble, which we paused in December 2022.

At the time of writing, in February 2025, the U.S. stock market is trading on nearly 38x cyclically adjusted earnings. That's in the top 1 percentile of its valuation range. The long-run prospects for the broad market look as poor as almost any other time in history. Simple arithmetic suggests you'll either have a dismal return forever or a hefty bear market followed by a normal return. It also seems likely that the after-effects of interest rate rises and the ridiculous speculation of 2020–21 and its return a couple of years later will eventually end in a recession. The U.S. market since at least 2020 has been in a bubble. How long a bubble lasts has always been variable and unpredictable. But all bubbles have always – so far – had one thing in common: they all, sooner or later, fall back to trend.

EPILOGUE

And You Thought the Stock Market Was Important!

Well, I can now tell you what I consider the essence of what I have learned over the years. It's how reluctant we humans are to face unpleasant facts and our fixation with the present. I would never have guessed that half a century ago. We fixate on current circumstances and refuse to face uncomfortable longer-term outcomes. This applies to all of life. It applies equally to environmental matters as it does to the stock market.

It takes little experience in the investment business to realize that investors prefer good news. As a bear in the bull market of 1999 I was banned from an institution's building for being "dangerously persuasive and totally wrong!" The investment industry also has a great incentive to encourage this optimistic bias, for little money would be made if the market ticked slowly upwards. Five steps forward and two back are far more profitable.

This bias is reflected in our drive for economic growth, regardless of the consequences. When dealing with realistic limits to growth it is also obvious how reluctant everyone is to accept the natural physical limits. As Kenneth Boulding pointed out, there simply cannot be permanent compound growth in a finite world. The entire economic and political system appears eager to encourage optimism on resources and on climate change for it is completely wedded to the virtues of quantitative growth forever. There is a complete refusal to face up to the fact that the profusion of toxic chemicals is causing fertility rates to collapse around the world.

Hard realities are inconvenient for vested interests and because the day of reckoning can always be seen as "later," politicians can always find a way to postpone necessary actions, as can we all: "Because markets are efficient, these high stock prices must be reflecting the remarkable potential of the internet"; "the U.S. housing market largely reflects a strong U.S. economy"; "the climate has always changed"; "how could mere mortals change something as immense as the weather"; "we have nearly infinite resources, it is only a question of price"; "the infinite capacity of the human brain will always solve our problems."

Having realized the seriousness of this bias over the last few decades, I have noticed how hard it is to effectively pass on a warning for the same reason: no one wants to hear this bad news. Our society's capacity for self-delusion is massive, beyond anything I would have guessed. It's clear that we in the U.S. in particular have a broad and heavy prejudice against unpleasant data. We are ready to be manipulated by vested interests in finance, politics and business, whose interests are better served by our believing optimistic stuff "that just ain't so."

A decade ago I gave a talk in the Somerset Club in Boston in which I bemoaned Americans' almost inexplicable inability to believe bad news even when the bad news is readily available from trusted sources. As I pointed out back then, they had a profound belief that the U.S. is the best place in the world, when in many things that matter most to most sensible people, the U.S. is often one of the worst. I came up with a list of propositions that were widely accepted by an educated audience but also happened to be totally wrong. It was my attempt to bring home how extreme our preference is for good news over accurate news.

For instance in the decades I had been in America, *Businessweek* and *The Wall Street Journal* had been telling us how incompetent at business the French were and how persistently we have been kicking their bottoms. If only they could get over their state socialism and their acute Eurosclerosis. As far as I could tell, Americans have generally accepted this thesis. Yet if one looks at the data, in the 50 years after 1970, France's real median hourly wage rose 186% – over 2% annualized – while in America the real median hourly wage has risen just 15%, or 0.2% annualized.

That's not all; the U.S. labor participation rate has declined over the years, while those of other developed countries have gone up. Since 1990 there has been a remarkable decline in the death rate for middle-aged people in other developed countries. For U.S. whites there is a slight increase. As for income inequality as measured by the Gini Ratio, only Turkey and Mexico outflank the U.S. as more unequal amongst the richer countries. These are the uncontestable facts (and are more widely accepted today than when I gave my talk). How is it possible that such views are given such credence in the face of the data, which is, after all, official and simple, not ingeniously manipulated by some perfidious Brit? (Yes, I admit it, I consider myself American or British depending on whether the context is favorable or not.)

Americans' views about politics are similarly skewed. "We have a democracy where people really count" is an idea that is built into the background cultural noise. Yet research shows that the probability of a bill passing through Congress is hardly affected by the general public's enthusiasm or horror toward it. In a nutshell, we, the people, have no influence on whether a law is passed at all. The financial elite, on the other hand, can double the chance of a bill passing and, much more disturbingly, completely block its passage. Clearly these facts are totally incompatible with the concept of participatory democracy and entirely at odds with the much more favorable and optimistic beliefs we share about our democracy. We really, really want to believe good news and to believe that we have a superior system that only needs fine-tuning. But, it ain't necessarily so.

It was only the pandemic that really nailed for me how desperately Americans want to believe good news and how easily manipulated we are, even by people who don't even think they're manipulating us. To everyone's presumed surprise, the U.S. and the U.K. did not do well with Covid despite their previous high standing in medical capability. We were in fact about the two worst countries in the developed world. But those of us living in Massachusetts believed that the local government was doing a decent job. Both the Mayor of Boston and the Governor of Massachusetts reported themselves as doing well and the apparently free press could pass that on or laugh at it.

Well, if Massachusetts had been a separate country, after the first six months it would have had the highest death rate in the world. It was, for example, 20 times worse than Japan, the country with the world's oldest population, in a pandemic where age had the highest correlation with mortality of any factor. I brought this up at every meeting and no one seemed aware. Yet the data were freely available, updated for nerds like me every day by Johns Hopkins. The facts were reported accurately, but people were not processing the negative data. If you belonged to a group of people who went around talking about how many people just died in Massachusetts, you would belong to a very small group and a very strange group. I spent half an hour every morning studying the data before I got out of bed but I could find no one else who gave a rat's tail.

We are dealing today with issues so important that they may affect the long-term viability of our global society and perhaps our species. It may well be necessary to our survival that we become more realistic, more willing to process the unpleasant and, above all, less easily manipulated through our need for good news.

LIVING IN THE PRESENT

There are almost no serious long-term thinkers out in the general public, or hardly any. They're all concentrated in these little clusters of cold-blooded rationalists. Those who can think about the long-term future seem to me, in a sense, cold-blooded. They're not overwhelmed by short-term considerations of advancement. They're willing to look three generations ahead. The short horizon of most people is key to almost everything that's wrong in the modern world. It's key to understanding the stock market, resource limits, pollution, even population and climate change. Everywhere one looks there is an unwillingness to think about the long term.

In the financial world this expresses itself through stock price bubbles, a lack of saving and too much debt. When I was a young man, corporations directed their resources toward building new plants, going for market share and aiming for long-term domination. That was the standard operating procedure. Now, they seek to maximize stock prices. They take on debt to repurchase their shares rather than build new plants.

Capitalism believes that its remit is exclusively to make maximum short-term profits. Corporations show an almost complete disregard for the long-term public good. They willingly produce things, knowing that they are dangerous, possibly existential threats and yet they still do it. They crank out hundreds of different products dripping in forever chemicals. These are chemicals that never go away naturally. You need to apply abnormal temperatures to get rid of them. Climate change is a classic example of the tragedy of the commons; corporations extract profits today while saddling future generations with enormous costs. Fifty years ago, Big Oil concealed from the general public its knowledge of the negative impact of carbon emissions on the Earth's atmosphere.

Any pushback on tobacco, lead, ozone, climate change and toxicity has been done by non-corporates. Karl Marx thought that capitalism would destroy itself and we would have rule of the people, whereas I think it's likely to destroy society and the environment first.

SHORT-TERMISM AND THE STOCK MARKET

Contrarianism serves a useful function in a world programmed for the short term. The contrarian questions the current consensus and focuses on the long term. In a world in which most people are extremely short-term-oriented, contrarians have an enormous amount to think about. But, as I discovered, investing for the long term in a short-term world is perilous.

Our "comfort model" showed that investors simply take today's economic conditions and extrapolate them forever. Extrapolation is the equivalent of saying that today's conditions are going to remain in place indefinitely. But it doesn't feel quite the same. Extrapolation actually makes people feel like they're doing something intellectual, useful or clever. Extrapolation is what drives the market. It drives the hiring and firing of fund managers, which guarantees momentum and pushes the market away from fair value.

The Yale economist Robert Shiller demonstrated long ago that the historic stream of dividends from U.S. stocks has been relatively stable compared to the wild oscillations of the market.* Given investors' tendency to extrapolate, the market switches from believing one day that it's the end of the world to the next moment thinking that profits will grow fabulously forever. If investors didn't extrapolate current conditions, the stock market would have been 17 times less volatile. But investors are not sensible. They assume today's conditions will last forever.

I'm interested in thinking about things that have a much longer horizon than is professionally useful. My own time horizon interest barely overlaps with anything in the market. Mine is several years and the market's outlook turns out to be very short. It's a very bad characteristic for a money manager to be so out of sync with what is moving the market. It's not good for the clients, nor the manager. I'd have made a lot more money for my clients and myself and had a more carefree existence if only my time horizon had been a bit shorter. That's my confession.

Career risk appears when the investment manager's time horizon differs from the clients'. You're holding out for things longer than the clients can stand. Even if you have the perfect portfolio, it can still take several years before the bets work out. But, as we discovered at GMO in the 1990s, you can get fired for underperforming, as we did, after just two and a quarter years. We stood our ground and winning our bets produced the most amazing burst of business for the firm. So dear Lord Keynes, there is an exception. If you stand your ground during a bubble market despite being fired by many clients, you can earn the reputation of being a strong-willed type who is prepared to do the right thing. At GMO we were independent so could survive the loss of business but other long-term investors were not so lucky.

---

* See Robert Shiller, "Do Stock Prices Move Too Much to be Justified by Subsequent Changes in Dividends?" *American Economic Review*, 1981.

I have always found investment an intellectual challenge. Managing a portfolio is interesting, as is discovering what works and doesn't work. Yet I've slowly but surely come to the view that investment management is a trivial activity. If I started out all over again I'd prefer to do something that has some socially redeeming features. Now, if you approached investment like the index pioneer Jack Bogle, that's a different story. Indexing is a useful idea for society and I'm happy to say I was involved in its early days. But it's been done. We are going to have desperately difficult years ahead. And I would urge young people with talent to do really seriously useful stuff: engineering, farming, metal bashing and serious science and research because we are going to need those kinds of skills.

Today, I'm working harder than ever. I have three jobs. The job I take most seriously is broadcasting to the world underrated long-term problems that are really important, i.e. they have to be either

Working at my home office in Boston in 2025 on the manuscript of this book. Picture taken by Harvard Business School for the 2025 HBS Alumni Lifetime Achievement Awards. With permission from Harvard Business School. Photo by Susan Youn.

existential or nearly existential. And there are so many of them that I don't have to worry about any other problems, because it takes more time than I have anyway. My second job is helping out GMO, writing occasional papers, commenting on the stock market and giving interviews. Job number three is running the Foundation, trying to keep up with some of our VC investments and grants.

The Foundation is investing in some new ventures that may save the day. What could be more interesting than that? They're risky, they're new, they're unproven and they're important, some really important if only they would just work. For instance, we are investing in a business that has had a technological breakthrough in developing greaseproof paper. Food often comes wrapped with toxin-leaching plastic chemicals. Pregnant women and their unborn babies are exposed to these toxins. They have found a way of coating ordinary harmless paper with a single molecule layer of grease. What that means is the paper is light and it's cheaper than plastic film. And it's non-toxic. So this is huge. We're very excited about it. We're also investing in several ventures that are developing geothermal energy. If geothermal works, we're off the hook. It could change everything. It doesn't run out and it's cheap, and we live happily ever after. Obviously, to make progress in something so important is more satisfying and exciting than the equivalent breakthrough in making money in the stock market.

DEBT

Our politicians are driven by short-term considerations, like everyone else. Their time horizon is measured by the length of their term in office. They're not willing to pay a political price to benefit people 50 years from now. So they under-invest in infrastructure. They run up the public debt. Policymakers believe that credit stimulates economic growth, but during recent decades growth has collapsed even as the level of debt has soared. In fact, debt is the ultimate aider and abettor of our focus on the current and the postponement of the unpleasant. It enables us to live beyond our means. And living beyond our means is a perfect description of our short-term approach.

Since the early 1980s, total U.S. debt relative to GDP has been trending upwards. Personal debt grew slowly at first but steadily accelerated, even though it can be easily demonstrated that consumers collectively are better off saving and that the only beneficiary of a heavily indebted society is the financial industry, whose growth throughout this period has been massive. Government debt was so high after World War II that it fell initially, but after 1974 it started to rise again, very slowly at first but then dramatically in recent years, to move back to WWII levels.

But this time, the catalyst was not a major war. The main cause was not Hitler and the Japanese High Command, but the broad-based incompetence of our financial leadership. Obligations have been piled on to future generations. Deferring gratification is apparently not easy for our species, and nowhere is this better demonstrated than in our disregard, even contempt, for the idea that we should consider our descendants and not just ourselves. Financially, they – our descendants – will soon face a population bind wherein a bigger load is placed on the workers to support a growing army of retirees.

It bears repeating that the best we can do to help them in this respect is to leave them with no national debt and an impeccably up-to-date infrastructure, which is, of course, the exact opposite of the current situation. But much more important is looking out for our great-grandchildren, and trying not to leave them with a resource crisis. When discussing conservation of all kinds, we frequently hear the cry that it costs too much to change our profligate ways. But that is precisely the point: by engaging in moderately and affordably higher cost steps now – mainly reducing consumption through increased efficiency and the use of brain power to modify lifestyles – we can mitigate an enormous rise in resource prices that our great-grandchildren will otherwise have to pay, increases that will bite deeply into their quality of life.

I LIKE IKE

More than 60 years have gone by since President Eisenhower left office. Historians may well look back on the period since then as the "Selfish Era" – a time when individualism and materialism steadily took precedence over social responsibility. Three days before his departure from the White House, Eisenhower gave a famous end-of-term address to the people in which he warns about the dangers posed by the military-industrial complex.

He makes a lot of other important remarks that are worth remembering. For instance, Ike opens his address with the point that over his term in office, "the Congress and the Administration have, on most vital issues, cooperated well, to serve the national good rather than mere partisanship, and so have assured that the business of the Nation should go forward." What a particularly bitter taste that thought leaves today, doesn't it? There may have been Congresses that were more partisan than our recent ones, but it would take a serious political historian to track them down. Eisenhower is suggesting that without bipartisan cooperation the "business of the Nation" is unlikely to go forward satisfactorily. Most of us would agree.

Ike then goes on to express a concern that the world community could become dominated by "dreadful fear and hate" rather than becoming one of "a proud confederation of mutual trust and respect."

This is bland enough, I suppose, although of course devoutly to be wished, but he goes on to say, "Such a confederation must be one of equals. The weakest must come to the conference table with the same confidence as do we, protected... by our moral, economic, and military strength." It is impossible to imagine recent American presidents, let alone the current one, expressing so benevolent an attitude.

Next, we have the most unexpected point: "As we peer into society's future, we – you and I, and our government – must avoid the impulse to live only for today, plundering, for our own ease and convenience, the precious resources of tomorrow. We cannot mortgage the material assets of our grandchildren without risking the loss also of their political and spiritual heritage." Wow! How is it possible that we collectively seem to have forgotten this clear warning? I have not once seen it referred to.

For make no mistake: our planet's resources are finite and we continue to mine them (and agriculture has become a form of mining) with reckless abandon. In stock markets, we consider accurate replacement cost to be the gold standard of true value. The true replacement cost of our non-replaceable patrimony of oil, gas and coal is their replacement – renewable energy sources. But we continue to price these resources on a very short horizon by using marginal cost of production. We continue to allow corporations to produce toxic materials. We continue emitting greenhouse gases at record levels. We continue getting further and further into debt. Our baby cohorts have been declining rapidly everywhere. And with that has come a steady decline in global economic growth. This decline will continue as the global population crashes, and as the growth rate drops the disgruntlement of typical voters will continue to rise. The public are turning against governments more often. And governments, in turn, are showing signs of desperation. Global geopolitical stability is decreasing steadily, and will likely continue to unravel.

But the worst outcomes are not certain. We have shown a shocking lack of long-term thinking. But we can and may do better. If we are to win this race of our lives, we had better start doing better right now. If our society is to survive and prosper, we must collectively aspire to be more like Ike.

A PARTING THOUGHT

As I've gotten older I have come to realize that one of the main things in life is purpose. Most people born in the history of man have not had any particular purpose other than staying alive. We have an opportunity to not just stay alive, earn a living and feed ourselves, but also an opportunity to change the outcome for future generations stretching out more or less forever. This is the purpose of all purposes, you lucky people. If you do not attach yourself to this problem, you're missing the point, you're not paying attention, you're not showing judgment. This is the issue that you should attach as much of your life to as you can. At least, that's what I do. In addition to purpose, it gives me intellectual challenges and camaraderie – it is, in fact, just plain fun!

Acknowledgements

The initial impetus for this book came from Peg McGetrick. A number of other GMOers have also offered their recollections, including Forrest Berkley, Chris Darnell, Ben Inker, Jody Shuman and Mason Smith. Sally McGregor put up with a lot of stories from her "Gasbag" brother. Hunter Lewis shared his memories about the early relationship between GMO and Cambridge Associates.

Barbara Wall's unpublished history of GMO contained much useful information. Cheryl Wakeham returned to her old role of carefully copy-editing the early drafts. Anthony Hene has overseen this project from GMO's end, providing invaluable support. Tucker Hewes read the final draft and made useful comments. Jamie Lee, who has assisted my research for the past 15 years, also read the early drafts and helped with charts and photographs. Melissa Stafford kept things moving along.

We would also like to thank our literary agent Jim Levine and Morgan Entrekin and colleagues at Grove Atlantic for taking on the book.

Index

NB entries in *italics* indicate illustrations

A.W. Gregory, 28–9
Ackman, Bill, 370
Acrow A shares, 50, 55–6
Africa, 323
Agtmael, Antoine van, 153–4
AI (artificial intelligence), 381–3
airline industry, 64
Albertsons, 86–7
"amateur's advantage", 104–6
Amazon (company), 213, 359, 383
AMC Entertainment, 374, 376
American Academy of Arts and Sciences, 316
American National Bank, 70, 74
American Raceways, 53–4, 56
Amherst, 131
anti-Semitism, 24–5
Appalachian Mountain Club, Beacon Hill, 208
Applegate, Jeffrey, 194, 229
ARKK fund, 376
Arnott, Rob, 142

Arthur D. Little, 47, 51
Attenborough, David, 314
Australia, 341
Australian Financial Review, 247
autism, 326–7
Avon, 85, 382
axioms, 225

Bangladesh, 323
Bangor Punta, 62–4
banks, 58, 251, 263, 273–5, 279–80
  bank executives, 274–5
Banque Nationale de Paris (BNP), 220
"barbaric double-counting", 363
Barings Bank, 140
Barra, 154
Barron's magazine, 161, 240, 242, 272, 365
Batterymarch Financial, 9, 68–71, 73, 87–9, 91–2, 94–6, 99, 117, 128–9, 137

Batterymarch Financial (*cont.*)
  Batterymarch Building, 94–5
  founding of, 65–8
  "index-matching service",
    74–6
  value investing, 76–8
"battleship GDP", 204, 356
Bayer, 343
Beacon Hill, Boston, 58
bear markets, 190–98, 217–19,
  224, 234, 236–8, 240, 268,
  373
Bear Stearns, 263, 273–4
Belash, Alexis, 125
Bell Atlantic, 133
Berkley, Forrest, 104, 133, 140,
  144, 149–50, 152, 220–21
Bernanke, Ben, 249–50, 273,
  280, 353–4
Biden, Joe, 371
  stimulus programs, 371, 373
Biggs, Barton, 176, 219
biodiversity, 293, 302, 306, 314,
  335
Birkhall, Scotland, 314
bitcoin, 369
"Black Swan" events, 261
Blackstone, 258
Blodget, Henry, 213
Bloomberg, 75, 316, 374
Bodenhamer, Lee, 69
Bogle, Jack, 74–5, 76, 391
bonds, 100–104, 167
  bond yields, 135
  emerging country debt, 214
  see also Treasury Inflation-
    Protected Securities (TIPS)
Bookstaber, Richard, 276
Booz Allen, 48
Borneo, 284
Boston Globe, 66
Boston, Massachusetts, 65–6,
  141, 158, 159, 58
Boston Security Analysts
  Society, 222
Boulding, Kenneth, 296, 298,
  384
bowling, 60–61
"Brains Trust", 151
Bridges, Harry, 36–7
Brinson, Gary, 210
Brunswick, 60–64
bubbles, 176–8, *178*, 180, 206–7,
  224–9, 233–9, 254–7, 278,
  288–9, 364, 366–9, 371–2,
  383
  AI bubble, 383
  Britain's railroad bubble
    (1840s), 382–3
  "chain-linked bubbles", 241
  global bubble, 253–62, *256*,
    367–8
  housing market bubbles,
    246–51, 273, 369, 375
  internet bubble, 290, 379, 383
Jackson Hole, 228
Japan, 180, 233, 236, 366,
  375

INDEX 401

Nifty Fifty bubble (1970s), 368
South Sea (1720), 151, 224, 233, 369, 372, 373
superbubbles, 366, 374–8
Tech Bubble, 184, 200–201, 206–9, 211–12, 214, 236, 239, 273, 287, 368, 375
"Bubbles for Fama" (Greenwood, Shleifer & You), 368
Buckingham Palace, visit to, 316
Buffett, Warren, 77, 205
bull markets, 190–98, 216, 227, 236–7, 239–40, 268, 289, 369
  "great bull market conspiracy", 204–5
  permabulls, 267–9
  propaganda, 231–2
Businessweek, 136–7, 386

C4 money, 303
Cabot, Walter, 131–2
California, 146
Cambridge Associates, 97, 112, 130, 139, 159, 345–6
Cameron, James, 302–3
Cap and Trade climate bill, 303
Capital Guardian, 130
Capital International, 129
  Capital International Perspective, 129
capitalism, 291–6, 298, 299, 362–3, 388–9
  deficiencies of, 287, 288
Capricorn, 345

carbon emissions, 348–9, 389
career risk, 86, 162, 184–7, 222, 269, 274, 317, 390
Carnegie Medal for Philanthropy, 316
Charles III, King of United Kingdom, 314, *315*
ChatGPT, 381
Chemical Bank, New York, 63
chemical pollution, 326–7, 336, 343, 385
Chesebrough-Ponds, 85
China, 309, 311, 381, 323, 325, 333, 334, 340, 344
Churchill, Winston, 290
Cisco Systems, 214
Citibank, 154, 273
civilizations, collapse of, 319–21, 338–9
climate change, 287, 291, 300–308, *304*, 313–14, 317–18, 321, 329–38, 344, 351–2, 389
  agriculture and, 287, 329–34
  erosion, 331–2
  global warming, 304, 306–8, 317, 343
  sea level rise, 329
  weather shocks, *329*, 330
Climate Tech 1.0, 345
CNBC, 371
Coca-Cola, 85, 145, 244
Cohen, Abby Joseph, 193–4, 202, 212, 229

Collins Associates Client Conference, 161
Columbia University, 154
commodity prices, 309–12
Common Fund, 131, 132
Common Stocks as Long-Term Investments (Smith), 191
compound growth, 297–9, 311
Congressional Budget Office, 357
Conning and Company, 95
conspiracy theorists, 307–8
consultancy, 48
contrarianism, 307, 389
Contrary Opinion Forum, 134, 136
Cooper, Tom, 173–4
Cooperman, Leon, 102
Copenhagen, Denmark, 325
Corning Glass, 98–9, 115, 139
"cornucopian" optimism, 351–2, 338–9
corporate power, 359–60
Corzine, Jon, 156–7
Costa Rica, 301
Count Down (Swan), 325
Covid-19 pandemic, 369–73, 387
Covid crash, 370–71
lockdown, 370
Cowen, Tyler, 375
Credit Suisse, 274
Cresap McCormick and Paget, 48–9

Crompton & Knowles Loom Works, 145
cryptocurrencies, 369, 374, 378
cyclicals, 103, 118–19

Dalio, Ray, 265
Damon, Matt, 302
Darnell, Chris, 108–11, 114–15, 124–5, 128–9, 130, 136, 137, 138–9, 142, 144–5, 172, 223
De Lamerie, Paul, 314
debt, 355–6, 392–4
democracy, 386–7
Demon of Our Own Design: Markets, Hedge Funds, and the Perils of Financial Innovation, A (Bookstaber), 276
discount rates, 292
Divecha, Arjun, 154, 158, 173, 219, 301
Divecha Centre for Climate Change, 301–2
Dogecoin, 374
Donaldson, Lufkin & Jenrette, 135
Doncaster, Yorkshire, 16
Douse, Henry, 12–13
"Dubious Achievement Award", 74
Durant, Kingsley, 94, *95*, 115, 211
Dye, Tony, 210

EAFE (Europe, Australasia, and the Far East) index, 132, 150–52, 218
earnings per share (EPS), 357–8
Eastman Kodak, 85, 86, 382
Economic Journal, 296
economic theory, 300, 301
Economist, The, 213, 255
Efficient Market Hypothesis (EMH), 219, 224–6, 232–3
Eisenhower, Dwight D., 394–5
Eli Lilly, 85
Ellis, Charley, 65
embezzlement, 216
emerging markets, 153–5
  emerging market equities, 214–15, 357
energy storage, 341–2
energy transition, 338–41
Enron, 216–17, 227
Environmental Defense Fund, 350
environmental issues, 288–96
  environmental research, 289, 290
Environmental Protection Agency, 326
equity markets, 179, 211, 228, 250, 255, 258
  international equities, 152
ESG (Environmental, Social and Governance), 342–3

Essay on the Principle of Population (Malthus), 297
European Union (EU), 313, 335–6
extrapolation, 389

Fama, Eugene, 70, 71, 225, 226
Federal Open Market Committee, 228
Federal Reserve, 205, 226, 227, 229, 246, 249–50, 260, 263, 273, 279–81, 354–5, 363
fertility rate, 322–3, 385
  sperm counts, 323–6, *324*
fertilizers, 333–4, 349
Fidelity, 49, 61–2, 142
Financial Analysts Journal, 142
Financial Times, 230, 260, 310, 325, 361
First Index Investment Trust, 74
First Index Mutual Fund (Bogle), 75
Fisher, Dick, 170
Fisher, Irving, 191, 234
Fisher, Kenneth, 267
Fisher-Lorie database, 79
Flynn, Jim, 98
Forbes magazine, 191, 198–9, 213, 267–8, 370
Ford Investor Services, 82
Formula 1 Grand Prix racing, 53–4
Forrest, Nathan Bedford, 296–7
Fortune magazine, 259

404 INDEX

fossil fuels, 292, 294–300, 338–40, 343–4, 352
France, 386
Franklin National Bank, 87
Freemasons, 17
French, Ken, 225

Galbraith, J.K., 216, 229
Galton, Francis, 115–16
"Gambler's Ruin", 134
GameStop, 374, 376
GDP (Gross Domestic Product), 277, 293–4, 295, 393
   global GDP volatility, 365
   growth, 193, 201–4, 354–61
General Motors, 372
General Theory (Keynes), 186
geothermal energy, 392
Gibbons, Ed, 62
Gibbons, Green, Van Amerongen (investment firm), 62
GIC, 265
Gillette, 85
Glasenberg, Ivan, 310
Glass, Norman, 24
Glenburn, New Zealand, 283
global bond markets, 380
Global Financial Crisis (2008), 44, 48, 184, 214, 262–3, 268–9, 272–5, 287, 288–9, 320
Global Investor, 218

Globalization, 359–61, 363
GMO (Grantham, Mayo, Van Otterloo), 94–128, 132, 135, 137–8, 140–43, 150, 155, 175, 187–90, 218–20, 260–62, 287, 290, 303, 357, 368, 375
   Asset Allocation, 158, 168–76, 179, 182–3, 187–8, 197, 219, 222, 245–6, 260
   BNP offer for, 220–21
   Bond Allocation Fund, 173
   bonds, 100–104, 105
   bubbles and, 176–87, *178*, 207–9
   client base, 181–3, 189
   client service, 189, 208
   Climate Change Fund, 344–5
   computers and, 110–12, 126
   cyclicals, 103, 118–19
   Emerging Country Debt Fund, 174–5
   emerging equities strategy, 154–5, 219
   Emerging Markets Fund, 219
   forecasts, 214–15, *215*
   Global Balanced Fund, 269
   Global Financial Crisis and, 268–9
   Growth Allocation Fund, 145
   Growth Fund, 147–8, 169
   HBS case study, 157–61
   hedge funds, 158, 222
   incorporation of, 94

informal organization, 143–4
International Active, 137–8,
   152, 153, 155, 158
International Intrinsic Value,
   152
International Quant, 149, 182
Japan fund, 152
mean reversion and, 115–19
Mean Reversion Fund, 245
"Microsoft effect", 120–21
momentum, 121–3
moves offices, 135
mutual fund structure, 138–9
"neglect", 124–7
quants and, 112–15, 125–7,
   137–48, 152–3, 155
reinvestment and, 269–71
Renewable Resources division,
   283
Resources Fund, 345
Rowes Wharf office, Boston,
   135, 160, 171
"Sausage Factory", 139–40
Sharpe Ratio, 175
Tactical Opportunities Fund,
   245
U.S. Active Fund, 137–8, 158,
   223
U.S. Core fund, 115, 139, 147,
   148
U.S. Quality Fund, 245
underperformance, 179–83,
   246, 260–61, 390
Yale, relationship with, 150

GMO Woolley, 140–41, 158
gold, investment in, 166
Goldman Sachs, 46, 102, 140,
   155–7, 176, 194, 263, 274–5,
   279–80, 377
Goltho, Lincolnshire, 11
Graham, Ben, 57, 77, 367
Grant, Jim, 205, 366
Grant's Interest Rate Observer,
   205, 366
Grantham Foundation for
   the Protection of the
   Environment, 300–301, 337,
   344–52, 377, 392
   "Covid trade", 370
   establishment of, 286
Grantham Prize, 302
Grantham Research Institute
   on Climate Change and the
   Environment, 301–2
Grantham, Robert Jeremy
   Goltho, *6, 14, 35, 95, 315,
   391*
   awards, 316
   "butterfly effect", 44–5
   childhood, 14–18
   Commander of the British
      Empire (CBE), 316
   "Death of Value" talk, 107
   debates, 190–96
   depression, 135
   "Dirty Secrets of International
      Investing" (essay), 150
   early investments, 50–57

Grantham, Robert Jeremy Goltho (*cont.*)
  environmental epiphany, 284–6
  "Everything I Know About the Market in 15 Minutes" (talk), 161–5
  father, 11–12, 17, 20, 27
  "Financial Innovation Boosts Economic Growth" debate, 276–9
  financial success, 285
  forestry and, 282–5
  gaming and, 22–5
  "Gasbag" nickname, 18–19
  grandparents, 13, 15–17
  idea generation, 44–5
  "Let the Wild Rumpus Begin" (paper), 377, 380
  mathematics and, 108
  media attention, 262
  military service and, 37–8
  mother, 12, 14–16, 27, *35*, 51
  permabear and, 267–9
  personality type, 46–7
  podcasts, 290–91
  propagandist, 287–8, 290, 303–4
  public speaking and, 38–9
  "Race of Our Lives" (paper), 337
  "Race of Our Lives Revisited" (paper), 337, 343
  "Reinvesting When Terrified" (letter), 269–71, 353, 370
  ruthlessness and, 34
  schooling, 17–25, *21*
  siblings, 18
  "Slowing Population Growth" (paper), 322
  small cap stocks and, 79–85
  sporting achievement and, 20–22, *21*
  stamp-trading venture, 24
  stepfather, 27–9
  travel, 247
  university, 25–8, 30–31
  "Waiting for the Last Dance" (paper), 373, 376
  wedding, 47–8
  "You Can't Fool All of the People All of the Time" (paper), 72n, 133, 171
  see also quarterly letters
Grantham, Hannelore (wife), 34–6, *35*, 52, 55, 313, 314, *315*
  career, 66
  environment and, 284, 285–6, 302, 309
  wedding, 47–8
Grantham, Isabel (daughter), 284, 309, *315*
Grantham, Jen (daughter-in-law), *315*
Grantham, Oliver (son), 284–5, *315*
Grantham, Redding, 20
Grantham, Rupert (son), 22, 284

Grantham, Sally (sister), 20
greaseproof paper, 392
Great Amwell, Hertfordshire, 11
Great Crash and After, The (Fisher), 191
Great Crash, The, (Galbraith), 216
Great Depression, 204, 243, 282, 354, 371, 375
"Great Moderation" (early 2000s), 254
"Great Paradigm Shift", 310–12, *312*
green investing, 288, 291, 342–4
Green Revolution, 333
green tech, 345–8, 372
greenhouse gas emissions, 300, 305
Greenspan, Alan, 167–8, 177, 205, 212, 226, 227–32, 234–5, 241, 248–50, 358
   "irrational exuberance" speech, 177
Greger, Eva, 283
Gross, Bill, 268
GTE (later Verizon), 175–6, 219
Guinness Peat, 155
"gunslingers" (investors), 53
Gurria, Angel, 313

Hagler, Jon, 9, 189
Harris, Britt, 176, 220
Hartford Steam Boiler Insurance and Inspection Company, 86
Harvard, 132
Harvard Business School (HBS), 20, 30–34, 36–44, 47, 67, 69, 115, 157, 286
   Baker Scholars, 39–40, 43, 67
   entrance test, 32–4
Harvard-Yenching Institute, 131–2
Haugen, Robert, 226
Hayek, Friedrich, 300
HBS, 316
heart disease, 327
Heat (documentary), 302
hedge funds, 250
Hedge-Hogging (Biggs), 219
Hedley's, 30
Hereditary Genius (Galton), 115
Hewes, Tucker, 269
Hicks, John, 27, 294
Hong Kong, 158
housing market, 242, 246–51, 258–62, 375, 380
   housing peak (2006), 375
   subprime market, 258–9, 275
Houston, Texas, 330
Hurricane Harvey, 330

IBM, 85, 86
Iceland, 275
Immoderate Greatness (Ophuls), 320
Imperial College, London, 301
income inequality, 386
indexing, 69–76, 391

India, 323, 340
industrial capacity, 358
Industrial Revolution, 294–5, 296, 298, 305
inflation, 200–202, 364–5, 378–80
Inker, Ben, 172–4, 201, 217, 221, 357–8, 364
Inker-Grantham comfort model, 365, 379–80, *379*
insect loss, 335–6
Institutional Investor magazine, 102
  "Portfolio Letter", 102–3
interest rates, 101–3, 241, 254–5, 356, 358–60
Internal Revenue Service (IRS), 303
International Active, 130–32
International Core (later International Intrinsic Value), 140
International Minerals and Chemicals (IMC), 40–42, 47–8
International Monetary Fund (IMF), 112–14, 127, 133, 139, 140, 145, 357
internet, 167–8
investment management, 58–60
investor behavior, 377–8
Iowa, 331

J.P. Morgan, 46, 176, 263

Japan, 149–53, 177, 326, 328, 330, 355, 387
Jeremy and Hannelore Grantham Environmental Trust, 286–7
John Hancock, 65
Johnson, Ned, 74, 134
Johnson & Johnson, 85, 244
Journal of Portfolio Management, 72
Joyce, Chuck, 245

Kagan, Michael, 125
Keynes, John Maynard, 77, 186–7, 192, 197, 234, 240, 264, 355, 367
Keystone, 49, 53, 58–66, 92
Keystone pipeline, 309
Khosla, Vinod, 345, 350
Kleiner Perkins, 345
Krugman, Paul, 228

LeBaron, Dean, 9–10, 64–8, 69–70, 73, 75, 89, 92–3, 94, 96
Lee Kuan Yew, 265
Lee, Jamie, 290, 309, 322, 350
Lehman Brothers, 194, 269, 273, 275, 369
Levitt, Theodore (Ted), 40–41
Lewis, Hunter, 97–9, 109, 159
Liang, Dr., 332
libertarians, 300, 306–7
life expectancy, 326, 386
Light, Jay, 129

London, England, 141, 158
London School of Economics (LSE), 301
Long-Term Capital Management, 278
long-term investment, 186–7
Longstreth, Bevis, 9

Mack, Consuelo, 291
Macmillan, Harold, 15
Mager, Ezra, 69
Magnificent Seven (MAG 7), 361, 363, 381–2
Malkiel, Burton, 104, 123
Malthus, Thomas Robert, 297–8, 322
Malthusians, 351–2
Mandelbrot, Benoit, 278
Manhattan, New York, 52
Market Monitor Data Systems, 54–6
Marketing Myopia (Levitt), 40
Martin, Michele, 350
Marx, Karl, 389
Massachusetts, 387
Mayo, Dick, 131–2, 134, 136–9, 147, 188, 218, 223
    Batterymarch and, 67–8, 92–3, 137
    bonds, 170
    GMO and, 94, *95*, 96–9, 101, 109–10, 113–14, 120, 128, 137–8, 144–5, 157–8
    oil and, 105–6

McGeary, Justine, 143
McGetrick, Peg, 132, 149, 158
McKinsey & Company, 48
mean reversion, 115–19, 362–3, 365, 368
Merck, 85
Mercury outboard motors, 61
Merrill Lynch 193, 213, 273
Merton, Robert, 225
Metcalf Institute, 302
Mexico, 173, 386
Microsoft, 120–21, 125, 244
Miller, Eric, 135
Minsky, Hyman, 254–5, 262, 272
(Mis)Behavior of Markets, The (Mandelbrot), 278
modern portfolio theory, 243, 256–7
"modified indexing", 133
Modigliani, Franco, 59, 200–201
monopolies, 118–19, 359–61, 363, 381
Monsanto, 343
Moody's, 243
Moore's Law, 339
Morgan Guaranty Trust (now J.P. Morgan), 58, 69
Morgan Stanley, 46, 170, 176, 219
Morgenstern, Oskar, 225
Morningstar, 219, 337
Morningstar Conference, Chicago, 265–6
Morocco, 334

Morse, David, 82–4, 86, 108, 110, 117, 121
Moss, Stirling, 53
Myers-Briggs personality test, 46–7

Nasdaq, 213–14, 230, 377
National Academy, U.S., 307
Nature (journal), 317
Nature, article in, 317–18
Nature Conservancy, The, 286, 350
Nemerever, Bill, 173
New Economy, 229–30
New England Journal of Medicine, 327
New Finance: The Case Against Efficient Markets (Haugen), 226
New York, 52–5, 58, 79
New York Times, 73–4, 228, 246
New Zealand, 247
Newton, Isaac, 307
Newton, Massachusetts, 54
Nifty Fifty, 84–93, 106, 209, 217, 243, 382
Nikkei index, 151, 152
Nobel Prize, 316–17
non-fungible tokens, 378

O.M. Scott, 41–2
Obama, Barack, 303, 360
Obamacare, 303
obesity, 326

Occupy Wall Street protest, 361–2
Ochoa, Hilda, 99, 153–4
Oddleifson, Eric, 283
oil, 105–6
  OPEC oil embargo (1970s), 310
Old Spice, 48
Ophuls, William, 320
Organisation for Economic Co-operation and Development (OECD), 300, 313
overvaluation, 364, 366–7, 373

Panama, 301
Panasonic, 372
paradigm shifts, 310
Parkinson's disease, 327
Paulson, Hank, 190
PBS Frontline, 302
Pensions and Investments, 74
permabears, 267–9
permabulls, 267–9
Phillips Exeter, 131
Pinker, Steven, 336
Planck, Max, 273
plastics, 335
Polaroid, 85, 382
Pomona College, California, 146
population growth, 322–7
portfolio insurance, 134
Prechter, Robert, 134–5
price acceleration, 368–9
price-to-book (P/B) ratios, 82, 106–7, 116, 120, 129–30

price-to-earnings (P/E) ratios, 59–60, 87, 106–7, 120, 130, 132, 149, 179–80, 192, 200–204, 364–5, 379
Princeton, 173, 174
Princeton Investment Committee, 169
Proceedings of the National Academy of Sciences, 331
Procter & Gamble, 30, 31, 85
productivity, 354–5, 361, 364–5
profit margins, 251, 259, 358–61, *359*, 362–3, 364–5
profitability, double counting of, 202–3, *203*
Prospect, 316
Pumatech, 211, 214, 240, 244

Quakers, 13, 15–16
quants, 137, 260–63
    funds, 112–15, 133
    models, 112, 114, 216–17
QuantumScape, 345, 348, 372–3, 376–7, 380
quarterly letters, 103, 206–10, 253, 258, 259, 264, 266–8, 273, 364
    "Bracing Yourself for a Possible Near-Term Melt-Up", 369
    "Everything You Need to Know About Global Warming in 5 Minutes", 304–8
    "It's Everywhere, In Everything: The First Truly Global Bubble", 255
    "Lessons from the Great Bubble", 231–8
    "Let's All Look Like Yale", 253
    "On the Road to Zero Growth" (letter), 356–7
    "Reaping the Whirlwind", 266
    "This Time Seems Very, Very Different", 365
    "Time Out Then Back to the Meat Grinder" (letter), 380
    "Time to Wake Up: Days of Abundant Resources and Falling Prices Are Over Forever", 309, 313

rainforests, 284
Ralston Purina, 102
Random Walk Down Wall Street, A (Malkiel), 104, 123
Rank, J. Arthur, 13
Rapaport, John, *315*
Rates of Return on Investments in Common Stocks (Fisher and Lorie), 79
Ravenel, Ramsay, 345, 350–51
Reader's Digest, 30
Real Estate Investment Trusts (REITs), 167–8, 209, 214–15

real estate *see* housing market
recession, 303, 381
regression, 235–6, 237
regression to the mean, 116, 166–7
renewable energy, 338–41, 395
resource limitations, 292–300, 309–13
Reynolds, Robert, 276
Ricardo, David, 80, 82
Roach, Stephen, 230, 241
Roberts, Carter, 286
Robertson, Julian, 210
Robinhood (stock trading app), 373
Rockefeller Family Fund, 9–10, 90
Rockefeller, Laurance, 9–10, 89, 90–91
Rocky Mountain Institute, 350
Roosevelt, Franklin D., 240
Ropes & Gray, 95
Rosenberg, Barr, 141–2
Rosenberg Capital Management, 141–2
Rothschild, Jacob, 4th Baron Rothschild, 314
Rowes Wharf, Boston Harbor, 135, 160
Royal Masonic Junior School for Boys, Bushey, Hertfordshire, 17–25
Royal Society, U.K., 307
Rwanda, 284
Ryan, Tony, 189–90

S&P 500, 91, 102–4, 134, 135–6, 147, 167, 171, 198–200, 207, 213–15, 218–19, 235, 237, 239, 243–4, 266–7, 364, 371, 377, 380
Safeway, 86–7
Samsonite, 70
Samuelson, Paul, 180, 191
San Francisco, 158
Schering-Plough, 85, 207
Schmidt, Eric, 337
Scholes, Myron, 276, 278
Schwartz, Charlie, 112–14
Schwarzenegger, Arnold, 302
Securities and Exchange Commission (SEC), 63–4, 139
Security Analysis (Graham and Dodd), 77
Security-Connecticut Life, 87–8, 89, 90
Selkovits, Larry, 40
"Seven Lean Years", 354–5
Sharpe, Bill, 225
Sheffield University, 26–7, 30–31, 302
Shell, 30–32, 36–7, 44, 51
Sherwood Medical Instruments, 61
Shiller, Robert, 204, 389
Shuman, Jody, 129, 189, 207
Siegel, Jeremy, 191–4
Siegel, Larry, 283
Sierra Club, 132
Singapore, 265

Smith, Alan, 143
Smith, Edgar, 191–2
Smith, Mason, 143, 144, 189
Smithers, Andrew, 185, 205
Solomon Brother, 140s, 151
Soucy, Rob, 138
South Croydon, London, 28, 34
South Korea, 328
Special Purpose Acquisition Companies (SPACs), 372–3
Spectator, The (magazine), 303
St James's Palace, London, 314
stability, 254–5
Stanford University, 154, 372
status, 42–4
Steinberg, Bruce, 193
Steinberg, Saul, 63
Stern, Nick, 301
Stern Review, 301
stock market, 50–57
   behavioralism and, 233–4
   price-to-earnings (P/E) ratio, 59–60, 234
   recovery, 239–40, 353–8, 364
   short-termism, 389–91
   stock market crash (1987), 135–6, 143, 169
   stock market crash (2000), 211–12, 217
   stock market lows, 100, 353–4
stocks, 97
   blue chip, 69, 89, 242–4, 280, 374, 376, 378
   electric vehicle-related, 378
   growth, 145–8, 167, 217, 235, 377
   international, 128–33
   Japanese, 149–53
   large cap, 99, 235
   low beta, 124
   meme, 374, 376–7, 378, 380
   momentum, 121–4
   "neglect", 124–7
   quality stocks, 86, 242–6, 263, 267
   small cap, 9–10, 59, 79–84, 87, 89–90, *91*, 99, 106, 116, 133, 152, 209, 214, 217–18
   speculative, 353, 376–7
   technology, 214, 217
   telecom, 214
   value, 23, 99, 106–8, 114, 120, 124, 167, 217–18, 235
Stocks for the Long Run (Siegel), 191
Summers, Larry, 233
sustainability, 313–14
Swan, Shanna, 325
Swarthmore College, Philadelphia, 98, 131
Swensen, David, 104, 150, 172, 252
Swiss Banking Corporation, 155
Sydney, Australia, 247–8

T. Rowe Price, 69
Takahashi, Dean, 104
Taleb, Nassim, 261

Tanzania, 284
tech stocks, 168, 211, 217, 240, 257
  green tech, 345–8, 372
  Tech Bubble, 184, 200–201, 206–9, 211–12, 214, 236, 239, 273, 287, 368, 375
  tech crash (1987), 370
  tech crash (2000), 366
Templeton, John, 131, 362, 365
Thatcher, Margaret, 36
3M, 131
Thurston, David, 344–6
Tidwell, Kevin, 350
timber market, 282–3
Tokyo real estate market, 151
toxicity, 326–7, 335, 385
Treasury Inflation-Protected Securities (TIPS), 167–8, 199, 209, 214
Trump, Donald, 318, 371
Turkey, 386
Tyco, 216

UBS, 155–6
Unconventional Success (Swensen), 252
Union Carbide, 102
Union Tank Car, 62–3
United Kingdom, 36, 37, 352, 370, 382
  Covid pandemic, 387
  government, 301
  stock market, 158

United Nations (UN), 311
  global food price index, 378
  Intergovernmental Panel on Climate Change, 318
United States, 130, 360–61, 385–8
  agriculture and, 333
  banks, 58, 263
  Covid pandemic, 370, 387
  environment and, 336
  economy, 193, 204–5, 227, 230, 385
  fossil fuels, 31–2, 342
  GDP growth, 356–7
  government/politics, 168, 303, 318, 360, 381
  health and longevity, 326–7
  housing market, 247–8, 250, 259, 269, 368–9, 375, 385
  Justice Department, 360
  presidential cycle, 240–42
  stock market, 100, 110, 135, 151, 167, 176–80, 197, 207–9, 211, 237, 239, 254, 267, 353, 368, 375, 381, 383
  Supreme Court, 360, 361
  venture capital, 346
  see also Federal Reserve
U.S. Steel, 119

value, 363, 366–7
value at risk (VAR), 254

Van Otterloo, Eijk, 94, *95*, 97, 109–10, 128–9, 130, 131, 132, 137–8, 149–50, 152–4, 158, 188
Vanderheiden, George, 210
Vanguard, 74–5
venture capital (VC), 344–50
Verizon *see* GTE
Vermont, 282
Volcker, Paul, 101, 278
Von Neumann, John, 225

Wakeham, Cheryl, 206
Walker, Jim, 263–4
Wall Street, 63, 110, 205
  ethics of, 278–9
  Occupy Wall Street protesters, 361
Wall Street Crash (1929), 106, 168, 207, 229, 233, 237, 367
Wall Street Digest, 51–2
Wall Street Journal, 255, 269, 386
Walmart, 85
Ward, Bob, 301
Ware, Hertfordshire, 11–12
Washington D.C., 308
Washington Post, 177
Wealthtrack podcast, 291
"weaseling", 216

Weintraub, Jerry, 302
Wellesley College, Massachusetts, 132
Wells Fargo, 70, 74
Western Sahara, 334
Wharton Business School, 191
White House, Washington, DC, 309
White, Lucas, 344
William, Prince of Wales, 316
Woolley, Paul, 112–13, 140–41, 145
World Bank, 99, 131, 133, 207
World War II (1939–45), 13–15, 18, 393
WorldCom, 216
WWF (World Wildlife Fund), 286, 350

Xerox, 85, 244, 382

Yale University, 104, 149–50, 245, 252–3
  Yale Investment Committee, 149–50
"Years of Living Dangerously" (documentary), 302–3

zero-sum game, 71–2, 74